The American Freshman

Twenty–Five Year Trends, 1966–1990

by

Eric L. Dey
Alexander W. Astin
William S. Korn

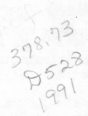

Higher Education Research Institute
Graduate School of Education
University of California, Los Angeles

September, 1991

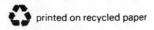

printed on recycled paper

Cooperative Institutional Research Program

The Cooperative Institutional Research Program (CIRP) is a national longitudinal study of the American higher education system. Established in 1966 at the American Council on Education, the CIRP is now the nation's largest and longest empirical study of higher education, involving data on some 1,300 institutions, over 7 million students, and more than 100,000 faculty. To maximize the use of these data in research and training, the CIRP was transferred to the Graduate School of Education at UCLA in 1973. The annual CIRP freshman and follow-up surveys are now administered by the Higher Education Research Institute at the University of California, Los Angeles, under the continuing sponsorship of the American Council on Education.

American Council on Education

The American Council on Education (ACE), founded in 1918, is a council of educational organizations and institutions. ACE seeks to advance education and educational methods through comprehensive voluntary and cooperative action on the part of American educational associations, organizations, and institutions.

Higher Education Research Institute
University of California, Los Angeles

The Higher Education Research Institute (HERI) is based in the Graduate School of Education at the University of California, Los Angeles. The Institute serves as an interdisciplinary center for research, evaluation, information, policy studies, and research training in postsecondary education. HERI's research program covers five broad areas: the outcomes of postsecondary education; academic administration and institutional management; faculty performance; federal and state policy assessment; and educational equity.

CIRP Project Staff

Alexander W. Astin, Professor and Director
Eric L. Dey, Associate Director
William S. Korn, Associate Director for Operations
Ellyne R. Riggs, HERI Office Manager   Robin Bailey, Assistant to the Director

CIRP Advisory Committee

Estela M. Bensimon
Center for the Study of Higher Education
The Pennsylvania State University

Peter Ewell
National Center for Higher Education
Management Systems

Hugh Fordyce, Director of Research
United Negro College Fund

Weldon Jackson, Vice President
Morehouse College

Charles McClain, Commissioner
Missouri Coordinating Board for Higher Education

George Neely, Jr., Executive Vice President
Fisk University

Amaury Nora
College of Education
University of Illinois at Chicago

Earl Richardson, President
Morgan State University

Deborah Teeter
Director, Institutional Research
University of Kansas

Robert H. Atwell (ex-officio)
President
American Council on Education

Elaine El-Khawas (ex-officio)
Vice President
American Council on Education

Published by the Higher Education Research Institute. Suggested citation:

Dey, E.L., Astin, A.W., & Korn, W.S. (1991). *The American Freshman: Twenty–Five Year Trends.* Los Angeles: Higher Education Research Institute, UCLA.

Additional copies of this report may be purchased from the Higher Education Research Institute, Graduate School of Education, 320 Moore Hall, University of California, Los Angeles, CA 90024-1521. Please remit $25.00 with your order.

ISBN 1–878477–07–2

The American Freshman

Twenty–Five Year Trends, 1966–1990

CONTENTS

TABLES

FIGURES

PREFACE

This report summarizes the results of the Cooperative Institutional Research Program's annual surveys of college freshmen over the past twenty–five years. The Cooperative Institutional Research Program (CIRP) was established at the American Council on Education as a longitudinal study of the American higher education system, and time has proven that CIRP data have been invaluable to educational researchers and policy makers. A recent study of the higher education literature showed that CIRP publications and research based on CIRP data are among the sources most cited by researchers (see Budd, 1990).

For those interested in American higher education, this report documents an array of demographic, attitudinal, and social changes involving students entering the nation's colleges since the survey's inception in 1966. Major findings from this report point to significant changes in students' academic skills, self–image, and personal goals, as well as their preferences for college majors and careers. This report is an extension of the earlier work of Astin, Green, and Korn (1987) which documented data trends from the first two decades of CIRP surveys. The added perspective afforded by an additional five years of data has highlighted a number of new and interesting trends.

This report presents separate normative data summaries for men, women, and all freshmen. We have been careful to note all instances in which changes in the question format or response options occurred. Additionally, data for some questions have been aggregated to create a consistent time–series for these items. Most questions which appear in fewer than four surveys have been omitted from this report, with the exception of items which have been recently introduced and are expected to remain part of our research program for the next several years.

As with all large research programs, the CIRP has benefitted substantially from the commitment and insight of a great many people throughout the years. These colleagues, listed below, have had principal roles in the collection, analysis, and management of the CIRP surveys at various times since 1966:

Alan E. Bayer	Carol Francis	John M. Light
Robert F. Boruch	Kenneth C. Green	Mary Jane Maier
David E. Drew	Margo King Hemond	Robert J. Panos
John A. Creager	Engin I. Holmstrom	Gerald T. Richardson
Penny Edgert	Sylvia Hurtado	Marilyn Schalit

The CIRP has also been fortunate to have many friends and supporters in and around the higher education community. A succession of presidents at the American Council on Education—Logan Wilson, Roger Heyns, Jack Peltason, and Robert Atwell—have provided continuing support for the CIRP. We are also indebted to Elaine El–Khawas, currently Vice President for Research and Policy Analysis at ACE, and to those on the CIRP advisory board who have provided strong direction and good advice over the years. Helen S. Astin, Kenneth C. Green, and Lewis C. Solmon have been critical colleagues over the past two and one–half decades, as was Allan M. Cartter prior to his untimely death over a decade ago. Allan also played a major role in establishing the CIRP in 1966 when he was Vice President of the American Council on Education. Grants from the Carnegie Corporation of New York, the Ford Foundation, the Sloan Foundation, the Exxon Education Foundation, the National Science Foundation, and the U.S. Department of Education have helped to support the CIRP and research based on the CIRP data over the past twenty–five years.

When federal funding was abruptly terminated five years ago, we turned to our "core" sample of institutions (those that have participated since 1966) for financial assistance to help us over a three–year period. Their response was generous and heartwarming. We also approached the Ford Foundation and Lilly Endowment for temporary assistance, and their subsequent support has been crucial in helping us make the transition to self–supporting status.

The CIRP would not have been possible without the continuing help of many campus presidents, institutional CIRP representatives, and the more than seven million students who have participated in the CIRP freshman surveys since 1966. Although the freshman survey data are processed at UCLA, they are collected at some 600 campuses across the country each year. Without this continuing institutional interest in and commitment to the CIRP, we would not have been able to generate the data upon which this report is based.

Finally, we owe special thanks to the staff of UCLA's Higher Education Research Institute. In addition to the generous and sustained support of our colleagues, we have been assisted in preparing this report by several HERI staffers who deserve special recognition. Linda Sax helped proof the data that appear in later sections of this report, while the careful readings of early drafts by Dr. Frank Ryan and Tamara Wingard helped improve this report immeasurably. The numerous details that accompany the publication of a report such as this were ably handled by Ellyne Riggs. Many thanks to all!

Eric L. Dey
Alexander W. Astin
William S. Korn

THE AMERICAN FRESHMAN: TWENTY–FIVE YEAR TRENDS, 1966–1990

Each fall since 1966 the Cooperative Institutional Research Program (CIRP) has collected survey data to profile the characteristics, attitudes, values, educational achievements, and future goals of the new students entering college in the United States. Compiling the results of these twenty–five consecutive surveys has yielded an extremely interesting and informative portrait of the changing character of American college students. While addressing changes that directly affect higher education, the trend data generated by these consecutive annual surveys can also be viewed as indicators of this country's changing social context. This report, then, provides an overview of the first twenty–five years of data from the CIRP, highlighting key findings and discussing the significance that these findings have for American higher education and society at large.

The first seven freshman surveys were conducted at the American Council on Education, with support from the Carnegie Corporation of New York and the Ford Foundation. Since 1972, the annual CIRP freshman surveys have been conducted by the Higher Education Research Institute (HERI) at the University of California, Los Angeles, with the continuing sponsorship of the American Council on Education (see Astin, Korn, & Berz, 1990). Each year the CIRP surveys some 250,000 full–time students who constitute the entering freshman classes at a nationally representative sample of about 600 two– and four–year colleges and universities across the United States. These data discussed below are presented under eight broad headings: Academic skills and preparation, demographic trends, high school activities and experiences, educational and career plans, majors and careers, attitudes, student values, and financing college.

Academic Skills and Preparation

One of the most persistent educational concerns during the past decade has been the quality of the academic skills of American secondary school students. Continuing changes in student performance on national college admissions tests over the past several decades (Grandy, 1987; Turnbull, 1985) and more recent evidence based on cross–national comparisons of student knowledge and academic performance (Educational Testing Service, 1989) have helped to fuel these concerns. While there are strongly differing opinions about what might explain these differences and, moreover, whether such comparisons are valid (see for example Rotberg, 1990; Bradburn, Haertel, Schwille, & Torney–Purta, 1991; Rotberg, 1991), a number of continuing trends in the annual CIRP surveys of entering freshmen seem to suggest that the academic preparation of students entering college has in fact declined.

The data in Table 1 provide additional evidence of the changing nature of academic skills and preparation of college freshmen. For example, the percentage of students who note that an "important" or "very important" reason for deciding to go to college is "to improve my reading and study skills" has steadily increased since the inception of the CIRP, nearly doubling between 1971 and 1990. In addition, the number of students who reported that there was a very good chance that they would get "tutoring in specific courses" doubled between 1976 and 1990.

Table 1
Changes in the Academic Skills and Preparation of Freshmen

	CIRP Freshman Survey Year				
	1971	1976	1981	1986	1990
Reason for attending college:					
Improve reading and study skills[1]	22.2	35.1	39.7	40.3	43.0
Student expects to get tutoring in specific courses[2]	—	7.8	9.8	11.0	15.9

[1]Noted as an 'Important' or 'Very important' reason for attending college.
[2]Noted as having 'A very good chance' of occurring during college.

The data on school–related activities provide additional evidence of a decline in academic preparation. Since new questions are introduced into the CIRP each year to reflect changing interests in the educational community, every question cannot be repeated each year. In order to simplify our analysis of how high school academic activities have changed over time, data are presented from two representative time periods, 1968–71 and 1987–90. In cases where data are available for several years during these periods, values have been averaged to provide a more stable estimate. This simplification makes it easier to see major changes between the late 1960s and the late 1980s.

About half of the items showed little variation over time, while the rest showed pronounced changes. (See Figure 1.) For example, the percentages of students who reported coming to class late, who did not complete homework on time, and who studied with or tutored other students were largely stable over time. In contrast, large declines—about one–fifth, or greater—were seen in the number of students who argued with a teacher in class, checked out books or journals from their school library, studied in a library, or were a guest in a teacher's home. Conversely, large increases were registered in the number of students who asked a teacher for advice after class. Evidence from studies currently in progress at HERI suggests that this last change may reflect an increase in the number of students who are experiencing academic difficulties. At the same time, it is interesting to note that the number of students who belonged to scholastic honor societies actually increased. While this finding seems to run counter to the trend of apparent declines in preparation, it may be that this increase is simply linked to either "grade inflation" or changing standards for admission to honor societies.

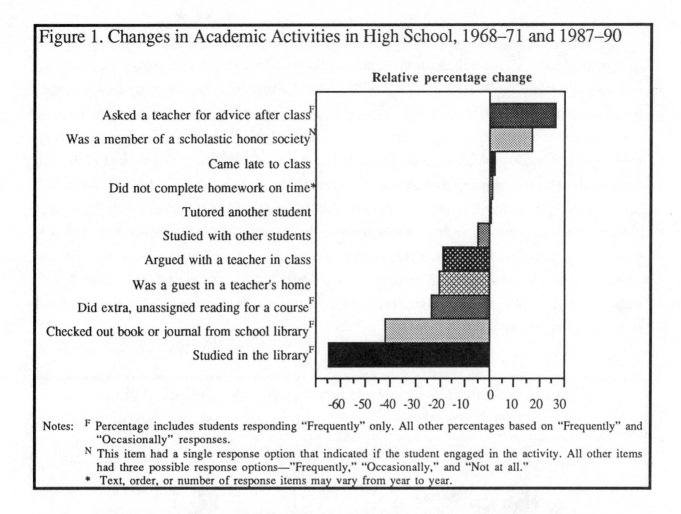

Figure 1. Changes in Academic Activities in High School, 1968–71 and 1987–90

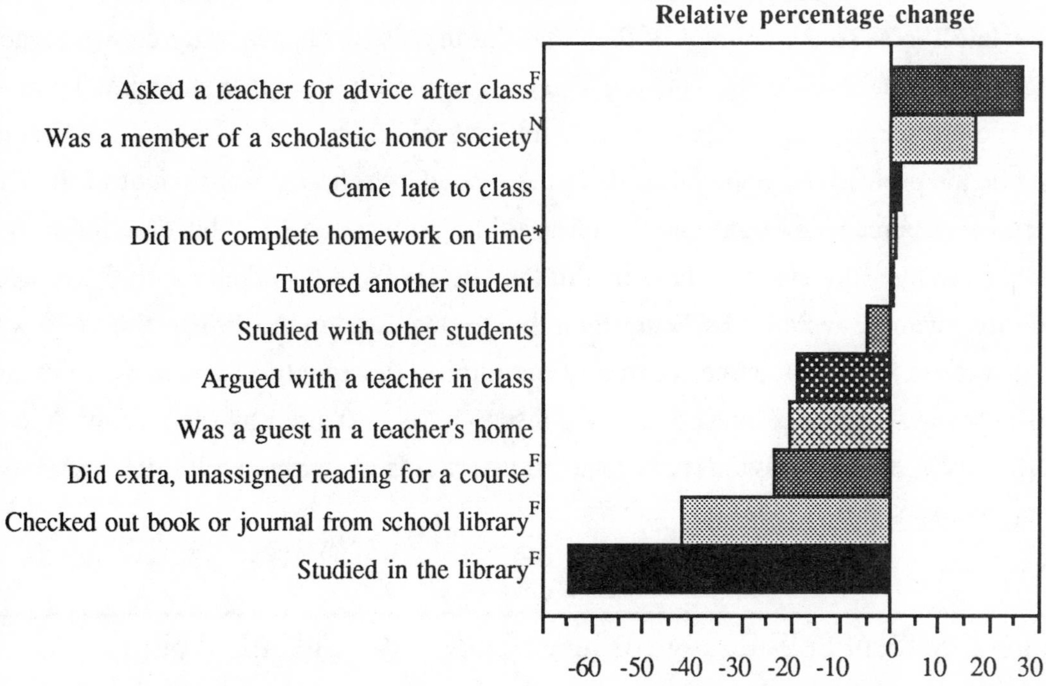

Notes: [F] Percentage includes students responding "Frequently" only. All other percentages based on "Frequently" and "Occasionally" responses.
[N] This item had a single response option that indicated if the student engaged in the activity. All other items had three possible response options—"Frequently," "Occasionally," and "Not at all."
* Text, order, or number of response items may vary from year to year.

Additional evidence that these declines in academic skills are real is found in the views of college faculty. When asked during the early 1980s about the quality of academic preparation of current students compared to those of the 1970s, more than 80 percent of a national sample of college faculty reported that the situation had either not improved or was worse than what it was in the 1970s (Minter & Bowen, 1982). For each professor who felt things had gotten better, there were two or more who felt that academic preparation had gotten worse. These perceptions applied regardless of the type of institution and regardless of the academic skill being rated (e.g., reading, writing, mathematics, sciences, etc.). A recent Carnegie Foundation (1989) survey of faculty showed that three–quarters of faculty thought students today are seriously underprepared in basic skills and nearly two–thirds (64 percent) believed today's students are "ill–suited for academic life." In addition, a large national survey of undergraduate teaching faculty conducted by the Higher Education Research Institute showed that only about one–quarter (27.4 percent) of college teachers felt that the students at their institution "were well–prepared academically" (see Astin, Korn, & Dey, 1991).

Despite these apparent declines in student preparation, the CIRP data show that students have more positive views of their academic and intellectual abilities. Figure 2 shows that following a decline in the late 1960s, student ratings of their abilities in these areas generally grew stronger, reaching a high point in the mid–1980s. One possible explanation for this apparent contradiction—declining levels of academic preparation coupled with increasingly positive views of intellectual ability—could be the problem of grade inflation in the secondary schools: Nearly half of the Fall 1986 freshmen (48.7 percent) thought that "grading in the high schools has become too easy." Moreover, data from the CIRP surveys show that in the late 1960s, the students with C averages outnumbered those with A averages by better than two to one. During the 1970s, this ratio was reversed, so that those with A averages currently outnumber those with C averages. In recent years, CIRP data show a slight resurgence of grade inflation (as measured by the ratio of A to C students entering college) to its previous peak level, although it is too early to tell if this trend will continue on into the 1990s[1].

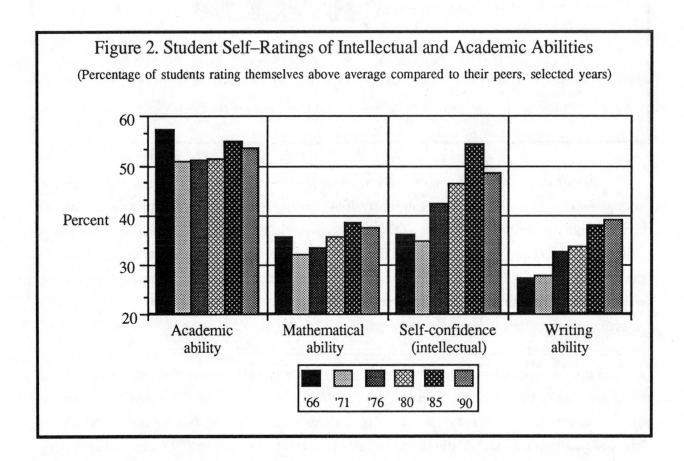

Figure 2. Student Self–Ratings of Intellectual and Academic Abilities

(Percentage of students rating themselves above average compared to their peers, selected years)

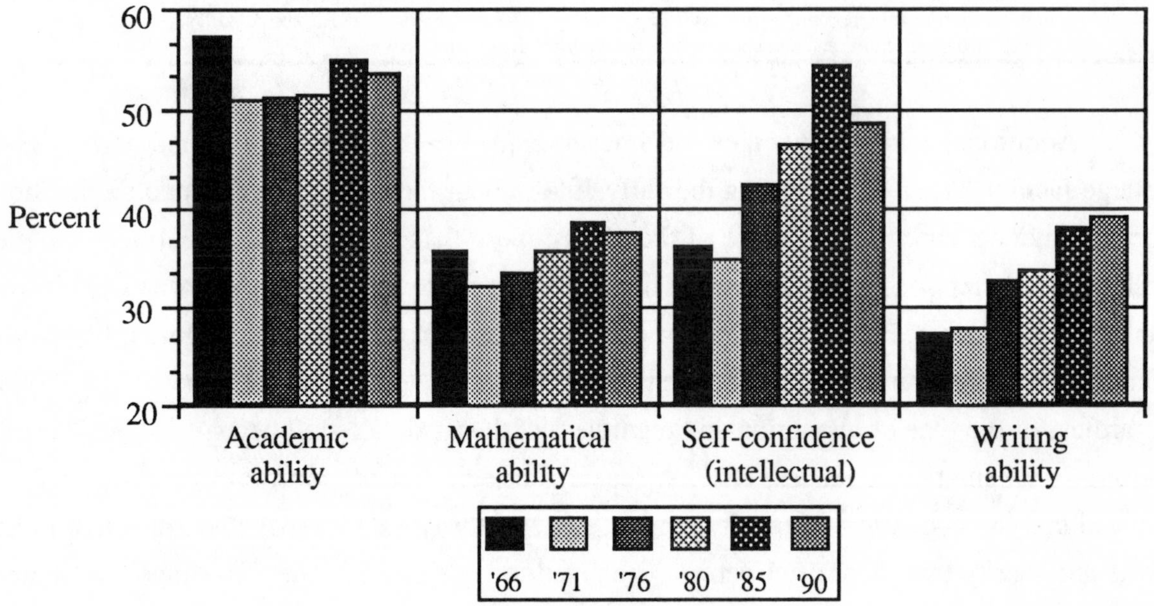

[1]Another possible interpretation is that changes in financial aid policy and more selective admissions guidelines have worked to exclude poorer—and less well prepared—students, thus resulting in the relative increase of A to C students we see in the late 1980s.

The National Commission on Excellence in Education (NCEE, 1982) performed a series of analyses which suggested that changes in the high school curriculum may have been partly responsible for declining levels of preparation and inflated grades. Students during the mid/late 1970s and early 1980s took fewer traditional academic courses (particularly in English and mathematics) and more "soft" electives such as band and driver training than did their counterparts in the late 1960s. Since the grading standards in these electives are likely to be less stringent than those in basic academic courses, this curricular shift would tend to inflate students' grade averages, while simultaneously impeding the development of basic academic skills.

It is interesting to note, however, that grade inflation has been rekindled even though college freshmen have been taking increasingly "academic" programs. The NCEE's report, *A Nation at Risk,* made recommendations concerning basic levels of high school preparation in various subject areas, and since then the CIRP has been tracking the number of students who meet or exceed these recommendations. As Figure 3 shows, the CIRP data indicate that the number of students taking more "academic" programs increased between 1983 and 1990, with the largest changes occurring in the level of foreign language preparation.

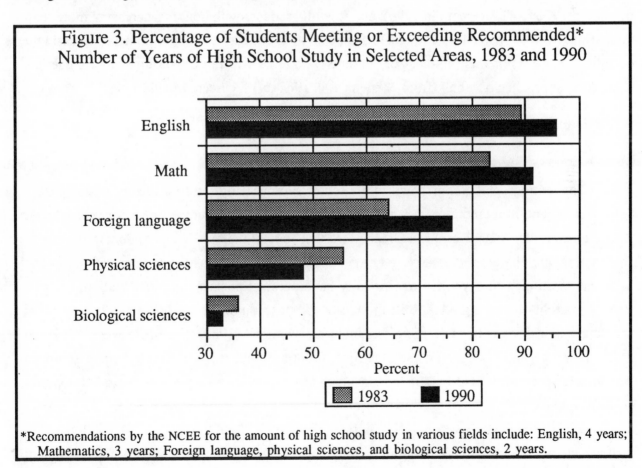

Figure 3. Percentage of Students Meeting or Exceeding Recommended* Number of Years of High School Study in Selected Areas, 1983 and 1990

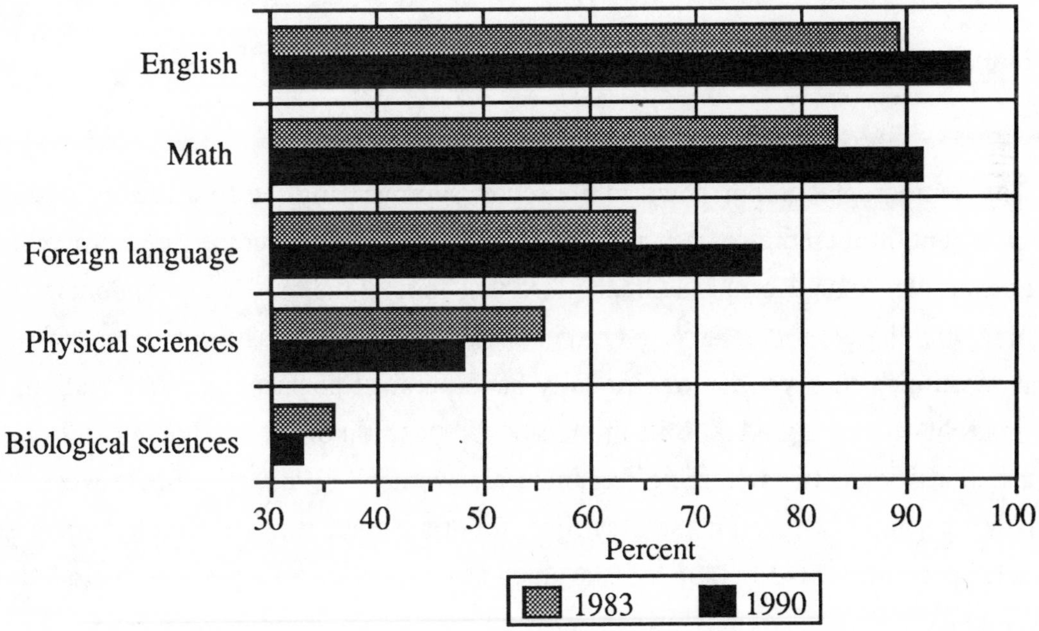

*Recommendations by the NCEE for the amount of high school study in various fields include: English, 4 years; Mathematics, 3 years; Foreign language, physical sciences, and biological sciences, 2 years.

While the CIRP data show that students are taking more academic courses in high school, one discouraging note for persons interested in America's international "competitiveness" is the declining level of scientific preparation among entering college students. During the past seven years, the number of students meeting the NCEE's recommended levels of preparation in the physical and biological sciences has dropped by about ten percent. It may be that as students seek to strengthen their skills in core academic areas such as English and math, they tend to balance their schedules with "soft" electives rather than "hard" electives such as science. If this is the case, efforts to increase rigor in certain fields (e.g., math and foreign language) may have inadvertently led to weakened preparation levels in others (e.g., natural sciences), with the number of "soft" electives remaining largely unchanged.

Other data from the CIRP indicate that decreased secondary school standards may encourage students to be very optimistic about their academic expectations for college. Since the inception of the CIRP there has been a dramatic increase in the proportion of students who believe that they: (a) will be elected to an academic honor society (nearly tripling, from 2.9 percent in 1967 to 8.1 percent in 1990); (b) will earn at least a B average in college (up by one–quarter, from 32.7 percent in 1972 to 41.3 percent in 1990); and (c) will graduate with honors (increasing more than three–fold, from 3.7 percent in 1967 to 13.5 percent in 1990). Concurrent with these increasingly optimistic expectations, the number of students who expect to fail any courses in college has dropped by more than one–half (from 2.9 percent in 1967 to 1.3 percent in 1990).

Demographic Trends

The demographic trends noted in the report summarizing the first twenty years of CIRP remain as salient, if not more so, today. Indeed, these trends have become more pronounced over time. For example, Astin, Korn, and Green noted that "one of the most widely publicized changes in demographic characteristics among entering college students was the reversal of sex ratios. Whereas more men than women traditionally have pursued postsecondary education, the past twenty years have seen a gradual shift in the sex composition of the freshman class to the point where a majority of today's entering freshmen are women" (1986, p. 10). Between 1969 and 1985, the proportion of women in the first–time, full–time student population had increased from 43.4 to 51.8 percent. By the Fall of 1990, women accounted for 53.8 percent of first–time, full–time freshmen.

While the changing sex ratio is important, the magnitude of this shift is small compared to striking changes in the racial and ethnic composition of the American undergraduate student population. Between the mid–1960s and the mid–1970s, the representation of minorities in entering freshman classes nearly doubled. Considering that the *absolute size* of the freshman class also increased by more than 40 percent during this period, such a sharp increase in the *proportion* of minorities among entering freshman classes is all the more remarkable. The largest increases were observed among blacks, although American Indians, Mexican–Americans, and Puerto Ricans also began to increase their representation in the early 1970s. In a study of these changes through 1981, Astin (1982) reported that minorities were best represented in education and the social sciences, and most underrepresented in the sciences and engineering. At the graduate level, the greatest improvement in minority representation occurred in the professional fields of medicine and law, while the greatest underrepresentations were in doctoral programs in the sciences and engineering. This same study indicated that the greatest loss of minorities from the American educational system occurred in the secondary schools.

During the 1980s, the trend toward increased minority enrollments in the first–time, full–time freshman class largely disappeared (also see Mortenson, 1991). For example, the representation of blacks among college freshmen increased from 9.2 to 9.6 percent between 1980 and 1990. The representation of Hispanics, on the other hand, actually declined over the same period: Mexican–Americans among first–time, full–time freshmen declined from 2.1 to 1.5 percent, while the percentage of Puerto Ricans dropped by nearly one–half, from 0.9 to 0.5 percent. In fact, the only nonwhite group with a substantially growing representation in the freshman class was Asian–Americans, who accounted for 1.4 percent in 1980 and 2.9 percent in 1990.

It seems likely that many of these enrollment trends can be attributed in part to changes in federal financial aid policies. During the Reagan–Bush years, there has been a pronounced shift in federal aid from grants to loans. As minority students are substantially more likely than whites to receive all forms of federal aid, these policy changes have likely had a disproportionate impact on minority students. In a recent study, for example, Astin (1990) reported CIRP trend data showing that the percentages of black and white students who picked their college because of "low tuition" was similar during the 1970s and early 1980s. Since then these percentages have diverged dramatically so that black students are now significantly more likely than white students to say that they picked their college because of low tuition. Moreover, by seeking institutions with low tuition, black students have increasingly been forced to attend their second– and lower–choice colleges at a higher rate than white students.

High School Activities and Experiences

The freshman survey instrument usually includes 15–20 items about the student's activities during the year prior to entering college. Some of the largest changes are found in the area of health–related behaviors such as smoking, drinking and drug use. The CIRP data show that the percentage of freshmen who frequently smoke cigarettes has declined by over one–third between 1966 and 1990 (from 16.6 to 10.6 percent, after reaching a low of 8.9 in 1987). The proportion reporting that they took sleeping pills also declined, from 5.9 percent in 1967 to 3.0 percent in 1989 (a 50 percent drop). Similarly, tranquilizer use declined more than 80 percent between 1967 and 1989, from 9.9 to 1.7 percent. The percentage of students reporting that they frequently or occasionally drank beer, on the other hand, showed a decidedly different pattern: The prevalence of beer drinking started increasing during the late 1970s, peaking at 75.2 percent in 1981, but then began to decline so that students today are only slightly more likely to drink beer than those who entered college in the mid–1960s (58.2 percent in 1990 versus 53.5 percent in 1966).

While these trends suggest that students are using these substances much less than in the recent past (although smoking has made somewhat of a rebound in the past few years, possibly due to controversial "youth–oriented" advertising campaigns sponsored by the tobacco industry), there are very important gender differences in these trends. For example, although freshmen men and women are less likely to smoke now than in 1966 the pattern of decline has been very different for men and women. As Figure 4 shows, freshman men entering college in 1966 were about 50 percent more likely to be smokers than were their women classmates; in 1990, women were about one–third more likely than men to be smokers (indeed, the percentage of women smokers substantially increased during the 1970s while the percentage of men smokers declined over the same period). Thus, while smoking among freshman men has declined by over one–half during the past twenty–five years, smoking among women has declined by only one–tenth. On the other hand, use of tranquilizers has declined for all freshmen, but the decrease was much larger for women. As noted above, the use of tranquilizers has dropped some 80 percent since 1967, but the decline of use among women has been twice as steep as that seen among men. As a result, usage for men and women has converged: Whereas women in 1967 were twice as likely to be frequent users of tranquilizers, reported levels of use for men and women were essentially the same in 1989.

Table 2 summarizes changes in many of the CIRP activity items. As noted above, new questions are introduced into the CIRP each year to reflect changing interests in the educational community so not all questions can be repeated every year. In order to simplify the presentation of trends among these activity items, data are presented from three time periods over the life of the

Figure 4. Substance Use Among College Freshmen, by Gender

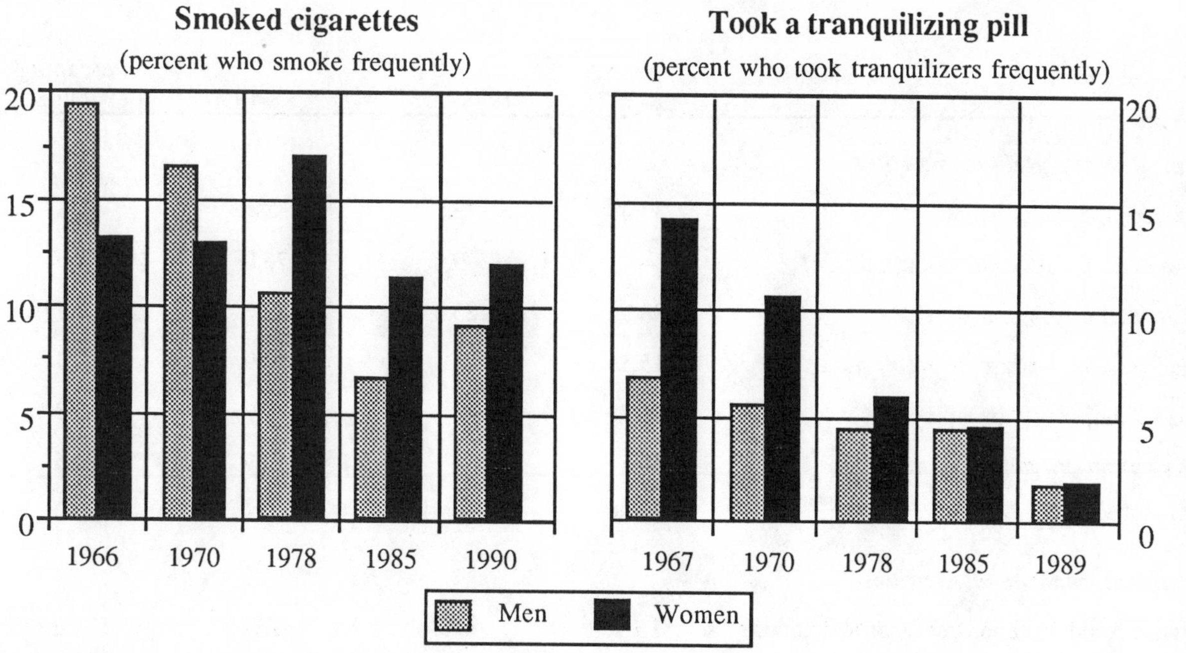

CIRP: 1968–71, 1978–81, and 1987–90. In cases where data are available for several years during one of this periods, the values have been averaged to provide a more stable estimate. (Readers interested in data on specific activities in specific years should consult the data that appear later in this report.)

The CIRP data in Table 2 show that consistent declines have occurred in the percentages of students who are involved in cultural and religious activities. Although some of these declines are modest—such as the 4.5 percent decline in the number of students attending public recitals and concerts—many are dramatic. The number of freshmen who "frequently" or "occasionally" visited an art gallery or museum in the year prior to entering college, for example, has declined by nearly one–quarter (from 69.3 percent in 1968–71 to 53.7 percent in 1987–90). The number of students who had original writings or poetry published, or had a major part in a play declined by more than 10 percent, suggesting that active participation in cultural activities has declined as well. One exception to this pattern is the number of students who played musical instruments in high school. While this percentage has declined only slightly since the late 1960s (from 39.0 percent in 1968–71 to 38.4 percent in 1990), it should be noted that the number of high school musicians has declined by about 10 percent since the early 1980s (following an approximately equivalent increase during the late 1970s). Participation in religious activities among freshmen has also been on the decline: The percentage attending religious services has dropped slightly, while the number who report having frequent discussions about religion has dropped by one–quarter.

Table 2
Activities of College Freshmen from Three Time Periods

	1968–1971	1978–1981	1987–1990	Relative Percentage Change
Cultural and Religious Activities				
Played a musical instrument	39.0	42.6	38.4	–1.5
Attended a public recital or concert*	—	79.6	76.0[1]	–4.5
Attended a religious service	88.5	85.4	82.6	–6.7
Had original writing or poetry published* N	15.5	—	13.9	–10.3
Had a major part in a play N	15.7	—	12.9	–17.8
Visited an art gallery or museum	69.3	—	53.7	–22.5
Discussed religion F	27.5	—	20.9	–24.0
Political and Social Activities				
Participated in organized demonstrations	16.3[2]	18.3	37.1	127.6
Discussed politics F	25.9	—	18.5	–28.6
Worked in a local, state, or national political campaign*	14.1	8.8	8.7	–38.3

Notes: N This item had a single response option that indicated if the student engaged in the activity. All other items had three possible response options—"Frequently," "Occasionally," and "Not at all."
F Percentage includes students responding "Frequently" only. All other percentages based on "Frequently" and "Occasionally" responses.
* Text, order, or number of response items may vary from year to year.
[1] Item not asked between 1987 and 1990. Percentage shown based upon data from the 1986 CIRP survey.
[2] Item not asked between 1968 and 1971. Percentage shown based upon data from the 1967 CIRP survey.

The CIRP data show similar declines in participation in political and social activities. The number of students who worked in political campaigns declined by about two–fifths between the late 1960s and late 1970s, while the number who report having frequent discussions about politics declined by about one–third between the late 1960s and late 1980s. These figures suggest that students are not politically active *in traditional ways*. Other data from the CIRP also suggests that students may be disillusioned with and alienated from traditional politics. For example: (a) the number of students who participated in organized demonstrations has more than doubled since the late 1960s (about 2 in 5 freshmen reported being involved in demonstrations in the 1990 survey); (b) students increasingly expect to be involved in future protests; and (c) students are becoming more interested in influencing social and political values (Astin, Korn, & Berz, 1990). These trends suggest that there is a rapidly expanding number of American college students who are dissatisfied with the status quo and with traditional political methods of bringing about social change.

Educational and Career Plans

The freshman survey data reveal that the proportion of freshmen planning to pursue graduate or professional degrees was fairly stable between 1970 and the mid–1980s (49.0 percent in 1970; 50.1 in 1978; and 50.4 in 1985). Since that time, however, interest in postgraduate study has been increasing regularly, setting record–high levels in each of the past five CIRP surveys. In 1990, three in five freshmen indicated that they planned to seek a master's, doctoral, medical, or law degree (60.7 percent).

While interest in law and medical degrees remained just below previous record levels, the popularity of the master's and doctoral degrees reached all–time highs in 1990 (37.2 percent and 12.4 percent, respectively). (See Figure 5.) The remarkable popularity of the doctoral degree is puzzling, considering that students continue to show little interest in scientific research (1.4 percent) and college teaching (0.4 percent), two fields where the Ph.D. is likely to be required. It may be that these high levels of degree aspiration reflect a strong need for achievement and status more than a switch in career interests (Astin, Korn, & Berz, 1990).

Figure 5. Freshman Interest in Postgraduate Degrees
(Percentages)

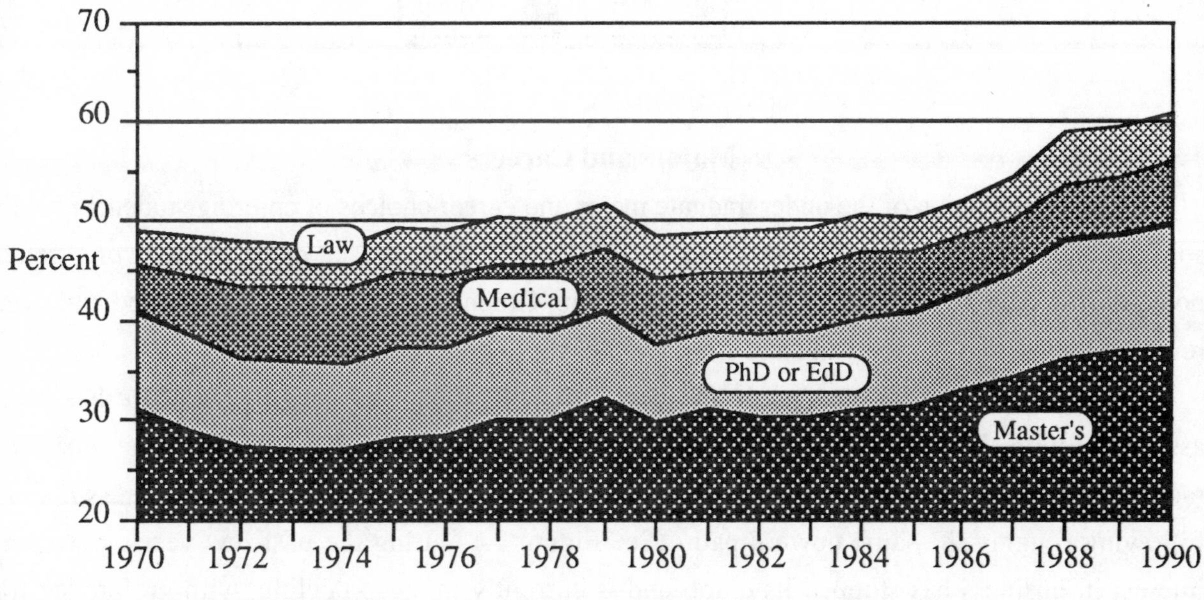

A closer look at the CIRP data reveals that changes in degree aspirations are not the same for men and women. (See Figure 6.) The strong effects of the Women's Movement on women's educational aspirations can be seen by comparing the 1970 and 1990 figures. While men's interest in doctoral, law, and medical degrees has remained steady or declined slightly in the 20–year period, women's interest has increased sharply. In 1970, women's relative interest in such degrees ranged from about one–half to one–eighth of the men's. By 1990 women showed a level of interest roughly equal to that of men.

Figure 6. Freshman Interest in Professional and Doctoral Degrees, by Gender
(Percentages)

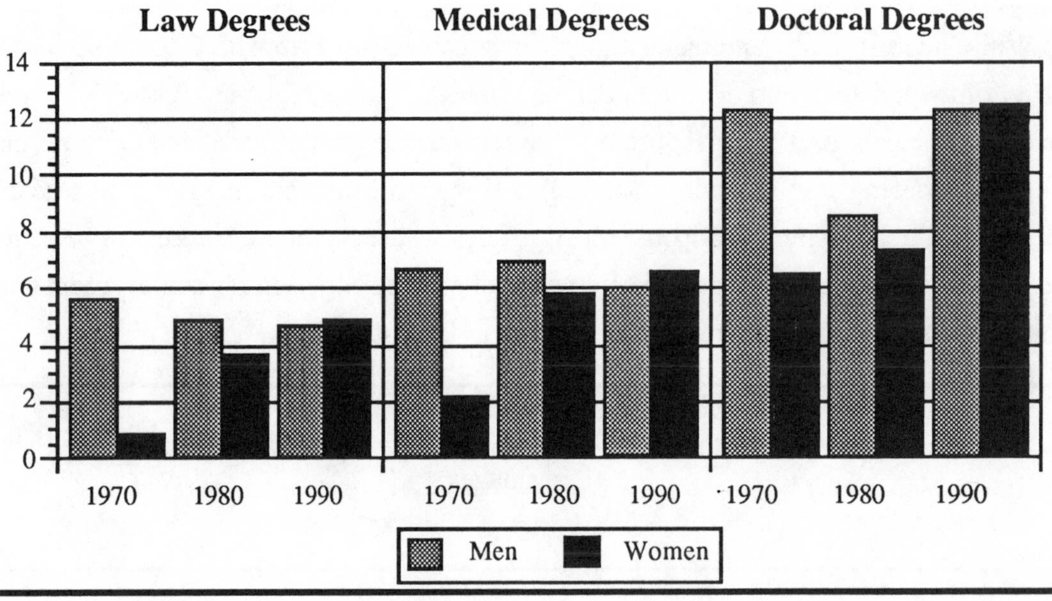

Majors and Careers

An examination of the undergraduate major and career choices of entering students reveals some of the most interesting changes contained in the CIRP data. In fact, many of the strong trends noted during the first 20 years of the CIRP (see Astin, Green, & Korn, 1986) have ended and even reversed themselves in surprising and striking ways during the past five years.

One of the largest changes in the popularity of fields measured by the CIRP has been associated with the field of business. The proportion of students interested in business careers more than doubled between 1966 and 1986 (from 11.6 to 24.1), with interest in business majors following roughly the same upward path. (See Figure 7.) During the past few years, however, interest in business has stopped its climb and is currently in steep decline, with preference for business careers dropping to 18.4 percent of 1990 freshmen (compared to 21.8 percent in 1989 and 24.6 percent in 1987, the peak year). Choice of business majors showed a similar decline, to 21.1 percent in 1990, compared to 24.5 percent in 1989 and 27.3 percent in 1987. While the reasons for this turnaround are not clear, it may be that competition for jobs has increased, or that many students are disillusioned by the field of business because of continuing revelations of business scandals such as insider trading, stock fraud, and the savings and loan debacle.

Figure 7. Freshman Interest in Business
(Percentages)

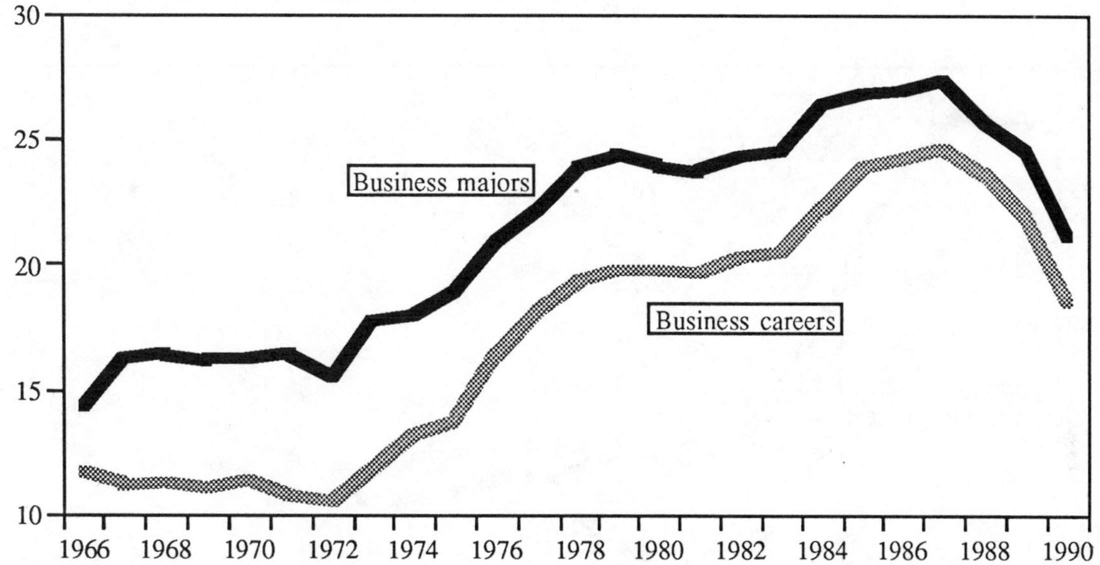

While interest in business is now in steep decline after a record–setting increase, interest in education majors and careers has slowly continued to rebound from the all–time low in the early 1980s. (See Figure 8.) The 1990 survey shows that 9.0 percent of freshmen were interested in teaching careers (up from 8.2 percent in 1989 and the low point of 4.7 percent in 1982). It should be noted that despite these increases, interest in teaching careers remains much lower than the level of interest registered in the late 1960s: Interest in secondary teaching careers is only about one–third of the all–time high, while interest in elementary teaching is about one–half of what it once was. Despite continuing claims that students interested in teaching careers should major in liberal arts fields rather than in education, interest in education majors has also been on the increase and is about equal to the level of interest registered in 1966 (10.6 percent in 1966 versus 9.9 percent in 1990). What this means, in essence, is that prospective teachers are more inclined than ever to major in education.

Interest in both science and engineering careers has continued to drop steadily in the past few years. (See Figure 9.) Student interest in engineering and computer science reached an all–time high in 1983, but their popularity—both as majors and as career choices—has declined sharply since then, by roughly one–half for computer science and by about one–quarter in engineering. While interest in majoring in biological or physical sciences has declined somewhat, interest in mathematics and statistics has experienced the largest relative decline, dropping from 4.5 percent in 1966 to a mere 0.7 percent in 1990. Although computer science may have captured some of the students who otherwise might have majored in mathematics or statistics, the recent 85 percent decline in the number of freshmen interested in math and statistics is quite alarming.

Figure 8. Freshman Interest in Teaching Careers
(Percentages)

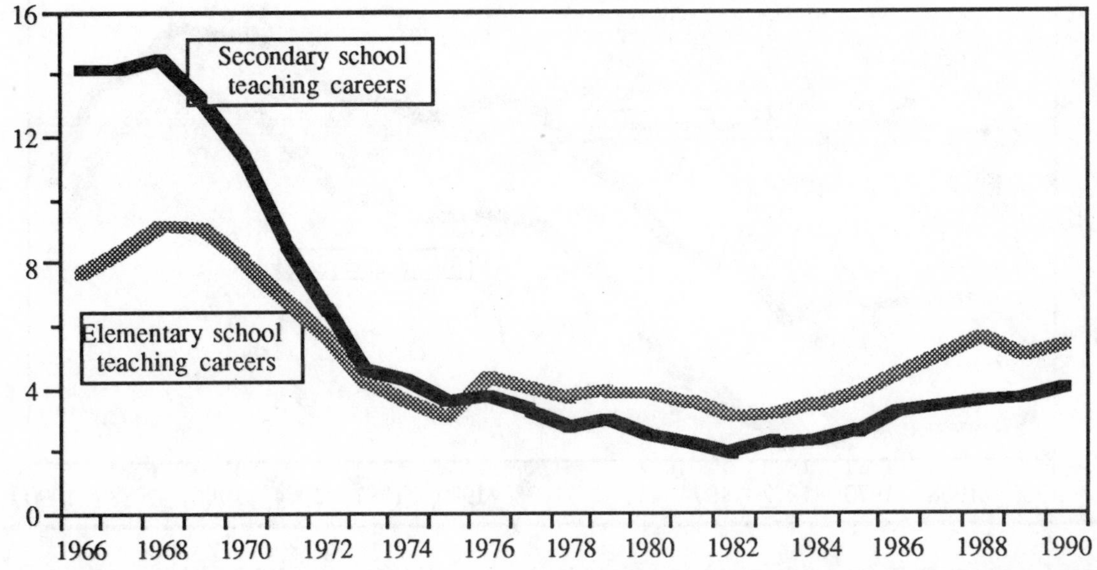

Figure 9. Freshman Interest in Engineering, Math, and Computer Science Majors
(Percentages)

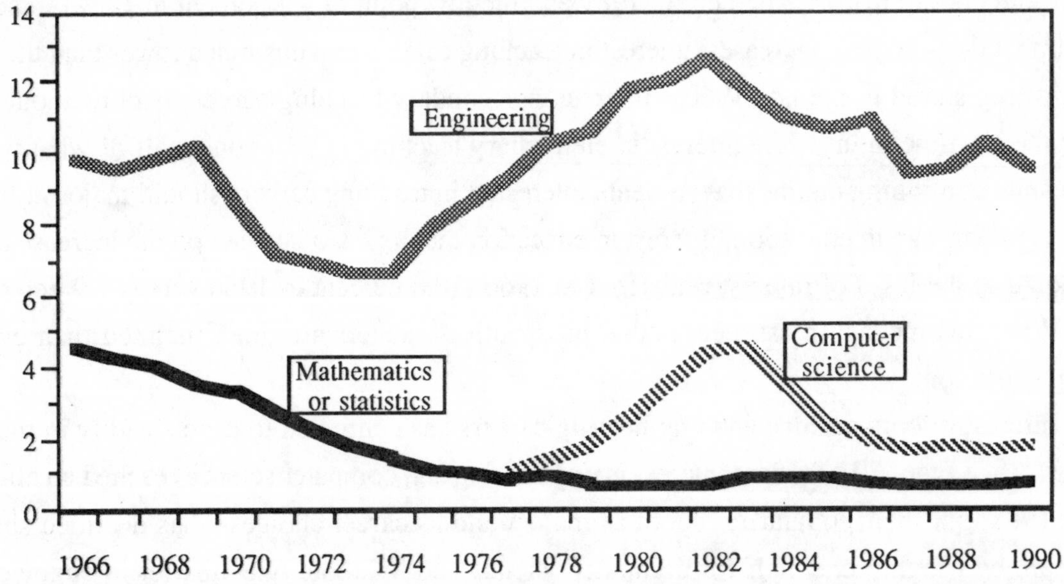

The first two decades of the CIRP recorded declining interest for most of the traditional liberal arts disciplines (especially in the humanities [English, literature, foreign language, philosophy, theology], the fine and performing arts [art, music, speech, and theater], and the social sciences [anthropology, economics, geography, history, political science, psychology, social work, and sociology]). However, the past five years have seen a slight recovery. Interest in the social sciences, for example, increased to 6.6 percent in the 1990 survey, up from 1982's all–time low of 3.9 percent. While the recovery in other liberal arts fields has not been as pronounced, the sharp declines recorded in the early 1980s have given way to a trend of slow growth.

Given the pronounced changes in the major field choices of freshmen, it is not surprising to find that career preferences have changed quite dramatically—especially among women. Figure 10, for example, shows how women's career choices have changed on a percentage basis, using choices from 1966 as the base year (given the wide range of percentage changes, Figure 10 displays these changes on a logarithmic scale). In addition to the decreased interest in educational careers discussed above, the figure shows that the number of women interested in engineering careers has increased more than ten–fold since 1966 (from 0.2 to 2.4 percent), while interest in law careers increased by over 750 percent. Interest in business careers has declined since the mid–1980s, although current interest is still five times what it was in 1966. Interest in nursing careers has rebounded somewhat from a low in the mid–1980s, with current levels of interest about one–quarter higher than they were in 1966.

Figure 10. Changing Career Preferences of Freshman Women
(Expressed as a percentage of 1966 choices)

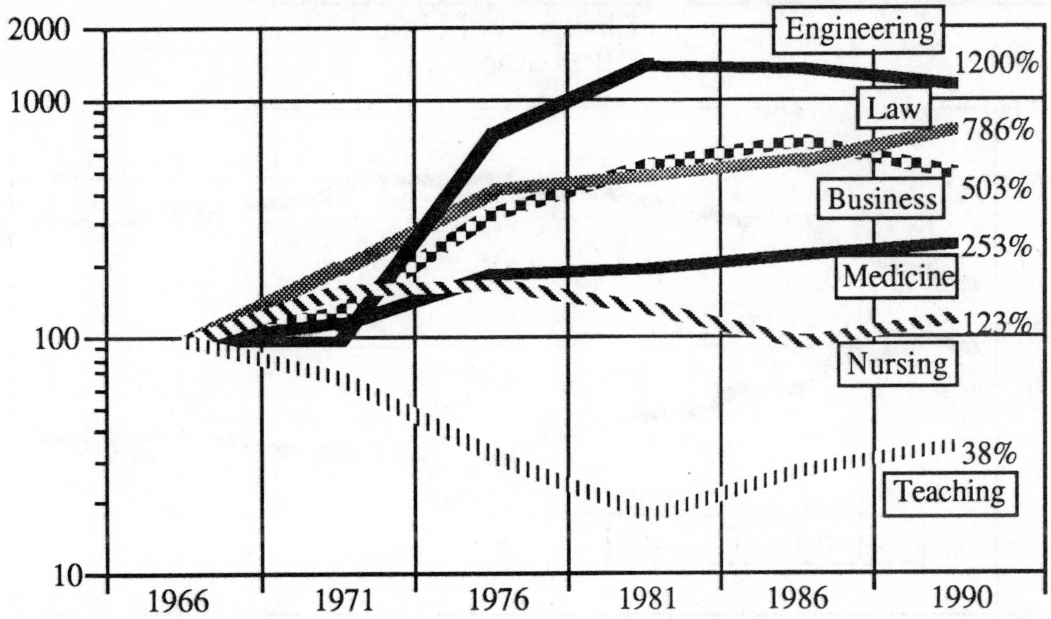

Attitudes

Each fall since 1967 the attitudes of the entering freshmen have been assessed by means of statements concerning a variety of controversial issues. The freshmen are asked to indicate whether they agree or disagree with each statement. Trends in freshman attitudes can be estimated by charting changes in the percent that agree ("strongly" or "somewhat") with each statement. Taken together, these data provide a fascinating 25–year profile of the changes not only in student attitudes but also in the attitudes and values of the larger society. To simplify the task of summarizing these results, the attitudinal statements are divided into three broad categories: Political orientation, personal and social issues, and sex, marriage and family.

Political Orientation

The recent and widespread publicity about the growing "conservatism" of American college students does not really describe the trends observed in the freshman survey. (See Figure 11.) While it is true that the percentage of freshmen identifying themselves as "liberal" or "far left" has decreased substantially since the high of 38.1 percent in 1971 (the 1990 figure is 24.4 percent), it has increased somewhat from its low of 19.7 percent in 1981. The percentage of freshmen identifying themselves as "conservative" or "far right," however, did not rise at a corresponding rate. Rising steadily from a low of 14.5 percent in 1973 to 20.7 percent in 1981, the trend in "right–wing" students has hovered in the range of 18.7—22.8 percent ever since. The trends for students identifying themselves at the extremes of the political orientation scale—either far left or far right—have been relatively flat, ranging from 1.6 to 3.1 percent for far left, and from 0.6 to 1.6 percent for far right.

Figure 11. Changes in Political View
(Percentages)

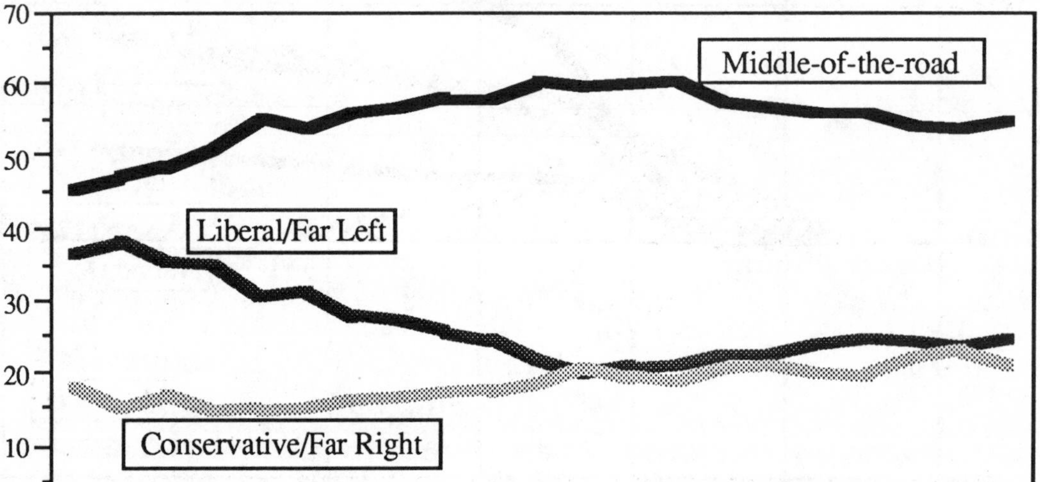

Striking changes in political identification have occurred in the "middle–of–the–road" category. From a low of 45.4 percent in 1970, the percentage of freshmen identifying themselves in this manner rose by almost one–third to 60.3 percent in 1983, then declined by one–tenth to 54.7 percent in 1990. While the gains in middle–of–the–road identification between 1973 and 1983 came almost exclusively at the cost of liberal/far left groups, the decline since 1983 has been matched by virtually equal increases in the liberal/far left and conservative/far right groups.

It is interesting to note that changes in political view among freshmen have not been the same for men and women. As Figure 12 shows, the decline in students identifying themselves as politically liberal was roughly equal for men and women, reaching bottom in the early 1980s. A strikingly different picture emerges when we consider the percentage of students identifying themselves as conservative or far right: While the percentage of women who are conservative has remained stable—about one in seven—over time, the percentage of men who label themselves as being conservative increased about 75 percent between 1971 and 1990 (from 16.2 to 25.8 percent, with a peak of 28.9 percent in 1989). Given the changes in the role of women in American society, it may be that this "gender gap" actually represents a backlash against the Women's Movement by men.

Figure 12. Changes in Political View, by Gender
(Percentages)

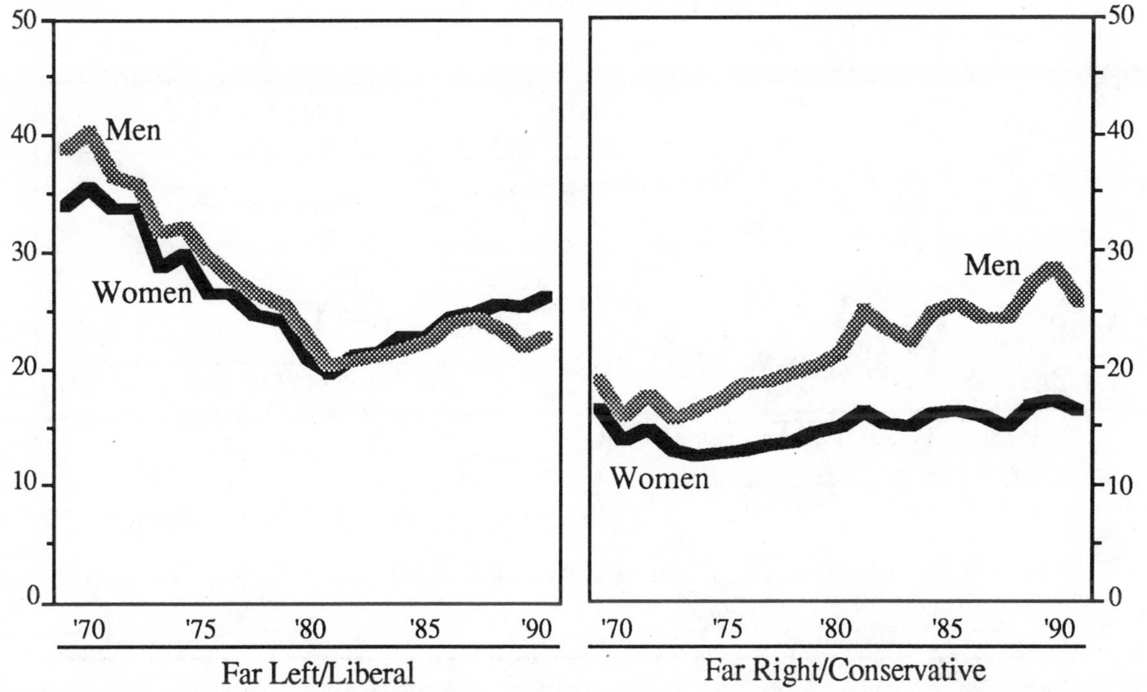

Personal and Social Issues

Despite these changes in the ways students identify themselves politically, there has been no monolithic trend away from positions traditionally considered as "liberal" or toward positions traditionally considered as "conservative." Indeed, our data point to a mixed bag of changes in student support for a variety of issues: While more students support "liberal" positions on environmental and health issues, their views have become more conservative on "law and order" issues. (See Figure 13.) The number of freshmen who believe that "the federal government is not doing enough to control environmental pollution" has been rising steadily since the mid–1980s (to 87.9 percent in 1990, up from the all–time low of 77.6 percent in 1981). Similarly, the percentage who say that it is "essential" or "very important" for them to "become involved in programs to clean up the environment" has more than doubled in the last four years (from a low of 15.9 percent in 1986 to 33.9 percent in 1990). Student support for a national health care plan has also increased, with nearly three–quarters of all freshmen agreeing that such a plan should be established to cover everyone's medical costs (up from a low of 54.8 in 1981). While such support might be indicative of increased liberalism among students, other trends show that students might be becoming more conservative: Student opposition to capital punishment declined by more than one–half between 1970 and 1990 (from 56.3 to 21.5 percent) while the number of students who believe that "there is too much concern in the courts for the rights of criminals" increased by one–quarter over the same period (from 51.6 to 66.3 percent).

Figure 13. Attitudes Toward Governmental Policies
(Percentages)

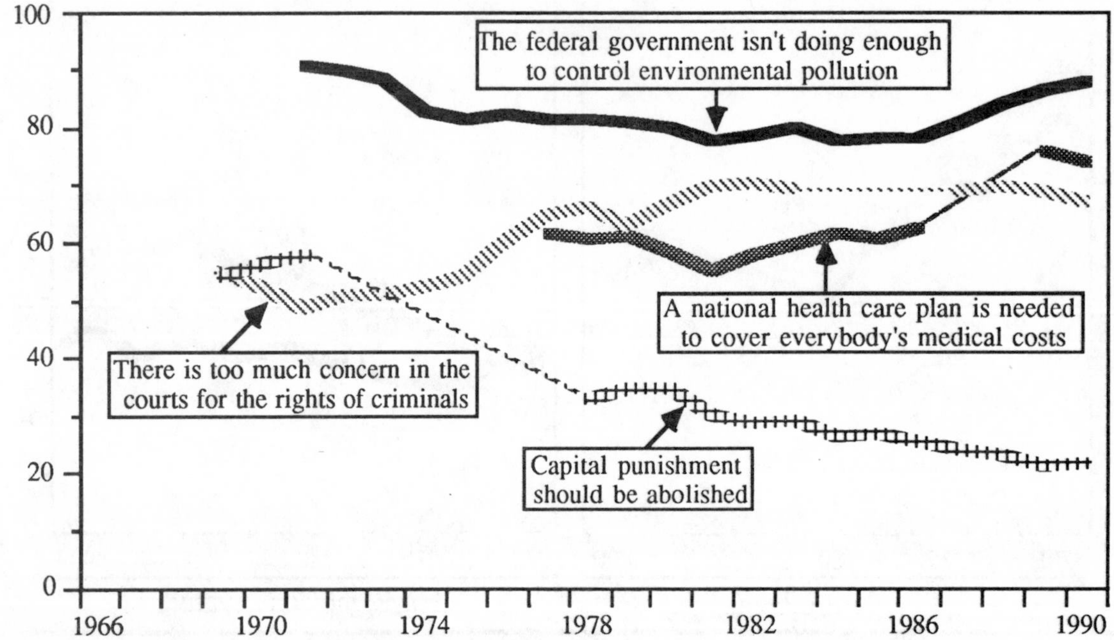

Note: Thin lines indicate interpolated values.

When considering issues of personal choice, student attitudes are again mixed. (See Figure 14.) Support for the legalization of marijuana rose sharply during the early to mid–1970s only to be followed by an equivalent decline since that time (from 19.4 percent in 1968 to 18.6 in 1990, with a peak of 52.9 percent in 1977). Surveys of high school students, college students, and young adults show that marijuana *usage* also peaked in the late 1970s, and has declined sharply since then (Johnston, O'Malley, & Bachman, 1991). Whether this recent decline in support for legalizing marijuana actually represents declining usage, a growing awareness of the potential health dangers of marijuana use, or both, is not clear. In this regard, it should be noted that the use of alcohol among college freshmen has decreased substantially during recent years while acceptance of mandatory drug testing for employees and job applicants has increased—from 71.0 percent in 1988, the first year it was asked, to 80.4 percent in 1990.

Nearly two–thirds of all freshmen currently support legal abortion—the 64.9 percent agreement recorded in 1990 is an all–time high. Our data also show that as a group, freshmen do not see this as a "women's issue": Men and women support legal abortion at equivalent rates (in 1990, 65.0 versus 64.8 percent for men and women, respectively). It is interesting to note that support for legal abortion jumped sharply in 1989, apparently in response to Supreme Court rulings that thrust the issue back into the political arena.

Figure 14. Attitudes Toward Social and Personal Issues
(Percentages)

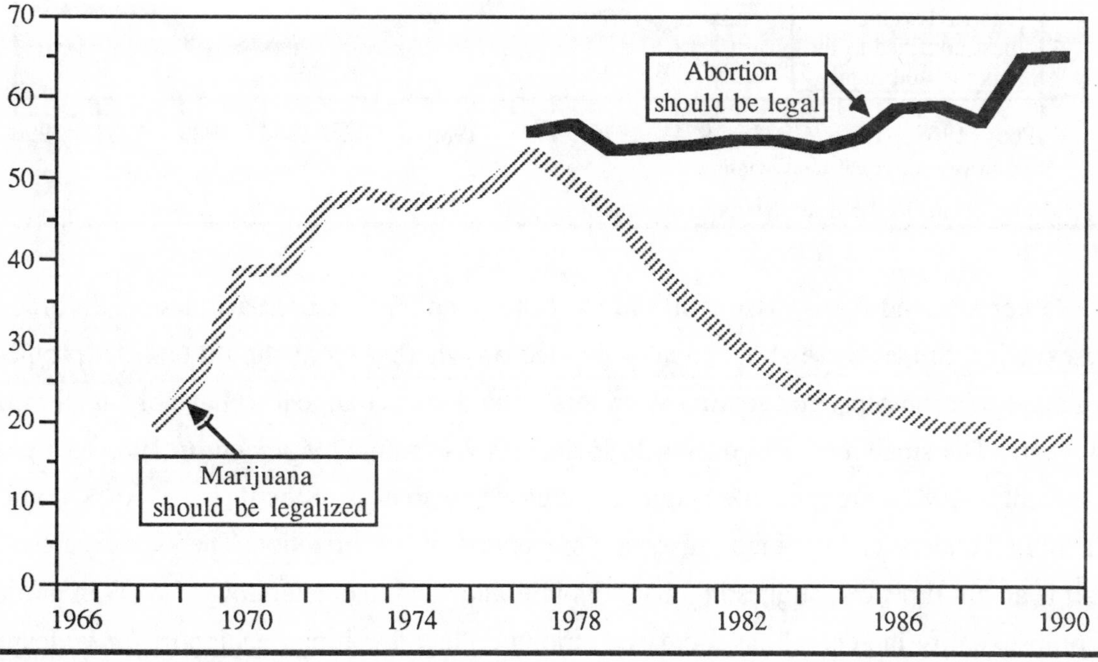

Sex, Marriage, and Family

Several survey items address student attitudes toward sex and marriage. The item showing the largest changes concerns the role of women: "The activities of married women are best confined to the home and family." Student endorsement of this traditional view of women declined sharply between 1967 and 1986, but has been increasing steadily since that time (25.2 percent in 1990, up from a low of 20.3 in 1986). Even though men are still more likely than women to support this view (30.6 versus 20.5 percent), the decline in support among men (66.5 to 30.6 percent) has been about as sharp as the decline among women (44.3 to 20.5 percent). (See Figure 15.)

Figure 15. Attitudes Toward Marriage, by Gender
(Percentage who 'Agree' or 'Strongly Agree')

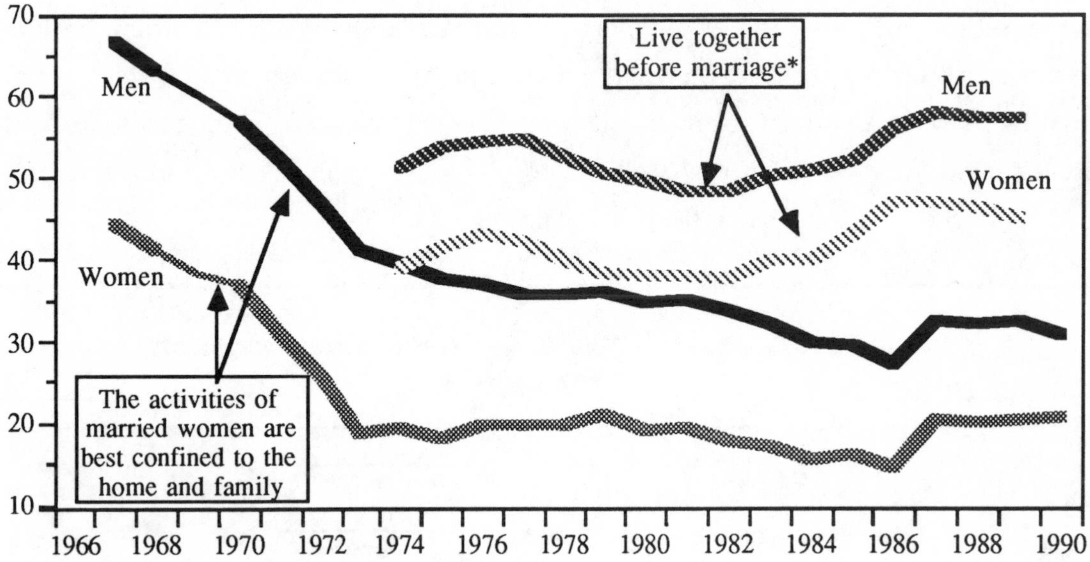

*See survey for actual item wording

Note: Thin lines indicate interpolated values.

Other sex and family issues in the CIRP have addressed premarital sex, divorce, and homosexuality. Students are about equally divided on whether there should be laws prohibiting homosexual relationships, and sentiment on this issue does not appear to have changed much in recent years. The small increases during 1986 and 1987—from 47.9 percent in 1985 to a peak of 53.2 percent in 1987—are most likely due to increased awareness of the threat of AIDS, combined with a limited understanding of the causes and prevention of HIV infection. The 1990 figure of 44.4 percent is an all–time low, suggesting that both tolerance and understanding of AIDS in particular and homosexuality in general has increased among college freshmen. (Support for widespread, mandatory testing to control AIDS also continues to decrease steadily.) Despite this increased tolerance overall, the CIRP data show that men are still much more likely than women to support such laws (in 1990, 56.0 versus 34.5 percent).

Since 1988, the CIRP has included an item measuring attitudes toward "date rape" (Students are asked whether they agree with the statement "Just because a man thinks that a women has 'led him on' does not entitle him to have sex with her"). Data from the last three CIRP surveys show that about 85 percent agree with this item, and this percentage is steadily increasing (among men agreement has risen from about three–quarters to four–fifths, while among women agreement has risen from 91.0 to 93.3 percent). These figures suggest that increased awareness of the problem of date rape—especially on college campuses—has led freshmen to be more sensitive to this issue. Nevertheless, the significant percentage of men who disagree with this statement (20.8 percent in 1990) suggests that much remains to be done to increase awareness of this problem.

About half the 1974 freshmen endorsed living together before marriage and this support has increased gradually since then, peaking at 52.1 in 1987. Similarly, acceptance of sexual relations among people who have known each other for a very short time has generally increased since 1977, with slightly more than half of all freshmen currently accepting this practice (51.0 in 1990). It is interesting to note that endorsement of this item has continued to grow despite increased publicity about the health risks associated with casual sexual relations. Yet here, as elsewhere in the data, we find profound differences between the sexes. (See Figure 15.) About two–thirds of men (66.3 percent) and slightly more than one–third of the women (37.9 percent) support the idea of sex between people who have known each other only for a short time. Men are also more likely than the women are to support living together before marriage (57.3 versus 45.0 percent in 1989). Thus, despite the changes in the views of both sexes toward traditional women's roles, men are still more likely than women to hold non–traditional views toward casual and premarital sexual relationships.

The number of freshmen who expect to marry in college or within a year of graduating declined during the late 1960s, but has remained fairly stable since the mid–1970s. Approximately 6.1 percent of 1975 freshmen estimated that there was a very good chance that they would marry in college, while 5.4 percent of 1990 freshmen gave similar odds. On the other hand, the percentage of students who reported that "raising a family" was an essential or very important goal has changed dramatically. (See Figure 16.) Following sharp declines in the early 1970s, interest in raising a family has steadily increased to a point that it has recovered much of its earlier popularity (69.5 percent in 1990 versus 71.4 in 1969). It is also interesting to note that the gap between men and women has been reduced, from about 10 percent in 1969 to less than 2 percent in 1990.

Figure 16. Freshman Interest in Raising a Family, by Gender
(Percentages)

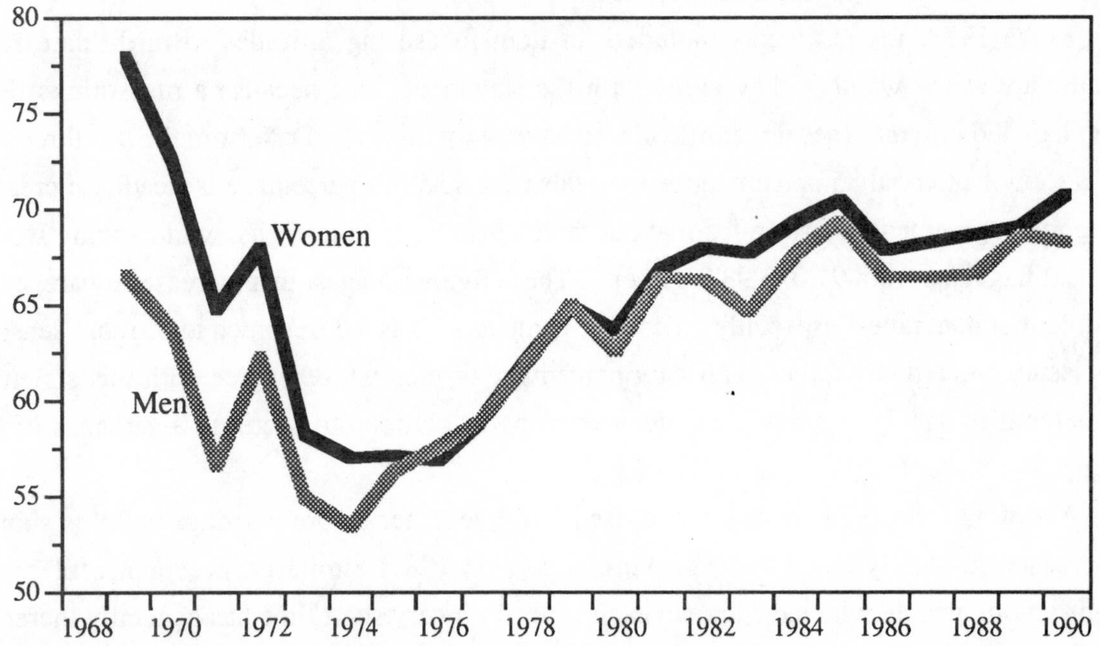

Student Values

Each year the freshman survey includes a list of fifteen to twenty items describing various personal values or "life goals." Although many of the value statements have waxed and waned in popularity since the 1960s, two of the items have shown especially consistent and contrasting trends. The item showing the strongest upward trend is "being very well–off financially." Between 1970 and 1987, student endorsement of this value increased from a low of 39.1 percent to an all–time high of 75.6 percent of the entering freshmen. Over the same period, the value showing the most precipitous decline in student endorsement is "developing a meaningful philosophy of life." (See Figure 17.) Although the latter was the most popular value in 1967, endorsed by 82.9 percent of the entering freshmen, it has been regularly decreasing throughout most of the history of the CIRP. It continued a steady decline until 1987, when it reached its low point of 39.4 percent. Since 1987, however, the trends have reversed: Interest in developing a meaningful philosophy of life has been increasing gradually while wanting to be very well–off financially has become slightly less popular. It may be that this recent reversal, coupled with the sharply declining interest in business careers and majors, are early signals of a shift away from a materialistic philosophy.

Figure 17. Freshman Life Goals
(Percentages)

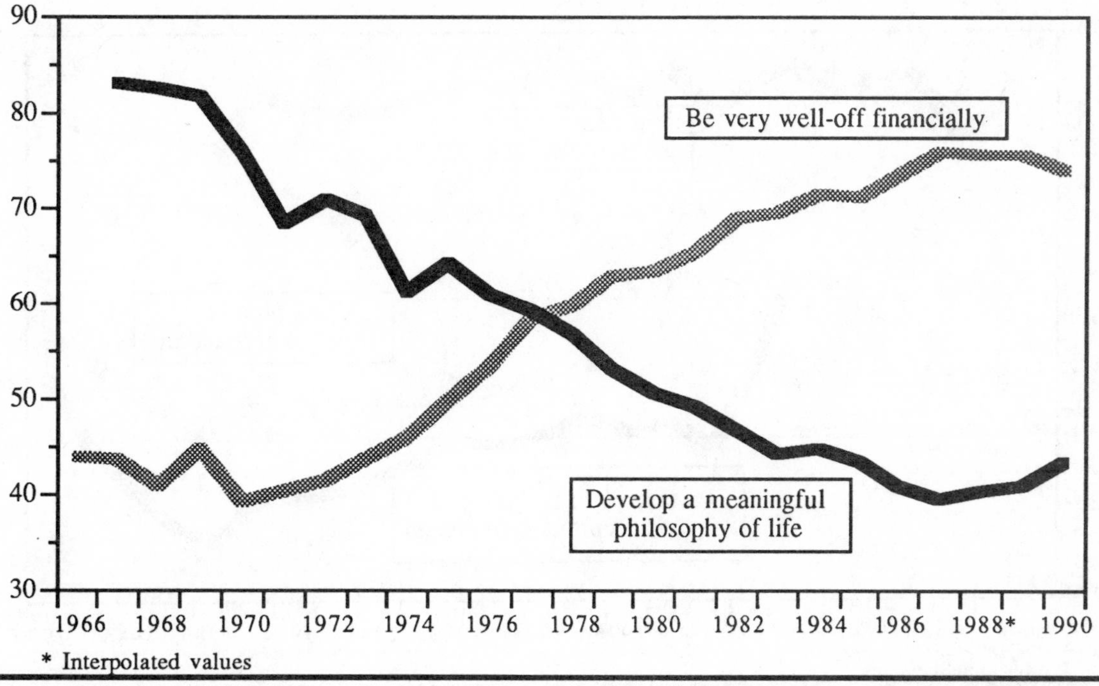

The freshman data also show that after a prolonged decline in interest in participating in altruistic activities, students have recently shown revived interest in such activities. As shown in Figure 18, student interest in helping others in difficulty has recently recovered somewhat from its 1986 low point of 57.2 percent, rebounding to 62.0 percent in 1990. Similar reversals have occurred with interest in helping to promote racial understanding and in participating in programs to clean up the environment. Both items declined during most of the 1970s and early 1980s, then rebounded sharply between 1986 and 1990. Interest in environmental activism more than doubled between 1986 and 1990 (from 15.9 to 33.9 percent).

Recent changes in the responses to several of the value questions also suggest that students are becoming increasingly interested in bringing about social change. Figure 19 shows that along with a declining interest in traditional politics (see above), there has recently been a sharp increase in the number of students who want to be personally involved in political and social action. Although there was little variation in the level of freshman interest in influencing political and social values through the 1970s and early 1980s, the data since the mid–1980s show that interest in these areas has climbed sharply. Interest in participating in community action programs has increased recently as well, rebounding to a level roughly equal to that registered in 1970 when it was first recorded.

Figure 18. Freshman Interest in Altruistic Activities
(Percentages)

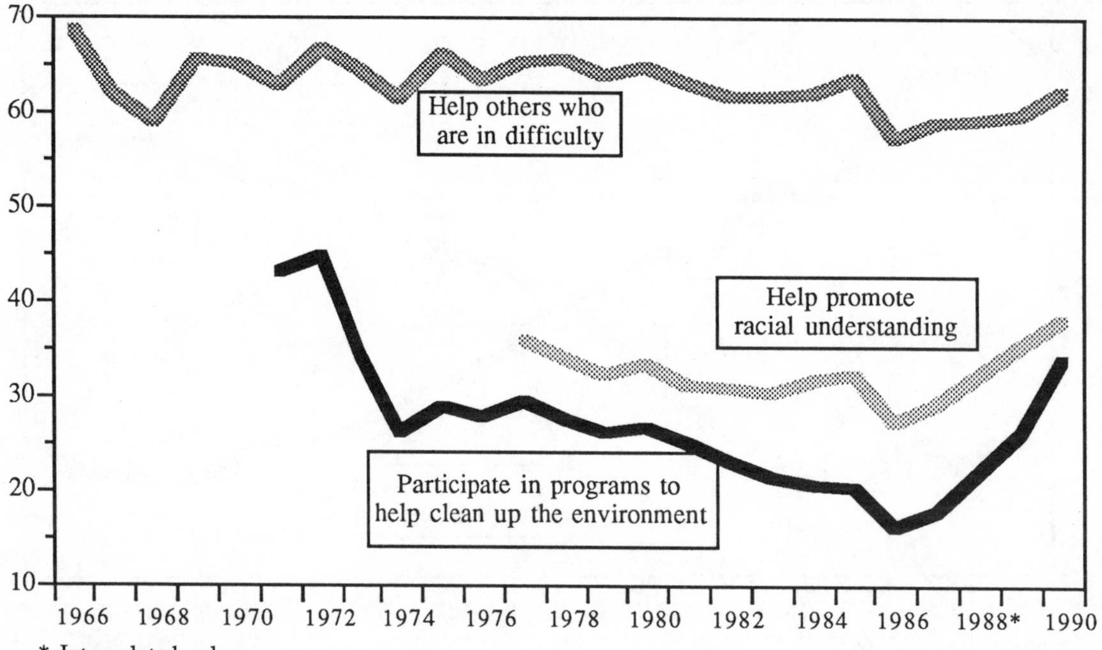

* Interpolated values

Figure 19. Freshman Interest in Political and Social Action
(Percentages)

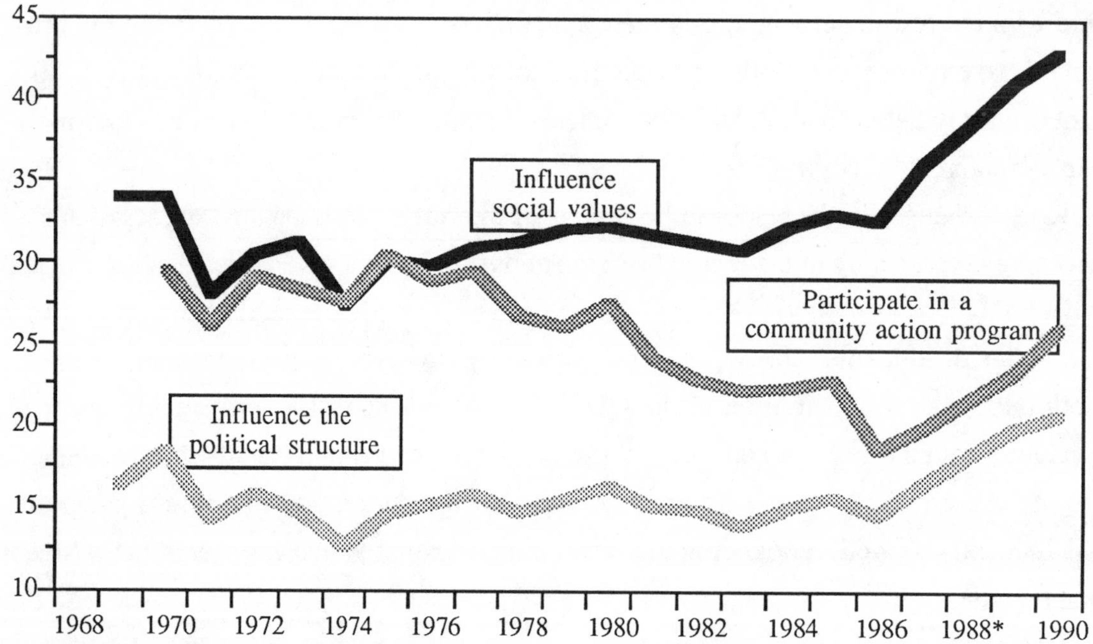

* Interpolated values

Financing College

The CIRP data reveal some significant trends in how students pay for college. The data show that students have had to become increasingly self–reliant as federal support has dwindled. Between 1978 and 1990, the CIRP data show steady increases in the numbers of students who relied upon parental support (from 71.8 to 78.7 percent) and summer work (from 47.1 to 55.5 percent) to pay their school–related expenses. Moreover, the percentage of students receiving $1,500 or more from these sources increased at a far greater rate during the same period—from 31.1 to 53.2 percent for parental support, and from 2.9 to 7.4 percent for summer work. Concurrently, there has been a sharp drop in the proportion receiving Pell Grants (from 31.5 in 1979 to 23.2 percent in 1990, with an all–time low of 16.9 percent in 1986), and a correspondingly sharp rise in reliance on Guaranteed Student Loans (from 10.4 percent in 1978 to 22.7 percent in 1990, with a peak of 26.3 percent in 1981). Finally, the data show an increased reliance on part–time employment during the mid– to late 1980s[2], other savings (from 20.5 to 31.7 percent), loans from the freshman college (3.6 to 6.0 percent), and loans from other sources (from 3.7 to 6.2).

It would appear that as federal student aid has shifted during the Reagan–Bush era from grants to loans, the nation's colleges have attempted to compensate, to some extent, for the loss of federal grant funds by providing more assistance from institutional resources. Other HERI research (Astin & Inouye, 1988) suggests that this greater demand on institutional resources is one of the major causes of rapidly increasing tuition, given that tuition revenues provide the principal source of student aid in most private colleges. Students have responded to the declining availability of federal grants by depending more on institutional and parental support and by taking on more part–time employment (as well as greater loan debt).

Other trends in the CIRP data suggest that in addition to forcing students and their parents to assume more of the financial burden for educational expenses, changes in financial aid programs may have forced many students out of higher education altogether. Figure 20, for example, shows the median parental income of college freshmen (in constant 1990 dollars) graphed with the percentage of students receiving Pell grants. As the number of Pell grant recipients has declined, the median parental income has increased. This suggests that, rather than taking out loans (which were intended to replace Pell grants), some individuals from less–advantaged backgrounds simply chose to forego college (at least as full–time students), thus forcing the median income upward.

The CIRP data also show that the median income of the parents of college freshmen is at near record–high levels: Between 1966 and 1988, the median family income of college freshmen increased about 15 percent, from $38,700 to $44,800 in constant 1990 dollars; the 1990 median income was $42,500. In addition, the relative difference between the median income of the parents

[2]The part–time employment item was changed in 1987, making direct comparisons to earlier years impossible.

of college freshmen and the median national household income is currently near its highest level (over 20 percent), and is equivalent to that first registered in 1966 by the CIRP. (See Figure 21.) Despite real progress toward equity in higher education (as measured by the gap in median income between those taking advantage of higher education and the national median) during the 1960s and 1970s, the record of the 1980s shows a reversal of the earlier gains.

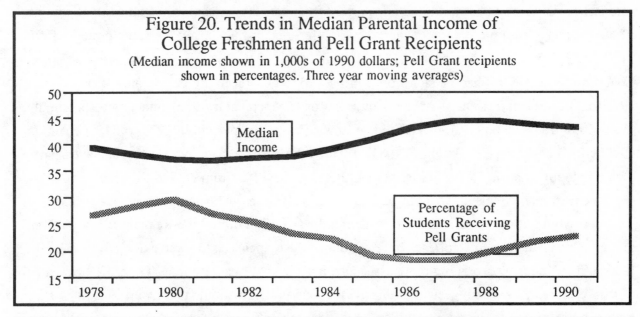

Figure 20. Trends in Median Parental Income of College Freshmen and Pell Grant Recipients
(Median income shown in 1,000s of 1990 dollars; Pell Grant recipients shown in percentages. Three year moving averages)

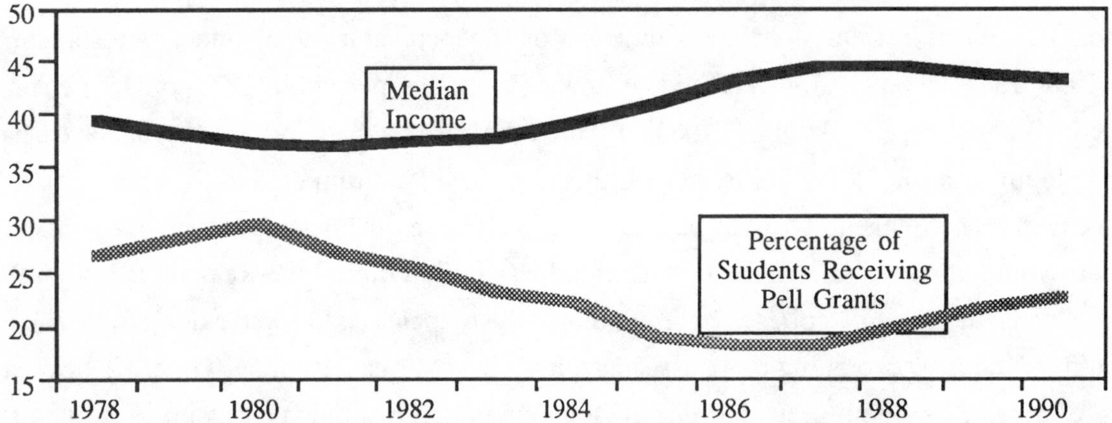

Figure 21. Trends in Median Family Income
(In 1,000s of 1990 dollars, three year moving average)

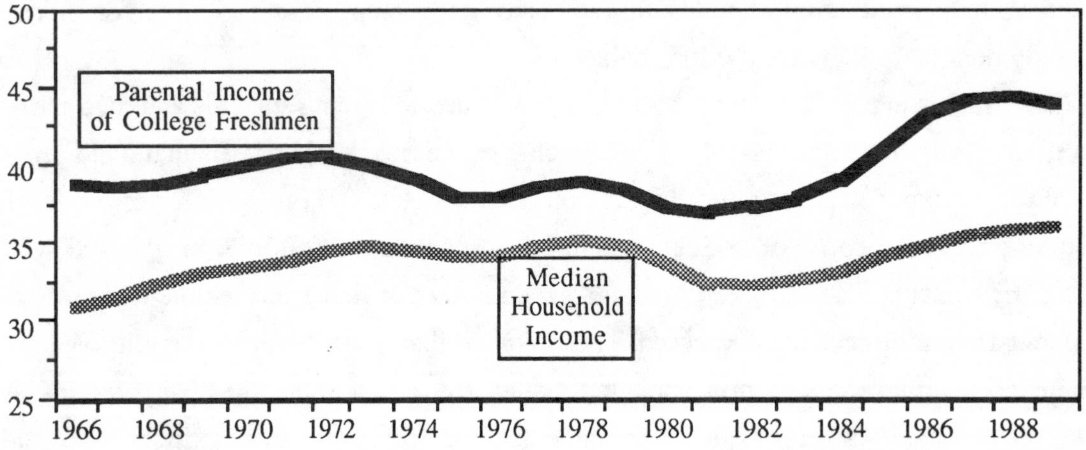

A Summary of Major Trends

The freshman survey data are a rich resource of information about changes in the nation's college students over the past twenty–five years. A summary of the major trends is offered below.

The Changing Role of Women

Perhaps the most dramatic changes revealed in our data concern the effects of the Women's Movement and the changing role of women in American society. Evidence of these changes comes to us from all directions:

a) ***Large shifts in preferences for majors and careers,*** away from the traditional fields of school teaching, nursing, social work, and homemaking, and toward business, law, medicine, science, and engineering; women also show greater interest in pursuing advanced degrees.

b) ***Behavioral changes,*** including increased cigarette smoking, decreased use of tranquilizers, and greater participation in competitive sports.

c) ***Attitudinal changes,*** including much greater support for job equality for women and rejection of the traditional homemaker role for married women.

d) ***Value changes,*** reflected in more widespread endorsement by women of traditionally male materialistic and power goals.

e) ***Demographic changes,*** reflected in more women entering higher education.

Major and Career Preferences

The field which has experienced the largest and most consistent surge in student popularity—and more recently an extremely sharp decline—has been business. Computer science showed strong growth from the mid–1970s through 1980 but has also dropped sharply since then. Engineering has been perhaps the most volatile of the major fields and career preferences: It nearly doubled in popularity between 1974 and 1983, but has dropped substantially since then.

The biggest overall losses have involved education and the traditional liberal arts and science fields: The humanities, fine and performing arts, social sciences, and the natural sciences. These declines have averaged 50 percent over the past twenty–five years; several fields lost as many as 80 percent of their prospective majors between 1966 and 1990.

The career field that has lost the largest absolute number of students has been school teaching. Despite a slight rebound since 1983, student interest in elementary and secondary school teaching is still only one–fourth of what it was in the late 1960s. Although the absolute numbers are smaller, interest among college freshmen in becoming college teachers or scientific researchers has declined more than 80 percent since the mid–1960s. Other career fields showing substantial declines in student interest involve almost all the human service occupations (such as the clergy, social work, nursing, and the allied health professions).

Given the nation's great historical reliance on its human and scientific resources, the substantial decline of student interest in all scientific fields—especially mathematics and statistics—and such careers as college teacher and scientific researcher should be viewed with some alarm. In the long run, this problem will only be exacerbated by the declining student interest in teaching at all levels. Moreover, given the expected declines in the overall size of the college–trained population entering the labor market through the year 2000, these declines in the proportions of students interested in scientific fields and careers can only extend existing shortages in the nation's talent pool of highly trained professionals.

Attitudes and Values

The freshman survey data show significant and complex changes in student attitudes and values over the past two and one–half decades:

a) ***Following increased interest in material and power goals, coupled with decreased social concern during the 1970s and early to mid–1980s, students today have shown a renewed interest in social action and altruism.*** These changes parallel the changes in college major and career preferences summarized above (especially the recent sharp reversal of interest in business fields).

b) ***A strong overall migration in political identification from liberal to middle–of–the–road, coupled with a strong increase in conservatism among men.*** It may be that these changes have been fueled by increased politicization of issues that cross traditional political orientation lines (see below).

c) ***Despite changes in the ways students identify themselves politically, there has been no monolithic trend away from liberal, or toward conservative, positions on specific personal and social issues.*** Our data point to a mixed bag of changes in student support for a variety of issues: Greater support for "liberal" positions on environmental and health issues, together with more conservative views on "law and order" issues. Support for legal abortions has jumped sharply in recent years, as has support for increased government action on environmental issues.

An Editorial Postscript*

We would like to close by considering the more practical question of what the academic community can—or should—do about these trends, particularly the changes in careers, majors, and values. Perhaps the best way to show how educators and policymakers can influence the shape of things to come is to speak for a moment about what is probably the most fashionable topic in education these days: The notion of *excellence*. All of us who work in academe inevitably adopt some perspective—at least implicitly, but hopefully explicitly—concerning what we regard as "excellent" education. For some time now, one of us has argued that our traditional notions of "excellence" in higher education do not serve us well (Astin, 1985). There are two favorite approaches which have dominated higher education policy over the years. The "reputational" approach, which equates excellence with an institution's ranking in national polls and surveys, amounts to a kind of popularity contest which may or may not tell us anything about the effectiveness of an institution's educational programs. Americans love to do competitive rankings of just about everything—from athletic teams to corporations to television shows—and our universities are no exception. The "resource" approach, which equates excellence with such things as the endowment, average faculty salaries, research grants, and the SATs of the entering freshmen, assumes that having a lot of such resources automatically guarantees an excellent educational program. These two traditional approaches are, of course, mutually reinforcing, since having a good reputation brings in additional resources and having abundant resources helps to enhance an institution's reputation. Unfortunately for the advocates of these traditional views, research on college student development shows that having a great reputation and a lot of resources does not assure an effective educational program; indeed, some of the most effective undergraduate education occurs at institutions with only modest reputations and resources.

We believe that these traditional ways of defining excellence should be replaced by one which directly reflects the institution's effectiveness in educating its students—a "talent development" approach. Basically, the talent development approach argues that true excellence resides in the ability of an institution to have a positive influence on its students' intellectual and personal development. In talent development terms, an "excellent" institution is one that develops the talents and abilities of its students to the fullest extent.

In certain respects these three approaches to excellence offer an interesting parallel to the changing patterns of student interests and values that we observed during much of the 1980s. The reputational and resources views, for example, parallel the increased student interest in money,

---

* This section is adapted from a forthcoming article by Alexander W. Astin, "The changing American college student: Implications for educational policy and practice," to be published in *Higher Education*. Portions have also been adapted from an earlier article in *Change* (Astin, A.W. "Competition or cooperation," September/October 1987).

power, status, and in business careers. In contrast, the talent development view parallels student concern for others and for the society and careers in the human service occupations. Under the reputational and resource approaches, the institution devotes its energies to enhancing its power, prestige, and possessions. Under the talent development approach, the institution invests its energy and resources into helping students develop their talents and abilities to the fullest.

Our support of the talent development approach is not intended to suggest that institutional reputations and resources are not important. Institutions obviously need resources to operate and they need reputations to attract both students and resources. The problem is really the relative emphasis that we give to these different conceptions, our tendency to treat reputations and resources as ends in themselves, and the naive assumption that the talent development problem will take care of itself. Research on student development shows that being prestigious or having a lot of resources by no means guarantees a high quality educational experience (Astin, 1977; Bowen, 1977).

Why do we tend to favor the resource and reputational approaches to excellence, and why hasn't the talent development approach—which seems so consistent with our educational mission—been more widely accepted and adopted? In large part the ultimate answer to this question seems to lie in the larger society and the particular philosophical or value perspective that holds sway at any point in time. We are speaking here, in other words, of how people view human nature and American society.

Some views of America maintain that our greatest achievements as a society are the result of our intense competitiveness and that it is only through our competitive spirit that we have been able to achieve greatness as a society. Free enterprise is certainly a competitive view, where individuals are given the maximum opportunity to compete with each other for the largest possible share of the resources and the rewards in the society. This competitive world view has deep roots in the history of western civilization, but the rise of Darwinism—with its emphasis on competition among species and the survival of the fittest—provided a scientific framework in which to view the development of the human species as a competitive enterprise. In Darwinian terms, the human species was able to survive and develop because we were more "fit" than any other species. This competitive world view also provides the basis for what the British sociologist Michael Young called the "meritocracy." In a pure meritocracy, the rewards and resources of the society are allocated in proportion to the abilities of each individual. "Rewards," in this context, are the social equivalent of survival. The more able persons get a disproportionate share of the resources and privileges, whereas the least able people get the smallest slice of the pie. It might be worth noting in passing that this competitive world view has implications not only for how we view education and the larger society, but also how we approach international relations and foreign policy.

A cooperative world view provides a vastly different frame of reference. Under this view, human progress and the development of the society is seen as depending upon the ability of individuals and groups to cooperate with each other. The survival and evolution of humankind is seen not as a victory in the struggle with other species or as a conquest of the environment, but rather as a manifestation of our ability to work cooperatively with each other toward common goals and to live in harmony with the environment.

It has become increasingly apparent to us that many of the issues that plague higher education these days can be better understood when viewed in terms of this cooperative–competitive framework. Take, for example, the different conceptions of excellence. The reputational approach is inherently competitive, since it fosters competition among institutions for higher and higher places in the pecking order. And the most obvious manifestation of this competition takes place in the arena of resources, where institutions compete with each other for the largest possible share of the resource pool. If my institution manages to improve its position in the pecking order by recruiting some of your faculty stars or National Merit Scholars, then your position in the reputational pecking order is proportionately diminished. In pursuing the resource approach to excellence, institutions inevitably compete with each other for funding, faculty stars, and students. Even within a single institution, the resource view breeds competition: Academic departments compete with each other over faculty positions and other resources, academic personnel compete with student affairs personnel over a finite resource pie, and trustees and administrators compete with faculty for a control over the resource allocation decisions. Claims for a larger share of resources are frequently buttressed by arguments about maintaining or enhancing quality or excellence. In short, it seems clear that both the reputational and resource approaches to excellence are manifestations of a competitive world view.

The talent development approach to excellence, on the other hand, symbolizes a very different value perspective. To this view, all institutions share a common purpose in trying to maximize the educational and personal development of their students. When an institution succeeds in its talent development mission, this success in no way diminishes what any other institution can do. Indeed, institutions can learn from each other by sharing information about their educational successes and failures. Under such a cooperative arrangement, the success of any one institution benefits and contributes to the success of all others.

What is particularly ironic about our inclination toward competitiveness in education is that the very institution that should be the most competitive in its mentality—American business—has been recently talking a lot about *cooperation.* Recent research suggests, for example, that one of the most striking features of an effectively managed business organization is its capacity for getting employees to work cooperatively toward common organizational goals. They see uncontrolled competition among employees as potentially destructive, particularly when it discourages teamwork and encourages employees to curry favor with higher management by making their peers "look bad." The key ingredient to developing a truly cooperative work environment, of course, is to develop a sense of trust among employees at all levels of the organization.

The capacity to be a good team member and to work cooperatively with co–workers should be one of the "basic skills" that we try to develop in our general education programs. Even in an academic setting, these qualities are becoming increasingly important. The expanding knowledge base, for example, has served to intensify the competition among disciplines for a piece of the curricular action, simply because there are now so many "worthy" items of knowledge to be learned, and because it's possible to make a plausible case for requiring almost any of these new items in a core curriculum. Clearly, the need for a cooperative approach has never been greater.

In many respects the undergraduate years are the ideal time to explore value issues such as cooperation versus competition, or materialism versus spirituality. If you ever find yourself entertaining the fantasy that there is any such thing as a "value–free" curriculum, recall Alan Bloom's *The Closing of the American Mind* or the recent flap over changes in the Stanford undergraduate curriculum, when then–Education Secretary Bennett attacked the Stanford faculty for "selling out" the Great Books tradition and for caving in to pressures from "special interest" groups such as women and minorities. It might be a useful exercise for each of us periodically to take a hard look at our curriculum with the following question in mind: To what extent does our current curriculum content reflect an awareness of and concern with issues such as environmental degradation, racism, poverty, world hunger, social justice, arms control, or world peace, and to what extent does it merely reflect a miscellaneous conglomerate of the faculty's specialized disciplinary and research interests? And what about curriculum objectives? While we hear a lot these days about developing such things as critical thinking and communication skills, we have not yet given enough attention to the *social* and *value* implications of such curriculum objectives. In the area of communications skills, for example, most of us focus on the improvement of writing and speaking, but few of us talk about the art of good *listening*. This neglected skill is not only of great practical importance in many career fields, but it also epitomizes the essence of the cooperative spirit. Being able to listen to and understand the thoughts and feelings of others is of vital importance in developing the trust and empathy which is so necessary for cooperative living.

The Implicit Curriculum

But most of us are inclined to forget that curricular content represents only a small portion of the "values education" that goes on in academe, and that our most important "teaching" may be independent of course content. This "implicit curriculum" includes the process of establishing a formal curriculum, the teaching methods we use, how we grade and test our students, how we run our institutions, and how we treat each other as professional colleagues.

Let's now consider the extent to which this implicit curriculum fosters the development of such qualities as cooperation, trust, social responsibility, and good citizenship. Does the implicit curriculum teach students the value and necessity of teamwork and cooperation? Does it show them *how* to cooperate? To what extent does it foster the development of contrary values, such as individualism and competitiveness?

Let's take pedagogical techniques as an example. Most lower division teaching, especially in our larger universities, still uses the traditional lecture format. Several national reports have criticized this traditional model of instruction on the grounds that it assigns students too passive a role, thereby reducing involvement and inhibiting the learning process. It has other serious deficiencies as well: It leads students to view learning as a solitary process, where each student works independently of every other student. Indeed, not only do students work independently, but also they are encouraged to compete with one another. This emphasis on competition is reinforced by the grading system, which is basically comparative or relativistic. The practice of grading "on the curve" does not tell us much about what a student has actually learned in a class; rather, it merely ranks students relative to one another. Under these conditions, one student's success signifies failure for some other student.

What is most regrettable about this heavy dependence on the traditional lecture format is that it ignores a growing body of research which suggests that "cooperative learning" models—where students teach each other or work together on joint projects—are clearly superior to competitive approaches. But the most important thing about cooperative learning is that it facilitates the development of teamwork skills and encourages the individual student to view each classmate as a potential helper rather than as a competitor. Under cooperative learning, students learn to work together toward common goals.

The limitations of competitive classroom learning are compounded by the fact that professors must grade students as well as teach them. The conflict of interest generated by the professor's dual role as mentor and judge was recognized many years ago by Robert Hutchins, who believed that the learning process should be separated from the testing and grading process. As president of the University of Chicago, Hutchins established the "Examiner's Office," where students could go when they felt ready to be tested or examined on some subject. Long since abandoned at Chicago, the Examiner's Office remains a largely untested concept which offers some real potential for effectuating a greater sense of trust and cooperation between professor and student.

What about collegial relations? Although students usually do not participate directly in faculty personnel actions, they are usually aware of the criteria used in hiring, promoting, and tenuring faculty. The peer review process provides a concrete example of how faculty members relate to each other. Since undergraduates are likely to see their professors as authority figures and even role models, the manner in which personnel actions are carried out helps to shape students' impressions about the nature of peer relationships among professional colleagues.

First, let us consider the criteria used. We are all familiar with the "publish or perish" syndrome. In effect, this dictum gives the greatest weight to a candidate's research and scholarship, relegating the functions of teaching, advising, colleagueship, and public service to second–class status. Scholarship is, of course, a highly competitive and individualistic activity, and the most productive scholars are accorded significant professional status and recognition. While some articles and books have multiple authors (signifying a cooperative or joint effort), such publications generally get *less* credit in the review process than do single–authored pieces. In other words, the process does not encourage scholarly collaboration.

Volumes have been written about how this skewed reward system negatively affects the quality of teaching, so we will not belabor the point here. Suffice it to say that under this system, professors have the strongest incentives to pursue their professional self–interest (publication and scholarly visibility) at the expense of both the student and the institution. While the scholarly and professional success of its faculty may further the reputational and resource "interests" of the research university, resulting in greater national prestige and increased access to research grants and contracts, this emphasis compromises the university's undergraduate teaching mission.

But the publish–or–perish philosophy exacts even higher costs. The typical faculty review process gives almost no weight to what might be termed "good colleagueship," yet good colleagueship is one of the most important, but least appreciated, talents that a faculty member can have. Besides service on departmental or institutional committees and task forces, good colleagueship is manifested in many ways. Some professors are excellent technical consultants, able and willing to confer informally with colleagues on a wide range of disciplinary issues. Others make themselves available to serve as trouble shooters or mediators. Still others simply provide positive and constructive inputs at meetings and in their daily interactions.

The point of all of this is that there is no way we can shield our students from the value implications of how we run our institutions and how we treat each other as colleagues.

Cognitive or Affective?

When we talk about cooperation or about the student's values and beliefs we are, of course, dealing with so–called "affective" outcomes. Educators have tended to shy away from discussing such outcomes because they are felt to be too "value–laden." However, the very act of deciding on a curriculum is itself a value judgment, and if you take the time to read through a few college catalogues it becomes clear that the concept of a liberal education is typically rationalized in terms of "affective" outcomes such as character and citizenship. The very idea of good citizenship in a democracy like ours necessarily includes the notion of an *informed* and *involved* electorate. Democracy is based fundamentally on a *cooperative* concept of governance. Yet recent national elections in the United States suggest that our citizenry is probably not very well informed and certainly not very involved in the democratic process. If we were able to effect just one change in our curriculum and our implicit curriculum, it would be to put much greater emphasis on the importance of producing graduates who appreciate the importance of being well informed and active participants in the democratic process.

Some of our higher education policy makers and leaders have recently become concerned about the extreme competitiveness of our students and our institutions and are openly advocating a greater emphasis on promoting cooperation, good citizenship and other affective outcomes. The Campus Compact Project, for example, is a consortium of some 200 institutions that are working together under the sponsorship of the Education Commission of the States to establish community service programs for undergraduates. In California, the legislature has passed a law requiring each campus of the University of California and the California State University to establish some kind of volunteer or public service program for undergraduates.

In his report to the Board of Overseers a few years ago, Harvard president Derek Bok said that "universities should be among the first to reaffirm the importance of basic values such as honesty, promise keeping, free expression, and nonviolence...[and] there is nothing odd or inappropriate...to make these values the foundation for a serious program to help students develop a strong set of moral standards." Bok also notes that "students must get help from their universities in developing moral standards or they are unlikely to get much assistance at all."

These trends would suggest that our political and higher education leaders are implicitly suggesting that social responsibility and concern for others are among the qualities that higher education institutions should try to foster in their students.

Recent Student Trends

Even the students seem to be reflecting some dissatisfaction with the status quo. It is important to realize that the rather depressing trends toward excessive materialism and competitiveness seemed to peak out a couple of years ago and have either remained level or declined somewhat during the past two years. A number of other findings from our most recent freshman surveys suggest that we may be seeing the emergence of some very different student tendencies. For example, we see that the most current crop of college freshmen appears to be more protest–prone even than students in the late 1960s. Not only have more of them participated in demonstrations in high school, but more of them anticipate getting involved in protests during their college years. In the same vein, during the past two years we have seen a resurgence of student interest in influencing social values and changing the political structure.

What specific issues are the students concerned about? Perhaps the single biggest issue for students these days is the environment. Interest in the environment bottomed out during the later years of the Reagan Administration, but has shown a substantial rebirth during the past couple of years. Although the level of interest and likely involvement among students is still below the environmental heyday of the early 1970s (when then first "Earth Day" was held), the environment is going to continue growing as a popular issue for students if these recent trends are maintained.

Two other areas where we find greater student concern in the past few years are the development of a national health care plan and abortion rights for women. Support for legalized abortions has remained steady during the years in which we have asked the question, with the exception of 1989 which witnessed a sharp increase in student support. This one–year change may well be a reaction to the U.S. Supreme Court's "Webster" decision. It seems likely that some of the students who were mildly opposed to legalized abortion in previous years may have jumped over to the support side when they began to realize that their or their partner's right to an abortion may indeed be taken away by the courts.

The past few years have seen increases in three other areas: Student altruism, support for school integration through busing, and interest in promoting racial understanding appear to be on the rise. These trends, together with those just discussed, suggest that we are witnessing the emergence of a small but rapidly growing minority of students who are concerned about a variety of social issues and who are inclined to become actively involved in working with these issues. Considering that the strong majority of students are still heavily focussed on business careers and on making money and achieving power and status, it is interesting to speculate on what is likely to happen on our college campuses during the next few years. Apparently, we have a rapidly growing minority of students who may well challenge the majority viewpoint on a number of political and social issues.

Conclusion

Considering that we are looking here only at trends from the past few years that were preceded by two decades of contrary changes, it may be wishful thinking to believe that America's long romance with greed and competitiveness may be beginning to reverse itself. But there *are* other signs on the horizon. The fall 1990 election showed that many people in the United States are fed up with politics as usual, and that a groundswell of public reaction may be developing against "the best government money can buy." Such sentiments have been fueled by a growing awareness that the much–maligned "tax and spend" politics of the left has been replaced by a "borrow and spend" politics of the right, which has really served to exacerbate rather than shrink existing disparities between rich and poor. There is also evidence of a growing national (and international) consciousness about the plight of the planet's ecosystem. Indeed, the environment, more than any other single issue, appears capable of galvanizing the most student interest and activist energy over the next decade.

Whether higher education is going to encourage such trends or merely continue its mindless pursuit of resources and reputation will depend largely on what we in the academy do. American academics are fond of complaining about "governmental threats to autonomy," but the fact remains that we still retain control over most of the decisions and policies that really matter: Whom to admit and on what basis, what to teach and how to teach it, how we test and grade students, how we hire and reward our professors and administrators, and how we structure our "implicit curriculum." Perhaps most important of all is whether we are going to continue to give the raising of money and the enhancement of our reputations greater priority than the development of our students' talents, and whether we are going to continue to ignore the so–called affective talents that seem to be so crucial to effective living in a multicultural and multinational community.

As we look around we see the great achievements of the intellect everywhere: Atomic energy, genetic engineering, modern agriculture, modern medicine, and computers and other electronic marvels of every conceivable type. It is truly astounding. And at the same time we see the great affective and emotional and spiritual divisions that threaten our very existence: Religious fanaticism and hatred, racial prejudice, ethnocentrism, nationalism and other political divisions, widespread criminal behavior in the land of opportunity, and massive poverty and starvation in the face of unprecedented affluence. What this suggests is that it is time to redress the balance. It is time to begin shifting some of our educational interest and energy in the direction of our affective side—to begin concerning ourselves much more directly with the development of beliefs and values that are going to heal our divisions, and which will help to create a society that is less materialistic, competitive, and selfish, and one that is more generous and cooperative.

References

Astin, A.W. (1977). *Four critical years.* San Francisco: Jossey–Bass.

Astin, A.W. (1982). *Minorities in American higher education.* San Francisco: Jossey–Bass.

Astin, A.W. (1985). *Achieving educational excellence.* San Francisco: Jossey–Bass.

Astin, A.W. (1990). *The Black undergraduate: Current status and trends in the characteristics of freshmen.* Los Angeles: Higher Education Research Institute, UCLA.

Astin, A.W., Green, K.C., & Korn, W.S. (1987). *The American freshman: Twenty year trends.* Los Angeles: Higher Education Research Institute, UCLA.

Astin, A.W. & Inouye, C.J. (1988). How public policy at the state level affects private higher education institutions. *Economics of Education Review, 7*(1), 47–63.

Astin, A.W., Korn, W.S., & Berz, E.R. (1990). *The American freshman: National norms for 1990.* Los Angeles: Higher Education Research Institute, UCLA.

Astin, A.W., Korn, W.S., & Dey, E.L. (1991). *The American college teacher.* Los Angeles: Higher Education Research Institute, UCLA.

Bradburn, N., Haertel, E., Schwille, J., & Torney–Purta, J. (1991, June). A rejoinder to 'I never promised you first place.' *Phi Delta Kappan,* 774–777.

Bowen, H.R. (1977). *Investment in learning.* San Francisco: Jossey–Bass.

Budd, J.M. (1990). Higher education literature: Characteristics of citation patterns. *The Journal of Higher Education, 61*(1), 84–97.

Carnegie Foundation. (1989). *The conditions of the professoriate: attitudes and trends, 1989.* Princeton, NJ: Carnegie Foundation for the Advancement of Teaching.

Educational Testing Service. (1989). *A world of differences: An international assessment of mathematics and science.* Princeton, NJ: Educational Testing Service.

Grandy, J. (1987). *Ten–year trends in SAT scores and other characteristics of high school seniors taking the SAT and planning to study mathematics, science, or engineering* (ETS–RR–87–49). Princeton, NJ: Educational Testing Service.

Johnston, L.D., O'Malley, P.M., & Bachman, J.G. (1991). *Trends in drug use and associated factors among American high school students, college students, and young adults: 1975–1989.* Ann Arbor, MI: Institute for Social Research, University of Michigan.

Minter, J.W. & Bowen, H.R. "Colleges' Achievements in Recent Years Came Out of the Hides of Professors." *The Chronicle of Higher Education,* May, 1982.

Mortenson, T.G. (1991). *Equity of higher educational opportunity for women, black, Hispanic, and low income students.* Iowa City: American College Testing.

National Commission on Excellence in Education. (1982). *A nation at risk.* Washington, DC: National Commission on Excellence in Education.

Rotberg, I.C. (1990, December). I never promised you first place. *Phi Delta Kappan,* 296–303.

Rotberg, I.C. (1991, June). How did all those dumb kids make all those smart bombs? *Phi Delta Kappan,* 778–781.

Turnbull, W.W. (1985). *Student change, program change: Why SAT scores kept falling* (CBR–85–2). New York: College Entrance Examination Board.

Twenty–Five Year Trends for Freshman Men

STUDENT'S DEMOGRAPHICS	1966	1967	1968	1969	1970	1971	1972	1973	1974	1975	1976	1977	1978
AGE													
16 or younger	--	0.2	0.1	0.1	0.1	0.1	0.1	0.1	0.1	0.1	0.1	0.1	0.1
17	--	3.9	3.7	3.1	3.2	2.6	3.0	3.3	2.6	2.7	2.9	2.5	2.5
18	--	73.4	72.4	70.0	70.4	70.5	71.1	71.9	71.9	70.6	71.5	71.7	72.5
19	--	16.4	16.2	17.0	16.5	18.6	18.2	17.9	18.8	19.4	19.2	19.9	20.2
20	--	2.2	2.6	2.7	2.4	2.6	2.6	2.4	2.7	2.6	2.6	2.6	2.3
21 or older [1]	--	4.0	5.1	7.1	7.4	5.7	5.1	4.4	4.0	4.6	3.9	3.3	2.5
RACIAL/ETHNIC BACKGROUND [2]													
White/Caucasian	90.9	90.1	88.3	91.6	[*]	92.1	88.4	89.1	89.4	87.2	87.1	87.9	89.3
African-American/Black [1]	4.5	3.9	4.7	5.1	[*]	5.5	7.6	7.0	6.5	8.0	7.3	7.8	7.2
American Indian	0.5	0.6	0.7	0.3	[*]	1.0	1.1	0.8	0.8	0.9	1.0	0.8	0.8
Oriental/Asian-American	0.8	0.9	1.2	1.8	[*]	0.5	1.1	1.2	1.0	1.6	2.2	1.2	1.2
Mexican-American/Chicano	--	--	--	--	--	1.1	1.6	1.3	1.6	1.8	1.6	1.4	1.0
Puerto Rican-American	--	--	--	--	--	0.2	0.6	0.5	0.6	0.7	0.6	0.9	0.9
Other	3.3	4.5	5.1	1.2	[*]	1.2	1.8	1.5	1.8	2.1	1.9	1.9	1.9
MARITAL STATUS													
No	--	--	--	--	--	97.0	97.7	97.9	98.2	97.9	98.4	98.8	99.1
Yes [1]	--	--	--	--	--	3.0	2.3	2.1	1.8	2.1	1.6	1.2	0.9
CITIZENSHIP STATUS													
Yes	--	--	--	97.7	98.2	--	97.6	97.5	--	--	--	--	--
No [1]	--	--	--	2.3	1.8	--	2.3	2.4	--	--	--	--	--
TWIN STATUS													
No	--	--	--	--	--	--	--	--	--	--	--	98.2	--
Yes, identical	--	--	--	--	--	--	--	--	--	--	--	0.6	--
Yes, fraternal	--	--	--	--	--	--	--	--	--	--	--	1.2	--
VETERAN STATUS													
No	--	--	--	--	93.9	95.0	96.3	96.9	96.4	96.0	96.7	97.4	98.1
Yes [1]	--	--	--	--	6.1	5.0	3.7	3.1	3.6	4.0	3.3	2.6	1.9
STUDENT'S CURRENT RELIGIOUS PREFERENCE (Aggregated) [3]													
Protestant	51.6	47.3	44.0	48.5	49.4	38.7	36.1	45.3	46.9	45.6	43.9	44.7	45.2
Roman Catholic	27.8	30.2	31.1	28.9	31.0	30.1	30.4	34.6	33.4	34.4	35.6	37.2	37.7
Jewish	4.1	4.9	4.1	3.4	4.4	2.8	3.6	5.0	3.8	3.7	3.9	4.0	4.3
Other	7.7	8.2	9.5	4.0	4.0	12.0	13.7	3.8	4.3	4.5	5.1	4.0	3.8
None	8.8	9.5	11.4	15.3	11.0	16.3	16.1	11.4	11.8	11.9	11.7	10.0	9.0
STUDENT'S CURRENT RELIGIOUS PREFERENCE (Disaggregated)													
Baptist	--	--	--	11.2	13.9	--	--	12.9	12.9	13.0	11.6	12.0	12.2
Buddhist	--	--	--	--	--	--	--	--	--	--	--	--	--
Congregational (United Church of Christ) [1]	--	--	--	3.7	2.1	--	--	1.7	1.8	1.6	1.7	2.0	1.8
Eastern Orthodox	--	--	--	--	0.5	--	--	0.6	0.5	0.7	0.6	0.8	0.7
Episcopal	--	--	--	3.1	3.0	--	--	2.9	2.8	2.6	2.6	2.8	3.0
Jewish	--	--	--	3.4	4.4	--	--	5.0	3.8	3.7	3.9	4.0	4.3
Latter Day Saints (Mormon)	--	--	--	0.8	0.2	--	--	0.3	0.5	0.3	0.3	0.2	0.2
Lutheran	--	--	--	6.6	6.4	--	--	5.6	6.5	5.8	6.1	5.5	5.6
Methodist	--	--	--	11.1	10.8	--	--	10.2	10.1	9.9	8.9	9.9	9.7
Muslim (Islamic) [1]	--	--	--	0.2	0.2	--	--	0.2	0.3	0.3	0.3	0.2	0.3
Presbyterian	--	--	--	6.1	6.2	--	--	5.7	5.7	5.8	5.4	5.5	5.8
Quaker (Society of Friends)	--	--	--	0.3	0.2	--	--	0.2	0.2	0.2	0.2	0.2	0.2
Roman Catholic	--	--	--	28.9	31.0	--	--	34.6	33.4	34.4	35.6	37.2	37.7
Seventh Day Adventist	--	--	--	0.3	0.3	--	--	0.3	0.3	0.5	0.6	0.3	0.4
Unitarian-Universalist	--	--	--	0.5	0.5	--	--	0.3	0.3	0.3	0.3	0.3	0.3
Other Protestant	--	--	--	4.8	5.3	--	--	4.6	5.3	4.9	5.6	5.2	5.3
Other religion	--	--	--	3.8	3.8	--	--	3.6	4.0	4.2	4.8	3.8	3.5
None	--	--	--	15.3	11.0	--	--	11.4	11.8	11.9	11.7	10.0	9.0
DISABILITIES [4]													
Hearing	--	--	--	--	--	--	--	--	--	--	--	--	--
Speech	--	--	--	--	--	--	--	--	--	--	--	--	--
Partially sighted/blind	--	--	--	--	--	--	--	--	--	--	--	--	--
Orthopedic	--	--	--	--	--	--	--	--	--	--	--	--	--
Learning disabled	--	--	--	--	--	--	--	--	--	--	--	--	--
Health related	--	--	--	--	--	--	--	--	--	--	--	--	--
Other	--	--	--	--	--	--	--	--	--	--	--	--	--
DISTANCE FROM HOME TO COLLEGE													
10 miles or less [1]	--	--	--	26.7	27.1	23.5	26.2	29.0	--	27.4	30.2	26.3	22.6
11-50 miles	--	--	--	23.9	25.3	26.7	24.4	24.2	--	25.2	25.1	25.6	26.1
51-100 miles	--	--	--	12.8	12.2	14.1	13.3	12.3	--	12.9	12.6	14.2	14.3
101-500 miles	--	--	--	26.4	26.5	27.1	26.2	25.3	--	25.7	24.0	26.0	28.2
More than 500 miles	--	--	--	10.2	8.9	8.6	10.0	9.1	--	8.9	8.1	7.8	8.9

[*] Results were not comparable to those of other years due to changes in question text or order.
[1] Text, order or number of response options may vary from year to year.
[2] Respondent allowed to mark all responses that apply from 1971-1990. Responses may sum to more than 100%.
[3] See Appendix D for a discussion of variation in question texts and aggregation procedures.
[4] Responses from 1978-1982 excluded because they were not recorded in a comparable manner.

1979	1980	1981	1982	1983	1984	1985	1986	1987	1988	1989	1990	***STUDENT'S DEMOGRAPHICS***
												AGE
0.1	0.1	0.1	0.0	0.0	0.0	0.0	0.1	0.1	0.1	0.0	0.0	16 or younger
2.2	2.0	1.8	1.9	1.9	2.0	2.0	2.1	2.1	2.1	2.1	1.7	17
71.0	69.1	70.6	70.7	69.3	69.9	68.7	68.7	68.6	70.1	67.4	63.6	18
20.9	22.1	22.4	22.3	23.0	22.7	23.7	22.8	23.2	22.4	25.2	28.5	19
2.6	2.7	2.4	2.4	2.5	2.6	2.5	2.5	2.6	2.3	2.7	3.2	20
3.3	4.0	2.8	2.7	3.3	2.8	2.9	3.8	3.3	3.0	2.4	3.0	21 or older [1]
												RACIAL/ETHNIC BACKGROUND [2]
87.2	87.0	89.5	89.0	88.0	86.9	87.3	86.9	87.6	84.7	85.6	85.2	White/Caucasian
8.2	8.0	7.5	7.6	7.8	8.6	8.1	7.3	7.2	8.0	7.8	8.5	African-American/Black [1]
1.0	0.8	1.1	1.0	1.0	1.0	1.0	0.9	0.9	0.8	0.8	1.2	American Indian
1.6	1.6	1.2	1.5	1.7	1.8	2.1	2.8	2.6	3.2	3.3	3.1	Oriental/Asian-American
1.1	2.1	0.9	0.9	0.9	0.9	1.0	1.2	0.9	1.5	1.2	1.4	Mexican-American/Chicano
1.1	0.8	0.6	0.9	0.7	0.8	0.6	0.8	0.9	1.2	0.8	0.5	Puerto Rican-American
2.2	1.8	1.8	1.5	1.8	1.7	1.5	1.9	1.6	2.2	2.1	1.8	Other
												MARITAL STATUS
98.9	98.8	99.0	99.0	98.9	99.1	99.0	98.8	--	--	--	--	No
1.1	1.3	1.0	1.0	1.1	0.9	1.0	1.2	--	--	--	--	Yes [1]
												CITIZENSHIP STATUS
--	--	--	97.4	97.1	96.9	97.4	96.8	98.2	97.6	96.8	97.3	Yes
--	--	--	2.6	2.9	3.1	2.6	3.2	1.8	2.3	3.2	2.7	No [1]
												TWIN STATUS
--	--	98.2	98.2	98.3	98.2	98.2	98.3	98.3	98.2	98.4	98.4	No
--	--	0.7	0.6	0.7	0.7	0.7	0.6	0.6	0.7	0.7	0.6	Yes, identical
--	--	1.1	1.1	1.1	1.1	1.1	1.0	1.1	1.1	0.9	1.1	Yes, fraternal
												VETERAN STATUS
97.8	97.5	98.2	98.2	--	--	--	--	--	--	--	--	No
2.2	2.5	1.8	1.8	--	--	--	--	--	--	--	--	Yes [1]
												STUDENT'S CURRENT RELIGIOUS PREFERENCE (Aggregated) [3]
33.0	33.3	34.9	33.2	31.6	42.7	45.1	29.7	44.1	40.8	44.5	45.8	Protestant
38.1	38.3	36.6	38.5	38.9	38.5	36.5	35.2	35.8	36.0	33.5	32.3	Roman Catholic
3.8	3.4	3.2	3.1	3.2	3.2	3.0	3.2	2.9	3.5	2.8	2.4	Jewish
15.8	15.2	16.4	16.5	17.1	5.9	5.5	19.9	5.3	5.7	5.6	5.8	Other
9.4	9.8	8.9	8.7	9.2	9.7	9.9	12.0	12.0	14.0	13.7	13.6	None
												STUDENT'S CURRENT RELIGIOUS PREFERENCE (Disaggregated)
--	--	--	--	--	14.0	14.0	--	11.9	12.0	14.1	17.0	Baptist
--	--	--	--	--	0.3	0.4	--	0.5	0.5	0.4	0.5	Buddhist
--	--	--	--	--	1.7	1.5	--	1.8	1.2	1.1	1.2	Congregational (United Church of Christ) [1]
--	--	--	--	--	0.8	0.6	--	0.6	0.7	0.6	0.6	Eastern Orthodox
--	--	--	--	--	--	2.5	--	2.5	2.3	2.4	2.2	Episcopal
--	--	--	--	--	3.2	3.0	--	2.9	3.5	2.8	2.4	Jewish
--	--	--	--	--	0.2	0.2	--	0.3	0.3	0.3	0.3	Latter Day Saints (Mormon)
--	--	--	--	--	5.6	5.8	--	8.2	6.2	6.3	5.7	Lutheran
--	--	--	--	--	9.8	9.5	--	8.6	8.0	9.2	9.1	Methodist
--	--	--	--	--	0.3	0.3	--	0.2	0.4	0.5	0.4	Muslim (Islamic) [1]
--	--	--	--	--	--	5.0	--	4.7	4.5	4.8	4.5	Presbyterian
--	--	--	--	--	0.2	0.2	--	0.2	0.2	0.2	0.2	Quaker (Society of Friends)
--	--	--	--	--	38.5	36.5	--	35.8	36.0	33.5	32.3	Roman Catholic
--	--	--	--	--	0.2	0.2	--	0.2	0.3	0.3	0.2	Seventh Day Adventist
--	--	--	--	--	0.2	--	--	--	--	--	--	Unitarian-Universalist
--	--	--	--	--	10.0	5.6	--	5.1	5.1	5.2	4.8	Other Protestant
--	--	--	--	--	5.3	4.8	--	4.6	4.8	4.7	4.9	Other religion
--	--	--	--	--	9.7	9.9	--	12.0	14.0	13.7	13.6	None
												DISABILITIES [4]
--	--	--	--	0.7	1.0	1.1	0.7	0.8	0.9	--	--	Hearing
--	--	--	--	0.3	0.4	0.4	0.2	0.3	0.4	--	--	Speech
--	--	--	--	2.2	2.2	2.2	1.8	2.1	2.1	--	--	Partially sighted/blind
--	--	--	--	0.9	1.0	0.9	0.7	0.8	0.9	--	--	Orthopedic
--	--	--	--	0.8	1.2	1.3	1.1	1.6	1.4	--	--	Learning disabled
--	--	--	--	0.8	1.0	1.1	0.8	1.0	1.0	--	--	Health related
--	--	--	--	1.3	1.5	1.4	1.1	1.2	1.4	--	--	Other
												DISTANCE FROM HOME TO COLLEGE
25.3	23.7	19.2	20.1	20.5	18.5	17.4	16.3	17.0	17.6	15.8	11.8	10 miles or less [1]
24.1	25.2	23.7	24.3	27.6	27.1	25.5	26.6	28.1	25.8	25.6	24.4	11-50 miles
14.5	15.1	16.7	16.3	16.0	15.9	16.8	16.5	16.3	14.1	15.9	18.4	51-100 miles
27.5	27.5	31.9	30.9	26.9	29.5	31.1	29.8	28.5	30.5	31.3	32.6	101-500 miles
8.6	8.5	8.5	8.3	8.9	8.9	9.3	10.8	10.0	12.0	11.3	12.7	More than 500 miles

[1] Text, order or number of response options may vary from year to year.
[2] Respondent allowed to mark all responses that apply from 1971-1990. Responses may sum to more than 100%.
[3] See Appendix D for a discussion of variation in question texts and aggregation procedures.
[4] Responses from 1978-1982 excluded because they were not recorded in a comparable manner.

STUDENT'S DEMOGRAPHICS	1966	1967	1968	1969	1970	1971	1972	1973	1974	1975	1976	1977	1978
RATED SELF ABOVE AVERAGE OR TOP 10% IN													
Academic ability	56.4	--	--	--	--	49.6	--	--	53.1	--	51.5	--	--
Athletic ability	45.6	--	--	--	--	45.8	--	--	50.6	--	51.7	--	--
Artistic ability	16.1	--	--	--	--	16.1	--	--	17.8	--	20.1	--	--
Drive to achieve	55.9	--	--	--	--	51.1	--	--	59.5	--	61.1	--	--
Emotional health	--	--	--	--	--	--	--	--	--	--	--	--	--
Leadership ability	40.7	--	--	--	--	38.6	--	--	45.8	--	47.2	--	--
Mathematical ability	43.5	--	--	--	--	37.6	--	--	39.4	--	40.0	--	--
Mechanical ability	36.6	--	--	--	--	34.7	--	--	37.0	--	37.2	--	--
Originality	37.6	--	--	--	--	34.8	--	--	38.3	--	40.1	--	--
Physical health	--	--	--	--	--	--	--	--	--	--	--	--	--
Political conservatism	17.9	--	--	--	--	10.4	--	--	13.0	--	15.2	--	--
Political liberalism	20.4	--	--	--	--	25.7	--	--	22.4	--	20.9	--	--
Popularity	34.7	--	--	--	--	31.9	--	--	33.7	--	34.5	--	--
Popularity with the opposite sex	32.3	--	--	--	--	30.2	--	--	32.7	--	34.5	--	--
Public speaking ability	23.9	--	--	--	--	21.3	--	--	23.2	--	23.9	--	--
Self-confidence (intellectual)	40.5	--	--	--	--	38.7	--	--	46.2	--	47.7	--	--
Self-confidence (social)	33.1	--	--	--	--	29.8	--	--	37.0	--	39.4	--	--
Sensitivity to criticism	24.6	--	--	--	--	23.0	--	--	22.8	--	22.4	--	--
Stubbornness	36.4	--	--	--	--	35.4	--	--	35.9	--	34.5	--	--
Understanding of others	55.0	--	--	--	--	58.4	--	--	61.4	--	61.4	--	--
Writing ability	25.7	--	--	--	--	26.5	--	--	28.9	--	30.5	--	--

PARENT'S DEMOGRAPHICS	1966	1967	1968	1969	1970	1971	1972	1973	1974	1975	1976	1977	1978
ESTIMATED PARENTAL INCOME													
Less than $6,000	19.1	[*]	16.1	14.0	12.6	11.3	12.8	10.2	9.3	9.8	9.3	8.5	7.0
$6,000-9,999	35.6	[*]	33.6	30.5	24.7	22.7	18.7	15.2	13.3	11.4	10.4	9.3	7.3
$10,000-14,999	25.1	[*]	27.7	29.4	32.3	33.1	31.6	30.5	29.5	25.7	23.2	20.3	17.0
$15,000-19,999	8.9	[*]	10.8	12.1	13.3	14.6	15.2	17.5	17.5	18.3	18.1	18.0	16.9
$20,000-24,999	4.2	[*]	4.9	5.9	7.0	7.9	8.8	10.9	12.2	13.0	14.1	15.6	17.2
$25,000-29,999	2.1	[*]	2.4	2.7	3.3	3.7	4.2	5.2	6.0	7.2	7.9	9.1	10.2
$30,000 or more	4.9	[*]	4.7	5.4	--	--	--	--	--	--	--	--	--
$30,000-34,999	--	--	--	--	2.1	2.2	2.8	3.4	3.8	4.7	5.6	6.5	8.0
$35,000-39,999	--	--	--	--	1.1	1.2	1.6	1.9	2.3	2.7	3.3	3.6	4.6
$40,000 or more	--	--	--	--	3.5	3.4	--	--	--	--	--	--	--
$40,000-49,999	--	--	--	--	--	--	1.6	1.9	2.2	2.6	2.9	3.4	4.5
$50,000 or more	--	--	--	--	--	--	2.7	3.4	4.0	4.6	5.1	5.7	7.3
$50,000-59,999	--	--	--	--	--	--	--	--	--	--	--	--	--
$50,000-99,999	--	--	--	--	--	--	--	--	--	--	--	--	--
$60,000-74,999	--	--	--	--	--	--	--	--	--	--	--	--	--
$75,000-99,999	--	--	--	--	--	--	--	--	--	--	--	--	--
$100,000 or more	--	--	--	--	--	--	--	--	--	--	--	--	--
$100,000-149,999	--	--	--	--	--	--	--	--	--	--	--	--	--
$150,000 or more	--	--	--	--	--	--	--	--	--	--	--	--	--
MEDIAN INCOME (in $1,000's)	**9.5**	**[*]**	**10.1**	**10.9**	**12.0**	**12.4**	**12.9**	**14.0**	**14.6**	**15.8**	**17.0**	**18.3**	**20.6**
NUMBER CURRENTLY DEPENDENT ON PARENTS FOR SUPPORT [1]													
One	--	--	--	--	--	--	--	--	--	--	--	--	6.0
Two	--	--	--	--	--	--	--	--	--	--	--	--	9.3
Three	--	--	--	--	--	--	--	--	--	--	--	--	19.1
Four	--	--	--	--	--	--	--	--	--	--	--	--	25.4
Five	--	--	--	--	--	--	--	--	--	--	--	--	22.5
Six or more	--	--	--	--	--	--	--	--	--	--	--	--	17.7
NUMBER OF DEPENDENTS CURRENTLY ATTENDING COLLEGE [2]													
None	--	--	--	--	--	--	--	--	--	--	--	--	66.6
One	--	--	--	--	--	--	--	--	--	--	--	--	24.9
Two	--	--	--	--	--	--	--	--	--	--	--	--	6.2
Three or more	--	--	--	--	--	--	--	--	--	--	--	--	2.3
PARENTS' MARITAL STATUS													
both alive and living with each other	--	--	--	--	--	--	83.9	--	--	--	--	--	--
both alive, divorced or separated	--	--	--	--	--	--	8.1	--	--	--	--	--	--
one or both deceased	--	--	--	--	--	--	8.0	--	--	--	--	--	--

[*] Results were not comparable to those of other years due to changes in question text or order.
[1] Including respondent and parents if applicable.
[2] Other than respondent.

1979	1980	1981	1982	1983	1984	1985	1986	1987	1988	1989	1990	***STUDENT'S DEMOGRAPHICS***
												RATED SELF ABOVE AVERAGE OR TOP 10% IN
--	52.6	--	--	--	--	57.8	57.8	57.8	60.9	59.7	57.5	Academic ability
--	54.6	--	--	--	--	--	--	--	--	--	--	Athletic ability
--	21.7	--	--	--	--	24.5	24.8	27.0	27.3	27.1	27.8	Artistic ability
--	63.6	--	--	--	--	62.4	61.4	60.0	66.7	66.8	67.7	Drive to achieve
--	--	--	--	--	--	65.2	63.7	63.0	63.3	62.9	63.3	Emotional health
--	50.2	--	--	--	--	56.2	56.8	55.6	57.5	56.2	56.5	Leadership ability
--	42.4	--	--	--	--	46.0	48.0	48.2	49.6	48.3	45.5	Mathematical ability
--	40.7	--	--	--	--	--	--	--	--	--	--	Mechanical ability
--	44.3	--	--	--	--	--	--	--	--	--	--	Originality
--	--	--	--	--	--	72.4	71.7	70.4	70.3	70.1	69.9	Physical health
--	17.4	--	--	--	--	--	--	--	--	--	--	Political conservatism
--	16.6	--	--	--	--	--	--	--	--	--	--	Political liberalism
--	37.3	--	--	--	--	49.2	50.2	50.3	51.3	49.9	50.3	Popularity
--	39.4	--	--	--	--	--	--	47.2	49.1	47.8	48.4	Popularity with the opposite sex
--	25.7	--	--	--	--	--	--	31.6	32.3	31.4	30.5	Public speaking ability
--	51.8	--	--	--	--	62.3	63.1	56.8	59.1	58.5	56.8	Self-confidence (intellectual)
--	43.3	--	--	--	--	51.6	52.7	48.6	49.5	48.8	49.3	Self-confidence (social)
--	23.0	--	--	--	--	--	--	--	--	--	--	Sensitivity to criticism
--	36.0	--	--	--	--	--	--	--	--	--	--	Stubbornness
--	64.4	--	--	--	--	--	--	--	--	--	63.0	Understanding of others
--	30.5	--	--	--	--	35.6	37.8	37.9	39.5	39.2	37.1	Writing ability

1979	1980	1981	1982	1983	1984	1985	1986	1987	1988	1989	1990	***PARENT'S DEMOGRAPHICS***
												ESTIMATED PARENTAL INCOME
6.6	6.2	4.8	4.3	4.5	4.8	3.8	3.3	2.9	3.0	2.5	2.4	Less than $6,000
7.2	6.3	5.3	4.5	4.7	4.5	3.5	3.2	2.7	2.3	2.3	2.3	$6,000-9,999
14.3	12.7	10.9	9.3	9.7	8.8	6.4	5.8	5.0	4.1	4.2	3.9	$10,000-14,999
14.5	12.4	10.4	8.7	8.6	7.7	6.8	6.0	5.5	4.8	4.5	4.7	$15,000-19,999
17.3	17.2	15.4	13.7	12.7	11.3	8.7	7.9	7.3	6.4	6.4	6.5	$20,000-24,999
10.8	11.4	12.1	12.2	10.8	10.4	8.9	8.4	7.3	6.7	6.8	6.1	$25,000-29,999
--	--	--	--	--	--	--	--	--	--	--	--	$30,000 or more
8.6	9.8	10.9	12.1	11.8	11.0	11.3	10.5	9.6	9.0	9.2	8.2	$30,000-34,999
5.6	6.4	8.1	8.8	8.7	9.1	9.7	9.6	9.8	9.2	8.9	8.7	$35,000-39,999
--	--	--	--	--	--	--	--	--	--	--	--	$40,000 or more
6.2	7.4	9.5	11.0	11.7	12.9	12.5	12.9	12.9	12.9	13.2	13.4	$40,000-49,999
--	--	--	--	--	--	--	--	--	--	--	--	$50,000 or more
--	--	--	--	--	--	9.9	10.6	11.3	12.2	12.3	12.1	$50,000-59,999
6.7	7.6	9.9	12.0	13.0	14.9	--	--	--	--	--	--	$50,000-99,999
--	--	--	--	--	--	7.3	9.7	10.1	11.3	11.2	12.2	$60,000-74,999
--	--	--	--	--	--	4.7	5.7	6.8	7.8	8.1	8.7	$75,000-99,999
2.2	2.4	2.9	3.5	3.7	4.5	--	--	--	--	--	--	$100,000 or more
--	--	--	--	--	--	3.3	3.9	4.6	5.4	5.5	5.8	$100,000-149,999
--	--	--	--	--	--	3.2	3.7	4.4	4.7	5.0	5.1	$150,000 or more
22.2	**23.6**	**26.3**	**28.9**	**30.0**	**31.1**	**35.3**	**37.6**	**39.9**	**43.5**	**43.9**	**45.3**	**MEDIAN INCOME (in $1,000's)**
												NUMBER CURRENTLY DEPENDENT ON PARENTS FOR SUPPORT [1]
7.2	7.0	6.4	6.4	7.1	7.2	7.8	8.4	10.1	--	--	--	One
10.9	10.7	10.8	11.6	13.1	13.2	13.9	15.3	18.6	--	--	--	Two
20.1	20.3	20.6	21.4	23.6	23.3	22.1	22.5	22.2	--	--	--	Three
24.6	25.5	26.5	27.1	28.6	29.1	27.8	27.8	26.1	--	--	--	Four
21.0	21.1	21.1	20.0	17.8	18.1	17.9	16.5	15.0	--	--	--	Five
16.2	15.4	14.6	13.6	9.8	9.1	10.6	9.6	7.9	--	--	--	Six or more
												NUMBER OF DEPENDENTS CURRENTLY ATTENDING COLLEGE [2]
66.3	66.4	65.6	65.2	66.4	67.9	68.7	69.2	68.9	--	--	--	None
24.4	24.6	24.7	25.1	24.5	23.5	23.6	23.4	23.5	--	--	--	One
6.5	6.5	6.9	6.9	6.5	6.2	5.7	5.5	5.7	--	--	--	Two
2.8	2.5	2.7	2.9	2.6	2.4	2.1	2.0	1.9	--	--	--	Three or more
												PARENTS' MARITAL STATUS
--	--	--	--	--	--	--	76.8	76.2	75.2	74.5	73.2	both alive and living with each other
--	--	--	--	--	--	--	17.8	18.8	20.1	20.8	21.7	both alive, divorced or separated
--	--	--	--	--	--	--	5.4	5.0	4.8	4.7	5.1	one or both deceased

[1] Including respondent and parents if applicable.
[2] Other than respondent.

PARENT'S DEMOGRAPHICS	1966	1967	1968	1969	1970	1971	1972	1973	1974	1975	1976	1977	1978
MOTHER'S EDUCATION													
Grammar school or less	6.3	6.6	6.8	6.5	7.2	5.3	5.9	4.6	4.7	4.9	4.5	4.2	3.5
Some high school	14.1	14.6	15.7	15.0	14.8	13.6	13.3	12.2	11.3	11.6	10.7	10.5	8.9
High school graduate	43.9	44.2	45.1	45.3	44.3	47.0	45.6	44.4	43.7	44.0	43.7	44.5	43.2
Postsecondary school other than college	--	--	--	--	--	--	--	6.0	6.2	5.8	6.2	6.2	6.7
Some college	18.6	17.9	17.5	17.3	17.2	16.8	16.7	13.7	14.3	13.3	13.3	13.2	13.9
College degree	14.5	13.9	12.6	13.2	13.7	14.4	12.7	13.0	13.6	13.8	14.7	14.5	15.8
Some graduate school	--	--	--	--	--	--	2.1	1.9	1.8	1.8	1.9	1.9	2.2
Graduate degree	2.6	2.7	2.3	2.6	2.8	2.8	3.7	4.2	4.3	4.7	4.9	5.0	5.8
MOTHER'S CURRENT OCCUPATION [1]													
Artist	--	--	--	--	--	--	--	--	--	--	1.1	1.2	1.1
Businesswoman	--	--	--	--	--	--	--	--	--	--	6.9	7.0	7.8
Business (clerical)	--	--	--	--	--	--	--	--	--	--	8.8	9.0	9.6
Clergy or religious worker	--	--	--	--	--	--	--	--	--	--	0.1	0.1	0.1
College teacher	--	--	--	--	--	--	--	--	--	--	0.3	0.3	0.3
Doctor or dentist	--	--	--	--	--	--	--	--	--	--	0.2	0.2	0.2
Educator (secondary school)	--	--	--	--	--	--	--	--	--	--	2.6	2.6	2.9
Elementary school teacher	--	--	--	--	--	--	--	--	--	--	5.4	5.4	5.6
Engineer	--	--	--	--	--	--	--	--	--	--	0.1	0.1	0.1
Farmer or forester	--	--	--	--	--	--	--	--	--	--	0.2	0.2	0.2
Health professional (non-MD)	--	--	--	--	--	--	--	--	--	--	1.4	1.4	1.4
Homemaker (full-time)	--	--	--	--	--	--	--	--	--	--	33.7	31.6	31.3
Lawyer	--	--	--	--	--	--	--	--	--	--	0.1	0.1	0.1
Nurse	--	--	--	--	--	--	--	--	--	--	5.8	6.4	6.7
Research scientist	--	--	--	--	--	--	--	--	--	--	0.1	0.1	0.1
Skilled worker	--	--	--	--	--	--	--	--	--	--	1.9	2.0	2.0
Semiskilled or unskilled worker	--	--	--	--	--	--	--	--	--	--	6.1	6.5	5.7
Social worker	--	--	--	--	--	--	--	--	--	--	--	1.1	1.1
Unemployed	--	--	--	--	--	--	--	--	--	--	10.2	10.2	9.5
Other	--	--	--	--	--	--	--	--	--	--	14.8	14.3	14.2
MOTHER'S CURRENT RELIGIOUS PREFERENCE (Aggregated) [2]													
Protestant	--	--	--	--	56.5	--	--	--	53.0	52.2	49.8	50.2	50.5
Roman Catholic	--	--	--	--	32.8	--	--	--	35.8	36.5	37.9	39.0	38.6
Jewish	--	--	--	--	5.1	--	--	--	4.3	4.2	4.3	4.4	4.8
Other	--	--	--	--	2.9	--	--	--	3.1	3.3	4.0	3.3	3.2
None	--	--	--	--	2.7	--	--	--	3.7	3.7	3.9	3.3	3.0
MOTHER'S CURRENT RELIGIOUS PREFERENCE (Disaggregated)													
Baptist	--	--	--	--	15.4	--	--	--	14.0	14.3	12.4	13.0	13.0
Buddhist	--	--	--	--	--	--	--	--	--	--	--	--	--
Congregational (United Church of Christ) [3]	--	--	--	--	2.6	--	--	--	2.1	1.9	2.0	2.2	2.1
Eastern Orthodox	--	--	--	--	0.6	--	--	--	0.6	0.7	0.7	0.9	0.8
Episcopal	--	--	--	--	3.7	--	--	--	3.4	3.3	3.2	3.4	3.5
Jewish	--	--	--	--	5.1	--	--	--	4.3	4.2	4.3	4.4	4.8
Latter Day Saints (Mormon)	--	--	--	--	0.3	--	--	--	0.4	0.3	0.3	0.2	0.2
Lutheran	--	--	--	--	7.1	--	--	--	7.4	6.6	6.9	6.1	6.1
Methodist	--	--	--	--	12.4	--	--	--	11.7	11.6	10.3	11.3	11.2
Muslim (Islamic) [3]	--	--	--	--	0.1	--	--	--	0.2	0.2	0.2	0.2	0.2
Presbyterian	--	--	--	--	7.6	--	--	--	6.8	7.0	6.5	6.4	6.9
Quaker (Society of Friends)	--	--	--	--	0.2	--	--	--	0.1	0.2	0.2	0.2	0.2
Roman Catholic	--	--	--	--	32.8	--	--	--	35.8	36.5	37.9	39.0	38.6
Seventh Day Adventist	--	--	--	--	0.3	--	--	--	0.3	0.6	0.6	0.3	0.4
Unitarian-Universalist	--	--	--	--	0.5	--	--	--	0.4	0.3	0.3	0.4	0.4
Other Protestant	--	--	--	--	5.8	--	--	--	5.8	5.4	6.4	5.8	5.7
Other religion	--	--	--	--	2.8	--	--	--	2.9	3.1	3.8	3.1	3.0
None	--	--	--	--	2.7	--	--	--	3.7	3.7	3.9	3.3	3.0

[1] Data for this item collected but not reported in 1969-1975
[2] See Appendix D for a discussion of variation in question texts and aggregation procedures.
[3] Text, order or number of response options may vary from year to year.

1979	1980	1981	1982	1983	1984	1985	1986	1987	1988	1989	1990	*PARENT'S DEMOGRAPHICS*
												MOTHER'S EDUCATION
3.8	3.9	2.6	2.6	2.9	3.1	2.6	2.4	2.2	2.5	2.3	2.3	Grammar school or less
9.5	8.9	7.8	7.5	7.5	7.1	6.7	6.0	4.9	5.3	4.9	4.7	Some high school
42.2	42.4	42.7	41.7	41.4	39.8	38.8	36.8	35.7	34.2	34.6	33.8	High school graduate
6.6	6.5	6.5	7.2	7.3	7.4	7.6	7.7	8.4	7.7	7.7	7.6	Postsecondary school other than college
14.2	14.0	14.1	14.3	14.7	15.1	16.0	16.0	16.0	16.3	16.4	17.0	Some college
15.5	16.3	17.5	17.6	16.9	17.7	17.6	19.0	20.0	20.5	20.9	20.9	College degree
2.2	2.1	2.1	2.2	2.3	2.3	2.6	3.0	3.1	3.2	3.0	3.1	Some graduate school
5.9	6.0	6.6	6.9	7.0	7.5	8.1	9.1	9.7	10.3	10.1	10.7	Graduate degree
												MOTHER'S CURRENT OCCUPATION [1]
1.1	1.1	1.3	1.4	1.4	1.4	1.6	1.7	1.5	1.6	1.5	1.4	Artist
8.3	8.9	9.8	10.1	10.8	11.2	12.5	13.3	14.2	14.1	14.5	14.2	Businesswoman
9.7	10.2	10.3	10.6	10.7	10.8	10.5	10.9	11.4	10.4	10.7	10.0	Business (clerical)
0.1	0.1	0.1	0.1	0.1	0.2	0.1	0.2	0.1	0.2	0.2	0.2	Clergy or religious worker
0.4	0.3	0.3	0.3	0.3	0.3	0.3	0.4	0.4	0.4	0.4	0.5	College teacher
0.2	0.2	0.3	0.3	0.3	0.4	0.4	0.4	0.5	0.5	0.5	0.5	Doctor or dentist
3.0	3.0	3.5	3.6	3.2	3.4	3.6	3.9	4.0	4.5	4.3	4.6	Educator (secondary school)
5.6	5.6	6.1	6.1	5.5	5.6	5.9	6.2	6.5	7.0	7.1	7.5	Elementary school teacher
0.1	0.1	0.1	0.1	0.2	0.2	0.1	0.2	0.2	0.3	0.3	0.2	Engineer
0.3	0.3	0.4	0.4	0.4	0.4	0.4	0.4	0.6	0.3	0.4	0.5	Farmer or forester
1.5	1.5	1.7	1.8	1.8	1.7	1.8	1.8	2.0	1.9	2.1	2.1	Health professional (non-MD)
29.2	28.1	23.4	23.1	25.2	24.0	21.9	20.3	18.0	17.5	15.5	14.1	Homemaker (full-time)
0.1	0.1	0.1	0.2	0.2	0.2	0.2	0.2	0.3	0.3	0.3	0.3	Lawyer
6.7	6.7	7.6	7.9	7.4	7.5	7.7	7.6	8.1	7.9	8.1	8.2	Nurse
0.1	0.1	0.1	0.1	0.2	0.1	0.1	0.1	0.2	0.1	0.1	0.2	Research scientist
2.1	2.1	2.1	2.2	2.2	2.4	2.2	2.3	2.6	2.3	2.7	2.7	Skilled worker
6.3	6.4	6.3	6.3	6.1	5.6	5.8	5.7	5.1	4.6	5.3	5.2	Semiskilled or unskilled worker
1.2	1.2	1.2	1.3	1.3	1.3	1.3	1.3	1.4	1.5	1.4	1.4	Social worker
9.4	8.9	9.0	8.4	7.3	7.4	7.3	7.0	6.4	6.5	6.2	5.8	Unemployed
14.7	14.8	16.3	15.9	15.4	16.1	16.3	16.4	16.7	18.0	18.3	20.5	Other
												MOTHER'S CURRENT RELIGIOUS PREFERENCE (Aggregated) [2]
36.7	36.8	38.2	36.6	34.7	46.7	49.3	33.4	48.8	45.8	49.5	50.3	Protestant
39.5	39.9	37.8	39.6	40.2	39.4	37.6	36.9	37.7	38.3	36.1	35.0	Roman Catholic
3.8	3.8	3.5	3.4	3.6	3.7	3.4	3.6	3.4	4.1	3.3	2.8	Jewish
15.9	15.4	16.6	16.7	17.5	5.9	5.2	10.6	4.9	5.8	5.2	5.5	Other
3.8	4.2	3.8	3.7	4.1	4.4	4.6	5.5	5.1	6.2	5.8	6.3	None
												MOTHER'S CURRENT RELIGIOUS PREFERENCE (Disaggregated)
--	--	--	--	--	14.4	14.3	--	12.5	12.7	14.6	17.1	Baptist
--	--	--	--	--	0.4	0.5	--	0.6	0.7	0.5	0.6	Buddhist
--	--	--	--	--	1.9	1.7	--	2.0	1.4	1.3	1.4	Congregational (United Church of Christ) [3]
--	--	--	--	--	1.0	0.7	--	0.6	0.7	0.7	0.6	Eastern Orthodox
--	--	--	--	--	--	2.8	--	3.0	2.8	2.9	2.7	Episcopal
--	--	--	--	--	3.7	3.4	--	3.4	4.1	3.3	2.8	Jewish
--	--	--	--	--	0.2	0.3	--	0.3	0.3	0.3	0.4	Latter Day Saints (Mormon)
--	--	--	--	--	6.2	6.3	--	9.0	7.0	7.1	6.4	Lutheran
--	--	--	--	--	11.0	10.7	--	9.8	9.1	10.4	10.2	Methodist
--	--	--	--	--	0.3	0.3	--	0.2	0.4	0.5	0.3	Muslim (Islamic) [3]
--	--	--	--	--	--	5.8	--	5.4	5.5	5.7	5.4	Presbyterian
--	--	--	--	--	0.2	0.2	--	0.2	0.2	0.3	0.3	Quaker (Society of Friends)
--	--	--	--	--	39.4	37.6	--	37.7	38.3	36.1	35.0	Roman Catholic
--	--	--	--	--	0.2	0.3	--	0.2	0.3	0.4	0.3	Seventh Day Adventist
--	--	--	--	--	0.3	--	--	--	--	--	--	Unitarian-Universalist
--	--	--	--	--	11.3	6.2	--	5.8	5.8	5.8	5.5	Other Protestant
--	--	--	--	--	5.2	4.4	--	4.1	4.7	4.2	4.6	Other religion
--	--	--	--	--	4.4	4.6	--	5.1	6.2	5.8	6.3	None

[1] Data for this item collected but not reported in 1969-1975
[2] See Appendix D for a discussion of variation in question texts and aggregation procedures.
[3] Text, order or number of response options may vary from year to year.

PARENT'S DEMOGRAPHICS	1966	1967	1968	1969	1970	1971	1972	1973	1974	1975	1976	1977	1978
FATHER'S EDUCATION													
Grammar school or less	10.0	11.0	10.8	10.1	10.8	8.8	9.0	7.2	7.4	7.3	7.0	6.2	5.3
Some high school	16.7	17.3	18.2	17.7	16.5	16.7	15.7	14.5	13.1	13.8	12.7	12.8	11.0
High school graduate	30.0	30.0	31.2	31.1	30.3	31.9	31.4	29.8	29.7	29.8	29.0	29.7	28.6
Postsecondary school other than college	--	--	--	--	--	--	--	3.9	4.3	3.8	4.1	4.1	4.4
Some college	18.2	17.1	17.1	16.8	16.6	16.4	15.8	13.9	14.0	13.5	13.3	13.2	13.5
College degree	16.0	15.4	15.0	16.1	16.8	17.6	15.5	16.8	17.3	17.6	18.6	19.1	20.2
Some graduate school	--	--	--	--	--	--	2.3	2.2	2.2	2.1	2.3	2.3	2.6
Graduate degree	9.1	9.2	7.8	8.3	8.9	8.7	10.2	11.7	11.9	12.0	12.9	12.6	14.4
FATHER'S CURRENT OCCUPATION [1]													
Artist	--	0.8	0.8	0.8	0.8	0.8	0.8	--	0.7	0.7	0.9	0.9	0.9
Businessman	--	30.8	29.9	29.5	30.1	29.7	30.2	--	28.1	27.0	29.8	29.7	30.8
Clergy or religious worker	--	1.0	0.8	0.9	1.0	0.8	0.9	--	1.0	1.1	1.1	1.1	1.1
College teacher	--	0.6	0.6	0.6	0.6	0.7	0.8	--	1.2	1.1	0.8	0.8	0.9
Doctor or dentist	--	2.3	1.9	1.9	2.0	1.8	1.9	--	2.0	2.1	2.3	2.1	2.4
Educator (secondary school)	--	1.9	1.9	1.9	2.2	2.1	2.4	--	2.0	2.0	3.1	3.1	3.4
Elementary school teacher	--	0.3	0.3	0.3	0.4	0.3	0.3	--	0.6	0.7	0.6	0.6	0.6
Engineer	--	6.8	6.7	7.0	7.0	7.5	7.7	--	6.6	6.7	8.9	8.7	9.4
Farmer or forester	--	7.2	6.9	5.9	5.8	6.7	5.9	--	5.0	4.4	3.7	3.4	3.1
Health professional (non-MD)	--	1.1	1.1	1.3	1.2	1.2	1.2	--	1.0	1.1	1.4	1.4	1.4
Lawyer	--	1.2	1.0	1.1	1.2	1.1	1.2	--	1.3	1.3	1.3	1.3	1.5
Military career	--	1.7	1.6	1.8	1.7	2.1	2.0	--	1.7	1.7	2.1	2.0	1.9
Research scientist	--	0.5	0.5	0.5	0.5	0.5	0.5	--	0.6	0.6	0.7	0.6	0.7
Skilled worker	--	13.8	14.1	14.6	13.1	13.5	13.2	--	18.7	18.0	12.0	12.1	11.8
Semiskilled or unskilled worker	--	12.8	14.0	13.4	13.5	12.2	12.0	--	9.7	10.0	10.5	10.5	8.8
Unemployed	--	0.8	1.0	1.1	1.3	1.2	1.9	--	2.0	3.0	2.2	2.2	2.1
Other	--	16.4	17.0	17.5	17.1	17.6	17.0	--	17.8	18.5	18.6	19.6	19.4
FATHER'S CURRENT RELIGIOUS PREFERENCE (Aggregated) [2]													
Protestant	--	--	--	--	--	--	--	--	51.2	50.3	47.9	48.4	48.7
Roman Catholic	--	--	--	--	--	--	--	--	34.2	35.1	36.2	37.7	37.5
Jewish	--	--	--	--	--	--	--	--	4.5	4.3	4.5	4.5	5.0
Other	--	--	--	--	--	--	--	--	3.0	3.0	3.9	3.0	2.9
None	--	--	--	--	--	--	--	--	7.3	7.2	7.4	6.3	5.9
FATHER'S CURRENT RELIGIOUS PREFERENCE (Disaggregated)													
Baptist	--	--	--	--	--	--	--	--	13.4	13.5	11.8	12.4	12.6
Buddhist	--	--	--	--	--	--	--	--	--	--	--	--	--
Congregational (United Church of Christ) [3]	--	--	--	--	--	--	--	--	2.0	1.8	1.9	2.1	1.9
Eastern Orthodox	--	--	--	--	--	--	--	--	0.6	0.8	0.7	0.9	0.8
Episcopal	--	--	--	--	--	--	--	--	3.1	3.0	2.9	3.1	3.1
Jewish	--	--	--	--	--	--	--	--	4.5	4.3	4.5	4.5	5.0
Latter Day Saints (Mormon)	--	--	--	--	--	--	--	--	0.4	0.2	0.2	0.2	0.1
Lutheran	--	--	--	--	--	--	--	--	7.2	6.5	6.8	6.1	6.0
Methodist	--	--	--	--	--	--	--	--	11.3	11.2	10.0	10.8	10.8
Muslim (Islamic) [3]	--	--	--	--	--	--	--	--	0.2	0.2	0.3	0.2	0.3
Presbyterian	--	--	--	--	--	--	--	--	6.7	7.0	6.4	6.2	6.7
Quaker (Society of Friends)	--	--	--	--	--	--	--	--	0.2	0.2	0.2	0.2	0.2
Roman Catholic	--	--	--	--	--	--	--	--	34.2	35.1	36.2	37.7	37.5
Seventh Day Adventist	--	--	--	--	--	--	--	--	0.3	0.4	0.5	0.3	0.4
Unitarian-Universalist	--	--	--	--	--	--	--	--	0.3	0.3	0.3	0.3	0.3
Other Protestant	--	--	--	--	--	--	--	--	5.7	5.4	6.2	5.8	5.8
Other religion	--	--	--	--	--	--	--	--	2.8	2.8	3.6	2.8	2.6
None	--	--	--	--	--	--	--	--	7.3	7.2	7.4	6.3	5.9

[1] Data for this item collected but not reported in 1973.
[2] See Appendix D for a discussion of variation in question texts and aggregation procedures.
[3] Text, order or number of response options may vary from year to year.

PARENT'S DEMOGRAPHICS

PARENT'S DEMOGRAPHICS	1979	1980	1981	1982	1983	1984	1985	1986	1987	1988	1989	1990
FATHER'S EDUCATION												
Grammar school or less	5.5	5.5	4.3	3.8	4.2	4.3	3.4	3.4	2.8	3.3	2.8	3.0
Some high school	11.2	11.2	9.7	9.3	9.9	9.1	8.6	7.7	7.1	6.6	6.8	6.3
High school graduate	28.5	29.5	29.3	29.6	29.1	28.6	28.4	26.8	26.1	25.6	26.4	26.6
Postsecondary school other than college	4.1	4.2	4.5	4.6	4.9	5.0	5.0	5.2	5.5	4.9	5.0	4.9
Some college	13.4	13.0	13.4	13.5	13.8	13.9	14.2	14.2	13.9	14.3	14.4	15.4
College degree	20.2	19.8	21.0	20.9	20.1	20.8	20.3	21.1	21.9	22.5	22.8	22.6
Some graduate school	2.4	2.3	2.4	2.4	2.4	2.4	2.8	2.8	2.9	2.9	2.7	2.5
Graduate degree	14.7	14.6	15.4	15.9	15.6	15.9	17.2	18.7	19.7	19.9	19.1	18.7
FATHER'S CURRENT OCCUPATION [1]												
Artist	0.8	0.9	0.9	1.0	0.9	0.9	0.9	0.9	0.9	0.9	0.9	0.7
Businessman	30.7	30.1	30.4	30.8	30.4	30.5	30.6	31.6	32.1	31.5	31.3	29.4
Clergy or religious worker	1.1	1.0	1.1	1.0	0.9	0.9	1.0	1.1	1.0	0.9	1.0	1.1
College teacher	0.9	0.9	0.9	0.9	0.9	1.0	0.9	1.0	1.0	0.9	0.9	0.8
Doctor or dentist	2.3	2.3	2.4	2.4	2.4	2.3	2.3	2.4	2.5	2.6	2.4	2.3
Educator (secondary school)	3.5	3.2	3.8	3.8	3.6	3.6	3.5	3.8	3.9	4.2	3.9	3.9
Elementary school teacher	0.6	0.6	0.7	0.6	0.7	0.6	0.8	0.9	0.9	1.0	1.0	1.0
Engineer	8.7	8.9	9.1	9.0	8.8	8.6	8.7	8.5	8.8	8.5	8.2	8.3
Farmer or forester	3.4	3.7	4.2	3.8	3.5	3.6	3.9	3.1	3.4	2.6	2.7	3.0
Health professional (non-MD)	1.4	1.3	1.4	1.4	1.4	1.3	1.3	1.6	1.4	1.4	1.4	1.5
Lawyer	1.5	1.6	1.5	1.6	1.5	1.6	1.6	1.8	1.8	2.0	1.8	1.7
Military career	2.0	1.8	2.0	1.8	1.9	1.7	1.6	1.7	1.8	1.8	1.9	2.4
Research scientist	0.6	0.7	0.6	0.6	0.7	0.5	0.6	0.7	0.6	0.7	0.6	0.5
Skilled worker	11.7	12.2	12.1	12.1	11.7	11.7	11.3	11.3	10.8	10.7	11.3	11.3
Semiskilled or unskilled worker	9.1	9.4	8.5	8.5	9.0	8.9	8.8	7.6	7.1	7.0	7.9	7.4
Unemployed	2.1	2.3	1.7	1.8	2.5	2.4	2.4	2.1	2.0	1.8	1.9	2.0
Other	19.6	19.1	18.9	18.8	19.3	19.9	19.6	20.2	19.9	21.4	20.9	22.7
FATHER'S CURRENT RELIGIOUS PREFERENCE (Aggregated) [2]												
Protestant	35.9	36.4	37.7	36.0	34.4	45.4	47.4	32.7	47.4	44.2	47.7	48.9
Roman Catholic	38.2	38.2	36.2	37.9	38.1	38.1	36.3	35.3	36.1	36.4	35.0	33.4
Jewish	4.2	3.9	3.6	3.5	3.7	3.7	3.5	3.6	3.5	4.3	3.5	3.0
Other	15.4	14.6	15.9	16.2	17.0	5.4	4.8	20.0	4.8	5.5	4.9	5.2
None	6.3	7.0	6.5	6.4	6.8	7.5	7.9	8.4	8.3	9.8	8.9	9.5
FATHER'S CURRENT RELIGIOUS PREFERENCE (Disaggregated)												
Baptist	--	--	--	--	--	14.1	13.7	--	12.2	12.3	14.1	16.9
Buddhist	--	--	--	--	--	0.3	0.4	--	0.6	0.6	0.5	0.6
Congregational (United Church of Christ) [3]	--	--	--	--	--	1.7	1.7	--	1.9	1.3	1.2	1.2
Eastern Orthodox	--	--	--	--	--	1.0	0.7	--	0.7	0.8	0.8	0.7
Episcopal	--	--	--	--	--	--	2.5	--	2.7	2.5	2.5	2.5
Jewish	--	--	--	--	--	3.7	3.5	--	3.5	4.3	3.5	3.0
Latter Day Saints (Mormon)	--	--	--	--	--	0.2	0.2	--	0.3	0.3	0.3	0.4
Lutheran	--	--	--	--	--	6.0	6.3	--	8.8	6.8	7.0	6.6
Methodist	--	--	--	--	--	10.5	10.1	--	9.6	8.7	10.0	9.5
Muslim (Islamic) [3]	--	--	--	--	--	0.3	0.3	--	0.3	0.5	0.6	0.5
Presbyterian	--	--	--	--	--	--	5.7	--	5.2	5.3	5.4	5.4
Quaker (Society of Friends)	--	--	--	--	--	0.2	0.2	--	0.1	0.2	0.2	0.2
Roman Catholic	--	--	--	--	--	38.1	36.3	--	36.1	36.4	35.0	33.4
Seventh Day Adventist	--	--	--	--	--	0.2	0.2	--	0.2	0.3	0.4	0.3
Unitarian-Universalist	--	--	--	--	--	0.3	--	--	--	--	--	--
Other Protestant	--	--	--	--	--	11.2	6.1	--	5.7	5.7	5.8	5.2
Other religion	--	--	--	--	--	4.8	4.1	--	3.9	4.4	3.8	4.1
None	--	--	--	--	--	7.5	7.9	--	8.3	9.8	8.9	9.5

[1] Data for this item collected but not reported in 1973.
[2] See Appendix D for a discussion of variation in question texts and aggregation procedures.
[3] Text, order or number of response options may vary from year to year.

HIGH SCHOOL EXPERIENCES AND ACHIEVEMENTS

HIGH SCHOOL EXPERIENCES AND ACHIEVEMENTS	1966	1967	1968	1969	1970	1971	1972	1973	1974	1975	1976	1977	1978
YEAR GRADUATED FROM HIGH SCHOOL													
Current year (year of the survey)	--	--	--	--	--	88.6	90.0	91.6	91.2	90.9	91.6	91.9	93.4
Last year	--	--	--	--	--	--	--	3.5	3.9	3.7	3.6	3.9	3.5
Two years ago	--	--	--	--	--	--	--	0.9	1.2	1.1	1.1	1.0	0.9
Three years ago	--	--	--	--	--	--	--	2.6	2.2	2.6	2.2	2.0	1.5
High school equivalency certificate	--	--	--	--	--	--	--	0.9	0.9	1.1	1.0	0.9	0.5
Never completed high school	--	--	--	--	--	--	--	0.5	0.6	0.7	0.5	0.3	0.2
TYPE OF SECONDARY SCHOOL													
Public	84.0	--	--	83.7	83.6	--	84.3	--	--	--	--	--	--
Private: nondenominational [1]	4.6	--	--	4.3	2.5	--	4.4	--	--	--	--	--	--
Private: denominational [1]	11.4	--	--	12.1	13.9	--	11.3	--	--	--	--	--	--
AVERAGE GRADE IN HIGH SCHOOL													
A or A+	4.2	3.9	3.4	3.2	4.2	4.3	5.1	5.9	6.2	6.3	6.7	6.8	8.5
A-	7.1	6.9	6.4	6.3	7.4	7.0	8.4	7.4	9.2	8.3	9.0	9.0	10.5
B+	13.6	13.3	12.5	12.3	14.6	13.8	15.6	17.0	16.0	16.2	17.7	17.6	17.6
B	19.8	20.5	20.0	20.6	21.6	22.4	24.2	24.1	24.8	24.3	25.7	26.6	25.7
B-	16.1	16.5	16.5	16.6	17.6	18.5	16.5	18.0	15.6	17.4	15.6	16.0	14.8
C+	19.6	19.6	20.0	20.3	18.9	19.3	17.7	14.0	15.9	15.0	14.6	14.3	13.4
C	18.3	18.2	19.8	19.4	14.5	13.7	11.8	13.1	11.5	11.8	10.1	9.1	9.0
D	1.3	1.2	1.4	1.3	1.1	0.9	0.7	0.6	0.7	0.7	0.6	0.6	0.5
ACADEMIC RANK IN HIGH SCHOOL													
Top quarter [1]	--	--	44.2	43.6	37.4	35.1	38.1	--	--	--	--	--	41.8
Second quarter	--	--	29.8	28.4	31.9	32.0	34.7	--	--	--	--	--	35.1
Third quarter	--	--	20.9	21.9	25.5	27.5	23.6	--	--	--	--	--	20.4
Fourth quarter	--	--	5.2	6.1	5.2	5.3	3.5	--	--	--	--	--	2.7
Top 20 percent	--	--	--	--	--	--	--	--	--	--	--	--	--
Second 20 percent	--	--	--	--	--	--	--	--	--	--	--	--	--
Middle 20 percent	--	--	--	--	--	--	--	--	--	--	--	--	--
Fourth 20 percent	--	--	--	--	--	--	--	--	--	--	--	--	--
Bottom 20 percent	--	--	--	--	--	--	--	--	--	--	--	--	--
HAVE MET/EXCEEDED RECOMMENDED YEARS OF HIGH SCHOOL STUDY [2]													
English (4 years)	--	--	--	--	--	--	--	--	--	--	--	--	--
Mathematics (3 years)	--	--	--	--	--	--	--	--	--	--	--	--	--
Foreign language (2 years)	--	--	--	--	--	--	--	--	--	--	--	--	--
Physical science (2 years)	--	--	--	--	--	--	--	--	--	--	--	--	--
Biological science (2 years)	--	--	--	--	--	--	--	--	--	--	--	--	--
History or American government (1 year)	--	--	--	--	--	--	--	--	--	--	--	--	--
Computer science (1/2 year)	--	--	--	--	--	--	--	--	--	--	--	--	--
Art and/or music (1 year)	--	--	--	--	--	--	--	--	--	--	--	--	--
HAVE HAD SPECIAL TUTORING OR REMEDIAL WORK IN													
English	--	--	--	--	--	--	--	--	--	--	--	--	--
Reading	--	--	--	--	--	--	--	--	--	--	--	--	--
Mathematics	--	--	--	--	--	--	--	--	--	--	--	--	--
Social studies	--	--	--	--	--	--	--	--	--	--	--	--	--
Science	--	--	--	--	--	--	--	--	--	--	--	--	--
Foreign language	--	--	--	--	--	--	--	--	--	--	--	--	--
WILL NEED SPECIAL TUTORING OR REMEDIAL WORK IN [1]													
English	--	--	--	--	--	--	--	--	--	--	--	14.5	16.0
Reading	--	--	--	--	--	--	--	--	--	--	--	8.0	9.1
Mathematics	--	--	--	--	--	--	--	--	--	--	--	22.6	21.9
Social studies	--	--	--	--	--	--	--	--	--	--	--	1.9	3.5
Science	--	--	--	--	--	--	--	--	--	--	--	7.3	10.1
Foreign language	--	--	--	--	--	--	--	--	--	--	--	12.6	15.7

[1] Text, order or number of response options may vary from year to year.
[2] Based on recommendations of the National Commission on Excellence in Education

HIGH SCHOOL EXPERIENCES AND ACHIEVEMENTS

1979	1980	1981	1982	1983	1984	1985	1986	1987	1988	1989	1990	
												YEAR GRADUATED FROM HIGH SCHOOL
92.0	91.3	93.1	93.1	92.5	93.2	93.1	91.9	92.5	93.6	93.2	92.9	Current year (year of the survey)
3.8	4.1	3.3	3.3	3.4	3.3	3.0	3.4	3.2	2.7	3.2	3.4	Last year
1.1	1.0	0.9	1.0	1.0	0.8	0.9	1.1	0.9	0.8	0.9	1.0	Two years ago
2.0	2.3	1.8	1.6	2.0	1.6	1.8	2.3	2.1	1.7	1.7	1.8	Three years ago
0.8	0.9	0.7	0.7	1.0	0.9	0.9	1.1	1.2	1.1	0.9	0.7	High school equivalency certificate
0.3	0.4	0.3	0.2	0.2	0.2	0.2	0.2	0.1	0.1	0.2	0.2	Never completed high school
												TYPE OF SECONDARY SCHOOL
85.3	85.5	--	--	84.0	82.9	--	--	--	--	--	--	Public
3.5	3.6	--	--	4.5	4.6	--	--	--	--	--	--	Private: nondenominational [1]
11.2	10.9	--	--	11.5	12.5	--	--	--	--	--	--	Private: denominational [1]
												AVERAGE GRADE IN HIGH SCHOOL
7.5	7.5	7.5	7.6	7.5	7.6	7.5	9.2	9.1	9.8	9.1	8.9	A or A+
9.6	9.7	9.4	9.5	9.2	9.0	10.2	10.4	9.5	11.3	11.5	11.2	A-
16.8	16.9	16.6	17.0	16.5	16.4	16.9	16.1	16.9	16.6	17.0	16.5	B+
25.8	25.5	25.4	25.3	24.4	23.8	24.1	23.4	20.6	23.5	24.6	24.3	B
16.1	15.5	16.6	15.9	16.2	16.1	15.7	15.9	19.3	15.9	16.4	16.2	B-
14.8	14.8	14.8	14.8	15.5	15.5	14.6	14.9	11.9	13.5	12.9	13.8	C+
9.0	9.5	9.2	9.3	10.0	10.8	10.3	9.4	12.0	8.9	8.0	8.6	C
0.5	0.6	0.5	0.6	0.7	0.7	0.7	0.6	0.6	0.5	0.5	0.5	D
												ACADEMIC RANK IN HIGH SCHOOL
--	--	--	--	--	--	--	--	--	--	--	--	Top quarter [1]
--	--	--	--	--	--	--	--	--	--	--	--	Second quarter
--	--	--	--	--	--	--	--	--	--	--	--	Third quarter
--	--	--	--	--	--	--	--	--	--	--	--	Fourth quarter
33.9	34.7	34.5	35.4	34.6	35.2	36.6	37.6	--	--	--	--	Top 20 percent
24.2	24.0	24.7	24.1	24.4	23.6	23.8	23.2	--	--	--	--	Second 20 percent
34.3	33.2	32.5	32.0	32.3	32.0	30.7	30.7	--	--	--	--	Middle 20 percent
6.5	6.8	7.2	7.2	7.4	7.9	7.6	7.1	--	--	--	--	Fourth 20 percent
1.1	1.3	1.1	1.3	1.4	1.4	1.3	1.3	--	--	--	--	Bottom 20 percent
												HAVE MET/EXCEEDED RECOMMENDED YEARS OF HIGH SCHOOL STUDY [2]
--	--	--	--	88.7	92.1	91.6	93.2	93.0	94.5	--	95.9	English (4 years)
--	--	--	--	86.6	87.8	87.7	90.1	90.4	92.9	--	92.6	Mathematics (3 years)
--	--	--	--	60.8	61.8	61.7	66.9	70.1	76.6	--	73.4	Foreign language (2 years)
--	--	--	--	62.2	57.6	60.9	59.6	55.1	56.1	--	53.4	Physical science (2 years)
--	--	--	--	34.4	31.6	33.1	34.2	31.9	32.8	--	32.0	Biological science (2 years)
--	--	--	--	--	98.6	99.0	98.9	99.2	99.1	--	98.8	History or American government (1 year)
--	--	--	--	--	57.7	62.1	63.7	63.2	63.2	--	57.1	Computer science (1/2 year)
--	--	--	--	--	55.7	54.9	57.2	58.4	62.3	--	68.2	Art and/or music (1 year)
												HAVE HAD SPECIAL TUTORING OR REMEDIAL WORK IN
7.4	8.1	6.1	6.3	--	6.6	--	--	--	--	6.8	--	English
7.3	8.1	5.8	6.0	--	6.3	--	--	--	--	6.3	--	Reading
8.4	8.9	7.3	7.6	--	9.0	--	--	--	--	9.9	--	Mathematics
6.0	7.2	4.4	4.6	--	4.7	--	--	--	--	4.9	--	Social studies
5.6	6.7	4.4	4.4	--	4.8	--	--	--	--	5.3	--	Science
4.6	4.6	3.3	3.7	--	4.1	--	--	--	--	5.2	--	Foreign language
												WILL NEED SPECIAL TUTORING OR REMEDIAL WORK IN [1]
13.5	13.7	13.3	13.4	--	14.2	--	--	--	--	13.0	--	English
5.7	5.9	5.3	5.1	--	5.4	--	--	--	--	5.4	--	Reading
19.5	18.8	19.2	20.1	--	21.7	--	--	--	--	22.5	--	Mathematics
2.3	2.5	2.2	2.3	--	2.5	--	--	--	--	2.5	--	Social studies
7.1	7.4	7.1	7.6	--	8.3	--	--	--	--	7.9	--	Science
9.4	9.8	8.4	8.5	--	10.0	--	--	--	--	10.6	--	Foreign language

[1] Text, order or number of response options may vary from year to year.
[2] Based on recommendations of the National Commission on Excellence in Education

HIGH SCHOOL EXPERIENCES AND ACHIEVEMENTS

ACTIVITIES REPORTED IN THE LAST YEAR	1966	1967	1968	1969	1970	1971	1972	1973	1974	1975	1976	1977	1978
Frequently or Occasionally [1]													
Played a musical instrument	43.7	39.3	36.0	37.3	36.1	34.7	--	--	--	--	--	--	38.6
Stayed up all night	59.1	63.1	58.2	64.4	61.3	60.4	--	--	--	--	--	--	66.4
Participated in organized demonstrations	16.0	17.1	--	--	--	--	--	--	--	--	--	--	15.7
Worked in a local, state, or national political campaign [4]	--	--	12.1	15.2	13.4	12.0	--	--	--	--	--	--	8.8
Came late to class	51.2	59.1	55.5	60.0	60.2	54.4	--	--	--	--	--	--	--
Attended a religious service	--	--	89.1	86.9	86.0	83.5	--	--	--	--	--	--	82.6
Attended a public recital or concert [4]	55.0	--	--	--	--	--	--	--	--	--	--	--	78.9
Overslept and missed a class or appointment	23.5	24.8	21.9	27.3	26.1	24.2	--	--	--	--	--	--	--
Argued with a teacher in class	--	58.1	57.4	59.6	57.3	55.4	--	--	--	--	--	--	--
Was a guest in a teacher's home	--	36.1	--	--	--	--	--	--	--	--	--	--	--
Studied with other students	--	89.4	--	--	--	--	--	--	--	--	--	--	--
Drank beer	63.9	64.9	63.1	66.9	67.3	71.0	--	--	--	--	--	--	80.3
Took sleeping pills	--	4.9	4.9	5.7	4.6	3.7	--	--	--	--	--	--	2.6
Took a tranquilizing pill	--	6.6	6.1	6.9	5.5	4.5	--	--	--	--	--	--	4.3
Took vitamins	--	58.1	56.6	58.3	54.4	54.7	--	--	--	--	--	--	54.1
Tutored another student	--	44.2	43.7	40.7	43.0	39.6	--	--	--	--	--	--	--
Visited an art gallery or museum	--	66.5	66.4	67.5	64.5	62.4	--	--	--	--	--	--	--
Played chess	--	54.7	53.9	53.9	51.7	51.8	--	--	--	--	--	--	--
Performed volunteer work	--	--	--	--	--	--	--	--	--	--	--	--	--
Had vocational counseling	--	57.6	59.8	56.8	51.8	45.2	--	--	--	--	--	--	--
Read poetry not connected with a course	--		44.3	46.4	44.9	45.5	--	--	--	--	--	--	--
Wore glasses or contact lenses	--	--	--	--	46.5	--	--	--	--	--	--	--	39.3
Did not complete homework on time [4]	--	79.0	68.5	77.4	76.2	72.3	--	--	--	--	--	--	--
Won a varsity letter in a sport [3]	47.3	47.5	45.5	44.8	44.7	46.9	--	--	--	--	--	--	--
Frequently Only [1]													
Did extra, unassigned reading for a course	--	12.1	8.7	11.0	13.2	11.8	--	--	--	--	--	--	--
Voted in a student election	66.9	69.4	74.4	63.8	64.9	61.5	--	--	--	--	--	--	--
Studied in the library	22.9	[*]	29.5	31.6	28.8	27.0	--	--	--	--	--	--	--
Checked out a book or journal from the school library	42.9	47.3	43.1	40.1	37.4	35.4	--	--	--	--	--	--	--
Missed school due to illness	--	2.1	1.9	2.4	2.2	2.1	--	--	--	--	--	--	--
Typed a homework assignment	18.7	20.3	15.3	17.4	15.8	15.9	--	--	--	--	--	--	--
Smoked cigarettes	19.4	19.1	18.4	17.9	16.5	16.8	--	--	--	--	--	--	10.6
Discussed religion	--	26.6	22.8	22.2	21.9	20.4	--	--	--	--	--	--	--
Discussed politics	--	26.8	32.0	28.2	29.8	23.7	--	--	--	--	--	--	--
Discussed sports	--	58.6	55.9	54.1	54.4	53.6	--	--	--	--	--	--	--
Asked a teacher for advice after class	--	25.0	20.6	23.0	21.5	20.0	--	--	--	--	--	--	--
Felt depressed	--	--	--	--	--	--	--	--	--	--	--	--	--
Felt overwhelmed	--	--	--	--	--	--	--	--	--	--	--	--	--
Used a personal computer	--	--	--	--	--	--	--	--	--	--	--	--	--
Noted [2]													
Was elected president of one or more student organizations	23.3	22.3	20.0	19.6	19.1	18.4	--	--	--	--	--	--	--
Received a high rating in a state or regional music contest	9.0	8.6	8.2	8.3	8.2	8.4	--	--	--	--	--	--	--
Competed in state or regional speech or debate contest	6.0	5.3	5.0	4.8	4.5	4.2	--	--	--	--	--	--	--
Had a major part in a play	18.5	16.9	16.2	15.5	14.8	14.4	--	--	--	--	--	--	--
Won an award in an art competition [4]	4.7	4.4	4.6	4.6	4.8	4.8	--	--	--	--	--	--	--
Edited a school publication [4]	9.0	8.4	8.0	7.9	8.2	8.2	--	--	--	--	--	--	--
Had original writing or poetry published [4]	13.2	13.2	12.6	12.9	13.2	12.5	--	--	--	--	--	--	--
Won an award in a state or regional science contest [4]	3.1	2.7	2.5	2.6	2.5	2.2	--	--	--	--	--	--	--
Was a member of a scholastic honor society	21.2	20.7	19.1	18.5	20.2	18.6	--	--	--	--	--	--	--

[*] Results were not comparable to those of other years due to changes in question text or order.
[1] Response options for these items were "frequently", "occasionally" and "not at all".
[2] Response option for these items was a single bubble to be marked if the student engaged in the indicated activity.
[3] In 1966-1971, response option was a single bubble as noted in [2]. In 1984-1990, response options were as in [1].
[4] Text, order or number of response options may vary from year to year.

HIGH SCHOOL EXPERIENCES AND ACHIEVEMENTS

ACTIVITIES REPORTED IN THE LAST YEAR	1979	1980	1981	1982	1983	1984	1985	1986	1987	1988	1989	1990
Frequently or Occasionally [1]												
Played a musical instrument	37.5	--	37.8	40.7	38.6	38.9	38.5	39.1	39.2	--	--	35.5
Stayed up all night	67.4	--	70.9	72.8	71.1	73.8	74.9	77.4	76.0	80.9	79.0	79.2
Participated in organized demonstrations	16.9	--	18.8	19.5	18.7	--	--	--	--	32.4	35.8	37.5
Worked in a local, state, or national political campaign [4]	8.5	--	8.7	8.1	7.4	8.7	--	--	--	8.7	--	--
Came late to class	--	--	--	--	--	--	--	--	--	--	--	58.9
Attended a religious service	82.1	--	83.4	83.4	82.4	82.1	82.4	80.0	80.7	78.3	78.7	79.7
Attended a public recital or concert [4]	76.6	--	75.6	73.9	71.3	69.0	73.3	72.7	74.9	--	--	--
Overslept and missed a class or appointment	--	--	--	--	24.1	27.4	29.6	31.7	31.1	--	--	--
Argued with a teacher in class	--	--	--	--	--	--	--	--	--	--	48.9	--
Was a guest in a teacher's home	--	--	--	--	--	--	32.4	32.8	--	30.1	28.5	30.1
Studied with other students	--	--	--	--	--	--	86.1	84.8	86.9	85.9	83.2	82.8
Drank beer	79.6	--	80.5	79.8	77.2	73.6	71.8	72.8	72.3	72.1	66.8	65.8
Took sleeping pills	2.7	--	2.8	2.9	2.6	--	--	--	--	--	2.9	--
Took a tranquilizing pill	4.9	--	5.1	4.9	4.3	4.3	--	--	--	--	1.7	--
Took vitamins	55.9	--	60.1	61.6	61.3	62.5	--	--	--	--	--	54.7
Tutored another student	--	--	--	--	--	--	40.9	40.0	42.4	44.7	44.0	44.4
Visited an art gallery or museum	--	--	--	--	--	--	--	--	--	--	52.6	50.8
Played chess	--	--	--	--	--	--	--	--	--	--	--	--
Performed volunteer work	--	--	--	--	--	68.1	68.7	67.4	--	--	58.8	60.5
Had vocational counseling	--	--	--	--	--	--	--	--	--	--	--	--
Read poetry not connected with a course	--	--	--	--	--	--	--	--	--	--	--	
Wore glasses or contact lenses	37.7	--	37.3	37.7	37.3	--	--	--	--	--	--	41.7
Did not complete homework on time [4]	--	--	--	--	63.9	72.3	72.8	72.9	73.0	73.0	72.8	72.6
Won a varsity letter in a sport [3]	--	--	--	--	--	53.8	54.2	54.4	55.7	55.2	56.7	59.5
Frequently Only [1]												
Did extra, unassigned reading for a course	--	--	--	--	--	9.9	9.2	9.6	8.4	9.0	8.5	8.4
Voted in a student election	--	--	--	--	--	--	--	--	--	--	--	--
Studied in the library	--	--	--	--	--	--	--	--	--	--	11.3	8.8
Checked out a book or journal from the school library	--	--	--	--	--	--	--	--	--	--	--	22.2
Missed school due to illness	--	--	--	--	--	2.4	2.6	2.9	2.6	--	--	--
Typed a homework assignment	--	--	--	--	--	--	--	--	--	--	--	--
Smoked cigarettes	9.7	--	8.6	8.5	8.0	7.1	6.6	7.9	7.3	8.2	8.6	9.1
Discussed religion	--	--	--	--	--	--	--	--	--	18.3	--	--
Discussed politics	--	--	--	--	--	--	--	--	--	22.0	--	--
Discussed sports	--	--	--	--	--	--	--	--	--	58.8	--	--
Asked a teacher for advice after class	--	--	--	--	--	--	21.7	--	--	--	--	25.5
Felt depressed	--	--	--	--	--	--	12.0	12.9	11.5	14.9	12.8	13.0
Felt overwhelmed	--	--	--	--	--	--	6.1	6.4	6.0	7.4	6.3	5.9
Used a personal computer	--	--	--	--	--	--	27.8	26.9	27.1	30.1	31.0	--
Noted [2]												
Was elected president of one or more student organizations	--	--	--	--	--	--	--	--	--	--	--	18.4
Received a high rating in a state or regional music contest	--	--	--	--	--	--	--	--	--	--	--	9.4
Competed in state or regional speech or debate contest	--	--	--	--	--	--	--	--	--	--	--	5.7
Had a major part in a play	--	--	--	--	--	--	--	--	--	--	--	12.0
Won an award in an art competition [4]	--	--	--	--	--	--	--	--	--	--	--	9.2
Edited a school publication [4]	--	--	--	--	--	--	--	--	--	--	--	9.0
Had original writing or poetry published [4]	--	--	--	--	--	--	--	--	--	--	--	11.7
Won an award in a state or regional science contest [4]	--	--	--	--	--	--	--	--	--	--	--	5.5
Was a member of a scholastic honor society	--	--	--	--	--	--	--	--	--	--	--	25.1

[1] Response options for these items were "frequently", "occasionally" and "not at all".
[2] Response option for these items was a single bubble to be marked if the student engaged in the indicated activity.
[3] In 1966-1971, response option was a single bubble as noted in [2]. In 1984-1990, response options were as in [1].
[4] Text, order or number of response options may vary from year to year.

COLLEGE CHOICE, APPLICATION AND MATRICULATION

COLLEGE CHOICE, APPLICATION AND MATRICULATION	1966	1967	1968	1969	1970	1971	1972	1973	1974	1975	1976	1977	1978
VERY IMPORTANT REASONS NOTED IN DECIDING TO GO TO COLLEGE [1]													
My parents wanted me to go	--	--	--	--	--	21.9	--	--	--	--	28.7	27.4	27.0
To be able to get a better job	--	--	--	--	--	77.0	--	--	--	--	71.7	76.8	75.1
Could not get a job	--	--	--	--	--	--	--	--	--	--	5.5	5.7	4.0
To get away from home	--	--	--	--	--	--	--	--	--	--	8.2	8.5	7.0
To gain a general education and appreciation of ideas	--	--	--	--	--	53.3	--	--	--	--	57.5	65.3	61.7
To improve my reading and study skills	--	--	--	--	--	21.7	--	--	--	--	32.8	40.6	35.0
There was nothing better to do	--	--	--	--	--	2.2	--	--	--	--	2.9	2.6	1.9
To make me a more cultured person	--	--	--	--	--	24.5	--	--	--	--	27.3	33.6	28.7
To be able to make more money	--	--	--	--	--	57.0	--	--	--	--	59.6	67.1	65.8
To learn more about things that interest me	--	--	--	--	--	64.5	--	--	--	--	67.5	75.1	69.0
To meet new and interesting people	--	--	--	--	--	36.3	--	--	--	--	44.7	51.8	48.1
To prepare myself for grad/prof school	--	--	--	--	--	38.9	--	--	--	--	44.3	46.3	44.0
VERY IMPORTANT REASONS NOTED FOR SELECTING FRESHMAN COLLEGE													
Relatives wanted me to come here [1]	--	--	--	--	--	6.3	[*]	[*]	6.2	6.9	5.9	5.5	5.0
Teacher advised me	--	--	--	--	--	--	--	5.1	5.1	4.6	4.4	4.2	3.8
College has a good academic reputation [1]	--	--	--	--	--	34.7	44.9	44.4	45.8	43.3	40.0	44.4	46.9
College has a good social reputation	--	--	--	--	--	--	--	--	--	--	--	--	--
Offered financial assistance	--	--	--	--	--	--	17.8	16.8	18.2	16.3	13.4	14.8	13.9
College offers special education programs	--	--	--	--	--	29.7	24.9	24.8	25.0	23.6	21.2	24.3	21.3
College has low tuition	--	--	--	--	--	18.9	19.1	26.4	27.1	24.3	17.7	19.3	16.5
Advice of guidance counselor	--	--	--	--	--	7.7	7.2	9.8	9.5	8.1	7.7	8.2	7.4
Wanted to live at home	--	--	--	--	--	12.2	11.6	13.5	12.8	13.9	11.1	11.2	9.7
Wanted to live near home	--	--	--	--	--	--	--	--	--	--	--	--	--
Friend suggested attending	--	--	--	--	--	--	--	--	--	6.7	6.7	7.5	6.1
College representative recruited me	--	--	--	--	--	--	--	--	--	5.0	4.5	5.3	5.1
Athletic department recruited me	--	--	--	--	--	--	--	--	--	--	--	--	--
Graduates go to top grad schools	--	--	--	--	--	--	--	--	--	--	--	--	--
Graduates get good jobs	--	--	--	--	--	--	--	--	--	50.0	--	--	--
Not accepted anywhere else	--	--	--	--	--	3.6	3.7	--	--	--	3.5	3.7	3.1
Advice of someone who attended	--	--	--	--	--	15.3	16.0	17.9	17.0	15.7	13.6	15.0	12.9
Not offered aid by first choice	--	--	--	--	--	--	--	--	--	--	--	--	--
Wanted to live away from home	--	--	--	--	--	--	14.2	11.7	10.8	10.7	--	--	--
THIS COLLEGE IS STUDENT'S													
First choice	--	--	--	--	--	--	--	--	75.2	77.2	76.0	74.0	75.0
Second choice	--	--	--	--	--	--	--	--	18.7	17.4	17.3	19.1	18.6
Less than second choice [1]	--	--	--	--	--	--	--	--	6.1	5.4	6.7	6.9	6.4
NUMBER OF APPLICATIONS SENT TO OTHER COLLEGES													
None (applied to only one college)	--	48.8	49.8	50.3	--	--	46.5	47.6	--	46.0	43.4	38.9	35.9
One	--	19.5	19.7	19.4	--	--	18.0	18.5	--	19.0	18.0	17.2	16.8
Two	--	14.4	14.0	14.1	--	--	15.1	14.7	--	14.4	14.8	16.8	17.8
Three	--	8.8	8.7	8.3	--	--	9.5	9.1	--	9.8	11.7	13.4	14.3
Four	--	4.5	4.1	4.2	--	--	5.1	4.9	--	5.2	5.8	6.6	7.2
Five	--	2.3	2.0	2.1	--	--	3.0	2.7	--	2.8	3.0	3.7	4.1
Six or more	--	1.8	1.6	1.7	--	--	2.8	2.5	--	2.7	3.2	3.5	3.9
NUMBER OF ACCEPTANCES FROM OTHER COLLEGES [2]													
None	--	--	--	--	--	--	--	--	--	30.6	29.1	26.3	22.3
One	--	--	--	--	--	--	--	--	--	30.4	28.5	28.8	29.4
Two	--	--	--	--	--	--	--	--	--	20.0	20.3	22.5	22.9
Three	--	--	--	--	--	--	--	--	--	10.9	12.8	13.1	14.7
Four	--	--	--	--	--	--	--	--	--	4.6	5.2	5.2	6.0
Five	--	--	--	--	--	--	--	--	--	1.7	2.0	2.2	2.5
Six or more	--	--	--	--	--	--	--	--	--	1.8	2.1	1.8	2.3

[*] Results were not comparable to those of other years due to changes in question text or order.
[1] Text, order or number of response options may vary from year to year.
[2] Students who applied to no other colleges not included.

COLLEGE CHOICE, APPLICATION AND MATRICULATION

	1979	1980	1981	1982	1983	1984	1985	1986	1987	1988	1989	1990
VERY IMPORTANT REASONS NOTED IN DECIDING TO GO TO COLLEGE [1]												
My parents wanted me to go	28.0	29.9	30.4	31.2	29.3	28.9	[*]	[*]	[*]	[*]	32.4	33.0
To be able to get a better job	77.5	76.6	75.7	77.0	74.9	74.4	[*]	[*]	[*]	[*]	75.4	77.9
Could not get a job	4.6	5.7	5.4	6.9	6.0	5.0	[*]	[*]	[*]	[*]	6.3	6.5
To get away from home	7.4	8.7	9.1	9.6	9.6	10.7	[*]	[*]	[*]	[*]	14.5	15.8
To gain a general education and appreciation of ideas	62.1	59.6	61.0	59.8	56.5	58.3	55.0	55.4	54.2	53.6	55.0	56.0
To improve my reading and study skills	36.3	36.0	36.5	36.6	37.8	37.8	36.9	36.4	36.4	35.6	35.8	38.4
There was nothing better to do	2.1	2.3	2.5	2.5	2.6	2.3	2.6	2.9	3.0	3.4	3.0	3.0
To make me a more cultured person	28.5	28.2	27.7	28.2	25.7	27.9	26.8	26.4	27.9	29.2	29.5	33.0
To be able to make more money	68.9	67.8	70.5	72.3	69.7	70.7	73.6	74.0	74.8	76.5	75.6	77.0
To learn more about things that interest me	68.8	68.9	68.6	67.9	66.3	67.3	68.8	69.7	68.1	69.3	67.9	68.4
To meet new and interesting people	48.4	47.0	46.7	46.2	46.6	48.5	--	--	--	--	--	--
To prepare myself for grad/prof school	44.8	43.9	43.4	43.9	44.3	45.1	43.9	44.1	44.3	46.1	47.3	48.5
VERY IMPORTANT REASONS NOTED FOR SELECTING FRESHMAN COLLEGE												
Relatives wanted me to come here [1]	5.1	5.9	5.4	5.7	5.5	6.1	5.3	6.8	6.3	6.2	7.6	8.1
Teacher advised me	4.0	4.5	4.0	4.2	4.0	4.1	4.2	4.6	3.9	4.1	3.9	4.5
College has a good academic reputation [1]	45.3	47.3	49.3	50.7	48.5	51.7	52.3	55.8	52.9	54.0	50.4	48.6
College has a good social reputation	--	--	--	--	19.6	21.3	22.3	26.8	26.6	23.0	22.5	21.5
Offered financial assistance	15.1	15.2	14.1	15.4	19.0	18.3	18.6	19.9	18.2	18.9	20.7	22.6
College offers special education programs	21.7	22.6	22.1	21.8	17.9	18.2	18.9	19.3	17.6	18.5	17.1	18.5
College has low tuition	16.0	16.2	16.6	19.7	19.9	19.5	20.1	20.9	19.8	20.1	20.3	21.3
Advice of guidance counselor	7.3	8.0	7.3	7.5	7.8	7.9	7.6	8.0	7.2	7.2	6.8	7.5
Wanted to live at home	10.2	10.4	9.4	10.2	--	--	--	--	--	--	--	--
Wanted to live near home	--	--	--	--	16.7	15.5	14.3	15.1	14.6	15.6	14.8	14.7
Friend suggested attending	6.4	6.9	6.5	6.9	6.4	6.5	6.9	7.9	7.8	7.9	7.8	8.3
College representative recruited me	5.6	5.8	5.7	5.3	3.2	3.4	4.0	4.2	3.7	3.9	4.2	4.6
Athletic department recruited me	--	--	--	--	6.4	6.4	6.8	7.0	6.7	6.6	7.1	7.5
Graduates go to top grad schools	--	--	--	--	23.8	24.5	24.3	23.9	25.3	--	22.6	23.0
Graduates get good jobs	--	--	--	--	44.4	44.4	45.0	45.5	45.6	[*]	43.3	41.8
Not accepted anywhere else	3.4	3.1	3.3	3.2	--	--	--	--	--	--	--	--
Advice of someone who attended	13.1	14.0	13.5	14.1	--	--	--	--	--	--	--	--
Not offered aid by first choice	--	--	--	--	--	3.9	4.0	4.7	4.0	4.5	5.1	--
Wanted to live away from home	--	--	--	--	--	--	--	--	--	--	--	--
THIS COLLEGE IS STUDENT'S												
First choice	74.8	74.8	73.5	72.7	72.6	72.4	71.9	71.5	69.4	67.5	69.0	70.4
Second choice	18.7	18.9	19.7	20.0	20.5	20.7	20.7	20.7	22.3	22.5	22.2	22.0
Less than second choice [1]	6.6	6.3	6.7	7.3	6.8	6.8	7.4	7.8	8.3	10.0	8.8	7.6
NUMBER OF APPLICATIONS SENT TO OTHER COLLEGES												
None (applied to only one college)	38.5	38.5	37.1	37.8	37.1	33.8	33.4	34.9	34.0	29.7	30.2	30.3
One	16.5	16.3	16.6	16.0	16.2	16.5	18.9	15.9	15.0	13.8	14.2	14.9
Two	16.5	16.6	17.0	16.5	16.8	17.4	16.7	15.8	15.7	16.5	16.8	16.5
Three	14.0	14.0	14.1	14.2	14.4	14.8	14.6	14.4	14.8	15.9	15.6	15.6
Four	6.6	6.9	7.2	7.2	7.1	8.1	7.5	8.3	9.0	10.1	9.7	9.6
Five	4.0	3.9	3.8	4.0	4.1	4.3	4.3	5.0	5.3	6.2	6.1	5.8
Six or more	3.9	3.9	4.2	4.4	4.3	5.0	4.7	5.6	6.3	7.7	7.5	7.2
NUMBER OF ACCEPTANCES FROM OTHER COLLEGES [2]												
None	24.1	22.1	21.6	[*]	19.8	18.9	18.8	19.4	17.9	15.7	16.3	--
One	28.6	28.7	29.1	[*]	28.7	28.3	28.2	27.4	27.1	26.5	25.9	--
Two	22.3	23.1	23.5	[*]	23.8	23.5	23.6	22.9	23.4	24.4	23.8	--
Three	14.4	15.1	14.8	[*]	15.7	16.2	16.4	15.9	16.8	17.3	17.1	--
Four	5.9	6.2	6.2	[*]	6.7	7.0	7.1	7.7	8.1	8.7	8.9	--
Five	2.4	2.5	2.4	[*]	2.7	3.0	2.9	3.3	3.4	3.7	4.0	--
Six or more	2.2	2.3	2.4	[*]	2.6	3.0	2.9	3.4	3.3	3.7	4.1	--

[*] Results were not comparable to those of other years due to changes in question text or order.
[1] Text, order or number of response options may vary from year to year.
[2] Students who applied to no other colleges not included.

DEGREE, MAJOR AND CAREER PLANS

DEGREE, MAJOR AND CAREER PLANS	1966	1967	1968	1969	1970	1971	1972	1973	1974	1975	1976	1977	1978
HIGHEST ACADEMIC DEGREE PLANNED AT ANY COLLEGE													
None	6.1	4.1	4.1	1.9	1.6	[*]	3.2	[*]	3.8	3.8	3.1	2.3	2.1
Vocational certificate	--	--	--	--	--	--	--	--	--	--	--	--	--
Associate or equivalent	4.1	5.6	5.4	7.1	5.4	[*]	6.5	[*]	6.3	6.3	6.7	6.6	6.0
Bachelor's degree (B.A., B.S., etc.)	32.5	32.3	33.7	33.7	33.9	[*]	33.9	[*]	34.6	32.7	34.2	34.8	35.8
Master's degree (M.A., M.S., etc.)	31.2	32.1	32.1	33.2	31.5	[*]	26.0	[*]	26.4	27.1	27.9	29.4	30.2
Ph.D. or Ed.D.	13.7	14.1	14.0	13.4	12.3	[*]	10.6	[*]	10.0	10.4	9.8	10.2	9.8
M.D., D.D.S., D.V.M., or D.O.	7.4	7.0	6.1	5.9	6.7	[*]	9.7	[*]	9.4	8.8	8.3	7.2	7.6
LL.B. or J.D. (law)	[*]	[*]	[*]	[*]	5.6	[*]	6.5	[*]	6.0	6.2	6.0	5.8	5.5
B.D. or M.Div. (divinity)	0.5	0.5	0.4	0.5	0.6	[*]	0.6	[*]	0.7	0.9	0.7	0.7	0.6
Other	2.1	1.8	2.0	2.1	2.4	[*]	2.9	[*]	2.7	3.9	3.3	2.9	2.4
HIGHEST ACADEMIC DEGREE AT FRESHMAN COLLEGE													
None	--	--	--	--	--	--	8.0	7.1	7.7	7.6	6.9	5.1	4.7
Vocational certificate	--	--	--	--	--	--	--	--	--	--	--	--	--
Associate or equivalent	--	--	--	--	--	--	25.6	27.1	29.7	29.1	27.5	26.6	23.8
Bachelor's degree (B.A., B.S., etc.)	--	--	--	--	--	--	49.5	48.4	46.3	45.3	47.7	50.0	52.5
Master's degree (M.A., M.S., etc.)	--	--	--	--	--	--	8.7	9.1	9.0	8.8	9.3	10.3	11.2
Ph.D. or Ed.D.	--	--	--	--	--	--	1.7	1.9	1.6	1.7	1.8	1.7	1.8
M.D., D.D.S., D.V.M., or D.O.	--	--	--	--	--	--	1.8	2.2	1.9	1.9	1.8	1.8	1.9
LL.B. or J.D. (law)	--	--	--	--	--	--	1.3	1.5	1.2	1.3	1.2	1.3	1.3
B.D. or M.Div. (divinity)	--	--	--	--	--	--	0.2	0.2	0.2	0.5	0.7	0.5	0.4
Other	--	--	--	--	--	--	3.2	2.4	2.4	3.7	3.1	2.6	2.4
MAJOR PLANS (AGGREGATED) [1,2]													
Agriculture (including forestry)	3.4	4.1	3.7	3.7	3.5	5.4	5.3	4.4	5.9	5.7	5.3	5.4	4.5
Biological sciences	4.2	4.2	4.1	3.8	4.1	4.4	4.7	8.2	7.7	7.1	6.7	4.8	4.8
Business	17.3	19.3	19.9	19.1	19.6	18.3	17.1	21.1	20.2	20.1	22.5	23.8	25.0
Education	4.7	4.6	5.5	4.8	5.0	4.6	3.5	5.2	4.7	4.6	4.5	3.8	3.3
Engineering	17.9	17.0	17.1	18.0	15.9	13.2	12.7	12.1	12.1	14.0	15.2	17.0	18.8
English	1.9	1.8	1.7	1.7	1.4	1.1	0.9	1.0	0.9	0.7	0.6	0.6	0.7
Health professions (nursing, pre-med, etc.)	1.5	1.4	1.4	1.5	1.9	2.6	3.4	4.6	1.9	1.8	1.5	5.1	5.2
History or political science	7.8	7.5	7.7	7.2	6.4	5.2	5.0	[*]	4.7	4.3	3.7	3.6	3.3
Humanities (other)	2.4	2.7	2.1	2.4	2.3	2.1	2.4	2.0	2.0	1.7	1.8	1.4	1.9
Fine arts (applied and performing)	6.8	7.1	7.1	7.4	8.2	8.4	7.9	[*]	6.5	6.0	6.0	5.4	4.5
Mathematics or statistics	4.6	4.1	3.8	3.3	3.2	2.6	2.2	1.8	1.6	1.1	1.1	1.0	1.1
Physical sciences	5.0	4.5	4.0	3.6	3.4	3.1	3.0	4.2	4.0	4.0	3.9	3.5	3.5
Pre-professional	11.3	10.4	9.6	9.4	10.7	12.4	13.3	--	--	--	--	--	--
Social sciences	[*]	[*]	[*]	[*]	5.8	5.6	4.9	[*]	4.3	3.7	3.2	3.2	2.6
Other technical	3.4	3.7	4.1	5.1	5.3	7.3	8.3	8.4	8.9	10.3	8.6	8.2	8.2
Other non-technical	0.6	0.6	0.7	1.0	1.3	1.4	1.0	7.1	10.2	10.2	11.2	9.2	8.8
Undecided	1.9	2.0	2.1	2.4	2.2	2.3	4.4	4.5	4.4	4.6	4.3	4.0	3.9
CAREER PLANS (AGGREGATED) [1,3]													
Artist (including performer)	4.6	4.1	4.2	4.3	5.1	4.9	5.2	2.7	4.5	4.1	5.5	5.5	4.9
Business	18.5	17.5	17.5	16.9	17.4	16.1	15.4	[*]	17.6	17.2	20.9	22.4	23.0
Clergy or other religious worker	1.2	1.9	1.1	1.4	1.3	1.0	1.0	1.0	1.3	1.0	0.9	0.8	0.8
College teacher	2.1	1.4	1.3	1.3	1.2	0.8	0.7	0.9	0.7	0.6	0.4	0.3	0.3
Doctor (M.D. or D.D.S.)	7.4	6.4	5.6	4.9	5.9	6.4	7.9	8.1	6.9	6.6	6.3	5.3	5.7
Education (elementary)	0.8	0.8	1.2	1.0	0.9	0.9	0.7	0.6	0.6	0.5	0.7	0.6	0.4
Education (secondary)	10.5	10.4	11.5	9.9	8.7	6.6	5.0	3.5	3.2	2.7	3.1	2.5	2.1
Engineer	16.3	15.0	14.6	14.5	13.3	9.7	9.6	9.4	8.5	10.2	13.7	15.1	16.5
Farmer, rancher, or forester	3.2	3.3	2.9	3.0	3.1	4.8	4.8	4.9	6.2	5.7	4.6	4.9	3.7
Health professional (non-M.D.)	3.1	2.6	2.8	2.7	2.9	3.8	4.6	5.4	5.5	5.2	4.0	3.7	3.4
Lawyer (or judge)	6.7	5.8	5.5	5.6	6.2	6.8	7.1	6.7	5.3	5.4	5.5	5.5	5.3
Nurse	0.1	0.1	0.1	0.1	0.1	0.3	0.2	0.3	0.3	0.3	0.3	0.3	0.2
Research scientist	4.9	3.9	3.8	3.3	3.5	3.3	3.1	3.7	2.7	2.5	3.0	2.8	2.7
Other	15.8	16.7	16.7	19.3	19.0	21.7	21.3	[*]	24.5	24.5	21.3	21.4	21.2
Undecided	[*]	10.2	11.3	11.6	11.5	12.9	13.4	10.8	12.3	13.5	9.7	8.8	9.6

[*] Results were not comparable to those of other years due to changes in question text or order.
[1] Figures for the years 1966-1976 are from annual Norms Reports. Figures from 1977-1990 computed from disaggregated majors/careers (see Appendix E)
[2] List of disaggregated majors was expanded in 1970, 1973, 1978 and 1982.
[3] List of careers for 1973-1976 not directly comparable to other years.

1979	1980	1981	1982	1983	1984	1985	1986	1987	1988	1989	1990	***DEGREE, MAJOR AND CAREER PLANS***
												HIGHEST ACADEMIC DEGREE PLANNED AT ANY COLLEGE
1.7	2.4	2.0	2.0	2.2	1.6	2.0	2.0	2.0	1.8	1.2	1.7	None
--	--	--	--	1.7	1.2	1.4	1.4	1.6	0.4	1.3	1.9	Vocational certificate
5.6	6.9	7.2	6.8	5.8	5.3	5.2	5.6	4.4	3.3	3.9	4.7	Associate or equivalent
35.4	37.2	37.5	37.8	36.4	37.8	38.3	37.2	35.9	34.0	33.1	30.7	Bachelor's degree (B.A., B.S., etc.)
32.4	29.3	30.9	30.8	30.1	31.2	31.5	32.1	34.1	35.8	36.3	36.1	Master's degree (M.A., M.S., etc.)
9.4	8.5	8.7	8.8	9.0	9.6	9.9	10.3	10.7	12.1	12.0	12.3	Ph.D. or Ed.D.
7.0	7.0	6.3	6.3	6.7	6.4	5.9	5.6	5.1	5.5	5.4	5.9	M.D., D.D.S., D.V.M., or D.O.
5.2	4.9	4.5	4.7	4.3	4.3	3.8	3.7	4.2	5.2	4.9	4.7	LL.B. or J.D. (law)
0.8	0.6	0.6	0.6	0.8	0.7	0.4	0.4	0.4	0.5	0.4	0.5	B.D. or M.Div. (divinity)
2.4	3.1	2.3	2.2	2.9	2.0	1.6	1.6	1.5	1.5	1.5	1.5	Other
												HIGHEST ACADEMIC DEGREE AT FRESHMAN COLLEGE
4.7	4.9	4.7	4.3	4.0	3.9	3.5	3.5	3.6	3.6	3.7	4.7	None
--	--	--	--	2.3	1.6	1.9	2.0	2.4	0.7	1.7	2.5	Vocational certificate
24.3	23.7	25.5	26.7	21.4	21.4	20.2	19.5	17.2	14.1	16.7	23.3	Associate or equivalent
52.2	52.6	52.0	51.1	53.0	54.8	56.1	57.6	57.4	59.7	58.9	51.0	Bachelor's degree (B.A., B.S., etc.)
11.4	11.1	11.1	11.2	11.0	11.6	12.3	12.2	13.7	15.5	13.3	12.7	Master's degree (M.A., M.S., etc.)
1.8	1.6	1.6	1.7	1.9	1.9	1.9	1.7	2.0	2.1	2.0	1.9	Ph.D. or Ed.D.
1.7	1.9	1.5	1.7	1.9	1.6	1.4	1.3	1.2	1.4	1.1	1.1	M.D., D.D.S., D.V.M., or D.O.
1.2	1.2	1.1	1.1	1.3	1.1	0.8	0.7	0.8	1.2	0.9	0.8	LL.B. or J.D. (law)
0.4	0.4	0.4	0.4	0.8	0.5	0.2	0.2	0.3	0.2	0.2	0.2	B.D. or M.Div. (divinity)
2.2	2.6	2.1	1.9	2.5	1.7	1.6	1.2	1.3	1.4	1.3	1.7	Other
												MAJOR PLANS (AGGREGATED) [1]
4.5	4.1	5.0	3.8	2.9	3.3	3.2	2.8	2.6	2.4	2.0	2.0	Agriculture (including forestry)
4.3	3.7	3.9	3.7	4.1	4.1	3.4	4.0	3.8	4.1	3.8	4.0	Biological sciences
25.1	22.9	22.7	22.3	22.7	25.1	25.7	26.6	28.6	27.6	25.9	22.1	Business
3.6	3.3	2.8	2.4	2.9	2.8	3.3	3.8	4.0	3.8	4.0	4.6	Education
19.2	21.0	21.3	22.3	20.6	20.1	19.3	19.7	17.0	17.5	18.8	17.8	Engineering
0.6	0.6	0.6	0.6	0.6	0.7	0.7	0.8	0.9	1.0	0.9	1.0	English
4.7	4.7	4.2	4.2	4.6	4.8	4.4	4.3	3.8	4.5	4.8	5.9	Health professions (nursing, pre-med, etc.)
3.2	3.0	2.9	2.9	2.7	3.2	3.4	3.5	3.7	4.3	4.2	4.3	History or political science
1.7	1.7	1.8	1.6	1.6	1.4	1.7	1.6	2.2	1.8	1.7	1.7	Humanities (other)
4.8	5.1	4.3	4.2	4.1	3.9	4.2	4.4	5.0	4.9	5.1	5.8	Fine arts (applied and performing)
0.7	0.7	0.6	0.6	0.8	0.8	0.8	0.9	0.6	0.6	0.7	0.7	Mathematics or statistics
3.2	2.9	2.9	2.6	2.5	2.5	2.3	2.2	2.3	2.3	2.4	2.3	Physical sciences
--	--	--	--	--	--	--	--	--	--	--	--	Pre-professional
2.7	2.3	2.2	2.0	2.2	2.8	2.7	2.8	3.0	3.4	3.1	3.4	Social sciences
8.9	10.9	12.3	14.6	15.5	12.2	10.4	8.9	7.4	6.4	7.7	7.7	Technical (other)
8.9	8.9	8.4	8.2	8.5	8.2	9.5	8.3	9.6	9.1	9.1	10.5	Nontechnical (other)
3.9	3.8	3.9	3.7	4.0	4.1	4.7	5.4	5.4	5.9	5.7	6.0	Undecided
												CAREER PLANS (AGGREGATED) [1]
5.6	5.5	5.3	5.1	5.1	4.9	5.5	5.5	6.5	6.1	5.5	5.2	Artist (including performer)
23.0	21.7	21.3	20.9	21.4	23.5	25.2	25.8	27.6	26.5	24.4	20.5	Business
0.7	0.7	0.7	0.5	0.5	0.4	0.5	0.4	0.4	0.4	0.4	0.4	Clergy or other religious worker
0.3	0.2	0.2	0.2	0.3	0.3	0.3	0.4	0.4	0.4	0.4	0.4	College teacher
5.2	5.3	4.9	5.0	5.4	5.2	4.8	4.6	4.2	4.6	4.6	4.5	Doctor (M.D. or D.D.S.)
0.5	0.5	0.4	0.4	0.3	0.4	0.5	0.6	0.7	0.7	0.7	0.9	Education (elementary)
2.2	2.0	1.7	1.5	1.9	1.9	2.2	2.7	2.8	2.9	3.0	3.2	Education (secondary)
16.8	19.1	19.5	20.6	18.8	18.5	17.7	17.4	15.2	15.7	16.5	14.9	Engineer
3.8	3.4	4.3	3.3	2.5	2.7	2.5	2.4	1.9	2.1	1.8	1.7	Farmer, rancher, or forester
3.1	2.9	2.5	2.4	2.9	2.9	2.8	2.7	2.8	3.0	3.0	3.5	Health professional (non-M.D.)
5.0	4.8	4.5	4.7	4.2	4.4	4.1	4.1	4.5	5.5	5.3	4.9	Lawyer (or judge)
0.2	0.2	0.2	0.2	0.3	0.2	0.1	0.2	0.2	0.3	0.3	0.7	Nurse
2.4	2.2	2.0	1.8	1.8	1.9	1.7	1.8	1.8	2.0	1.9	1.7	Research scientist
21.9	22.8	23.7	25.4	25.8	23.4	22.8	21.4	20.9	20.3	22.2	26.9	Other
9.4	8.9	8.8	8.1	8.8	9.2	9.2	9.9	9.9	9.8	10.0	10.3	Undecided

[1] Figures for the years 1966-1976 are from annual Norms Reports. Figures from 1977-1990 computed from disaggregated majors/careers (see Appendix E)

[2] List of disaggregated majors was expanded in 1970, 1973, 1978 and 1982.

[3] List of careers for 1973-1976 not directly comparable to other years.

DEGREE, MAJOR AND CAREER PLANS

DEGREE, MAJOR AND CAREER PLANS	1966	1967	1968	1969	1970	1971	1972	1973	1974	1975	1976	1977	1978
MAJOR PLANS (DISAGGREGATED) [1]													
Arts and Humanities													
Art, fine and applied	--	--	--	--	--	--	--	--	--	--	--	1.5	1.1
English, language and literature	--	--	--	--	--	--	--	--	--	--	--	0.6	0.7
History	--	--	--	--	--	--	--	--	--	--	--	1.0	0.9
Journalism	--	--	--	--	--	--	--	--	--	--	--	0.9	1.0
Language (except English)	--	--	--	--	--	--	--	--	--	--	--	0.2	0.2
Music	--	--	--	--	--	--	--	--	--	--	--	1.6	1.5
Philosophy	--	--	--	--	--	--	--	--	--	--	--	0.2	0.2
Theater or drama	--	--	--	--	--	--	--	--	--	--	--	--	0.6
Speech or drama	--	--	--	--	--	--	--	--	--	--	--	0.5	--
Speech	--	--	--	--	--	--	--	--	--	--	--	--	0.1
Theology or religion	--	--	--	--	--	--	--	--	--	--	--	0.5	0.5
Other arts and humanities	--	--	--	--	--	--	--	--	--	--	--	0.5	0.4
Biological Sciences													
Biology (general)	--	--	--	--	--	--	--	--	--	--	--	2.0	2.0
Biochemistry or biophysics	--	--	--	--	--	--	--	--	--	--	--	0.5	0.6
Botany	--	--	--	--	--	--	--	--	--	--	--	0.2	0.2
Marine (life) sciences	--	--	--	--	--	--	--	--	--	--	--	0.9	0.7
Microbiology or bacteriology	--	--	--	--	--	--	--	--	--	--	--	0.2	0.2
Zoology	--	--	--	--	--	--	--	--	--	--	--	0.4	0.4
Other biological sciences	--	--	--	--	--	--	--	--	--	--	--	0.6	0.7
Business													
Accounting	--	--	--	--	--	--	--	--	--	--	--	7.1	7.2
Business administration (general)	--	--	--	--	--	--	--	--	--	--	--	8.9	9.2
Finance	--	--	--	--	--	--	--	--	--	--	--	0.8	0.9
Marketing	--	--	--	--	--	--	--	--	--	--	--	1.3	1.5
Management	--	--	--	--	--	--	--	--	--	--	--	4.8	5.3
Secretarial studies	--	--	--	--	--	--	--	--	--	--	--	0.0	0.0
Other business	--	--	--	--	--	--	--	--	--	--	--	0.9	0.9
Education													
Business education	--	--	--	--	--	--	--	--	--	--	--	0.1	0.1
Elementary education	--	--	--	--	--	--	--	--	--	--	--	0.3	0.3
Music or art education	--	--	--	--	--	--	--	--	--	--	--	0.3	0.2
Physical education or recreation	--	--	--	--	--	--	--	--	--	--	--	2.1	1.9
Secondary education	--	--	--	--	--	--	--	--	--	--	--	0.7	0.5
Special education	--	--	--	--	--	--	--	--	--	--	--	0.2	0.2
Other education	--	--	--	--	--	--	--	--	--	--	--	0.1	0.1
Engineering													
Aeronautical or astronautical	--	--	--	--	--	--	--	--	--	--	--	1.3	1.7
Civil	--	--	--	--	--	--	--	--	--	--	--	2.1	2.3
Chemical	--	--	--	--	--	--	--	--	--	--	--	1.1	1.4
Electrical or electronic	--	--	--	--	--	--	--	--	--	--	--	5.9	6.0
Industrial	--	--	--	--	--	--	--	--	--	--	--	0.7	0.8
Mechanical	--	--	--	--	--	--	--	--	--	--	--	3.4	3.7
Other engineering	--	--	--	--	--	--	--	--	--	--	--	2.5	2.9
Physical Sciences													
Astronomy	--	--	--	--	--	--	--	--	--	--	--	0.2	0.2
Atmospheric sciences	--	--	--	--	--	--	--	--	--	--	--	0.1	0.2
Chemistry	--	--	--	--	--	--	--	--	--	--	--	1.2	1.2
Earth science	--	--	--	--	--	--	--	--	--	--	--	0.5	0.5
Marine sciences	--	--	--	--	--	--	--	--	--	--	--	0.5	0.4
Mathematics	--	--	--	--	--	--	--	--	--	--	--	0.9	1.0
Physics	--	--	--	--	--	--	--	--	--	--	--	0.8	0.8
Statistics	--	--	--	--	--	--	--	--	--	--	--	0.1	0.1
Other physical sciences										--	--	0.2	0.2
Professional													
Architecture or urban planning	--	--	--	--	--	--	--	--	--	--	--	1.8	1.8
Home economics	--	--	--	--	--	--	--	--	--	--	--	0.1	0.1
Health technology	--	--	--	--	--	--	--	--	--	--	--	1.0	0.8
Library or archival sciences	--	--	--	--	--	--	--	--	--	--	--	0.0	0.0
Nursing	--	--	--	--	--	--	--	--	--	--	--	0.2	0.2
Pharmacy	--	--	--	--	--	--	--	--	--	--	--	0.7	0.6
Predentistry, premedicine, prevet	--	--	--	--	--	--	--	--	--	--	--	3.8	4.0
Therapy (physical, occupational, etc.)	--	--	--	--	--	--	--	--	--	--	--	0.4	0.4
Other professional	--	--	--	--	--	--	--	--	--	--	--	1.6	1.4

[1] Data collected in disaggregated form but not reported in 1966-1976.

DEGREE, MAJOR AND CAREER PLANS

	1979	1980	1981	1982	1983	1984	1985	1986	1987	1988	1989	1990
MAJOR PLANS (DISAGGREGATED) [1]												
Arts and Humanities												
Art, fine and applied	1.5	1.6	1.5	1.5	1.7	1.4	1.5	1.6	2.2	1.8	1.7	1.6
English, language and literature	0.6	0.6	0.6	0.6	0.6	0.7	0.7	0.8	0.9	1.0	0.9	1.0
History	0.9	0.8	0.8	0.7	0.7	0.9	0.9	1.0	1.1	1.1	1.1	1.3
Journalism	1.3	1.2	1.3	1.2	1.0	1.1	1.1	1.1	1.1	1.1	1.0	0.9
Language (except English)	0.2	0.1	0.2	0.2	0.2	0.2	0.2	0.2	0.2	0.3	0.2	0.2
Music	1.4	1.4	1.3	1.1	1.1	1.0	1.1	1.2	1.1	1.1	1.1	1.1
Philosophy	0.2	0.2	0.2	0.2	0.2	0.2	0.2	0.2	0.3	0.3	0.3	0.2
Theater or drama	0.6	0.6	0.5	0.5	0.5	0.4	0.5	0.5	0.5	0.5	0.5	0.5
Speech or drama	--	--	--	--	--	--	--	--	--	--	--	--
Speech	0.1	0.1	0.1	0.1	0.1	0.1	0.1	0.1	0.1	0.1	0.1	0.1
Theology or religion	0.4	0.4	0.5	0.3	0.3	0.2	0.3	0.3	0.3	0.2	0.2	0.3
Other arts and humanities	0.3	0.4	0.4	0.4	0.4	0.4	0.5	0.4	0.9	0.5	0.5	0.5
Biological Sciences												
Biology (general)	1.8	1.7	1.7	1.6	1.8	1.8	1.7	1.8	1.7	1.8	1.8	1.8
Biochemistry or biophysics	0.5	0.5	0.5	0.5	0.6	0.6	0.5	0.6	0.6	0.6	0.5	0.5
Botany	0.1	0.1	0.1	0.1	0.1	0.1	0.0	0.1	0.1	0.1	0.1	0.1
Marine (life) sciences	0.7	0.5	0.5	0.4	0.4	0.5	0.3	0.5	0.4	0.5	0.5	0.6
Microbiology or bacteriology	0.2	0.1	0.2	0.2	0.3	0.2	0.2	0.2	0.2	0.2	0.2	0.1
Zoology	0.4	0.3	0.3	0.4	0.3	0.3	0.3	0.3	0.2	0.3	0.2	0.3
Other biological sciences	0.6	0.5	0.6	0.5	0.6	0.6	0.4	0.5	0.6	0.6	0.5	0.6
Business												
Accounting	6.3	5.9	5.3	5.5	5.5	5.7	5.7	5.5	5.7	5.6	5.6	4.6
Business administration (general)	9.4	8.2	8.5	7.9	7.8	8.5	8.2	8.3	8.8	8.4	7.4	6.5
Finance	0.9	0.8	1.0	1.2	1.4	1.7	2.1	2.5	3.2	3.0	2.8	2.1
Marketing	1.8	1.7	1.6	1.7	1.9	2.2	2.4	2.7	3.3	3.1	3.2	2.8
Management	5.6	5.3	5.2	5.0	5.1	5.9	6.2	6.2	6.1	5.9	5.4	4.8
Secretarial studies	0.0	0.0	0.0	0.0	0.0	0.0	0.0	0.0	0.0	0.0	0.0	0.0
Other business	1.1	1.0	1.1	1.0	1.0	1.1	1.1	1.4	1.5	1.6	1.5	1.3
Education												
Business education	0.1	0.1	0.1	0.1	0.1	0.1	0.3	0.3	0.3	0.2	0.2	0.2
Elementary education	0.3	0.3	0.3	0.2	0.2	0.3	0.4	0.5	0.5	0.5	0.5	0.7
Music or art education	0.2	0.3	0.2	0.2	0.2	0.2	0.2	0.2	0.3	0.2	0.2	0.4
Physical education or recreation	2.2	1.7	1.5	1.2	1.5	1.4	1.4	1.6	1.5	1.3	1.5	1.5
Secondary education	0.5	0.6	0.5	0.5	0.7	0.6	0.8	1.0	1.2	1.4	1.4	1.5
Special education	0.2	0.2	0.1	0.1	0.1	0.1	0.1	0.1	0.1	0.1	0.1	0.1
Other education	0.1	0.1	0.1	0.1	0.1	0.1	0.1	0.1	0.1	0.1	0.1	0.2
Engineering												
Aeronautical or astronautical	1.8	2.0	2.2	2.3	2.2	2.5	2.4	3.0	2.8	3.0	2.9	2.5
Civil	2.2	2.2	2.0	1.6	1.4	1.6	1.6	1.6	1.6	1.8	2.0	2.5
Chemical	1.5	1.6	1.7	1.7	1.4	1.0	1.0	1.0	0.8	0.8	0.9	1.0
Electrical or electronic	6.2	7.3	6.8	7.4	7.9	7.8	7.4	7.2	5.9	5.6	5.9	4.8
Industrial	0.9	0.8	0.8	0.8	0.7	0.6	0.6	0.6	0.5	0.5	0.5	0.5
Mechanical	3.8	4.3	4.5	4.8	4.1	4.0	4.0	3.8	3.4	3.6	4.0	4.0
Other engineering	2.8	2.8	3.3	3.7	2.9	2.6	2.3	2.5	2.0	2.2	2.6	2.5
Physical Sciences												
Astronomy	0.1	0.1	0.1	0.1	0.1	0.1	0.1	0.1	0.2	0.1	0.2	0.1
Atmospheric sciences	0.2	0.2	0.1	0.1	0.1	0.1	0.1	0.1	0.2	0.2	0.2	0.1
Chemistry	1.1	1.1	1.1	0.9	1.0	1.0	0.9	0.9	0.7	0.8	0.7	0.8
Earth science	0.5	0.4	0.5	0.5	0.3	0.3	0.2	0.2	0.2	0.2	0.2	0.2
Marine sciences	0.4	0.2	0.2	0.2	0.2	0.2	0.2	0.1	0.1	0.1	0.2	0.2
Mathematics	0.7	0.7	0.6	0.6	0.8	0.8	0.8	0.8	0.6	0.6	0.7	0.7
Physics	0.7	0.7	0.7	0.6	0.6	0.7	0.7	0.7	0.7	0.7	0.7	0.7
Statistics	0.0	0.0	0.0	0.0	0.0	0.0	0.0	0.1	0.0	0.0	0.0	0.0
Other physical sciences	0.2	0.2	0.2	0.2	0.2	0.1	0.1	0.1	0.2	0.2	0.2	0.2
Professional												
Architecture or urban planning	1.8	2.0	1.4	1.5	1.2	1.4	1.5	1.5	1.6	1.9	2.2	3.0
Home economics	0.2	0.1	0.0	0.0	0.1	0.0	0.0	0.1	0.1	0.1	0.0	0.0
Health technology	0.8	0.8	0.6	0.6	0.8	0.7	0.7	0.6	0.6	0.6	0.6	0.6
Library or archival sciences	0.0	0.0	0.0	0.0	0.0	0.0	0.0	0.0	0.0	0.0	0.0	0.0
Nursing	0.2	0.2	0.2	0.2	0.3	0.3	0.1	0.2	0.1	0.3	0.3	0.7
Pharmacy	0.5	0.4	0.3	0.3	0.4	0.5	0.5	0.5	0.4	0.7	0.7	0.9
Predentistry, premedicine, prevet	3.6	3.6	3.1	3.2	3.3	3.2	3.1	2.9	2.5	2.6	2.8	2.9
Therapy (physical, occupational, etc.)	0.4	0.5	0.6	0.5	0.6	0.8	0.7	0.7	0.8	0.9	1.0	1.4
Other professional	1.4	1.4	1.3	1.2	1.2	1.1	1.1	1.0	1.4	1.2	1.1	1.1

[1] Data collected in disaggregated form but not reported in 1966-1976.

DEGREE, MAJOR AND CAREER PLANS

DEGREE, MAJOR AND CAREER PLANS	1966	1967	1968	1969	1970	1971	1972	1973	1974	1975	1976	1977	1978
MAJOR PLANS (DISAGGREGATED) [1]													
Social Sciences													
Anthropology	--	--	--	--	--	--	--	--	--	--	--	0.1	0.1
Economics	--	--	--	--	--	--	--	--	--	--	--	0.5	0.5
Geography	--	--	--	--	--	--	--	--	--	--	--	0.1	0.0
Political science	--	--	--	--	--	--	--	--	--	--	--	2.6	2.4
Psychology	--	--	--	--	--	--	--	--	--	--	--	1.4	1.2
Social work	--	--	--	--	--	--	--	--	--	--	--	0.5	0.4
Sociology	--	--	--	--	--	--	--	--	--	--	--	0.4	0.2
Other social sciences	--	--	--	--	--	--	--	--	--	--	--	0.2	0.2
Ethnic studies	--	--	--	--	--	--	--	--	--	--	--	--	--
Women's studies	--	--	--	--	--	--	--	--	--	--	--	--	--
Technical Fields													
Building trades	--	--	--	--	--	--	--	--	--	--	--	0.9	1.2
Data processing/computer programming	--	--	--	--	--	--	--	--	--	--	--	1.7	1.8
Drafting or design	--	--	--	--	--	--	--	--	--	--	--	0.9	0.9
Electronics	--	--	--	--	--	--	--	--	--	--	--	1.7	1.5
Mechanics	--	--	--	--	--	--	--	--	--	--	--	0.9	0.9
Other technical	--	--	--	--	--	--	--	--	--	--	--	0.8	0.7
Other Majors													
Agriculture	--	--	--	--	--	--	--	--	--	--	--	3.3	3.1
Communications (radio, T.V.)	--	--	--	--	--	--	--	--	--	--	--	1.7	1.7
Computer science	--	--	--	--	--	--	--	--	--	--	--	1.2	1.6
Forestry	--	--	--	--	--	--	--	--	--	--	--	2.1	1.4
Law enforcement	--	--	--	--	--	--	--	--	--	--	--	2.7	2.3
Military science	--	--	--	--	--	--	--	--	--	--	--	0.2	0.2
Other fields	--	--	--	--	--	--	--	--	--	--	--	1.1	0.9
Undecided	--	--	--	--	--	--	--	--	--	--	--	4.0	3.9
CAREER PLANS (DISAGGREGATED) [1]													
Accountant or actuary	--	--	--	--	--	--	--	--	--	--	--	6.7	6.4
Actor or entertainer	--	--	--	--	--	--	--	--	--	--	--	0.8	0.8
Architect or urban planner	--	--	--	--	--	--	--	--	--	--	--	2.6	2.5
Artist	--	--	--	--	--	--	--	--	--	--	--	1.4	1.0
Business, clerical	--	--	--	--	--	--	--	--	--	--	--	0.3	0.3
Business executive	--	--	--	--	--	--	--	--	--	--	--	10.6	11.3
Business owner	--	--	--	--	--	--	--	--	--	--	--	4.0	4.1
Business, sales	--	--	--	--	--	--	--	--	--	--	--	1.1	1.2
Clergy or other religious worker	--	--	--	--	--	--	--	--	--	--	--	0.8	0.8
Clinical psychologist	--	--	--	--	--	--	--	--	--	--	--	0.6	0.5
College teacher	--	--	--	--	--	--	--	--	--	--	--	0.3	0.3
Computer programmer	--	--	--	--	--	--	--	--	--	--	--	3.2	4.0
Conservationist or forester	--	--	--	--	--	--	--	--	--	--	--	2.9	1.9
Dentist (including orthodontist)	--	--	--	--	--	--	--	--	--	--	--	1.4	1.4
Dietitian or home economist	--	--	--	--	--	--	--	--	--	--	--	0.1	0.1
Engineer	--	--	--	--	--	--	--	--	--	--	--	15.1	16.5
Farmer, rancher, or forester	--	--	--	--	--	--	--	--	--	--	--	2.0	1.8
Foreign service worker	--	--	--	--	--	--	--	--	--	--	--	0.3	0.3
Homemaker (full-time)	--	--	--	--	--	--	--	--	--	--	--	0.0	0.0
Interior decorator	--	--	--	--	--	--	--	--	--	--	--	0.1	0.1
Interpreter (translator)	--	--	--	--	--	--	--	--	--	--	--	0.0	0.1
Laboratory technician or hygienist	--	--	--	--	--	--	--	--	--	--	--	0.9	0.7
Law enforcement officer	--	--	--	--	--	--	--	--	--	--	--	2.4	2.2
Lawyer (or judge)	--	--	--	--	--	--	--	--	--	--	--	5.5	5.3
Military service (career)	--	--	--	--	--	--	--	--	--	--	--	1.7	1.8
Musician (performer, composer)	--	--	--	--	--	--	--	--	--	--	--	1.7	1.6
Nurse	--	--	--	--	--	--	--	--	--	--	--	0.3	0.2
Optometrist	--	--	--	--	--	--	--	--	--	--	--	0.3	0.3
Pharmacist	--	--	--	--	--	--	--	--	--	--	--	0.8	0.7
Physician	--	--	--	--	--	--	--	--	--	--	--	3.9	4.3
School counselor	--	--	--	--	--	--	--	--	--	--	--	0.2	0.1
School principal, superintendent	--	--	--	--	--	--	--	--	--	--	--	0.0	0.0
Research scientist	--	--	--	--	--	--	--	--	--	--	--	2.8	2.7
Social or welfare worker	--	--	--	--	--	--	--	--	--	--	--	0.8	0.6
Statistician	--	--	--	--	--	--	--	--	--	--	--	0.1	0.1
Therapist (occupational, physical, etc.)	--	--	--	--	--	--	--	--	--	--	--	0.5	0.5
Elementary teacher	--	--	--	--	--	--	--	--	--	--	--	0.6	0.4
Secondary teacher	--	--	--	--	--	--	--	--	--	--	--	2.3	2.0
Veterinarian	--	--	--	--	--	--	--	--	--	--	--	1.1	1.1
Writer or journalist	--	--	--	--	--	--	--	--	--	--	--	1.5	1.4
Skilled worker	--	--	--	--	--	--	--	--	--	--	--	3.5	3.1
Other	--	--	--	--	--	--	--	--	--	--	--	5.9	5.7
Undecided	--	--	--	--	--	--	--	--	--	--	--	8.8	9.6

[1] Data collected in disaggregated form but not reported in 1966-1976.

DEGREE, MAJOR AND CAREER PLANS	1979	1980	1981	1982	1983	1984	1985	1986	1987	1988	1989	1990
MAJOR PLANS (DISAGGREGATED) [1]												
Social Sciences												
Anthropology	0.1	0.1	0.1	0.1	0.1	0.1	0.1	0.1	0.1	0.1	0.1	0.1
Economics	0.5	0.5	0.5	0.5	0.5	0.6	0.5	0.6	0.7	0.8	0.7	0.6
Geography	0.1	0.0	0.0	0.0	0.0	0.1	0.1	0.0	0.0	0.0	0.0	0.1
Political science	2.3	2.2	2.1	2.2	2.0	2.3	2.5	2.5	2.6	3.2	3.1	3.0
Psychology	1.3	1.1	1.1	1.0	1.2	1.4	1.5	1.6	1.6	1.9	1.7	1.8
Social work	0.3	0.3	0.2	0.2	0.2	0.2	0.2	0.2	0.3	0.2	0.2	0.3
Sociology	0.2	0.2	0.1	0.1	0.1	0.2	0.2	0.2	0.2	0.2	0.2	0.3
Other social sciences	0.2	0.1	0.2	0.1	0.1	0.2	0.1	0.1	0.1	0.2	0.2	0.2
Ethnic studies	--	--	--	0.0	0.0	0.0	0.0	0.0	0.0	0.0	0.0	0.0
Women's studies	--	--	--	0.0	0.0	0.0	0.0	0.0	0.0	0.0	0.0	0.0
Technical Fields												
Building trades	0.8	1.1	0.7	0.6	0.6	0.5	0.9	0.7	0.4	0.3	0.9	1.9
Data processing/computer programming	2.1	2.5	3.1	4.3	4.4	2.9	2.6	1.9	1.4	1.3	1.2	1.0
Drafting or design	1.0	1.0	1.0	0.9	1.0	1.0	0.9	1.0	0.5	0.6	0.9	0.9
Electronics	1.3	2.0	1.5	1.9	1.4	1.2	1.1	0.9	0.6	0.5	0.8	0.7
Mechanics	0.9	1.2	1.1	1.0	1.3	0.9	0.9	1.0	1.2	0.5	1.1	1.2
Other technical	0.7	0.7	1.1	1.0	1.2	1.2	1.1	0.9	0.8	0.5	0.8	1.3
Other Majors												
Agriculture	3.1	3.1	3.5	2.7	2.0	2.5	2.1	1.7	2.1	1.5	1.3	1.3
Communications (radio, T.V.)	1.9	2.0	2.2	2.0	2.2	1.9	2.4	2.3	2.8	2.6	2.4	2.1
Computer science	2.1	2.7	3.9	4.9	5.4	4.3	3.1	2.6	2.3	2.4	2.3	2.0
Forestry	1.4	1.0	1.5	1.1	0.9	0.8	1.1	1.1	0.5	0.9	0.7	0.7
Law enforcement	2.0	1.9	1.5	2.1	2.2	2.1	2.4	1.8	2.3	2.2	2.1	2.6
Military science	0.2	0.2	0.2	0.2	0.2	0.2	0.3	0.2	0.2	0.2	0.2	0.4
Other fields	1.1	1.0	1.2	0.9	1.0	1.3	1.3	1.1	1.3	1.4	1.4	1.5
Undecided	3.9	3.8	3.9	3.7	4.0	4.1	4.7	5.4	5.4	5.9	5.7	6.0
CAREER PLANS (DISAGGREGATED) [1]												
Accountant or actuary	5.6	5.4	4.9	5.1	5.0	5.2	5.5	5.1	5.3	5.4	5.2	4.0
Actor or entertainer	0.9	0.9	0.8	0.7	0.8	0.7	0.9	0.9	1.1	1.0	0.9	0.8
Architect or urban planner	2.8	2.8	2.2	2.2	1.9	2.2	2.3	2.3	2.5	2.8	3.0	3.9
Artist	1.3	1.4	1.3	1.3	1.5	1.3	1.4	1.4	2.0	1.7	1.6	1.5
Business, clerical	0.4	0.3	0.3	0.3	0.3	0.4	0.4	0.3	0.4	0.3	0.3	0.3
Business executive	11.6	11.1	11.2	10.8	11.3	12.5	13.6	13.9	14.9	14.0	12.8	10.6
Business owner	4.5	4.1	4.1	3.9	4.0	4.5	4.7	5.3	5.7	5.7	5.0	4.5
Business, sales	1.3	1.1	1.1	1.1	1.1	1.3	1.4	1.5	1.7	1.4	1.4	1.4
Clergy or other religious worker	0.7	0.7	0.7	0.5	0.5	0.4	0.5	0.4	0.4	0.4	0.4	0.4
Clinical psychologist	0.5	0.4	0.4	0.3	0.5	0.5	0.5	0.6	0.6	0.7	0.6	0.6
College teacher	0.3	0.2	0.2	0.2	0.3	0.3	0.3	0.4	0.4	0.4	0.4	0.4
Computer programmer	4.7	5.6	7.5	9.7	10.2	7.7	5.7	4.6	3.7	3.8	3.5	3.1
Conservationist or forester	1.8	1.4	1.9	1.3	1.1	1.1	1.3	1.4	1.0	1.3	1.0	0.9
Dentist (including orthodontist)	1.2	1.2	0.9	0.9	0.9	0.7	0.7	0.7	0.6	0.6	0.6	0.6
Dietitian or home economist	0.1	0.1	0.1	0.1	0.1	0.1	0.1	0.0	0.1	0.0	0.0	0.0
Engineer	16.8	19.1	19.5	20.6	18.8	18.5	17.7	17.4	15.2	15.7	16.5	14.9
Farmer, rancher, or forester	2.0	2.0	2.4	2.0	1.4	1.6	1.2	1.0	0.9	0.8	0.8	0.8
Foreign service worker	0.3	0.4	0.4	0.4	0.4	0.5	0.6	0.6	0.7	0.7	0.6	0.6
Homemaker (full-time)	0.0	0.1	0.0	0.0	0.0	0.0	0.1	0.0	0.0	0.0	0.0	0.1
Interior decorator	0.1	0.1	0.0	0.1	0.1	0.1	0.1	0.1	0.1	0.1	0.0	0.1
Interpreter (translator)	0.0	0.0	0.0	0.1	0.0	0.0	0.1	0.1	0.1	0.1	0.1	0.1
Laboratory technician or hygienist	0.6	0.6	0.4	0.5	0.7	0.4	0.4	0.3	0.3	0.3	0.3	0.2
Law enforcement officer	1.7	1.8	1.4	1.9	1.8	1.8	2.0	1.7	2.1	2.0	1.9	2.4
Lawyer (or judge)	5.0	4.8	4.5	4.7	4.2	4.4	4.1	4.1	4.5	5.5	5.3	4.9
Military service (career)	1.9	1.7	1.8	1.6	2.0	2.1	2.0	2.3	1.9	2.1	1.7	2.4
Musician (performer, composer)	1.6	1.5	1.5	1.4	1.2	1.2	1.5	1.5	1.5	1.4	1.4	1.3
Nurse	0.2	0.2	0.2	0.2	0.3	0.2	0.1	0.2	0.2	0.3	0.3	0.7
Optometrist	0.3	0.2	0.2	0.2	0.2	0.3	0.3	0.2	0.2	0.3	0.2	0.3
Pharmacist	0.6	0.5	0.4	0.3	0.5	0.5	0.5	0.6	0.5	0.8	0.8	0.9
Physician	4.0	4.1	4.0	4.1	4.5	4.5	4.1	3.9	3.6	4.0	4.0	3.9
School counselor	0.1	0.1	0.1	0.1	0.1	0.1	0.1	0.1	0.1	0.1	0.1	0.2
School principal, superintendent	0.0	0.0	0.0	0.0	0.0	0.0	0.0	0.0	0.0	0.1	0.1	0.0
Research scientist	2.4	2.2	2.0	1.8	1.8	1.9	1.7	1.8	1.8	2.0	1.9	1.7
Social or welfare worker	0.6	0.6	0.4	0.3	0.4	0.4	0.3	0.4	0.4	0.3	0.3	0.3
Statistician	0.1	0.1	0.1	0.1	0.1	0.1	0.1	0.1	0.1	0.1	0.1	0.1
Therapist (occupational, physical, etc.)	0.6	0.6	0.6	0.5	0.7	0.9	0.8	0.9	1.1	1.0	1.2	1.6
Elementary teacher	0.5	0.5	0.4	0.4	0.3	0.4	0.5	0.6	0.7	0.7	0.7	0.9
Secondary teacher	2.1	1.9	1.6	1.4	1.8	1.8	2.1	2.6	2.7	2.7	2.8	3.0
Veterinarian	0.9	0.9	0.8	0.8	0.7	0.7	0.7	0.7	0.6	0.6	0.5	0.5
Writer or journalist	1.7	1.6	1.7	1.6	1.5	1.6	1.6	1.6	1.8	1.9	1.6	1.5
Skilled worker	2.7	3.2	3.1	2.9	2.7	2.4	2.9	2.6	2.3	1.2	2.5	4.1
Other	6.2	5.8	6.1	5.6	5.5	5.3	5.8	5.8	6.1	6.2	7.6	8.9
Undecided	9.4	8.9	8.8	8.1	8.8	9.2	9.2	9.9	9.9	9.8	10.0	10.3

[1] Data collected in disaggregated form but not reported in 1966-1976.

COLLEGE EXPERIENCES AND EXPECTATIONS

COLLEGE EXPERIENCES AND EXPECTATIONS	1966	1967	1968	1969	1970	1971	1972	1973	1974	1975	1976	1977	1978
PLANNED RESIDENCE FOR FALL													
With parents or relatives	--	--	--	--	--	--	--	43.1	42.7	40.8	44.9	42.2	37.2
Other private home, apartment or room	--	--	--	--	--	--	--	6.7	6.5	8.4	7.6	7.7	6.6
College dormitory	--	--	--	--	--	--	--	46.7	47.9	47.3	44.3	46.7	52.7
Fraternity or sorority house	--	--	--	--	--	--	--	0.8	1.1	0.8	0.8	0.8	0.9
Other campus student housing	--	--	--	--	--	--	--	1.4	1.0	1.7	1.5	1.7	1.8
Other type of housing	--	--	--	--	--	--	--	1.3	0.8	1.1	0.9	0.9	0.9
PREFERRED RESIDENCE FOR FALL													
With parents or relatives	--	--	--	--	--	--	--	--	23.7	23.9	23.9	23.3	20.4
Other private home, apartment or room	--	--	--	--	--	--	--	--	30.3	28.8	30.5	27.4	25.8
College dormitory	--	--	--	--	--	--	--	--	35.3	36.6	34.2	38.5	42.3
Fraternity or sorority house	--	--	--	--	--	--	--	--	4.4	3.5	4.1	4.3	5.0
Other campus student housing	--	--	--	--	--	--	--	--	3.2	3.8	3.8	3.8	3.8
Other type of housing	--	--	--	--	--	--	--	--	3.0	3.5	3.5	2.7	2.6
STUDENTS ESTIMATE CHANCES ARE VERY GOOD THAT THEY WILL [1]													
Be satisfied with this college	--	--	--	--	61.6	--	54.7	48.7	47.1	48.3	45.3	48.9	50.4
Make at least a B average	--	--	--	--	--	--	31.7	33.7	35.8	38.2	40.1	40.3	41.0
Graduate with honors	--	4.2	4.2	4.6	5.6	--	8.8	10.6	10.6	11.7	11.9	12.7	12.6
Be elected to an academic honor society	--	2.8	2.5	2.2	2.5	--	4.5	4.8	5.2	5.5	6.3	7.0	7.3
Get a bachelor's degree (B.A., B.S., etc)	--	--	--	--	--	--	59.9	60.6	58.8	61.4	61.6	63.1	64.9
Be elected to a student office	--	2.6	2.4	2.3	2.2	--	2.3	2.3	2.2	2.3	2.4	2.8	2.8
Join social fraternity, sorority or club	--	28.9	25.1	21.1	19.1	--	15.7	13.3	11.8	13.3	13.3	15.3	15.6
Change major field	--	16.0	13.8	15.5	15.3	--	16.3	14.3	12.0	11.8	10.6	11.7	11.5
Change career choice	--	17.3	14.9	16.5	15.6	--	16.4	13.3	11.1	11.3	10.2	10.9	10.6
Need extra time to complete degree	--	--	--	--	--	--	5.0	5.2	4.7	4.9	4.7	4.8	4.6
Fail one or more courses	--	3.5	2.4	2.9	3.9	--	3.2	2.8	2.4	2.4	2.1	2.2	1.9
Get tutoring help in specific courses	--	--	--	--	--	--	--	--	--	6.3	7.1	8.0	8.2
Live in a coeducational dorm	--	--	--	--	--	--	--	17.9	17.6	18.7	20.5	24.1	26.4
Seek vocational counseling	--	--	--	--	--	--	12.2	9.6	8.4	7.6	6.2	6.3	5.9
Seek personal counseling	--	--	--	--	--	--	6.4	6.2	5.1	5.4	4.0	4.4	4.2
Get a job to help pay for college expenses	--	--	--	--	--	--	--	--	--	--	39.9	42.4	40.1
Have to work at an outside job	--	--	--	--	--	--	35.0	33.1	32.0	30.8	25.1	25.4	22.6
Work full-time while attending college	--	--	--	--	--	--	--	--	--	--	--	--	--
Participate in student protests or demonstrations	--	5.1	4.3	--	--	--	--	--	--	--	--	--	3.4
Transfer to another college	--	12.9	12.2	12.6	11.9	--	12.2	12.6	13.6	13.0	13.1	11.8	10.7
Drop out of this college temporarily (excluding transferring)	--	1.0	0.8	1.0	1.2	--	1.7	1.8	1.6	1.7	1.5	1.4	1.2
Drop out permanently	--	0.4	0.4	0.4	0.6	--	1.0	1.1	1.0	1.1	1.0	0.9	0.9
Get married while in college	--	6.8	6.0	7.2	6.6	--	6.4	5.6	5.1	5.0	4.3	3.9	3.6
Get married within a year after college	--	19.3	16.6	18.2	17.2	--	15.3	15.6	15.2	14.8	14.0	13.2	13.1
Enlist in the Armed Services before graduating	--	--	--	1.7	2.5	--	3.8	2.2	2.2	--	--	--	--
Be more successful after graduating than most students attending this college	--	--	--	13.8	14.3	--	20.9	22.8	21.7	--	--	--	--
Play varsity athletics	--	--	--	--	--	--	--	--	--	--	--	--	--
Find a job after college graduation in the field for which you were trained	--	--	--	--	--	[*]	52.4	57.1	54.2	58.0	58.0	63.8	65.7
CONCERN ABOUT ABILITY TO FINANCE COLLEGE EDUCATION													
None (I am confident that I will have sufficient funds)	34.9	34.3	35.4	35.2	35.0	35.3	37.3	37.9	41.7	40.1	38.6	37.3	38.5
Some concern (but I will probably have enough funds)	57.0	57.6	56.7	55.4	54.9	55.0	48.5	46.7	44.7	45.1	46.6	47.6	48.3
Major concern (not sure I will have enough funds to complete college)	8.1	8.1	7.9	9.4	10.2	9.7	14.1	15.4	13.7	14.8	14.8	15.1	13.2

[1] Text, order or number of response options may vary from year to year.

1979	1980	1981	1982	1983	1984	1985	1986	1987	1988	1989	1990	COLLEGE EXPERIENCES AND EXPECTATIONS
												PLANNED RESIDENCE FOR FALL
37.5	36.0	30.2	33.0	35.8	32.4	29.9	29.0	30.0	30.2	28.1	20.7	With parents or relatives
8.4	8.7	6.9	7.0	7.3	5.7	6.4	8.9	8.3	7.2	8.1	5.8	Other private home, apartment or room
50.4	51.1	58.9	56.3	53.6	58.8	60.2	58.0	57.7	58.3	59.3	69.1	College dormitory
1.1	1.1	1.2	1.0	0.8	0.8	0.8	0.9	1.2	1.1	0.8	0.5	Fraternity or sorority house
1.7	2.1	1.9	1.7	1.8	1.7	2.1	2.4	2.1	2.6	3.1	3.1	Other campus student housing
0.9	1.0	0.8	1.0	0.7	0.6	0.7	0.8	0.6	0.6	0.6	0.7	Other type of housing
												PREFERRED RESIDENCE FOR FALL
21.9	21.7	19.1	20.1	20.3	19.0	17.6	17.1	15.1	15.1	14.3	--	With parents or relatives
25.9	24.6	26.2	27.1	28.2	27.2	28.1	30.0	32.0	32.7	34.4	--	Other private home, apartment or room
40.5	42.0	42.7	41.3	38.8	40.7	40.4	38.0	37.3	36.0	34.9	--	College dormitory
5.0	5.1	5.4	5.0	5.5	6.4	6.8	7.4	8.2	8.2	7.8	--	Fraternity or sorority house
3.6	3.9	4.0	3.8	4.5	4.7	4.6	4.9	5.1	5.6	6.0	--	Other campus student housing
3.2	2.7	2.6	2.7	2.7	2.0	2.5	2.6	2.3	2.4	2.6	--	Other type of housing
												STUDENTS ESTIMATE CHANCES ARE VERY GOOD THAT THEY WILL [1]
48.7	48.1	50.3	50.2	48.6	49.4	48.6	47.2	47.1	46.4	44.8	45.3	Be satisfied with this college
39.7	39.9	39.4	40.0	38.9	39.4	39.1	39.0	38.7	42.1	41.4	41.8	Make at least a B average
12.5	12.5	12.3	12.6	12.5	12.6	13.0	12.0	12.8	13.2	13.6	14.8	Graduate with honors
7.2	7.3	7.1	6.4	6.5	6.8	6.9	6.4	6.9	7.5	7.3	8.2	Be elected to an academic honor society
64.3	62.5	64.3	64.2	63.3	66.2	66.0	66.0	67.2	67.6	66.7	64.5	Get a bachelor's degree (B.A., B.S., etc)
3.1	3.0	2.9	2.9	2.9	3.2	3.5	3.2	3.5	3.6	3.5	3.6	Be elected to a student office
14.6	14.0	15.1	12.8	13.4	13.8	15.1	14.4	15.8	16.0	15.5	15.2	Join social fraternity, sorority or club
11.7	11.0	11.1	11.0	11.1	11.6	11.9	12.0	12.9	13.4	12.2	12.0	Change major field
10.4	10.1	9.9	9.5	9.6	10.0	10.6	10.4	11.2	11.4	10.4	10.6	Change career choice
5.0	5.2	5.7	5.2	5.2	5.2	6.1	6.3	6.6	6.6	7.2	8.0	Need extra time to complete degree
2.1	2.0	1.9	1.7	1.5	1.6	1.7	1.6	1.8	1.6	1.5	1.8	Fail one or more courses
8.3	8.3	8.9	8.4	8.3	9.3	9.9	9.3	9.0	10.2	10.5	13.3	Get tutoring help in specific courses
26.7	26.8	29.4	28.7	26.7	29.3	28.8	--	--	--	--	--	Live in a coeducational dorm
5.9	5.2	5.3	5.1	5.0	4.8	5.2	4.6	4.6	4.2	3.9	4.5	Seek vocational counseling
4.6	4.0	3.9	3.4	3.6	3.3	3.7	3.3	3.3	3.1	3.0	3.5	Seek personal counseling
39.0	37.9	38.3	37.5	34.2	34.8	34.8	33.5	35.4	31.9	31.0	32.9	Get a job to help pay for college expenses
21.8	21.8	21.3	19.1	18.0	17.6	17.9	17.2	18.4	16.7	16.9	16.9	Have to work at an outside job
--	--	--	3.4	3.4	3.6	3.5	3.8	3.7	3.5	3.4	3.8	Work full-time while attending college
4.1	4.8	4.0	4.2	3.6	4.1	4.9	4.7	5.5	4.9	5.5	5.9	Participate in student protests or demonstrations
12.0	10.5	10.9	10.7	10.3	10.5	10.3	9.9	10.4	11.3	10.9	13.3	Transfer to another college
1.4	1.3	1.3	1.1	1.2	1.3	1.3	1.4	1.2	1.2	1.3	1.3	Drop out of this college temporarily (excluding transferring)
1.2	1.0	1.1	0.9	1.1	0.9	0.9	0.9	0.9	1.0	1.0	1.3	Drop out permanently
3.8	3.9	3.9	3.5	3.2	3.2	3.3	3.2	2.9	3.0	3.5	3.9	Get married while in college
13.4	14.2	14.6	13.9	12.8	12.8	13.1	12.6	11.4	12.3	--	--	Get married within a year after college
--	--	--	--	--	--	--	--	--	--	--	--	Enlist in the Armed Services before graduating
--	--	--	--	--	--	--	--	--	--	--	--	Be more successful after graduating than most students attending this college
--	--	--	--	19.5	20.5	20.5	19.1	19.9	19.8	19.5	20.8	Play varsity athletics
66.3	67.2	69.0	67.6	65.4	67.9	66.6	66.3	66.4	67.6	66.4	66.9	Find a job after college graduation in the field for which you were trained
												CONCERN ABOUT ABILITY TO FINANCE COLLEGE EDUCATION
37.8	36.8	37.0	36.1	38.3	38.4	40.7	41.6	42.7	42.1	39.9	--	None (I am confident that I will have sufficient funds)
49.4	49.4	49.3	49.0	48.8	49.2	47.5	46.5	45.9	45.9	49.3	--	Some concern (but I will probably have enough funds)
12.8	13.8	13.7	14.9	12.9	12.4	11.8	11.9	11.3	11.9	10.8	--	Major concern (not sure I will have enough funds to complete college)

[1] Text, order or number of response options may vary from year to year.

ATTITUDES AND VALUES	1966	1967	1968	1969	1970	1971	1972	1973	1974	1975	1976	1977	1978
PRESENT POLITICAL VIEWS													
Far left	--	--	--	--	3.7	3.5	2.9	2.7	2.6	2.6	2.6	2.0	2.0
Liberal	--	--	--	--	35.1	36.7	33.6	33.2	29.0	29.4	26.7	25.7	24.3
Middle of the road	--	--	--	--	42.0	43.6	45.6	48.2	51.9	50.6	51.9	53.0	53.7
Conservative	--	--	--	--	18.0	15.3	16.9	15.0	15.6	16.5	17.6	18.2	18.9
Far right	--	--	--	--	1.3	0.9	1.0	0.8	1.0	0.9	1.3	1.0	1.0
OBJECTIVES CONSIDERED TO BE ESSENTIAL OR VERY IMPORTANT													
Become accomplished in one of the performing arts (acting, dancing, etc)	8.7	8.7	7.0	9.5	11.1	9.9	10.1	[*]	9.9	10.4	10.2	11.3	11.0
Become an authority in my field	70.3	71.0	61.2	62.9	71.7	64.8	64.8	67.0	66.5	73.0	73.5	77.5	75.3
Obtain recognition from colleagues for contributions to my special field	48.0	46.2	41.1	45.3	45.3	42.1	41.2	--	43.1	47.0	49.4	51.8	53.4
Influence the political structure	--	--	--	19.6	21.8	17.3	18.7	17.9	15.3	17.6	18.5	19.2	17.9
Influence social values	--	--	--	31.5	32.3	26.5	29.0	29.2	25.2	28.4	27.9	29.0	28.6
Raise a family	--	--	--	66.5	63.5	56.5	62.2	54.8	53.3	56.2	57.5	58.8	61.8
Have administrative responsibility for the work of others	34.6	30.6	27.5	29.8	27.4	25.2	29.7	32.0	29.3	34.3	35.1	37.9	38.6
Be very well-off financially	54.1	54.2	51.3	54.1	48.3	50.2	50.6	[*]	54.4	57.8	61.0	65.6	67.1
Help others who are in difficulty	59.2	52.3	49.7	58.2	57.4	55.2	59.4	56.0	52.9	58.4	54.9	57.3	56.9
Make a theoretical contribution to science	18.2	15.8	14.2	14.0	13.4	11.9	13.6	--	15.5	16.5	16.9	17.4	17.8
Write original works (poems, novels, etc)	11.8	11.5	10.9	11.8	12.4	11.5	12.0	--	10.5	10.6	11.0	11.7	10.7
Create artistic work (painting, sculpture, decorating, etc.)	10.1	10.2	9.5	11.3	11.9	11.2	12.7	--	10.6	10.9	11.2	12.3	10.9
Become involved in programs to clean up the environment	--	--	--	--	--	43.9	45.5	35.8	27.8	30.4	29.2	31.1	28.9
Be successful in my own business	63.8	57.3	55.3	55.5	53.9	53.0	55.2	51.6	47.6	52.7	54.1	55.5	55.7
Develop a meaningful philosophy of life	--	79.1	78.8	78.5	72.6	63.6	67.3	64.7	57.4	60.7	57.7	56.4	53.8
Participate in a community action program	--	--	--	--	27.0	23.7	26.6	--	24.8	27.3	25.7	26.5	23.9
Help promote racial understanding	--	--	--	--	--	--	--	--	--	--	--	31.9	29.7
Keep up to date with political affairs	58.0	51.8	51.7	52.5	54.7	44.8	50.6	43.7	38.8	41.7	40.5	44.5	41.4
Become an expert in finance and commerce	19.9	17.5	15.3	22.5	21.7	19.0	21.9	--	--	--	--	--	--
Participate in an organization like the Peace Corps or Vista	13.3	11.6	11.8	--	14.3	11.3	11.3	--	--	--	--	--	--
Become a community leader	30.3	27.7	24.8	20.4	18.3	16.1	17.7	--	--	--	--	--	--
Never be obligated to people	29.0	26.2	24.9	26.0	24.2	22.8	24.9	--	--	--	--	--	--
PERCENT WHO STRONGLY AGREE OR AGREE SOMEWHAT [1]													
Academic/Campus Issues													
Chief benefit of a college education is that it increases one's earning power	--	63.7	64.9	59.8	71.2	66.2	65.6	61.6	--	--	--	--	--
Faculty promotions should be based in part on student evaluations	--	63.4	64.1	68.5	71.8	76.2	76.5	74.4	72.9	71.8	71.0	72.2	71.6
Colleges would be improved if organized sports were de-emphasized	--	20.9	--	--	--	26.9	26.7	26.1	29.7	28.6	28.4	27.6	27.7
College officials have the right to regulate student behavior off campus	--	--	23.0	20.4	17.2	14.1	13.3	12.5	14.9	15.3	15.2	15.1	15.8
Student publications should be cleared by college officials	--	51.1	55.8	52.0	43.0	32.6	32.6	31.2	32.6	33.6	33.9	35.2	35.1
College officials have the right to ban persons with extreme views from speaking on campus	--	42.3	34.0	34.7	35.4	29.9	28.0	25.7	25.0	26.4	27.3	27.1	26.9
Most college officials have been too lax dealing with student protests on campus	--	51.2	57.8	63.3	61.0	49.7	45.7	40.3	38.0	--	--	--	--
Grading in the high schools is too easy	--	--	--	--	--	--	--	--	--	--	57.6	61.6	63.3
College grades should be abolished	--	--	--	--	42.9	41.7	37.9	35.1	30.3	26.4	23.0	21.2	17.8
Students from disadvantaged social backgrounds should be given preferential treatment in college admissions	--	45.3	43.2	43.3	45.7	41.4	41.6	39.5	39.1	38.5	38.1	38.3	36.2
Open admissions (admitting anyone who applies) should be adopted by all publicly supported colleges	--	--	--	--	--	37.7	38.0	36.7	40.6	37.3	35.7	35.5	33.6
Even if it employs open admissions, a college should use the same performance standards in awarding degrees to all students	--	--	--	--	--	78.5	80.6	79.0	78.5	77.1	77.9	78.5	79.3
All college graduates should be able to demonstrate some minimal competency in written English and mathematics	--	--	--	--	--	--	--	--	--	--	--	--	--

[*] Results were not comparable to those of other years due to changes in question text or order.

[1] Text, order or number of response options may vary from year to year.

1979	1980	1981	1982	1983	1984	1985	1986	1987	1988	1989	1990	*ATTITUDES AND VALUES*
												PRESENT POLITICAL VIEWS
2.2	2.2	1.9	2.1	2.2	2.4	2.2	2.5	2.9	2.7	2.4	2.3	Far left
23.1	20.3	18.1	18.5	18.7	19.1	19.9	21.2	21.4	20.5	19.3	20.3	Liberal
54.1	55.8	55.0	55.9	56.8	53.7	52.2	51.9	51.3	49.5	49.5	51.7	Middle of the road
19.4	20.0	23.5	22.0	20.7	23.0	23.5	22.4	22.4	24.8	26.6	24.0	Conservative
1.2	1.7	1.6	1.5	1.6	1.8	2.1	2.0	2.0	2.5	2.3	1.8	Far right
												OBJECTIVES CONSIDERED TO BE ESSENTIAL OR VERY IMPORTANT
10.9	10.7	10.2	10.6	10.5	9.8	9.9	9.7	11.1	9.8	10.7	10.3	Become accomplished in one of the performing arts (acting, dancing, etc)
75.3	74.7	74.5	75.1	73.2	74.5	73.1	72.4	78.1	73.6	67.8	67.4	Become an authority in my field
54.7	56.4	56.3	57.1	56.2	56.5	57.1	55.1	59.5	56.9	56.1	56.0	Obtain recognition from colleagues for contributions to my special field
19.1	20.1	18.5	18.1	16.8	17.9	18.9	17.1	19.5	19.8	22.4	22.9	Influence the political structure
29.8	29.4	29.0	28.6	28.1	29.4	30.5	29.3	32.8	32.7	35.2	36.3	Influence social values
65.0	62.5	66.3	66.2	64.6	67.6	69.3	66.3	[*]	66.5	68.5	68.2	Raise a family
39.5	40.5	41.5	41.9	41.5	43.5	44.7	45.2	47.0	[*]	44.9	44.2	Have administrative responsibility for the work of others
69.1	69.4	70.5	73.1	73.4	75.6	75.4	76.9	79.5	[*]	79.5	77.7	Be very well-off financially
55.4	56.0	54.3	53.5	53.2	53.4	55.1	48.0	50.0	[*]	49.0	50.9	Help others who are in difficulty
17.6	18.5	18.0	18.1	18.0	16.8	17.0	16.0	15.9	[*]	20.7	20.3	Make a theoretical contribution to science
10.9	11.1	11.0	11.1	10.7	10.7	11.3	11.0	12.8	[*]	12.2	11.8	Write original works (poems, novels, etc)
11.3	12.1	10.9	10.9	11.0	10.3	10.6	10.0	12.6	[*]	12.4	12.3	Create artistic work (painting, sculpture, decorating, etc.)
27.6	28.1	27.0	25.3	23.7	23.2	23.4	18.7	20.8	--	28.3	33.5	Become involved in programs to clean up the environment
55.9	55.4	55.0	54.7	54.1	56.4	56.2	53.5	55.4	[*]	50.1	49.5	Be successful in my own business
51.0	48.7	47.5	46.0	42.5	44.0	43.6	40.7	39.6	[*]	40.0	41.8	Develop a meaningful philosophy of life
23.5	24.1	22.0	21.2	20.3	20.2	20.8	16.3	17.7	[*]	20.2	22.1	Participate in a community action program
28.9	30.1	28.7	28.7	28.4	29.7	30.8	25.3	27.6	[*]	32.5	34.1	Help promote racial understanding
43.2	45.4	44.9	43.4	39.9	43.1	--	--	--	--	43.4	46.5	Keep up to date with political affairs
--	--	--	--	--	--	30.7	30.1	34.5	[*]	--	--	Become an expert in finance and commerce
--	--	--	--	--	--	--	--	--	--	--	--	Participate in an organization like the Peace Corps or Vista
--	--	--	--	--	--	--	--	--	--	--	--	Become a community leader
--	--	--	--	--	--	--	--	--	--	--	--	Never be obligated to people
												PERCENT WHO STRONGLY AGREE OR AGREE SOMEWHAT [1]
												Academic/Campus Issues
--	--	--	--	--	--	74.4	74.3	73.8	73.9	75.6	76.0	Chief benefit of a college education is that it increases one's earning power
70.4	71.1	70.1	69.9	69.6	70.3	70.9	70.4	--	--	--	74.9	Faculty promotions should be based in part on student evaluations
--	--	--	--	--	--	--	--	--	--	--	34.9	Colleges would be improved if organized sports were de-emphasized
16.8	16.6	16.3	15.9	16.9	16.4	15.7	13.7	--	--	--	--	College officials have the right to regulate student behavior off campus
39.3	40.0	40.0	39.3	39.6	--	--	--	--	--	--	--	Student publications should be cleared by college officials
27.6	27.9	28.3	26.3	27.5	24.2	27.5	28.0	--	--	--	--	College officials have the right to ban persons with extreme views from speaking on campus
--	--	--	--	--	--	--	--	--	--	--	--	Most college officials have been too lax dealing with student protests on campus
59.9	61.5	59.3	55.1	58.2	53.7	50.6	49.7	--	--	--	--	Grading in the high schools is too easy
18.4	17.7	17.4	17.1	17.3	16.6	--	--	--	--	--	--	College grades should be abolished
39.0	38.6	37.7	36.2	37.6	39.0	--	--	--	--	--	--	Students from disadvantaged social backgrounds should be given preferential treatment in college admissions
36.3	35.8	34.5	--	--	--	--	--	--	--	--	--	Open admissions (admitting anyone who applies) should be adopted by all publicly supported colleges
78.7	--	--	--	--	--	--	--	--	--	--	--	Even if it employs open admissions, a college should use the same performance standards in awarding degrees to all students
--	89.7	89.6	89.8	89.8	89.5	--	--	--	--	--	--	All college graduates should be able to demonstrate some minimal competency in written English and mathematics

[*] Results were not comparable to those of other years due to changes in question text or order.
[1] Text, order or number of response options may vary from year to year.

ATTITUDES AND VALUES	1966	1967	1968	1969	1970	1971	1972	1973	1974	1975	1976	1977	1978
PERCENT WHO STRONGLY AGREE OR AGREE SOMEWHAT [1]													
Political/Governance Issues													
Federal government is not doing enough to control environmental pollution	--	--	--	--	--	90.3	89.6	86.7	80.8	79.0	80.3	79.0	78.7
Federal government is not doing enough to protect the consumer from faulty goods and services	--	--	--	--	--	76.2	75.4	75.6	72.9	71.3	71.2	68.7	70.3
Government is not promoting disarmament	--	--	--	--	--	--	--	--	--	--	--	--	--
Increase Federal military spending	--	--	--	--	--	--	--	--	--	--	--	--	--
Federal government is not doing enough to promote school desegregation	--	--	--	--	--	50.6	46.9	46.3	--	--	--	--	--
The Federal government should do more to discourage energy consumption	--	--	--	--	--	--	--	--	--	78.8	77.0	79.8	79.3
Federal government should raise taxes to reduce the deficit	--	--	--	--	--	--	--	--	--	--	--	--	--
The Federal government should do more to control the sale of handguns	--	--	--	--	--	--	--	--	--	--	--	--	--
Wealthy people should pay a larger share of taxes than they do now	--	--	--	--	--	--	75.8	75.8	78.0	78.4	78.5	77.1	75.2
A national health care plan is needed to cover everybody's medical costs	--	--	--	--	--	--	--	--	--	--	--	60.4	58.6
Inflation is our biggest domestic problem	--	--	--	--	--	--	--	--	--	--	--	--	--
Abortion should be legal	--	--	--	--	--	--	--	--	--	--	--	55.8	56.5
Marijuana should be legalized	--	--	21.4	28.1	41.0	41.7	49.6	50.9	49.7	50.7	51.6	56.6	52.1
Capital punishment should be abolished	--	--	--	50.0	53.4	53.2	--	--	--	--	--	--	26.8
Women should receive the same salary and opportunities for advancement as men in comparable positions	--	--	--	--	76.5	82.7	87.8	88.0	88.2	88.7	88.2	88.2	88.7
It is important to have laws prohibiting homosexual relationships	--	--	--	--	--	--	--	--	--	--	55.0	56.7	54.4
Divorce laws should be liberalized	--	--	--	46.5	55.2	--	--	--	--	--	--	--	51.5
Personal/Social Issues													
The activities of married women are best confined to the home and family	--	66.5	--	--	57.0	51.9	46.7	40.9	39.5	37.4	36.8	35.5	35.5
Live together before marriage	--	--	--	--	--	--	--	--	51.2	53.7	54.3	54.5	52.3
Sex is OK if people like each other	--	--	--	--	--	--	--	--	60.9	65.0	65.1	66.5	65.5
People should not obey laws which violate their personal values	--	--	--	--	--	--	--	--	35.4	33.6	34.2	33.9	34.1
Parents should be discouraged from having large families	--	48.8	--	--	--	69.3	68.9	67.1	64.1	61.8	60.0	57.2	53.1
Scientists should publish their findings regardless of the possible consequences	--	47.8	57.7	58.7	63.6	--	--	--	--	--	--	--	--
Realistically, an individual can do little to bring about changes in our society	--	35.3	35.3	39.5	42.3	46.4	46.6	44.6	47.5	51.9	47.5	47.2	--
There is too much concern in the courts for the rights of criminals	--	--	--	60.0	57.5	53.9	56.4	55.7	56.9	59.1	64.8	69.2	70.3
Busing is OK if it helps to achieve racial balance in the schools	--	--	--	--	--	--	--	--	--	--	35.1	38.4	39.2
Nuclear disarmament is attainable	--	--	--	--	--	--	--	--	--	--	--	--	--
Employers should be allowed to require drug testing of employees or job applicants	--	--	--	--	--	--	--	--	--	--	--	--	--
The only way to control AIDS is through widespread, mandatory testing	--	--	--	--	--	--	--	--	--	--	--	--	--
Just because a man thinks that a woman has "led him on"" does not entitle him to have sex with her	--	--	--	--	--	--	--	--	--	--	--	--	--
Young more idealistic than old	--	--	--	--	--	--	--	--	74.6	73.7	--	--	--

[1] Text, order or number of response options may vary from year to year.

ATTITUDES AND VALUES

PERCENT WHO STRONGLY AGREE OR AGREE SOMEWHAT [1]

	1979	1980	1981	1982	1983	1984	1985	1986	1987	1988	1989	1990
Political/Governance Issues												
Federal government is not doing enough to control environmental pollution	77.3	75.8	73.2	74.9	77.6	74.9	75.8	76.3	79.1	82.3	84.8	87.0
Federal government is not doing enough to protect the consumer from faulty goods and services	70.8	71.6	65.7	64.4	61.9	57.7	58.2	58.5	62.0	61.0	64.7	64.7
Government is not promoting disarmament	--	--	--	--	--	58.1	58.5	58.6	63.5	56.9	58.8	--
Increase Federal military spending	--	--	--	47.9	45.8	40.2	34.4	34.8	32.7	33.1	30.2	29.0
Federal government is not doing enough to promote school desegregation	--	--	--	--	--	--	--	--	--	--	--	--
The Federal government should do more to discourage energy consumption	80.6	80.1	76.5	74.5	71.6	69.4	68.6	67.0	--	--	--	--
Federal government should raise taxes to reduce the deficit	--	--	--	--	--	--	26.2	27.4	28.9	32.0	32.6	33.8
The Federal government should do more to control the sale of handguns	--	--	--	--	--	--	--	--	--	--	67.2	65.5
Wealthy people should pay a larger share of taxes than they do now	71.9	71.1	71.3	72.4	70.8	69.9	73.5	72.8	--	--	--	--
A national health care plan is needed to cover everybody's medical costs	59.0	55.3	51.7	54.4	56.4	58.0	57.3	58.8	--	--	72.1	69.7
Inflation is our biggest domestic problem	78.6	78.6	76.0	75.9	63.8	--	--	--	--	--	--	--
Abortion should be legal	53.0	53.3	53.0	53.7	54.7	53.3	54.5	58.3	58.7	56.8	63.6	65.0
Marijuana should be legalized	48.6	42.1	36.3	32.5	28.4	25.8	24.8	25.0	23.1	22.8	20.1	21.7
Capital punishment should be abolished	28.0	28.0	24.7	23.1	23.9	22.2	22.6	21.4	20.4	19.6	18.4	18.5
Women should receive the same salary and opportunities for advancement as men in comparable positions	88.4	89.9	88.6	88.2	88.3	87.8	86.4	87.3	--	--	--	--
It is important to have laws prohibiting homosexual relationships	56.2	58.1	57.8	57.0	58.3	57.9	58.3	62.5	62.5	59.7	57.3	56.0
Divorce laws should be liberalized	51.6	49.4	47.3	46.8	46.6	--	--	--	--	--	--	--
Personal/Social Issues												
The activities of married women are best confined to the home and family	35.9	34.7	35.0	33.6	32.0	29.8	29.5	27.0	32.3	32.1	32.3	30.6
Live together before marriage	50.3	49.5	48.1	48.3	50.1	50.8	52.1	56.0	58.0	57.3	57.3	--
Sex is OK if people like each other	65.7	64.6	62.8	64.0	64.5	63.0	--	--	66.4	65.1	65.1	66.3
People should not obey laws which violate their personal values	35.7	34.9	35.3	--	--	--	--	--	--	--	--	--
Parents should be discouraged from having large families	51.1	50.1	47.1	42.4	40.9	--	--	--	--	--	--	--
Scientists should publish their findings regardless of the possible consequences	--	--	--	--	--	--	--	--	--	--	--	57.1
Realistically, an individual can do little to bring about changes in our society	--	--	--	--	--	--	39.9	--	--	--	--	--
There is too much concern in the courts for the rights of criminals	68.1	70.5	74.2	74.3	72.5	--	--	--	71.4	72.7	71.9	69.8
Busing is OK if it helps to achieve racial balance in the schools	41.5	43.3	40.8	43.8	47.8	50.8	51.6	53.6	53.5	52.3	56.1	56.4
Nuclear disarmament is attainable	--	--	--	--	--	--	51.7	52.7	56.4	59.5	--	61.4
Employers should be allowed to require drug testing of employees or job applicants	--	--	--	--	--	--	--	--	--	69.8	76.5	78.5
The only way to control AIDS is through widespread, mandatory testing	--	--	--	--	--	--	--	--	--	67.7	66.9	66.5
Just because a man thinks that a woman has "led him on"" does not entitle him to have sex with her	--	--	--	--	--	--	--	--	--	75.4	79.0	79.2
Young more idealistic than old	--	--	--	--	--	--	--	--	--	--	--	--

[1] Text, order or number of response options may vary from year to year.

FINANCIAL AID

	1966	1967	1968	1969	1970	1971	1972	1973	1974	1975	1976	1977	1978
RECEIVED ANY AID FOR FIRST YEAR EDUCATIONAL EXPENSES [1]													
Personal or Family Resources													
Parents and family	--	--	--	--	--	--	--	--	--	--	--	--	70.1
Spouse's income	--	--	--	--	--	--	--	--	--	--	--	--	0.7
Savings from summer work	--	--	--	--	--	--	--	--	--	--	--	--	48.5
Other savings	--	--	--	--	--	--	--	--	--	--	--	--	20.7
Part-time work while attending college	--	--	--	--	--	--	--	--	--	--	--	--	26.1
Part-time work on campus	--	--	--	--	--	--	--	--	--	--	--	--	--
Other part-time work while in college	--	--	--	--	--	--	--	--	--	--	--	--	--
Full-time work while in college	--	--	--	--	--	--	--	--	--	--	--	--	2.7
Aid Which Need Not Be Repaid													
Pell Grant (BEOG prior to 1982) [2]	--	--	--	--	--	--	--	--	--	--	--	--	21.3
Supp. Educational Oppty. Grant (SEOG) [2]	--	--	--	--	--	--	--	--	--	--	--	--	5.6
State scholarship or grant [2]	--	--	--	--	--	--	--	--	--	--	--	--	14.7
College grant or scholarship	--	--	--	--	--	--	--	--	--	--	--	--	12.2
College Work-Study Grant [2]	--	--	--	--	--	--	--	--	--	--	--	--	10.1
Private grant or scholarship	--	--	--	--	--	--	--	--	--	--	--	--	6.7
Student's GI benefits	--	--	--	--	--	--	--	--	--	--	--	--	1.0
GI benefits awarded to student's parent	--	--	--	--	--	--	--	--	--	--	--	--	1.1
GI/military benefits (student's or parents')	--	--	--	--	--	--	--	--	--	--	--	--	--
Social Security dependent's benefits	--	--	--	--	--	--	--	--	--	--	--	--	4.9
Other gov't aid (ROTC, Soc. Sec.,BIA,etc.)	--	--	--	--	--	--	--	--	--	--	--	--	--
Aid Which Must Be Repaid													
Stafford/Guaranteed Student Loan [2]	--	--	--	--	--	--	--	--	--	--	--	--	10.9
Perkins Loan (NDSL prior to 1990) [2]	--	--	--	--	--	--	--	--	--	--	--	--	7.5
College loan	--	--	--	--	--	--	--	--	--	--	--	--	3.6
Loan(s) from other sources	--	--	--	--	--	--	--	--	--	--	--	--	3.4
From sources other than those cited above	--	--	--	--	--	--	--	--	--	--	--	--	4.1
RECEIVED $1,500+ AID FOR FIRST YEAR EDUCATIONAL EXPENSES [1]													
Personal or Family Resources													
Parents and family	--	--	--	--	--	--	--	--	--	--	--	--	29.2
Spouse's income	--	--	--	--	--	--	--	--	--	--	--	--	0.1
Savings from summer work	--	--	--	--	--	--	--	--	--	--	--	--	4.0
Other savings	--	--	--	--	--	--	--	--	--	--	--	--	2.1
Part-time work while attending college	--	--	--	--	--	--	--	--	--	--	--	--	1.0
Part-time work on campus	--	--	--	--	--	--	--	--	--	--	--	--	--
Other part-time work while in college	--	--	--	--	--	--	--	--	--	--	--	--	--
Full-time work while in college	--	--	--	--	--	--	--	--	--	--	--	--	0.5
Aid Which Need Not Be Repaid													
Pell Grant (BEOG prior to 1982) [2]	--	--	--	--	--	--	--	--	--	--	--	--	3.1
Supp. Educational Oppty. Grant (SEOG) [2]	--	--	--	--	--	--	--	--	--	--	--	--	0.3
State scholarship or grant [2]	--	--	--	--	--	--	--	--	--	--	--	--	1.6
College grant or scholarship	--	--	--	--	--	--	--	--	--	--	--	--	2.9
College Work-Study Grant [2]	--	--	--	--	--	--	--	--	--	--	--	--	0.3
Private grant or scholarship	--	--	--	--	--	--	--	--	--	--	--	--	0.8
Student's GI benefits	--	--	--	--	--	--	--	--	--	--	--	--	0.5
GI benefits awarded to student's parent	--	--	--	--	--	--	--	--	--	--	--	--	0.3
GI/military benefits (student's or parents')	--	--	--	--	--	--	--	--	--	--	--	--	--
Social Security dependent's benefits	--	--	--	--	--	--	--	--	--	--	--	--	1.0
Other gov't aid (ROTC, Soc. Sec.,BIA,etc.)	--	--	--	--	--	--	--	--	--	--	--	--	--
Aid Which Must Be Repaid													
Stafford/Guaranteed Student Loan [2]	--	--	--	--	--	--	--	--	--	--	--	--	4.6
Perkins Loan (NDSL prior to 1990) [2]	--	--	--	--	--	--	--	--	--	--	--	--	0.9
College loan	--	--	--	--	--	--	--	--	--	--	--	--	1.0
Loan(s) from other sources	--	--	--	--	--	--	--	--	--	--	--	--	1.2
From sources other than those cited above	--	--	--	--	--	--	--	--	--	--	--	--	1.9

[1] Response and processing options rendered data from 1973-1977 not comparable to 1978-1990.
[2] In 1987-1990, highest response option of "$3,000 or more" was dropped, since these programs have upper limits less than $3,000.

1979	1980	1981	1982	1983	1984	1985	1986	1987	1988	1989	1990	*FINANCIAL AID*
												RECEIVED ANY AID FOR FIRST YEAR EDUCATIONAL EXPENSES [1]
												Personal or Family Resources
66.7	67.7	68.1	70.8	69.7	68.6	69.0	71.9	76.9	77.8	80.4	79.5	Parents and family
0.7	0.8	0.8	0.8	0.8	0.8	0.9	1.2	1.1	1.1	1.0	1.1	Spouse's income
44.3	43.9	44.6	42.8	41.8	47.2	49.7	51.3	56.8	56.4	56.3	57.1	Savings from summer work
18.1	18.6	19.0	18.4	18.5	20.0	21.9	26.1	28.6	28.8	28.7	31.6	Other savings
25.1	25.3	23.6	23.4	23.3	26.4	28.5	31.4	--	--	--	--	Part-time work while attending college
--	--	--	--	--	--	--	--	17.3	17.7	18.4	19.4	Part-time work on campus
--	--	--	--	--	--	--	--	23.7	22.3	22.8	21.2	Other part-time work while in college
2.7	2.9	2.3	2.2	2.1	2.0	2.5	2.8	2.3	2.2	2.2	2.4	Full-time work while in college
												Aid Which Need Not Be Repaid
30.0	29.7	24.7	22.2	25.4	18.6	18.4	15.8	16.2	17.5	19.9	20.6	Pell Grant (BEOG prior to 1982) [2]
7.3	7.8	5.7	5.5	6.5	5.1	4.5	5.1	5.7	5.2	5.8	6.3	Supp. Educational Oppty. Grant (SEOG) [2]
14.5	15.5	13.3	13.9	15.2	13.1	13.2	12.9	15.4	13.5	14.3	15.1	State scholarship or grant [2]
10.8	12.2	10.7	11.3	12.7	15.3	17.0	16.5	12.4	18.2	18.7	20.5	College grant or scholarship
10.6	13.0	10.6	11.0	12.1	8.0	8.6	9.1	8.5	8.4	8.7	9.3	College Work-Study Grant [2]
6.2	6.7	6.3	6.7	6.8	5.9	5.3	6.6	9.1	8.9	8.9	10.3	Private grant or scholarship
1.3	1.5	1.1	0.9	0.8	0.7	0.9	1.3	--	--	--	--	Student's GI benefits
1.1	1.2	1.0	0.8	0.9	0.7	0.5	0.6	--	--	--	--	GI benefits awarded to student's parent
--	--	--	--	--	--	--	--	1.7	--	--	--	GI/military benefits (student's or parents')
4.7	5.2	5.1	2.8	2.5	--	--	--	--	--	--	--	Social Security dependent's benefits
--	--	--	--	--	2.6	2.3	2.7	2.5	3.7	3.7	4.6	Other gov't aid (ROTC, Soc. Sec.,BIA,etc.)
												Aid Which Must Be Repaid
14.0	22.0	27.1	21.0	21.8	23.5	22.8	25.1	21.5	21.2	22.5	21.8	Stafford/Guaranteed Student Loan [2]
7.4	8.7	7.2	5.9	6.2	5.7	5.4	5.9	4.6	3.0	2.6	7.7	Perkins Loan (NDSL prior to 1990) [2]
3.6	4.5	3.8	3.6	3.8	3.7	3.7	4.4	5.5	6.2	7.8	6.5	College loan
3.4	3.8	4.0	4.0	3.7	3.7	3.7	4.1	5.0	5.1	6.2	6.2	Loan(s) from other sources
4.1	4.1	3.8	3.3	3.7	2.3	2.1	2.2	2.9	2.6	3.0	2.7	From sources other than those cited above
												RECEIVED $1,500+ AID FOR FIRST YEAR EDUCATIONAL EXPENSES [1]
												Personal or Family Resources
27.1	27.4	30.9	36.1	36.4	40.6	41.8	45.5	51.2	53.3	54.5	54.9	Parents and family
0.1	0.3	0.3	0.3	0.2	0.2	0.3	0.4	0.4	0.4	0.3	0.3	Spouse's income
4.3	4.2	4.9	5.7	5.4	6.1	6.7	6.4	7.7	9.1	8.9	9.6	Savings from summer work
2.1	2.5	2.6	2.9	3.0	3.5	3.7	4.7	5.3	5.7	6.0	6.5	Other savings
1.4	1.5	1.3	1.4	1.4	1.3	1.4	1.8	--	--	--	--	Part-time work while attending college
--	--	--	--	--	--	--	--	0.7	0.9	0.9	1.2	Part-time work on campus
--	--	--	--	--	--	--	--	1.4	1.5	1.4	1.3	Other part-time work while in college
0.7	0.6	0.5	0.4	0.5	0.4	0.6	0.7	0.6	0.6	0.6	0.6	Full-time work while in college
												Aid Which Need Not Be Repaid
4.5	4.7	4.5	4.0	6.5	4.6	4.7	3.8	4.1	4.9	5.5	6.3	Pell Grant (BEOG prior to 1982) [2]
0.6	0.6	0.5	0.6	0.8	0.8	0.7	0.9	1.0	1.0	1.1	1.4	Supp. Educational Oppty. Grant (SEOG) [2]
1.6	1.8	1.6	0.6	2.1	1.7	2.2	2.1	3.4	3.2	3.5	3.8	State scholarship or grant [2]
2.3	3.0	3.1	3.7	4.4	5.9	6.6	6.8	5.4	8.3	8.7	9.6	College grant or scholarship
0.4	0.6	0.4	0.7	1.0	0.6	0.8	0.8	0.8	1.0	1.0	1.3	College Work-Study Grant [2]
0.9	1.2	1.1	1.2	1.2	1.1	1.0	1.4	2.1	2.0	2.3	2.8	Private grant or scholarship
0.6	0.6	0.5	0.4	0.4	0.4	0.4	0.6	--	--	--	--	Student's GI benefits
0.3	0.3	0.3	0.3	0.2	0.3	0.1	0.3	--	--	--	--	GI benefits awarded to student's parent
--	--	--	--	--	--	--	--	0.8	--	--	--	GI/military benefits (student's or parents')
1.1	1.3	1.4	0.7	1.2	--	--	--	--	--	--	--	Social Security dependent's benefits
--	--	--	--	--	1.7	1.3	1.9	1.8	0.7	2.4	2.9	Other gov't aid (ROTC, Soc. Sec.,BIA,etc.)
												Aid Which Must Be Repaid
7.3	12.9	19.5	13.5	14.0	16.8	15.7	15.5	12.3	12.1	13.0	13.0	Stafford/Guaranteed Student Loan [2]
1.2	1.9	2.3	1.7	2.0	1.8	1.8	1.7	1.4	1.1	1.0	2.2	Perkins Loan (NDSL prior to 1990) [2]
1.2	1.8	1.8	1.6	1.5	1.8	1.8	1.9	2.4	2.2	3.7	3.5	College loan
1.2	1.6	2.1	1.8	1.8	1.1	1.9	2.0	2.5	2.6	3.2	3.5	Loan(s) from other sources
2.1	1.8	1.7	1.6	1.6	1.2	0.9	0.9	1.3	1.1	1.6	1.3	From sources other than those cited above

[1] Response and processing options rendered data from 1973-1977 not comparable to 1978-1990.
[2] In 1987-1990, highest response option of "$3,000 or more" was dropped, since these programs have upper limits less than $3,000.

Twenty–Five Year Trends for Freshman Women

STUDENT'S DEMOGRAPHICS	1966	1967	1968	1969	1970	1971	1972	1973	1974	1975	1976	1977	1978
AGE													
16 or younger	--	0.2	0.1	0.1	0.1	0.1	0.1	0.2	0.2	0.2	0.1	0.2	0.1
17	--	5.4	5.5	4.8	4.6	4.3	5.3	6.2	5.2	4.8	4.9	4.0	4.0
18	--	81.3	79.9	79.3	76.6	78.4	77.7	77.8	77.2	77.1	77.0	77.0	77.9
19	--	10.0	10.1	10.6	11.8	12.8	12.8	12.3	13.0	13.7	13.7	14.2	14.4
20	--	1.0	1.4	1.3	1.6	1.4	1.3	1.2	1.5	1.4	1.5	1.6	1.3
21 or older [1]	--	2.1	3.1	3.9	5.3	3.0	2.8	2.4	2.9	2.9	2.7	3.2	2.3
RACIAL/ETHNIC BACKGROUND [2]													
White/Caucasian	90.5	89.6	86.0	90.0	[*]	90.6	85.9	87.9	87.8	85.6	85.2	86.0	87.6
African-American/Black [1]	5.6	4.8	7.2	7.1	[*]	7.2	10.0	8.6	8.5	10.1	9.6	9.8	9.0
American Indian	0.6	0.7	0.7	0.3	[*]	0.9	1.2	1.0	1.0	0.8	0.9	0.7	0.8
Oriental/Asian-American	0.7	0.7	1.0	1.5	[*]	0.4	1.1	1.0	0.9	1.3	1.9	1.0	1.1
Mexican-American/Chicano	--	--	--	--	--	1.1	1.5	1.2	1.4	1.6	1.7	1.4	1.0
Puerto Rican-American	--	--	--	--	--	0.2	0.7	0.4	0.7	0.6	0.5	1.0	0.8
Other	2.7	4.2	5.1	1.0	[*]	1.1	1.8	1.5	1.7	1.7	1.7	1.6	1.5
MARITAL STATUS													
No	--	--	--	--	--	97.4	97.7	98.2	98.0	97.8	98.0	98.0	98.5
Yes [1]	--	--	--	--	--	2.6	2.3	1.8	2.0	2.2	2.0	2.0	1.5
CITIZENSHIP STATUS													
Yes	--	--	--	98.4	98.7	--	97.9	98.0	--	--	--	--	--
No [1]	--	--	--	1.6	1.3	--	2.1	2.0	--	--	--	--	--
TWIN STATUS													
No	--	--	--	--	--	--	--	--	--	--	--	98.2	--
Yes, identical	--	--	--	--	--	--	--	--	--	--	--	0.7	--
Yes, fraternal	--	--	--	--	--	--	--	--	--	--	--	1.2	--
VETERAN STATUS													
No	--	--	--	--	99.7	99.8	99.8	99.8	99.2	99.1	99.1	99.2	99.3
Yes [1]	--	--	--	--	0.3	0.2	0.1	0.1	0.8	0.9	0.9	0.8	0.7
STUDENT'S CURRENT RELIGIOUS PREFERENCE (Aggregated) [3]													
Protestant	56.7	51.9	48.4	51.7	53.2	44.8	40.7	48.4	49.9	49.4	47.9	47.7	48.6
Roman Catholic	28.5	30.9	31.6	30.2	30.2	28.7	29.6	33.9	33.3	33.6	35.3	37.6	37.3
Jewish	3.9	4.7	4.7	3.7	4.5	2.9	4.0	5.1	3.5	3.9	3.4	3.4	3.8
Other	6.1	6.6	8.0	3.9	4.0	11.4	13.5	3.7	4.3	4.5	5.0	4.3	4.1
None	4.7	6.0	7.3	10.6	8.2	12.2	12.2	8.8	9.0	8.5	8.3	6.9	6.2
STUDENT'S CURRENT RELIGIOUS PREFERENCE (Disaggregated)													
Baptist	--	--	--	11.8	14.7	--	--	13.5	13.7	14.7	13.7	14.1	13.8
Buddhist	--	--	--	--	--	--	--	--	--	--	--	--	--
Congregational (United Church of Christ) [1]	--	--	--	3.9	2.5	--	--	1.8	2.1	1.7	1.8	1.9	2.0
Eastern Orthodox	--	--	--	--	0.5	--	--	0.6	0.5	0.6	0.6	0.6	0.6
Episcopal	--	--	--	4.2	4.2	--	--	3.6	3.3	3.3	3.2	3.2	3.4
Jewish	--	--	--	3.7	4.5	--	--	5.1	3.5	3.9	3.4	3.4	3.8
Latter Day Saints (Mormon)	--	--	--	0.6	0.3	--	--	0.3	0.3	0.3	0.3	0.3	0.2
Lutheran	--	--	--	6.8	6.3	--	--	5.7	6.7	5.9	6.4	5.7	5.4
Methodist	--	--	--	11.0	10.8	--	--	10.9	10.9	11.0	9.7	10.2	10.8
Muslim (Islamic) [1]	--	--	--	0.1	0.1	--	--	0.1	0.2	0.1	0.1	0.1	0.2
Presbyterian	--	--	--	6.7	6.6	--	--	6.1	5.8	6.0	5.5	5.3	5.8
Quaker (Society of Friends)	--	--	--	0.4	0.3	--	--	0.2	0.2	0.2	0.2	0.2	0.2
Roman Catholic	--	--	--	30.2	30.2	--	--	33.9	33.3	33.6	35.3	37.6	37.3
Seventh Day Adventist	--	--	--	0.4	0.4	--	--	0.4	0.4	0.5	0.5	0.3	0.4
Unitarian-Universalist	--	--	--	0.9	0.8	--	--	0.5	0.5	0.4	0.4	0.3	0.3
Other Protestant	--	--	--	5.0	5.8	--	--	4.8	5.5	4.8	5.6	5.6	5.7
Other religion	--	--	--	3.8	3.9	--	--	3.6	4.1	4.4	4.9	4.2	3.9
None	--	--	--	10.6	8.2	--	--	8.8	9.0	8.5	8.3	6.9	6.2
DISABILITIES [4]													
Hearing	--	--	--	--	--	--	--	--	--	--	--	--	--
Speech	--	--	--	--	--	--	--	--	--	--	--	--	--
Partially sighted/blind	--	--	--	--	--	--	--	--	--	--	--	--	--
Orthopedic	--	--	--	--	--	--	--	--	--	--	--	--	--
Learning disabled	--	--	--	--	--	--	--	--	--	--	--	--	--
Health related	--	--	--	--	--	--	--	--	--	--	--	--	--
Other	--	--	--	--	--	--	--	--	--	--	--	--	--
DISTANCE FROM HOME TO COLLEGE													
10 miles or less [1]	--	--	--	26.2	27.2	22.8	26.6	27.3	--	25.5	28.9	26.7	21.4
11-50 miles	--	--	--	25.2	24.6	26.9	25.6	25.5	--	26.2	26.9	27.4	26.9
51-100 miles	--	--	--	13.6	13.2	15.3	14.4	13.3	--	14.0	13.4	14.6	15.7
101-500 miles	--	--	--	26.2	26.7	28.4	25.9	26.5	--	26.8	23.8	24.5	28.1
More than 500 miles	--	--	--	8.8	8.3	6.7	7.4	7.4	--	7.5	6.9	6.8	7.8

[*] Results were not comparable to those of other years due to changes in question text or order.
[1] Text, order or number of response options may vary from year to year.
[2] Respondent allowed to mark all responses that apply from 1971-1990. Responses may sum to more than 100%.
[3] See Appendix D for a discussion of variation in question texts and aggregation procedures.
[4] Responses from 1978-1982 excluded because they were not recorded in a comparable manner.

STUDENT'S DEMOGRAPHICS	1979	1980	1981	1982	1983	1984	1985	1986	1987	1988	1989	1990
AGE												
16 or younger	0.1	0.1	0.1	0.1	0.1	0.1	0.1	0.1	0.1	0.1	0.1	0.1
17	3.5	3.2	3.1	3.1	2.9	3.2	2.9	3.4	2.8	3.0	2.6	2.3
18	77.2	75.9	77.4	77.7	76.0	76.6	75.4	75.3	74.7	76.1	75.1	72.4
19	14.9	15.8	15.5	15.6	16.7	15.7	16.9	15.5	16.5	15.8	17.6	18.8
20	1.5	1.7	1.3	1.3	1.5	1.4	1.3	1.4	1.6	1.3	1.6	1.8
21 or older [1]	2.7	3.2	2.6	2.2	2.8	3.0	3.4	4.3	4.2	3.7	3.0	4.7
RACIAL/ETHNIC BACKGROUND [2]												
White/Caucasian	85.4	85.1	87.6	87.5	85.9	84.6	85.1	84.8	84.5	81.9	83.3	83.5
African-American/Black [1]	10.1	10.3	9.6	9.4	10.1	10.9	10.0	9.6	10.0	10.7	10.3	10.6
American Indian	1.0	0.7	1.0	0.9	1.1	0.9	1.0	0.8	0.9	0.8	1.0	1.4
Oriental/Asian-American	1.2	1.2	1.0	1.3	1.4	1.5	1.8	2.3	2.1	2.5	2.6	2.8
Mexican-American/Chicano	1.2	2.0	0.9	0.9	0.9	1.1	1.4	1.3	1.1	2.0	1.5	1.5
Puerto Rican-American	1.0	0.9	0.6	0.9	0.7	0.8	0.7	0.9	1.5	1.5	0.9	0.6
Other	1.8	1.6	1.2	1.3	1.5	1.7	1.5	1.3	1.7	2.2	2.0	1.7
MARITAL STATUS												
No	98.4	98.1	98.3	98.5	98.2	98.2	98.0	97.4	--	--	--	--
Yes [1]	1.6	1.9	1.7	1.5	1.8	1.8	2.0	2.6	--	--	--	--
CITIZENSHIP STATUS												
Yes	--	--	--	97.9	97.7	97.1	97.7	96.9	98.3	97.7	97.2	97.8
No [1]	--	--	--	2.1	2.3	2.9	2.3	3.1	1.7	2.2	2.8	2.2
TWIN STATUS												
No	--	--	98.1	98.2	98.2	98.2	98.2	98.3	98.2	98.2	98.4	98.0
Yes, identical	--	--	0.6	0.6	0.7	0.6	0.7	0.6	0.7	0.7	0.7	0.8
Yes, fraternal	--	--	1.2	1.2	1.1	1.2	1.1	1.1	1.2	1.0	0.9	1.2
VETERAN STATUS												
No	99.1	99.2	99.2	99.2	--	--	--	--	--	--	--	--
Yes [1]	0.9	0.8	0.8	0.8	--	--	--	--	--	--	--	--
STUDENT'S CURRENT RELIGIOUS PREFERENCE (Aggregated) [3]												
Protestant	34.3	34.7	35.8	34.2	32.4	44.5	47.4	29.4	47.3	44.5	48.4	49.3
Roman Catholic	38.2	39.0	37.4	39.3	39.6	40.0	37.6	36.8	36.1	36.4	33.6	31.8
Jewish	3.5	2.9	2.8	2.9	3.0	2.9	2.7	3.2	2.5	3.0	2.5	1.9
Other	17.5	17.0	18.2	17.8	18.7	6.3	5.5	22.4	5.7	6.6	6.0	6.7
None	6.6	6.5	5.8	5.9	6.2	6.4	7.0	8.2	8.4	9.6	9.3	10.3
STUDENT'S CURRENT RELIGIOUS PREFERENCE (Disaggregated)												
Baptist	--	--	--	--	--	14.5	15.0	--	14.3	14.5	16.4	19.3
Buddhist	--	--	--	--	--	0.2	0.2	--	0.3	0.3	0.2	0.3
Congregational (United Church of Christ) [1]	--	--	--	--	--	1.9	1.6	--	1.5	1.2	1.1	1.1
Eastern Orthodox	--	--	--	--	--	0.6	0.6	--	0.5	0.5	0.7	0.5
Episcopal	--	--	--	--	--	--	2.8	--	2.8	2.8	2.6	2.4
Jewish	--	--	--	--	--	2.9	2.7	--	2.5	3.0	2.5	1.9
Latter Day Saints (Mormon)	--	--	--	--	--	0.2	0.2	--	0.2	0.2	0.3	0.3
Lutheran	--	--	--	--	--	5.6	6.0	--	8.2	6.3	6.5	6.0
Methodist	--	--	--	--	--	10.7	10.3	--	9.7	9.4	10.4	10.2
Muslim (Islamic) [1]	--	--	--	--	--	0.2	0.1	--	0.2	0.2	0.3	0.2
Presbyterian	--	--	--	--	--	--	5.1	--	5.0	4.5	4.9	4.5
Quaker (Society of Friends)	--	--	--	--	--	0.2	0.1	--	0.1	0.2	0.2	0.2
Roman Catholic	--	--	--	--	--	40.0	37.6	--	36.1	36.4	33.6	31.8
Seventh Day Adventist	--	--	--	--	--	0.3	0.3	--	0.2	0.3	0.4	0.3
Unitarian-Universalist	--	--	--	--	--	0.2	--	--	--	--	--	--
Other Protestant	--	--	--	--	--	10.3	5.4	--	4.8	4.6	4.9	4.5
Other religion	--	--	--	--	--	5.9	5.2	--	5.2	6.1	5.5	6.2
None	--	--	--	--	--	6.4	7.0	--	8.4	9.6	9.3	10.3
DISABILITIES [4]												
Hearing	--	--	--	--	0.7	0.8	0.7	0.6	0.6	0.7	--	--
Speech	--	--	--	--	0.2	0.2	0.1	0.1	0.1	0.2	--	--
Partially sighted/blind	--	--	--	--	2.1	1.7	2.0	1.6	1.8	1.7	--	--
Orthopedic	--	--	--	--	0.9	0.9	0.9	0.7	0.8	1.0	--	--
Learning disabled	--	--	--	--	0.5	0.7	0.9	0.5	0.8	0.9	--	--
Health related	--	--	--	--	0.9	1.1	1.4	0.8	1.0	1.3	--	--
Other	--	--	--	--	1.1	1.1	1.0	0.7	0.9	1.3	--	--
DISTANCE FROM HOME TO COLLEGE												
10 miles or less [1]	24.9	23.9	20.0	21.0	21.8	20.3	20.1	18.5	18.3	18.5	18.4	14.6
11-50 miles	26.0	27.7	26.5	26.8	30.2	29.8	28.5	28.8	28.8	27.7	27.9	29.9
51-100 miles	15.4	15.4	16.5	16.3	15.9	16.0	17.3	16.8	16.9	15.2	15.9	17.9
101-500 miles	26.7	25.6	29.6	28.3	24.4	26.0	26.1	26.3	26.6	28.2	28.2	27.7
More than 500 miles	7.0	7.4	7.4	7.6	7.7	7.9	8.0	9.5	9.3	10.4	9.6	9.9

[1] Text, order or number of response options may vary from year to year.
[2] Respondent allowed to mark all responses that apply from 1971-1990. Responses may sum to more than 100%.
[3] See Appendix D for a discussion of variation in question texts and aggregation procedures.
[4] Responses from 1978-1982 excluded because they were not recorded in a comparable manner.

STUDENT'S DEMOGRAPHICS	1966	1967	1968	1969	1970	1971	1972	1973	1974	1975	1976	1977	1978
RATED SELF ABOVE AVERAGE OR TOP 10% IN													
Academic ability	58.5	--	--	--	--	51.9	--	--	52.8	--	50.8	--	--
Athletic ability	24.3	--	--	--	--	24.3	--	--	25.5	--	26.1	--	--
Artistic ability	21.6	--	--	--	--	19.7	--	--	21.2	--	22.9	--	--
Drive to achieve	57.9	--	--	--	--	54.0	--	--	60.4	--	61.8	--	--
Emotional health	--	--	--	--	--	--	--	--	--	--	--	--	--
Leadership ability	35.0	--	--	--	--	30.4	--	--	36.3	--	39.2	--	--
Mathematical ability	26.0	--	--	--	--	25.5	--	--	26.8	--	26.6	--	--
Mechanical ability	10.5	--	--	--	--	8.2	--	--	9.5	--	9.8	--	--
Originality	36.3	--	--	--	--	33.4	--	--	36.4	--	37.7	--	--
Physical health	--	--	--	--	--	--	--	--	--	--	--	--	--
Political conservatism	12.2	--	--	--	--	6.6	--	--	7.8	--	8.8	--	--
Political liberalism	17.5	--	--	--	--	19.8	--	--	17.6	--	16.3	--	--
Popularity	28.5	--	--	--	--	26.0	--	--	26.4	--	26.8	--	--
Popularity with the opposite sex	24.6	--	--	--	--	23.6	--	--	25.7	--	25.4	--	--
Public speaking ability	20.7	--	--	--	--	17.1	--	--	18.0	--	19.4	--	--
Self-confidence (intellectual)	30.7	--	--	--	--	30.3	--	--	34.8	--	36.7	--	--
Self-confidence (social)	26.0	--	--	--	--	24.5	--	--	30.5	--	32.9	--	--
Sensitivity to criticism	29.8	--	--	--	--	28.2	--	--	27.5	--	26.3	--	--
Stubbornness	37.5	--	--	--	--	37.4	--	--	38.1	--	37.3	--	--
Understanding of others	66.0	--	--	--	--	67.3	--	--	70.7	--	71.6	--	--
Writing ability	28.9	--	--	--	--	29.3	--	--	32.3	--	34.8	--	--

PARENT'S DEMOGRAPHICS	1966	1967	1968	1969	1970	1971	1972	1973	1974	1975	1976	1977	1978
ESTIMATED PARENTAL INCOME													
Less than $6,000	19.7	[*]	17.4	15.2	14.9	13.1	15.7	12.3	12.2	12.5	12.4	11.8	9.2
$6,000-9,999	32.4	[*]	30.8	29.4	23.2	21.9	18.3	14.8	14.1	12.2	11.5	10.9	9.3
$10,000-14,999	25.2	[*]	26.4	27.6	29.4	31.3	28.7	28.5	28.4	25.2	23.4	21.5	18.1
$15,000-19,999	10.1	[*]	11.9	13.1	13.1	13.9	14.3	16.0	15.4	16.2	16.1	16.3	15.6
$20,000-24,999	5.2	[*]	5.8	6.6	7.6	8.4	9.0	10.9	11.8	12.1	12.9	14.0	15.4
$25,000-29,999	2.7	[*]	2.8	3.0	4.0	4.0	4.5	5.4	5.8	6.8	7.1	7.7	9.4
$30,000 or more	4.6	[*]	4.9	5.0	--	--	--	--	--	--	--	--	--
$30,000-34,999	--	--	--	--	2.8	2.7	3.0	4.1	4.1	4.6	5.4	5.8	7.5
$35,000-39,999	--	--	--	--	1.5	1.5	2.0	2.4	2.5	3.1	3.3	3.6	4.6
$40,000 or more	--	--	--	--	3.6	3.3	--	--	--	--	--	--	--
$40,000-49,999	--	--	--	--	--	--	1.8	2.0	2.2	2.8	3.2	3.3	4.2
$50,000 or more	--	--	--	--	--	--	2.8	3.5	3.6	4.5	4.8	5.1	6.7
$50,000-59,999	--	--	--	--	--	--	--	--	--	--	--	--	--
$50,000-99,999	--	--	--	--	--	--	--	--	--	--	--	--	--
$60,000-74,999	--	--	--	--	--	--	--	--	--	--	--	--	--
$75,000-99,999	--	--	--	--	--	--	--	--	--	--	--	--	--
$100,000 or more	--	--	--	--	--	--	--	--	--	--	--	--	--
$100,000-149,999	--	--	--	--	--	--	--	--	--	--	--	--	--
$150,000 or more	--	--	--	--	--	--	--	--	--	--	--	--	--
MEDIAN INCOME (in $1,000's)	**9.7**	**[*]**	**10.3**	**11.0**	**12.0**	**12.4**	**12.8**	**14.0**	**14.2**	**15.0**	**15.8**	**16.8**	**19.3**
NUMBER CURRENTLY DEPENDENT ON PARENTS FOR SUPPORT [1]													
One	--	--	--	--	--	--	--	--	--	--	--	--	4.1
Two	--	--	--	--	--	--	--	--	--	--	--	--	7.8
Three	--	--	--	--	--	--	--	--	--	--	--	--	19.3
Four	--	--	--	--	--	--	--	--	--	--	--	--	25.8
Five	--	--	--	--	--	--	--	--	--	--	--	--	22.6
Six or more	--	--	--	--	--	--	--	--	--	--	--	--	20.4
NUMBER OF DEPENDENTS CURRENTLY ATTENDING COLLEGE [2]													
None	--	--	--	--	--	--	--	--	--	--	--	--	66.4
One	--	--	--	--	--	--	--	--	--	--	--	--	24.9
Two	--	--	--	--	--	--	--	--	--	--	--	--	6.2
Three or more	--	--	--	--	--	--	--	--	--	--	--	--	2.5
PARENTS' MARITAL STATUS													
both alive and living with each other	--	--	--	--	--	--	82.1	--	--	--	--	--	--
both alive, divorced or separated	--	--	--	--	--	--	9.4	--	--	--	--	--	--
one or both deceased	--	--	--	--	--	--	8.5	--	--	--	--	--	--

[*] Results were not comparable to those of other years due to changes in question text or order.
[1] Including respondent and parents if applicable.
[2] Other than respondent.

1979	1980	1981	1982	1983	1984	1985	1986	1987	1988	1989	1990	***STUDENT'S DEMOGRAPHICS***
												RATED SELF ABOVE AVERAGE OR TOP 10% IN
--	50.4	--	--	--	--	52.3	52.1	50.9	51.9	52.5	50.3	Academic ability
--	26.8	--	--	--	--	--	--	--	--	--	--	Athletic ability
--	22.7	--	--	--	--	21.1	21.8	23.1	22.5	22.2	22.6	Artistic ability
--	65.1	--	--	--	--	60.9	60.5	58.6	61.1	61.9	65.2	Drive to achieve
--	--	--	--	--	--	55.9	54.2	51.2	49.9	50.8	51.7	Emotional health
--	43.9	--	--	--	--	46.0	46.8	46.0	46.5	46.6	46.1	Leadership ability
--	29.2	--	--	--	--	31.7	32.5	32.3	32.9	32.8	30.4	Mathematical ability
--	11.2	--	--	--	--	--	--	--	--	--	--	Mechanical ability
--	42.3	--	--	--	--	--	--	--	--	--	--	Originality
--	--	--	--	--	--	51.7	51.6	48.8	48.1	48.6	48.7	Physical health
--	9.5	--	--	--	--	--	--	--	--	--	--	Political conservatism
--	12.7	--	--	--	--	--	--	--	--	--	--	Political liberalism
--	30.5	--	--	--	--	37.5	38.9	37.5	36.8	36.8	36.8	Popularity
--	29.6	--	--	--	--	--	--	35.8	35.6	35.4	35.1	Popularity with the opposite sex
--	22.0	--	--	--	--	--	--	27.3	27.1	27.6	26.7	Public speaking ability
--	40.9	--	--	--	--	47.0	47.1	41.2	41.7	42.7	40.9	Self-confidence (intellectual)
--	38.0	--	--	--	--	43.7	44.1	39.5	38.9	39.3	39.5	Self-confidence (social)
--	25.0	--	--	--	--	--	--	--	--	--	--	Sensitivity to criticism
--	38.2	--	--	--	--	--	--	--	--	--	--	Stubbornness
--	76.1	--	--	--	--	--	--	--	--	--	70.1	Understanding of others
--	36.4	--	--	--	--	39.8	40.9	39.6	40.0	40.5	40.6	Writing ability

1979	1980	1981	1982	1983	1984	1985	1986	1987	1988	1989	1990	***PARENT'S DEMOGRAPHICS***
												ESTIMATED PARENTAL INCOME
9.0	8.4	6.6	5.9	6.6	6.6	5.3	4.5	4.4	4.3	3.5	3.6	Less than $6,000
9.0	8.0	6.6	6.2	5.9	5.6	4.9	4.2	3.7	3.4	3.3	3.6	$6,000-9,999
16.0	14.7	12.9	11.2	11.5	10.8	7.8	7.0	6.3	6.0	5.4	5.8	$10,000-14,999
13.4	12.3	10.7	9.5	8.7	8.3	7.4	6.9	6.4	6.0	5.9	5.8	$15,000-19,999
15.9	15.8	15.0	12.8	12.6	11.3	8.4	8.0	7.8	7.3	7.5	7.2	$20,000-24,999
9.7	10.4	10.9	10.8	10.3	10.0	8.7	7.9	7.6	7.3	7.1	6.7	$25,000-29,999
--	--	--	--	--	--	--	--	--	--	--	--	$30,000 or more
7.8	9.0	10.1	11.8	10.8	10.8	11.2	10.4	9.8	9.1	9.3	9.4	$30,000-34,999
5.5	5.9	7.6	8.2	8.4	9.1	9.8	9.9	9.5	9.0	9.1	8.7	$35,000-39,999
--	--	--	--	--	--	--	--	--	--	--	--	$40,000 or more
5.8	6.8	8.5	10.1	10.6	11.4	11.2	11.9	12.0	12.0	12.5	12.0	$40,000-49,999
--	--	--	--	--	--	--	--	--	--	--	--	$50,000 or more
--	--	--	--	--	--	9.2	9.8	10.5	11.1	11.2	11.2	$50,000-59,999
5.9	6.6	8.5	10.5	11.5	12.4	--	--	--	--	--	--	$50,000-99,999
--	--	--	--	--	--	6.7	8.0	9.1	10.1	10.4	10.7	$60,000-74,999
--	--	--	--	--	--	3.9	4.9	5.6	6.3	6.4	6.8	$75,000-99,999
--	--	--	--	--	--	2.7	3.3	3.8	4.2	4.2	4.4	$100,000 or more
1.9	2.0	2.5	3.0	3.1	3.5	--	--	--	--	--	--	$100,000-149,999
--	--	--	--	--	--	2.7	3.4	3.6	4.0	4.0	4.2	$150,000 or more
20.8	**22.1**	**24.4**	**27.0**	**27.3**	**28.7**	**33.3**	**35.5**	**37.1**	**38.7**	**39.4**	**39.5**	**MEDIAN INCOME (in $1,000's)**
												NUMBER CURRENTLY DEPENDENT ON PARENTS FOR SUPPORT [1]
5.1	4.9	4.5	5.3	5.6	5.4	6.0	6.7	8.4	--	--	--	One
9.1	9.1	9.3	9.8	11.2	11.8	12.5	13.7	16.4	--	--	--	Two
19.5	20.9	20.7	21.1	23.5	23.8	22.1	22.2	22.9	--	--	--	Three
25.8	25.9	26.8	27.7	29.1	29.6	28.7	28.5	27.7	--	--	--	Four
21.6	21.5	22.2	20.8	19.2	18.6	18.3	17.7	15.8	--	--	--	Five
18.9	17.8	16.5	15.4	11.5	10.8	12.3	11.1	8.9	--	--	--	Six or more
												NUMBER OF DEPENDENTS CURRENTLY ATTENDING COLLEGE [2]
66.2	66.1	65.5	65.6	66.6	68.0	69.2	69.3	70.1	--	--	--	None
24.6	24.9	25.0	24.9	24.5	23.6	23.2	23.2	23.0	--	--	--	One
6.5	6.4	6.7	6.7	6.3	6.0	5.5	5.5	5.0	--	--	--	Two
2.7	2.5	2.7	2.8	2.6	2.4	2.1	2.0	1.9	--	--	--	Three or more
												PARENTS' MARITAL STATUS
--	--	--	--	--	--	--	72.8	71.5	70.8	70.4	69.6	both alive and living with each other
--	--	--	--	--	--	--	20.9	22.1	23.2	24.2	24.7	both alive, divorced or separated
--	--	--	--	--	--	--	6.4	6.3	6.0	5.4	5.8	one or both deceased

[1] Including respondent and parents if applicable.
[2] Other than respondent.

PARENT'S DEMOGRAPHICS	1966	1967	1968	1969	1970	1971	1972	1973	1974	1975	1976	1977	1978
MOTHER'S EDUCATION													
Grammar school or less	5.5	6.0	6.2	6.3	7.0	5.4	6.2	4.5	5.2	5.1	5.3	5.0	4.0
Some high school	12.7	13.0	14.4	13.7	13.9	13.2	13.0	11.7	11.7	11.6	11.7	12.0	10.2
High school graduate	40.2	40.3	41.2	41.6	40.5	42.6	41.8	40.1	39.8	40.2	40.6	41.4	40.6
Postsecondary school other than college	--	--	--	--	--	--	--	7.7	7.9	7.2	7.3	7.1	7.5
Some college	22.5	21.6	20.4	20.5	19.7	19.3	18.5	15.3	14.9	14.7	14.2	13.6	14.4
College degree	16.3	16.0	14.9	14.9	15.6	16.2	13.9	14.1	14.2	14.2	14.4	14.0	15.4
Some graduate school	--	--	--	--	--	--	2.4	2.2	2.0	2.1	1.9	1.9	2.1
Graduate degree	2.8	3.0	2.8	3.0	3.2	3.4	4.3	4.4	4.4	4.9	4.7	5.0	5.8
MOTHER'S CURRENT OCCUPATION [1]													
Artist	--	--	--	--	--	--	--	--	--	--	1.3	1.2	1.3
Businesswoman	--	--	--	--	--	--	--	--	--	--	6.6	6.8	7.7
Business (clerical)	--	--	--	--	--	--	--	--	--	--	11.3	11.0	11.2
Clergy or religious worker	--	--	--	--	--	--	--	--	--	--	0.0	0.0	0.1
College teacher	--	--	--	--	--	--	--	--	--	--	0.3	0.3	0.3
Doctor or dentist	--	--	--	--	--	--	--	--	--	--	0.2	0.1	0.2
Educator (secondary school)	--	--	--	--	--	--	--	--	--	--	2.4	2.3	2.5
Elementary school teacher	--	--	--	--	--	--	--	--	--	--	5.2	5.1	5.5
Engineer	--	--	--	--	--	--	--	--	--	--	0.1	0.1	0.1
Farmer or forester	--	--	--	--	--	--	--	--	--	--	0.2	0.2	0.2
Health professional (non-MD)	--	--	--	--	--	--	--	--	--	--	1.6	1.6	1.5
Homemaker (full-time)	--	--	--	--	--	--	--	--	--	--	34.0	32.1	31.5
Lawyer	--	--	--	--	--	--	--	--	--	--	0.1	0.1	0.1
Nurse	--	--	--	--	--	--	--	--	--	--	6.1	6.4	6.4
Research scientist	--	--	--	--	--	--	--	--	--	--	0.1	0.1	0.1
Skilled worker	--	--	--	--	--	--	--	--	--	--	1.6	1.7	1.8
Semiskilled or unskilled worker	--	--	--	--	--	--	--	--	--	--	5.4	5.4	4.8
Social worker	--	--	--	--	--	--	--	--	--	--	--	1.0	1.0
Unemployed	--	--	--	--	--	--	--	--	--	--	8.3	8.8	7.8
Other	--	--	--	--	--	--	--	--	--	--	15.4	15.6	16.2
MOTHER'S CURRENT RELIGIOUS PREFERENCE (Aggregated) [2]													
Protestant	--	--	--	--	58.3	--	--	--	54.6	54.1	52.0	51.5	52.0
Roman Catholic	--	--	--	--	30.6	--	--	--	34.5	34.7	36.6	38.2	37.8
Jewish	--	--	--	--	5.2	--	--	--	4.0	4.3	3.8	3.7	4.1
Other	--	--	--	--	3.0	--	--	--	3.0	3.5	4.0	3.5	3.4
None	--	--	--	--	3.1	--	--	--	3.6	3.6	3.8	3.0	2.9
MOTHER'S CURRENT RELIGIOUS PREFERENCE (Disaggregated)													
Baptist	--	--	--	--	15.6	--	--	--	14.3	15.5	14.1	14.5	13.9
Buddhist	--	--	--	--	--	--	--	--	--	--	--	--	--
Congregational (United Church of Christ) [3]	--	--	--	--	2.9	--	--	--	2.3	1.9	2.0	2.2	2.1
Eastern Orthodox	--	--	--	--	0.5	--	--	--	0.6	0.7	0.7	0.7	0.7
Episcopal	--	--	--	--	4.8	--	--	--	4.0	3.9	3.7	3.7	3.8
Jewish	--	--	--	--	5.2	--	--	--	4.0	4.3	3.8	3.7	4.1
Latter Day Saints (Mormon)	--	--	--	--	0.3	--	--	--	0.3	0.2	0.3	0.3	0.2
Lutheran	--	--	--	--	6.9	--	--	--	7.2	6.4	7.0	6.2	5.9
Methodist	--	--	--	--	12.4	--	--	--	12.3	12.3	10.9	11.2	11.8
Muslim (Islamic) [3]	--	--	--	--	0.1	--	--	--	0.1	0.1	0.1	0.1	0.1
Presbyterian	--	--	--	--	7.6	--	--	--	7.0	7.1	6.5	6.0	6.6
Quaker (Society of Friends)	--	--	--	--	0.2	--	--	--	0.2	0.2	0.2	0.2	0.2
Roman Catholic	--	--	--	--	30.6	--	--	--	34.5	34.7	36.6	38.2	37.8
Seventh Day Adventist	--	--	--	--	0.4	--	--	--	0.3	0.5	0.6	0.3	0.5
Unitarian-Universalist	--	--	--	--	0.6	--	--	--	0.5	0.5	0.5	0.4	0.4
Other Protestant	--	--	--	--	6.1	--	--	--	5.6	4.9	5.5	5.8	5.9
Other religion	--	--	--	--	2.9	--	--	--	2.9	3.4	3.9	3.4	3.3
None	--	--	--	--	3.1	--	--	--	3.6	3.6	3.8	3.0	2.9

[1] Data for this item collected but not reported in 1969-1975
[2] See Appendix D for a discussion of variation in question texts and aggregation procedures.
[3] Text, order or number of response options may vary from year to year.

1979	1980	1981	1982	1983	1984	1985	1986	1987	1988	1989	1990	***PARENT'S DEMOGRAPHICS***
												MOTHER'S EDUCATION
4.7	4.5	3.5	3.3	3.7	3.7	3.6	3.5	3.4	3.6	3.0	3.1	Grammar school or less
11.1	10.4	9.4	8.4	8.9	8.6	8.4	7.5	6.5	6.8	6.4	7.3	Some high school
39.9	40.9	40.8	40.8	39.8	39.0	37.7	35.8	35.7	34.4	34.9	35.0	High school graduate
6.9	7.1	7.0	7.4	7.7	7.9	7.9	7.8	8.8	8.2	8.3	7.6	Postsecondary school other than college
14.6	14.3	14.9	14.8	15.0	15.2	16.1	16.8	16.4	17.1	16.9	16.9	Some college
15.0	14.9	16.0	16.4	15.7	16.5	16.4	17.3	17.7	17.9	18.4	18.2	College degree
2.1	2.0	2.1	2.1	2.1	2.3	2.5	2.7	2.8	2.8	2.8	2.7	Some graduate school
5.8	5.8	6.2	6.7	7.2	6.8	7.5	8.4	8.8	9.2	9.3	9.1	Graduate degree
												MOTHER'S CURRENT OCCUPATION [1]
1.3	1.2	1.3	1.4	1.4	1.3	1.4	1.5	1.5	1.4	1.4	1.5	Artist
8.1	8.6	9.7	10.0	10.7	11.1	12.6	13.5	14.3	14.2	14.2	13.8	Businesswoman
11.4	12.0	12.3	12.4	11.8	12.2	11.6	11.7	12.4	11.7	11.5	10.5	Business (clerical)
0.1	0.1	0.1	0.1	0.1	0.1	0.1	0.1	0.1	0.1	0.1	0.1	Clergy or religious worker
0.3	0.3	0.3	0.3	0.3	0.3	0.3	0.4	0.4	0.4	0.3	0.4	College teacher
0.2	0.2	0.2	0.2	0.3	0.2	0.3	0.3	0.3	0.3	0.3	0.3	Doctor or dentist
2.5	2.6	2.9	3.0	2.7	2.8	3.2	3.3	3.5	3.5	3.7	3.5	Educator (secondary school)
5.5	5.1	5.5	5.6	5.0	5.3	5.4	5.6	5.9	6.5	6.5	6.4	Elementary school teacher
0.1	0.1	0.1	0.1	0.1	0.1	0.2	0.2	0.2	0.1	0.2	0.2	Engineer
0.2	0.3	0.4	0.3	0.3	0.3	0.3	0.3	0.3	0.3	0.3	0.4	Farmer or forester
1.6	1.7	1.8	1.9	1.9	1.9	1.8	1.8	1.9	1.8	2.0	2.1	Health professional (non-MD)
28.0	28.0	23.1	22.5	25.1	23.6	22.6	20.8	18.2	18.5	16.7	15.9	Homemaker (full-time)
0.1	0.1	0.1	0.1	0.1	0.2	0.2	0.2	0.2	0.2	0.2	0.2	Lawyer
6.6	6.7	7.4	7.5	7.4	7.7	7.4	7.3	7.4	7.4	7.6	7.9	Nurse
0.1	0.1	0.1	0.1	0.1	0.1	0.1	0.1	0.1	0.1	0.1	0.1	Research scientist
1.7	1.8	1.8	1.9	1.8	1.6	1.7	1.9	2.4	1.8	1.8	1.9	Skilled worker
5.4	5.3	5.3	5.4	5.3	5.3	4.9	4.8	4.6	4.2	4.9	5.1	Semiskilled or unskilled worker
1.2	1.1	1.1	1.1	1.1	1.2	1.1	1.1	1.2	1.3	1.4	1.2	Social worker
8.5	8.3	8.0	7.5	6.8	6.8	6.8	6.4	6.1	5.8	5.4	5.7	Unemployed
17.2	16.5	18.5	18.5	17.5	18.1	18.1	18.6	19.0	20.1	21.3	23.0	Other
												MOTHER'S CURRENT RELIGIOUS PREFERENCE (Aggregated) [2]
36.8	37.1	38.0	36.5	34.5	46.9	49.9	31.8	50.4	47.9	51.8	51.9	Protestant
38.7	39.4	37.5	39.2	39.7	40.0	37.6	37.1	36.6	37.2	34.9	33.7	Roman Catholic
3.8	3.2	3.1	3.2	3.3	3.2	2.9	3.5	2.8	3.4	2.8	2.3	Jewish
17.2	16.8	18.0	17.8	18.8	6.0	5.4	22.4	5.5	6.4	5.7	6.4	Other
3.5	3.5	3.4	3.3	3.6	3.8	4.2	5.1	4.6	5.2	4.8	5.6	None
												MOTHER'S CURRENT RELIGIOUS PREFERENCE (Disaggregated)
--	--	--	--	--	14.5	14.9	--	14.5	14.7	16.2	18.2	Baptist
--	--	--	--	--	0.2	0.3	--	0.4	0.5	0.5	0.5	Buddhist
--	--	--	--	--	2.0	1.7	--	1.6	1.3	1.2	1.2	Congregational (United Church of Christ) [3]
--	--	--	--	--	0.7	0.6	--	0.5	0.6	0.7	0.6	Eastern Orthodox
--	--	--	--	--	--	3.1	--	3.1	3.1	3.0	2.8	Episcopal
--	--	--	--	--	3.2	2.9	--	2.8	3.4	2.8	2.3	Jewish
--	--	--	--	--	0.2	0.2	--	0.2	0.3	0.3	0.2	Latter Day Saints (Mormon)
--	--	--	--	--	6.1	6.4	--	8.6	6.8	7.2	6.7	Lutheran
--	--	--	--	--	11.4	11.0	--	10.7	10.2	11.5	11.3	Methodist
--	--	--	--	--	0.2	0.2	--	0.2	0.2	0.3	0.2	Muslim (Islamic) [3]
--	--	--	--	--	--	5.6	--	5.6	5.3	5.7	5.3	Presbyterian
--	--	--	--	--	0.2	0.2	--	0.1	0.2	0.2	0.3	Quaker (Society of Friends)
--	--	--	--	--	40.0	37.6	--	36.6	37.2	34.9	33.7	Roman Catholic
--	--	--	--	--	0.3	0.3	--	0.3	0.3	0.5	0.3	Seventh Day Adventist
--	--	--	--	--	0.3	--	--	--	--	--	--	Unitarian-Universalist
--	--	--	--	--	11.2	5.9	--	5.2	5.1	5.3	5.0	Other Protestant
--	--	--	--	--	5.6	4.9	--	4.9	5.7	4.9	5.7	Other religion
--	--	--	--	--	3.8	4.2	--	4.6	5.2	4.8	5.6	None

[1] Data for this item collected but not reported in 1969-1975
[2] See Appendix D for a discussion of variation in question texts and aggregation procedures.
[3] Text, order or number of response options may vary from year to year.

PARENT'S DEMOGRAPHICS	1966	1967	1968	1969	1970	1971	1972	1973	1974	1975	1976	1977	1978
FATHER'S EDUCATION													
Grammar school or less	8.6	9.5	9.9	9.8	10.7	8.8	9.6	7.1	8.2	7.6	8.0	7.6	6.4
Some high school	14.4	14.9	15.8	15.5	15.3	14.9	14.3	13.4	13.2	13.2	13.2	13.3	11.8
High school graduate	28.0	27.9	28.6	28.9	27.5	29.7	28.9	26.9	28.0	27.9	28.0	29.3	28.0
Postsecondary school other than college	--	--	--	--	--	--	--	4.8	4.6	4.5	4.4	4.5	4.5
Some college	20.3	19.1	18.8	18.5	17.5	17.4	16.8	14.9	14.3	13.9	13.4	13.2	13.5
College degree	18.1	17.9	17.3	17.7	18.8	19.4	16.7	17.7	17.4	18.0	18.4	17.9	19.5
Some graduate school	--	--	--	--	--	--	2.5	2.5	2.2	2.2	2.3	2.1	2.5
Graduate degree	10.5	10.8	9.5	9.5	10.2	10.0	11.2	12.6	12.1	12.6	12.3	12.2	13.9
FATHER'S CURRENT OCCUPATION [1]													
Artist	--	0.9	0.8	0.9	0.9	0.8	0.8	--	0.7	0.7	0.9	0.9	0.8
Businessman	--	31.5	30.4	29.4	30.0	29.7	29.9	--	27.1	25.8	28.2	27.3	28.5
Clergy or religious worker	--	1.1	0.9	1.0	1.2	0.9	1.0	--	1.0	1.0	1.0	1.0	1.2
College teacher	--	0.8	0.8	0.9	0.9	0.9	1.0	--	1.2	1.2	0.9	0.9	0.9
Doctor or dentist	--	2.6	2.2	2.2	2.2	2.0	2.1	--	2.1	2.3	2.1	1.9	2.2
Educator (secondary school)	--	2.2	2.0	2.2	2.1	2.3	2.3	--	2.0	2.0	2.9	2.8	3.1
Elementary school teacher	--	0.3	0.3	0.3	0.5	0.4	0.3	--	0.5	0.7	0.5	0.5	0.5
Engineer	--	7.3	7.3	7.3	7.1	7.5	7.7	--	6.7	7.1	8.7	8.3	9.0
Farmer or forester	--	6.5	6.2	6.0	5.6	6.8	5.9	--	5.5	4.4	4.4	4.1	3.9
Health professional (non-MD)	--	1.0	1.0	1.3	1.1	1.2	1.1	--	1.0	1.1	1.2	1.2	1.2
Lawyer	--	1.6	1.3	1.3	1.4	1.3	1.4	--	1.5	1.5	1.4	1.3	1.4
Military career	--	1.6	1.5	1.5	1.6	1.8	1.6	--	1.3	1.5	1.9	1.8	1.8
Research scientist	--	0.6	0.6	0.5	0.7	0.6	0.6	--	0.6	0.6	0.6	0.5	0.7
Skilled worker	--	11.3	11.5	12.2	11.5	11.0	11.5	--	17.6	17.0	10.4	10.7	10.3
Semiskilled or unskilled worker	--	10.2	11.6	11.4	11.5	10.5	10.4	--	9.3	9.0	9.4	9.6	8.0
Unemployed	--	0.9	1.3	1.3	1.5	1.7	2.1	--	2.3	3.1	2.6	2.9	2.7
Other	--	19.5	20.1	20.4	20.0	20.7	20.2	--	19.7	21.0	22.9	24.1	23.7
FATHER'S CURRENT RELIGIOUS PREFERENCE (Aggregated) [2]													
Protestant	--	--	--	--	--	--	--	--	51.9	51.2	49.5	48.7	49.3
Roman Catholic	--	--	--	--	--	--	--	--	33.1	33.2	34.7	37.1	36.3
Jewish	--	--	--	--	--	--	--	--	4.2	4.5	4.0	3.9	4.2
Other	--	--	--	--	--	--	--	--	2.7	3.1	3.7	3.3	3.2
None	--	--	--	--	--	--	--	--	8.0	8.1	8.4	6.9	6.9
FATHER'S CURRENT RELIGIOUS PREFERENCE (Disaggregated)													
Baptist	--	--	--	--	--	--	--	--	13.5	14.5	13.4	13.5	13.3
Buddhist	--	--	--	--	--	--	--	--	--	--	--	--	--
Congregational (United Church of Christ) [3]	--	--	--	--	--	--	--	--	2.2	1.8	1.9	1.9	1.9
Eastern Orthodox	--	--	--	--	--	--	--	--	0.6	0.6	0.7	0.7	0.7
Episcopal	--	--	--	--	--	--	--	--	3.5	3.5	3.3	3.3	3.3
Jewish	--	--	--	--	--	--	--	--	4.2	4.5	4.0	3.9	4.2
Latter Day Saints (Mormon)	--	--	--	--	--	--	--	--	0.3	0.2	0.3	0.2	0.1
Lutheran	--	--	--	--	--	--	--	--	7.2	6.2	6.9	6.0	5.7
Methodist	--	--	--	--	--	--	--	--	11.7	11.9	10.3	10.8	11.2
Muslim (Islamic) [3]	--	--	--	--	--	--	--	--	0.1	0.1	0.2	0.1	0.2
Presbyterian	--	--	--	--	--	--	--	--	6.7	6.7	6.1	5.9	6.3
Quaker (Society of Friends)	--	--	--	--	--	--	--	--	0.1	0.2	0.2	0.2	0.2
Roman Catholic	--	--	--	--	--	--	--	--	33.1	33.2	34.7	37.1	36.3
Seventh Day Adventist	--	--	--	--	--	--	--	--	0.3	0.4	0.5	0.2	0.4
Unitarian-Universalist	--	--	--	--	--	--	--	--	0.5	0.4	0.4	0.3	0.4
Other Protestant	--	--	--	--	--	--	--	--	5.3	4.8	5.5	5.7	5.8
Other religion	--	--	--	--	--	--	--	--	2.6	3.0	3.5	3.2	3.0
None	--	--	--	--	--	--	--	--	8.0	8.1	8.4	6.9	6.9

[1] Data for this item collected but not reported in 1973.
[2] See Appendix D for a discussion of variation in question texts and aggregation procedures.
[3] Text, order or number of response options may vary from year to year.

1979	1980	1981	1982	1983	1984	1985	1986	1987	1988	1989	1990	***PARENT'S DEMOGRAPHICS***
												FATHER'S EDUCATION
6.9	6.8	5.8	5.1	5.6	5.4	5.2	4.7	4.5	4.8	3.9	4.5	Grammar school or less
13.0	12.2	11.2	10.7	10.9	10.3	10.2	9.5	8.7	8.0	8.1	8.3	Some high school
27.6	29.4	29.2	29.7	29.4	29.9	28.6	27.9	28.1	28.0	28.7	29.2	High school graduate
4.5	4.3	4.6	4.6	4.8	5.2	5.0	4.8	5.1	4.8	5.1	4.8	Postsecondary school other than college
13.4	12.9	13.3	13.4	13.6	13.7	13.9	13.9	14.2	14.6	14.7	15.2	Some college
18.7	18.5	19.3	19.2	18.8	19.0	19.0	19.5	19.8	19.8	20.7	19.9	College degree
2.3	2.3	2.4	2.3	2.2	2.3	2.6	2.6	2.6	2.6	2.4	2.4	Some graduate school
13.6	13.6	14.3	15.0	14.6	14.2	15.7	17.0	17.0	17.4	16.4	15.8	Graduate degree
												FATHER'S CURRENT OCCUPATION [1]
0.9	0.8	0.8	0.8	0.8	0.8	0.8	0.8	0.8	0.9	0.8	0.7	Artist
28.0	27.6	27.7	28.5	28.0	27.9	27.9	28.9	29.5	28.3	28.4	25.9	Businessman
1.0	1.0	1.0	0.9	1.0	0.9	0.9	0.9	0.9	0.9	1.0	1.1	Clergy or religious worker
1.0	1.0	1.0	1.0	0.9	0.9	0.9	1.0	0.9	1.0	0.9	0.8	College teacher
2.1	2.1	2.1	2.1	2.1	1.9	2.0	2.2	2.2	2.3	2.0	2.0	Doctor or dentist
3.1	3.1	3.4	3.3	3.3	3.2	3.4	3.4	3.4	3.6	3.5	3.3	Educator (secondary school)
0.6	0.5	0.6	0.6	0.6	0.6	0.7	0.6	0.7	0.8	0.8	0.8	Elementary school teacher
8.5	8.5	8.5	9.0	8.4	8.5	8.3	8.4	7.8	7.9	7.3	7.3	Engineer
4.0	4.1	4.7	4.0	4.2	3.8	4.0	3.1	3.3	3.2	3.0	3.3	Farmer or forester
1.2	1.1	1.3	1.3	1.2	1.3	1.2	1.2	1.2	1.2	1.1	1.2	Health professional (non-MD)
1.5	1.4	1.5	1.6	1.4	1.4	1.5	1.7	1.6	1.7	1.5	1.5	Lawyer
1.5	1.6	1.9	1.8	1.6	1.6	1.6	1.6	1.8	1.6	1.7	2.0	Military career
0.5	0.6	0.5	0.5	0.6	0.5	0.5	0.5	0.5	0.5	0.5	0.4	Research scientist
10.1	10.4	9.9	10.1	9.8	10.2	9.6	9.7	9.5	9.6	9.4	9.5	Skilled worker
8.7	9.2	7.9	8.0	8.3	8.1	8.6	7.6	7.5	7.1	7.9	8.4	Semiskilled or unskilled worker
2.8	3.0	2.5	2.5	3.7	3.2	3.1	3.0	2.7	2.7	2.7	2.8	Unemployed
24.5	24.0	24.7	24.0	24.1	25.4	25.1	25.5	25.6	26.7	27.5	28.9	Other
												FATHER'S CURRENT RELIGIOUS PREFERENCE (Aggregated) [2]
35.8	35.9	37.0	35.5	33.5	44.7	47.0	30.4	48.1	45.1	49.3	49.1	Protestant
37.2	38.0	35.9	37.7	37.9	38.7	36.5	35.5	35.1	35.6	33.8	32.6	Roman Catholic
3.9	3.3	3.2	3.4	3.5	3.4	3.1	3.8	3.0	3.4	3.0	2.5	Jewish
16.3	15.8	17.1	16.8	18.0	5.4	4.8	21.5	4.9	5.8	5.1	5.9	Other
6.8	6.9	6.7	6.6	7.2	7.6	8.5	8.8	8.8	10.0	8.7	9.9	None
												FATHER'S CURRENT RELIGIOUS PREFERENCE (Disaggregated)
--	--	--	--	--	13.7	14.0	--	13.7	14.0	15.5	17.9	Baptist
--	--	--	--	--	0.2	0.3	--	0.4	0.4	0.4	0.5	Buddhist
--	--	--	--	--	1.8	1.5	--	1.4	1.2	1.1	1.0	Congregational (United Church of Christ) [3]
--	--	--	--	--	0.8	0.7	--	0.6	0.6	0.8	0.7	Eastern Orthodox
--	--	--	--	--	--	2.7	--	2.8	2.7	2.6	2.5	Episcopal
--	--	--	--	--	3.4	3.1	--	3.0	3.4	3.0	2.5	Jewish
--	--	--	--	--	0.2	0.2	--	0.2	0.2	0.2	0.2	Latter Day Saints (Mormon)
--	--	--	--	--	6.1	6.2	--	8.7	6.6	7.1	6.6	Lutheran
--	--	--	--	--	10.9	10.5	--	10.0	9.6	10.8	10.2	Methodist
--	--	--	--	--	0.2	0.2	--	0.2	0.3	0.4	0.3	Muslim (Islamic) [3]
--	--	--	--	--	--	5.3	--	5.4	4.9	5.6	4.7	Presbyterian
--	--	--	--	--	0.2	0.1	--	0.1	0.2	0.2	0.2	Quaker (Society of Friends)
--	--	--	--	--	38.7	36.5	--	35.1	35.6	33.8	32.6	Roman Catholic
--	--	--	--	--	0.3	0.2	--	0.2	0.2	0.4	0.2	Seventh Day Adventist
--	--	--	--	--	0.2	--	--	--	--	--	--	Unitarian-Universalist
--	--	--	--	--	10.7	5.6	--	5.0	4.9	5.0	4.9	Other Protestant
--	--	--	--	--	5.0	4.3	--	4.3	5.1	4.3	5.1	Other religion
--	--	--	--	--	7.6	8.5	--	8.8	10.0	8.7	9.9	None

[1] Data for this item collected but not reported in 1973.
[2] See Appendix D for a discussion of variation in question texts and aggregation procedures.
[3] Text, order or number of response options may vary from year to year.

HIGH SCHOOL EXPERIENCES AND ACHIEVEMENTS

	1966	1967	1968	1969	1970	1971	1972	1973	1974	1975	1976	1977	1978
YEAR GRADUATED FROM HIGH SCHOOL													
Current year (year of the survey)	--	--	--	--	--	92.6	93.5	94.7	93.4	93.9	93.7	93.4	94.8
Last year	--	--	--	--	--	--	--	2.2	2.8	2.5	2.6	2.7	2.4
Two years ago	--	--	--	--	--	--	--	0.6	0.8	0.7	0.8	0.8	0.6
Three years ago	--	--	--	--	--	--	--	1.4	1.7	1.6	1.7	1.9	1.3
High school equivalency certificate	--	--	--	--	--	--	--	0.5	0.6	0.6	0.7	0.8	0.6
Never completed high school	--	--	--	--	--	--	--	0.7	0.8	0.6	0.5	0.4	0.3
TYPE OF SECONDARY SCHOOL													
Public	83.5	--	--	83.4	82.7	--	84.8	--	--	--	--	--	--
Private: nondenominational [1]	3.1	--	--	3.5	2.6	--	3.9	--	--	--	--	--	--
Private: denominational [1]	13.4	--	--	13.1	14.7	--	11.3	--	--	--	--	--	--
AVERAGE GRADE IN HIGH SCHOOL													
A or A+	7.4	6.9	6.2	5.8	6.6	7.4	8.5	9.3	9.0	10.0	10.3	10.3	12.4
A-	12.8	12.0	11.6	10.7	11.3	12.0	13.3	12.4	13.6	12.7	13.8	13.2	14.9
B+	21.1	20.9	20.3	19.9	20.7	21.7	22.6	24.7	22.5	22.7	23.8	23.1	22.5
B	25.2	26.4	27.0	27.8	27.5	28.1	27.8	27.4	28.7	28.2	27.6	28.6	27.0
B-	13.3	13.8	14.1	14.5	14.5	13.9	11.9	12.7	11.4	12.2	10.6	11.2	10.7
C+	11.9	11.7	12.0	12.6	12.2	10.8	10.2	7.4	9.2	8.0	8.5	8.5	7.7
C	8.0	7.9	8.4	8.4	6.9	5.8	5.6	6.0	5.5	6.1	5.3	5.0	4.6
D	0.3	0.2	0.3	0.3	0.3	0.2	0.2	0.1	0.2	0.2	0.2	0.2	0.2
ACADEMIC RANK IN HIGH SCHOOL													
Top quarter [1]	--	--	60.6	59.7	48.1	49.7	49.8	--	--	--	--	--	49.3
Second quarter	--	--	24.7	24.2	30.6	30.4	32.1	--	--	--	--	--	33.1
Third quarter	--	--	12.4	13.4	18.4	17.5	16.3	--	--	--	--	--	15.9
Fourth quarter	--	--	2.3	2.7	2.9	2.4	1.8	--	--	--	--	--	1.6
Top 20 percent	--	--	--	--	--	--	--	--	--	--	--	--	--
Second 20 percent	--	--	--	--	--	--	--	--	--	--	--	--	--
Middle 20 percent	--	--	--	--	--	--	--	--	--	--	--	--	--
Fourth 20 percent	--	--	--	--	--	--	--	--	--	--	--	--	--
Bottom 20 percent	--	--	--	--	--	--	--	--	--	--	--	--	--
HAVE MET/EXCEEDED RECOMMENDED YEARS OF HIGH SCHOOL STUDY [2]													
English (4 years)	--	--	--	--	--	--	--	--	--	--	--	--	--
Mathematics (3 years)	--	--	--	--	--	--	--	--	--	--	--	--	--
Foreign language (2 years)	--	--	--	--	--	--	--	--	--	--	--	--	--
Physical science (2 years)	--	--	--	--	--	--	--	--	--	--	--	--	--
Biological science (2 years)	--	--	--	--	--	--	--	--	--	--	--	--	--
History or American government (1 year)	--	--	--	--	--	--	--	--	--	--	--	--	--
Computer science (1/2 year)	--	--	--	--	--	--	--	--	--	--	--	--	--
Art and/or music (1 year)	--	--	--	--	--	--	--	--	--	--	--	--	--
HAVE HAD SPECIAL TUTORING OR REMEDIAL WORK IN													
English	--	--	--	--	--	--	--	--	--	--	--	--	--
Reading	--	--	--	--	--	--	--	--	--	--	--	--	--
Mathematics	--	--	--	--	--	--	--	--	--	--	--	--	--
Social studies	--	--	--	--	--	--	--	--	--	--	--	--	--
Science	--	--	--	--	--	--	--	--	--	--	--	--	--
Foreign language	--	--	--	--	--	--	--	--	--	--	--	--	--
WILL NEED SPECIAL TUTORING OR REMEDIAL WORK IN [1]													
English	--	--	--	--	--	--	--	--	--	--	--	11.1	12.1
Reading	--	--	--	--	--	--	--	--	--	--	--	6.7	7.1
Mathematics	--	--	--	--	--	--	--	--	--	--	--	28.6	27.7
Social studies	--	--	--	--	--	--	--	--	--	--	--	3.1	4.5
Science	--	--	--	--	--	--	--	--	--	--	--	13.1	15.6
Foreign language	--	--	--	--	--	--	--	--	--	--	--	10.5	12.9

[1] Text, order or number of response options may vary from year to year.
[2] Based on recommendations of the National Commission on Excellence in Education

HIGH SCHOOL EXPERIENCES AND ACHIEVEMENTS

	1979	1980	1981	1982	1983	1984	1985	1986	1987	1988	1989	1990
YEAR GRADUATED FROM HIGH SCHOOL												
Current year (year of the survey)	93.6	92.9	94.5	94.8	94.1	93.7	93.7	92.5	92.5	93.6	93.5	92.1
Last year	2.8	2.8	2.1	2.3	2.3	2.5	2.3	2.3	2.5	1.9	2.5	2.4
Two years ago	0.7	0.9	0.6	0.6	0.7	0.6	0.6	0.6	0.7	0.7	0.6	0.8
Three years ago	1.6	2.0	1.6	1.4	1.7	1.8	1.9	2.6	2.4	2.0	1.9	3.0
High school equivalency certificate	0.8	0.9	0.7	0.7	1.0	1.1	1.3	1.6	1.6	1.6	1.2	1.7
Never completed high school	0.4	0.5	0.4	0.3	0.2	0.2	0.3	0.4	0.2	0.2	0.3	0.2
TYPE OF SECONDARY SCHOOL												
Public	86.2	86.8	--	--	85.0	84.2	--	--	--	--	--	--
Private: nondenominational [1]	2.9	2.8	--	--	4.1	4.2	--	--	--	--	--	--
Private: denominational [1]	10.9	10.4	--	--	11.0	11.6	--	--	--	--	--	--
AVERAGE GRADE IN HIGH SCHOOL												
A or A+	10.8	10.7	10.8	11.5	11.3	10.9	10.6	12.0	11.5	12.1	11.6	11.4
A-	13.4	13.5	13.3	13.2	12.7	12.3	13.0	13.1	12.3	13.7	13.9	13.5
B+	21.7	21.5	21.8	21.5	20.6	20.7	21.0	20.3	21.6	20.1	20.3	19.9
B	28.1	28.4	27.9	27.7	27.2	26.5	26.8	26.1	23.9	26.0	26.8	26.1
B-	11.4	11.2	11.9	11.9	12.2	12.8	12.1	12.5	14.9	12.7	12.7	13.0
C+	8.9	8.9	9.1	9.3	10.0	10.7	10.1	10.3	8.3	9.8	9.6	10.8
C	5.4	5.7	5.1	4.9	5.7	6.0	6.1	5.4	7.3	5.4	4.9	5.2
D	0.2	0.2	0.2	0.1	0.3	0.2	0.3	0.2	0.2	0.3	0.2	0.1
ACADEMIC RANK IN HIGH SCHOOL												
Top quarter [1]	--	--	--	--	--	--	--	--	--	--	--	--
Second quarter	--	--	--	--	--	--	--	--	--	--	--	--
Third quarter	--	--	--	--	--	--	--	--	--	--	--	--
Fourth quarter	--	--	--	--	--	--	--	--	--	--	--	--
Top 20 percent	42.3	43.0	43.8	43.7	44.0	44.1	45.1	45.6	--	--	--	--
Second 20 percent	22.0	22.0	22.5	22.2	21.3	21.2	21.4	21.5	--	--	--	--
Middle 20 percent	30.3	29.6	28.4	29.1	28.9	28.3	27.3	27.0	--	--	--	--
Fourth 20 percent	4.7	4.6	4.7	4.4	5.1	5.6	5.4	5.1	--	--	--	--
Bottom 20 percent	0.7	0.7	0.6	0.6	0.7	0.8	0.8	0.8	--	--	--	--
HAVE MET/EXCEEDED RECOMMENDED YEARS OF HIGH SCHOOL STUDY [2]												
English (4 years)	--	--	--	--	89.7	93.1	93.1	94.0	94.0	95.2	--	95.6
Mathematics (3 years)	--	--	--	--	80.3	83.2	83.1	86.2	86.6	90.3	--	90.4
Foreign language (2 years)	--	--	--	--	67.4	69.3	68.9	74.9	76.3	80.3	--	78.4
Physical science (2 years)	--	--	--	--	49.5	46.6	48.6	48.2	44.3	43.8	--	43.4
Biological science (2 years)	--	--	--	--	37.4	35.9	46.7	36.8	36.0	36.3	--	34.0
History or American government (1 year)	--	--	--	--	--	--	99.1	99.0	99.2	99.0	--	98.7
Computer science (1/2 year)	--	--	--	--	--	47.2	53.4	55.1	52.9	53.8	--	50.7
Art and/or music (1 year)	--	--	--	--	--	66.2	66.9	68.1	69.2	70.6	--	75.8
HAVE HAD SPECIAL TUTORING OR REMEDIAL WORK IN												
English	5.3	5.3	4.4	4.3	--	4.7	--	--	--	--	4.6	--
Reading	5.6	5.6	4.4	4.3	--	4.5	--	--	--	--	4.4	--
Mathematics	7.2	7.6	6.7	7.5	--	9.0	--	--	--	--	10.8	--
Social studies	4.5	5.0	3.3	3.2	--	3.4	--	--	--	--	3.4	--
Science	4.1	4.7	3.4	3.3	--	3.8	--	--	--	--	4.1	--
Foreign language	3.6	3.5	2.8	3.0	--	3.3	--	--	--	--	3.9	--
WILL NEED SPECIAL TUTORING OR REMEDIAL WORK IN [1]												
English	10.1	10.1	10.0	9.4	--	10.0	--	--	--	--	9.9	--
Reading	4.6	4.6	4.1	3.8	--	4.2	--	--	--	--	4.4	--
Mathematics	24.2	23.3	23.5	24.0	--	27.4	--	--	--	--	29.9	--
Social studies	3.2	3.3	2.9	2.9	--	3.3	--	--	--	--	3.7	--
Science	11.4	11.4	10.9	11.1	--	12.2	--	--	--	--	11.7	--
Foreign language	8.1	7.7	6.8	6.5	--	7.5	--	--	--	--	9.3	--

[1] Text, order or number of response options may vary from year to year.
[2] Based on recommendations of the National Commission on Excellence in Education

HIGH SCHOOL EXPERIENCES AND ACHIEVEMENTS

ACTIVITIES REPORTED IN THE LAST YEAR	1966	1967	1968	1969	1970	1971	1972	1973	1974	1975	1976	1977	1978
Frequently or Occasionally [1]													
Played a musical instrument	60.4	51.2	44.4	43.2	41.4	41.4	--	--	--	--	--	--	48.9
Stayed up all night	61.6	63.6	56.2	63.1	61.1	59.3	--	--	--	--	--	--	67.5
Participated in organized demonstrations	14.9	15.3	--	--	--	--	--	--	--	--	--	--	17.8
Worked in a local, state, or national political campaign [4]	--	--	13.5	17.9	15.1	14.2	--	--	--	--	--	--	9.1
Came late to class	46.8	54.3	51.0	56.1	56.7	51.1	--	--	--	--	--	--	--
Attended a religious service	--	--	93.4	92.1	89.6	89.0	--	--	--	--	--	--	88.1
Attended a public recital or concert [4]	75.2	--	--	--	--	--	--	--	--	--	--	--	84.2
Overslept and missed a class or appointment	16.8	16.8	14.8	19.3	19.2	17.2	--	--	--	--	--	--	--
Argued with a teacher in class	--	44.0	42.4	46.3	44.6	42.5	--	--	--	--	--	--	--
Was a guest in a teacher's home	--	38.8	--	--	--	--	--	--	--	--	--	--	--
Studied with other students	--	92.3	--	--	--	--	--	--	--	--	--	--	--
Drank beer	41.3	42.1	38.5	42.8	43.7	48.3	--	--	--	--	--	--	66.4
Took sleeping pills	--	7.1	6.8	7.4	6.0	5.0	--	--	--	--	--	--	3.2
Took a tranquilizing pill	--	14.0	12.0	13.0	10.5	8.4	--	--	--	--	--	--	5.8
Took vitamins	--	64.6	62.4	65.1	63.4	63.7	--	--	--	--	--	--	63.2
Tutored another student	--	49.6	50.3	47.2	47.8	46.9	--	--	--	--	--	--	--
Visited an art gallery or museum	--	77.5	76.9	76.5	74.0	70.6	--	--	--	--	--	--	--
Played chess	--	25.1	23.8	23.8	22.4	22.5	--	--	--	--	--	--	--
Performed volunteer work	--	--	--	--	--	--	--	--	--	--	--	--	--
Had vocational counseling	--	60.3	60.8	59.0	54.3	48.5	--	--	--	--	--	--	--
Read poetry not connected with a course	--	--	71.4	72.9	71.9	75.5	--	--	--	--	--	--	--
Wore glasses or contact lenses	--	--	--	--	57.9	--	--	--	--	--	--	--	52.8
Did not complete homework on time [4]	--	67.8	51.9	66.6	65.8	60.2	--	--	--	--	--	--	--
Won a varsity letter in a sport [3]	13.2	13.8	13.2	13.5	13.6	16.0	--	--	--	--	--	--	--
Frequently Only [1]													
Did extra, unassigned reading for a course	--	17.2	14.1	16.9	18.5	17.2	--	--	--	--	--	--	--
Voted in a student election	75.3	77.2	80.1	71.9	71.9	67.9	--	--	--	--	--	--	--
Studied in the library	32.8	[*]	38.1	42.1	37.4	36.2	--	--	--	--	--	--	--
Checked out a book or journal from the school library	61.9	63.2	59.7	57.2	52.6	50.9	--	--	--	--	--	--	--
Missed school due to illness	--	4.5	4.1	5.2	4.8	4.6	--	--	--	--	--	--	--
Typed a homework assignment	32.3	34.4	27.2	31.7	28.7	30.0	--	--	--	--	--	--	--
Smoked cigarettes	13.2	13.2	12.0	12.5	12.9	12.7	--	--	--	--	--	--	17.1
Discussed religion	--	41.9	37.7	35.6	33.0	32.1	--	--	--	--	--	--	--
Discussed politics	--	20.8	27.1	22.9	23.3	18.0	--	--	--	--	--	--	--
Discussed sports	--	27.3	27.5	28.4	27.2	27.6	--	--	--	--	--	--	--
Asked a teacher for advice after class	--	27.7	22.7	25.8	23.9	23.8	--	--	--	--	--	--	--
Felt depressed	--	--	--	--	--	--	--	--	--	--	--	--	--
Felt overwhelmed	--	--	--	--	--	--	--	--	--	--	--	--	--
Used a personal computer	--	--	--	--	--	--	--	--	--	--	--	--	--
Noted [2]													
Was elected president of one or more student organizations	23.3	22.3	20.6	19.9	18.8	18.4	--	--	--	--	--	--	--
Received a high rating in a state or regional music contest	13.7	12.4	12.1	11.9	11.1	12.2	--	--	--	--	--	--	--
Competed in state or regional speech or debate contest	7.8	6.8	6.4	6.3	5.5	5.0	--	--	--	--	--	--	--
Had a major part in a play	20.6	18.7	17.5	16.6	15.5	15.4	--	--	--	--	--	--	--
Won an award in an art competition [4]	6.3	6.5	6.4	6.4	6.3	6.4	--	--	--	--	--	--	--
Edited a school publication [4]	17.0	16.3	15.3	15.2	14.6	15.5	--	--	--	--	--	--	--
Had original writing or poetry published [4]	20.9	20.4	19.7	19.6	18.2	18.1	--	--	--	--	--	--	--
Won an award in a state or regional science contest [4]	2.6	2.3	2.2	2.1	2.1	1.7	--	--	--	--	--	--	--
Was a member of a scholastic honor society	36.7	35.2	33.2	31.8	30.8	31.5	--	--	--	--	--	--	--

[*] Results were not comparable to those of other years due to changes in question text or order.
[1] Response options for these items were "frequently", "occasionally" and "not at all".
[2] Response option for these items was a single bubble to be marked if the student engaged in the indicated activity.
[3] In 1966-1971, response option was a single bubble as noted in [2]. In 1984-1990, response options were as in [1].
[4] Text, order or number of response options may vary from year to year.

HIGH SCHOOL EXPERIENCES AND ACHIEVEMENTS

1979	1980	1981	1982	1983	1984	1985	1986	1987	1988	1989	1990	ACTIVITIES REPORTED IN THE LAST YEAR
												Frequently or Occasionally [1]
46.1	--	45.6	50.2	47.5	45.9	45.8	44.9	44.4	--	--	40.8	Played a musical instrument
68.3	--	71.2	74.0	71.8	73.2	73.8	75.7	74.5	81.1	78.4	79.0	Stayed up all night
19.2	--	21.4	23.2	22.3	--	--	--	--	37.4	37.5	41.1	Participated in organized demonstrations
8.6		9.0	8.3	7.7	9.0	--	--	--	8.6	--	--	Worked in a local, state, or national political campaign [4]
--	--	--	--	--	--	--	--	--	--	--	55.5	Came late to class
87.1	--	88.3	88.3	88.0	86.5	87.3	86.1	85.8	84.5	85.2	85.8	Attended a religious service
81.3	--	80.8	80.7	78.3	77.1	79.6	79.0	80.9	--	--	--	Attended a public recital or concert [4]
--	--	--	--	24.7	27.0	27.7	29.8	29.5	--	--	--	Overslept and missed a class or appointment
--	--	--	--	--	--	--	--	--	--	35.8	--	Argued with a teacher in class
--	--	--	--	--	--	32.9	32.9	--	30.5	29.2	29.8	Was a guest in a teacher's home
--	--	--	--	--	--	90.1	89.3	89.2	88.5	87.3	86.4	Studied with other students
65.7	--	70.1	70.5	67.5	62.5	61.6	60.7	59.9	59.5	54.8	51.7	Drank beer
3.1	--	3.0	2.9	2.8	--	--	--	--	--	3.2	--	Took sleeping pills
5.6	--	5.2	4.9	4.4	4.2	--	--	--	--	1.8	--	Took a tranquilizing pill
64.1	--	69.1	70.7	70.0	70.5	--	--	--	--	--	58.6	Took vitamins
--	--	--	--	--	--	43.7	43.1	44.3	45.1	45.0	46.4	Tutored another student
--	--	--	--	--	--	--	--	--	--	57.0	53.9	Visited an art gallery or museum
--	--	--	--	--	--	--	--	--	--	--	--	Played chess
--	--	--	--	--	71.4	72.0	71.1	--	--	64.8	65.3	Performed volunteer work
--	--	--	--	--	--	--	--	--	--	--	--	Had vocational counseling
--	--	--	--	--	--	--	--	--	--	--	--	Read poetry not connected with a course
50.5	--	50.0	49.6	49.6	--	--	--	--	--	--	55.3	Wore glasses or contact lenses
--	--	--	--	57.7	63.4	64.8	65.0	64.9	65.1	65.3	63.8	Did not complete homework on time [4]
--	--	--	--	--	37.7	38.2	38.5	40.3	39.2	41.2	42.6	Won a varsity letter in a sport [3]
												Frequently Only [1]
--	--	--	--	--	14.6	13.3	13.7	12.2	12.6	11.5	11.9	Did extra, unassigned reading for a course
--	--	--	--	--	--	--	--	--	--	--	--	Voted in a student election
--	--	--	--	--	--	--	--	--	--	15.0	11.2	Studied in the library
--	--	--	--	--	--	--	--	--	--	--	30.5	Checked out a book or journal from the school library
--	--	--	--		5.3	5.7	5.8	5.6	--	--	--	Missed school due to illness
--	--	--	--	--	--	--	--	--	--	--	--	Typed a homework assignment
16.7	--	15.0	14.8	13.6	11.8	11.3	11.5	10.4	11.8	11.5	11.9	Smoked cigarettes
--	--	--	--	--	--	--	--	--	23.1	--	--	Discussed religion
--	--	--	--	--	--	--	--	--	15.5	--	--	Discussed politics
--	--	--	--	--	--	--	--	--	29.0	--	--	Discussed sports
--	--	--	--	--	--	26.2	--	--	--	--	31.0	Asked a teacher for advice after class
--	--	--	--	--	--	19.6	21.6	20.7	27.2	24.7	26.5	Felt depressed
--	--	--	--	--	--	10.2	10.3	10.4	13.2	11.3	10.6	Felt overwhelmed
--	--	--	--	--	--	22.3	21.8	22.4	25.1	28.0	--	Used a personal computer
												Noted [2]
--	--	--	--	--	--	--	--	--	--	--	22.1	Was elected president of one or more student organizations
--	--	--	--	--	--	--	--	--	--	--	13.7	Received a high rating in a state or regional music contest
--	--	--	--	--	--	--	--	--	--	--	6.6	Competed in state or regional speech or debate contest
--	--	--	--	--	--	--	--	--	--	--	13.6	Had a major part in a play
--	--	--	--	--	--	--	--	--	--	--	9.3	Won an award in an art competition [4]
--	--	--	--	--	--	--	--	--	--	--	15.4	Edited a school publication [4]
--	--	--	--	--	--	--	--	--	--	--	15.8	Had original writing or poetry published [4]
--	--	--	--	--	--	--	--	--	--	--	3.7	Won an award in a state or regional science contest [4]
--	--	--	--	--	--	--	--	--	--	--	32.6	Was a member of a scholastic honor society

[1] Response options for these items were "frequently", "occasionally" and "not at all".
[2] Response option for these items was a single bubble to be marked if the student engaged in the indicated activity.
[3] In 1966-1971, response option was a single bubble as noted in [2]. In 1984-1990, response options were as in [1].
[4] Text, order or number of response options may vary from year to year.

COLLEGE CHOICE, APPLICATION AND MATRICULATION

COLLEGE CHOICE, APPLICATION AND MATRICULATION	1966	1967	1968	1969	1970	1971	1972	1973	1974	1975	1976	1977	1978
VERY IMPORTANT REASONS NOTED IN DECIDING TO GO TO COLLEGE [1]													
My parents wanted me to go	--	--	--	--	--	24.1	--	--	--	--	30.0	30.3	30.1
To be able to get a better job	--	--	--	--	--	70.1	--	--	--	--	70.4	77.2	75.7
Could not get a job	--	--	--	--	--	--	--	--	--	--	5.8	6.4	4.8
To get away from home	--	--	--	--	--	--	--	--	--	--	10.1	9.6	8.5
To gain a general education and appreciation of ideas	--	--	--	--	--	66.8	--	--	--	--	70.9	76.6	74.5
To improve my reading and study skills	--	--	--	--	--	22.7	--	--	--	--	37.5	44.6	40.2
There was nothing better to do	--	--	--	--	--	2.3	--	--	--	--	2.4	2.3	1.7
To make me a more cultured person	--	--	--	--	--	34.0	--	--	--	--	38.6	44.4	39.2
To be able to make more money	--	--	--	--	--	41.5	--	--	--	--	47.6	56.9	55.3
To learn more about things that interest me	--	--	--	--	--	73.9	--	--	--	--	78.6	83.6	78.8
To meet new and interesting people	--	--	--	--	--	55.3	--	--	--	--	62.4	67.0	64.6
To prepare myself for grad/prof school	--	--	--	--	--	29.3	--	--	--	--	43.4	45.6	44.4
VERY IMPORTANT REASONS NOTED FOR SELECTING FRESHMAN COLLEGE													
Relatives wanted me to come here [1]	--	--	--	--	--	9.5	[*]	[*]	9.1	9.3	7.8	7.3	6.6
Teacher advised me	--	--	--	--	--	--	--	5.3	5.4	5.0	4.0	4.4	4.0
College has a good academic reputation [1]	--	--	--	--	--	37.7	52.5	54.2	55.4	52.4	46.5	51.6	54.4
College has a good social reputation	--	--	--	--	--	--	--	--	--	--	--	--	--
Offered financial assistance	--	--	--	--	--	--	17.2	16.9	19.0	17.2	13.9	16.1	15.0
College offers special education programs	--	--	--	--	--	35.9	29.4	34.2	36.3	33.5	29.8	33.9	30.2
College has low tuition	--	--	--	--	--	18.7	20.2	27.5	28.0	25.2	18.3	19.6	17.0
Advice of guidance counselor	--	--	--	--	--	6.6	6.6	9.2	9.3	8.7	7.4	8.3	7.8
Wanted to live at home	--	--	--	--	--	12.2	13.7	14.3	13.7	14.3	12.1	12.7	10.4
Wanted to live near home	--	--	--	--	--	--	--	--	--	--	--	--	--
Friend suggested attending	--	--	--	--	--	--	--	--	--	7.6	7.7	8.7	7.0
College representative recruited me	--	--	--	--	--	--	--	--	--	3.3	3.3	3.6	3.3
Athletic department recruited me	--	--	--	--	--	--	--	--	--	--	--	--	--
Graduates go to top grad schools	--	--	--	--	--	--	--	--	--	--	--	--	--
Graduates get good jobs	--	--	--	--	--	--	--	--	--	51.9	--	--	--
Not accepted anywhere else	--	--	--	--	--	2.5	3.1	--	--	--	2.3	2.7	2.3
Advice of someone who attended	--	--	--	--	--	16.2	18.3	19.9	18.6	17.7	15.4	17.4	14.8
Not offered aid by first choice	--	--	--	--	--	--	--	--	--	--	--	--	--
Wanted to live away from home	--	--	--	--	--	--	22.2	19.6	17.0	17.8	--	--	--
THIS COLLEGE IS STUDENT'S													
First choice	--	--	--	--	--	--	--	--	75.9	79.4	77.8	76.4	76.7
Second choice	--	--	--	--	--	--	--	--	19.2	16.4	17.1	18.2	18.4
Less than second choice [1]	--	--	--	--	--	--	--	--	4.8	4.3	5.0	5.4	5.0
NUMBER OF APPLICATIONS SENT TO OTHER COLLEGES													
None (applied to only one college)	--	51.8	51.7	52.6	--	--	48.0	47.7	--	46.5	45.0	41.2	38.1
One	--	20.0	20.8	20.7	--	--	19.5	19.8	--	21.7	20.5	19.7	19.4
Two	--	14.0	13.7	13.6	--	--	14.6	14.4	--	14.0	14.9	16.6	17.8
Three	--	8.0	7.7	7.4	--	--	8.4	8.7	--	8.6	10.1	11.2	12.6
Four	--	3.6	3.4	3.3	--	--	4.3	4.7	--	4.3	4.7	5.5	5.9
Five	--	1.7	1.7	1.5	--	--	2.8	2.6	--	2.6	2.5	3.2	3.2
Six or more	--	0.9	1.0	0.9	--	--	2.5	2.1	--	2.3	2.3	2.7	3.0
NUMBER OF ACCEPTANCES FROM OTHER COLLEGES [2]													
None	--	--	--	--	--	--	--	--	--	27.3	25.0	23.7	19.0
One	--	--	--	--	--	--	--	--	--	34.5	33.2	32.4	32.7
Two	--	--	--	--	--	--	--	--	--	20.9	21.5	22.9	24.3
Three	--	--	--	--	--	--	--	--	--	10.3	12.0	12.6	14.3
Four	--	--	--	--	--	--	--	--	--	4.2	4.9	5.1	5.8
Five	--	--	--	--	--	--	--	--	--	1.6	1.9	1.9	2.3
Six or more	--	--	--	--	--	--	--	--	--	1.3	1.5	1.4	1.7

[*] Results were not comparable to those of other years due to changes in question text or order.
[1] Text, order or number of response options may vary from year to year.
[2] Students who applied to no other colleges not included.

COLLEGE CHOICE, APPLICATION AND MATRICULATION

1979	1980	1981	1982	1983	1984	1985	1986	1987	1988	1989	1990	
												VERY IMPORTANT REASONS NOTED IN DECIDING TO GO TO COLLEGE [1]
31.3	33.0	34.6	34.9	34.6	34.3	[*]	[*]	[*]	[*]	36.2	37.1	My parents wanted me to go
78.0	77.6	76.8	78.8	77.3	76.9	[*]	[*]	[*]	[*]	76.3	78.6	To be able to get a better job
5.6	5.9	6.2	7.8	6.4	5.5	[*]	[*]	[*]	[*]	7.5	7.6	Could not get a job
8.1	9.1	10.0	10.7	10.9	11.5	[*]	[*]	[*]	[*]	15.5	16.2	To get away from home
74.5	73.2	73.4	72.3	70.9	71.3	67.0	67.1	66.6	65.6	68.9	69.1	To gain a general education and appreciation of ideas
41.7	42.4	42.8	42.3	45.5	45.1	43.8	43.8	42.9	42.7	44.4	46.9	To improve my reading and study skills
1.9	1.9	2.1	2.1	2.1	1.8	2.2	2.2	2.1	2.4	1.9	1.8	There was nothing better to do
39.0	40.2	39.0	39.1	37.6	39.2	37.8	37.5	38.5	40.7	40.8	45.7	To make me a more cultured person
59.2	59.3	63.6	67.4	63.9	65.2	66.1	67.6	68.2	69.2	69.3	70.0	To be able to make more money
78.4	79.8	77.8	76.9	76.8	76.8	77.7	78.2	76.4	77.6	76.2	77.0	To learn more about things that interest me
63.8	64.8	63.6	62.7	62.2	63.1	--	--	--	--	--	--	To meet new and interesting people
45.9	47.9	47.3	46.8	49.6	50.5	48.0	49.7	49.9	53.1	55.1	57.1	To prepare myself for grad/prof school
												VERY IMPORTANT REASONS NOTED FOR SELECTING FRESHMAN COLLEGE
6.7	6.9	7.6	7.3	7.1	7.6	6.7	8.6	7.7	7.9	9.3	9.4	Relatives wanted me to come here [1]
4.0	4.2	4.2	3.8	4.0	4.5	4.1	4.2	3.7	4.1	3.6	3.8	Teacher advised me
52.8	54.1	56.5	56.3	56.6	59.5	57.6	62.3	59.0	57.7	54.9	53.5	College has a good academic reputation [1]
--	--	--	--	21.6	23.1	22.6	27.6	26.7	22.2	22.3	20.9	College has a good social reputation
16.7	17.1	16.5	18.0	22.6	21.5	21.7	23.0	21.9	23.6	24.7	27.5	Offered financial assistance
30.8	31.6	30.9	29.1	25.7	25.9	25.2	27.2	26.0	25.0	23.0	24.5	College offers special education programs
17.2	17.7	18.6	21.5	22.6	22.1	22.4	23.8	21.9	22.3	23.3	25.2	College has low tuition
7.7	8.2	7.8	7.9	8.4	8.2	7.9	8.8	7.6	7.8	7.3	7.6	Advice of guidance counselor
11.8	11.7	11.5	12.0	--	--	--	--	--	--	--	--	Wanted to live at home
--	--	--	--	22.5	21.6	20.4	22.1	20.9	22.2	22.5	24.1	Wanted to live near home
7.5	7.6	7.8	7.6	7.0	7.4	7.9	8.8	8.4	8.5	8.7	9.6	Friend suggested attending
3.8	4.0	3.6	3.4	2.9	2.9	3.4	3.3	3.2	3.4	3.3	3.5	College representative recruited me
--	--	--	--	2.1	1.9	2.4	2.4	2.4	2.6	2.6	2.9	Athletic department recruited me
--	--	--	--	27.7	27.8	27.0	27.5	29.6	--	25.1	25.0	Graduates go to top grad schools
--	--	--	--	48.4	48.2	46.4	47.9	49.2	[*]	44.0	43.0	Graduates get good jobs
2.5	2.0	2.1	2.1	--	--	--	--	--	--	--	--	Not accepted anywhere else
15.7	16.1	16.1	15.7	--	--	--	--	--	--	--	--	Advice of someone who attended
--	--	--	--	--	4.1	4.3	4.7	4.3	4.7	5.3	--	Not offered aid by first choice
--	--	--	--	--	--	--	--	--	--	--	--	Wanted to live away from home
												THIS COLLEGE IS STUDENT'S
76.4	76.7	75.5	74.5	74.7	74.2	72.7	71.4	71.1	68.3	68.7	71.0	First choice
18.4	18.1	19.2	19.7	19.9	20.1	21.0	21.9	21.9	23.4	23.4	22.3	Second choice
5.2	5.3	5.4	5.7	5.4	5.7	6.3	6.7	7.0	8.4	7.8	6.7	Less than second choice [1]
												NUMBER OF APPLICATIONS SENT TO OTHER COLLEGES
40.5	40.8	38.8	39.4	38.5	36.0	34.0	35.7	36.3	32.5	32.3	33.3	None (applied to only one college)
18.8	17.9	19.2	17.4	19.0	19.1	22.8	18.4	16.9	16.1	16.2	16.3	One
17.0	16.9	17.5	16.8	17.1	17.4	16.8	16.1	15.8	16.7	16.6	16.8	Two
12.1	12.4	12.5	13.0	12.3	13.3	12.6	13.6	13.6	14.6	14.8	14.3	Three
5.5	5.8	6.1	6.4	6.1	6.7	6.3	7.2	7.6	8.4	8.4	8.2	Four
3.2	3.2	3.1	3.4	3.5	3.8	3.7	4.5	4.7	5.3	5.4	5.1	Five
3.0	2.9	2.9	3.5	3.5	3.8	3.6	4.6	5.1	6.4	6.3	6.0	Six or more
												NUMBER OF ACCEPTANCES FROM OTHER COLLEGES [2]
21.5	18.2	17.7	[*]	16.9	17.5	16.9	17.1	16.4	14.5	15.4	--	None
31.9	31.9	32.4	[*]	32.2	31.3	31.5	30.0	30.0	29.1	28.1	--	One
23.4	24.5	25.2	[*]	24.5	24.2	24.1	23.9	23.4	24.5	23.7	--	Two
13.9	14.9	14.7	[*]	15.1	15.6	15.7	15.8	16.6	17.0	16.9	--	Three
5.4	6.2	5.9	[*]	6.4	6.5	6.7	7.4	7.6	8.1	8.4	--	Four
2.2	2.3	2.3	[*]	2.6	2.7	2.9	3.3	3.3	3.7	3.9	--	Five
1.6	1.9	1.8	[*]	2.3	2.2	2.3	2.6	2.8	3.1	3.6	--	Six or more

[*] Results were not comparable to those of other years due to changes in question text or order.
[1] Text, order or number of response options may vary from year to year.
[2] Students who applied to no other colleges not included.

DEGREE, MAJOR AND CAREER PLANS

DEGREE, MAJOR AND CAREER PLANS	1966	1967	1968	1969	1970	1971	1972	1973	1974	1975	1976	1977	1978
HIGHEST ACADEMIC DEGREE PLANNED AT ANY COLLEGE													
None	4.8	4.4	4.1	2.3	2.7	[*]	3.6	[*]	3.9	3.7	3.3	2.3	2.3
Vocational certificate	--	--	--	--	--	--	--	--	--	--	--	--	--
Associate or equivalent	7.3	9.3	8.4	10.9	10.3	[*]	10.1	[*]	10.9	9.4	9.7	10.2	9.3
Bachelor's degree (B.A., B.S., etc.)	46.1	43.7	44.2	44.0	43.6	[*]	41.3	[*]	39.2	37.0	37.2	36.4	38.5
Master's degree (M.A., M.S., etc.)	32.3	32.9	33.1	32.6	30.8	[*]	28.9	[*]	28.0	29.6	29.4	30.8	29.9
Ph.D. or Ed.D.	5.2	5.7	6.1	6.1	6.5	[*]	6.8	[*]	6.9	7.6	7.6	8.0	8.1
M.D., D.D.S., D.V.M., or D.O.	1.9	1.9	1.7	1.8	2.2	[*]	4.3	[*]	5.3	5.5	5.7	5.2	5.6
LL.B. or J.D. (law)	[*]	[*]	[*]	[*]	0.9	[*]	2.1	[*]	2.6	3.1	3.5	3.7	3.6
B.D. or M.Div. (divinity)	0.1	0.1	0.2	0.2	0.1	[*]	0.2	[*]	0.1	0.4	0.4	0.4	0.3
Other	1.8	1.8	2.1	1.9	2.9	[*]	2.7	[*]	3.0	3.7	3.3	3.0	2.4
HIGHEST ACADEMIC DEGREE AT FRESHMAN COLLEGE													
None	--	--	--	--	--	--	8.5	7.1	8.6	6.7	6.6	5.2	4.8
Vocational certificate	--	--	--	--	--	--	--	--	--	--	--	--	--
Associate or equivalent	--	--	--	--	--	--	27.4	28.6	31.5	29.0	29.2	30.3	28.0
Bachelor's degree (B.A., B.S., etc.)	--	--	--	--	--	--	51.1	51.2	46.6	48.9	49.2	49.3	52.6
Master's degree (M.A., M.S., etc.)	--	--	--	--	--	--	7.7	8.6	7.9	9.2	8.4	9.3	9.4
Ph.D. or Ed.D.	--	--	--	--	--	--	1.0	1.1	0.9	1.1	1.1	1.2	1.2
M.D., D.D.S., D.V.M., or D.O.	--	--	--	--	--	--	0.8	0.9	1.0	1.0	1.1	1.0	1.2
LL.B. or J.D. (law)	--	--	--	--	--	--	0.4	0.4	0.4	0.7	0.6	0.7	0.7
B.D. or M.Div. (divinity)	--	--	--	--	--	--	0.1	0.0	0.1	0.3	0.4	0.3	0.2
Other	--	--	--	--	--	--	3.0	2.0	2.9	3.1	3.4	2.6	1.9
MAJOR PLANS (AGGREGATED) [1,2]													
Agriculture (including forestry)	0.1	0.2	0.1	0.2	0.3	0.7	0.8	1.0	1.6	1.9	2.0	2.0	2.0
Biological sciences	3.1	3.1	3.1	2.7	2.9	2.7	3.0	5.7	5.6	5.5	5.7	4.5	4.4
Business	10.9	12.2	12.1	12.5	12.3	14.2	13.7	14.0	15.5	18.9	17.5	19.2	23.1
Education	17.5	17.6	19.3	19.2	19.1	15.9	11.5	19.6	16.4	15.5	14.3	13.6	12.1
Engineering	0.3	0.3	0.3	0.4	0.4	0.3	0.4	0.7	1.0	1.3	1.6	1.8	2.3
English	7.3	6.8	6.4	6.1	4.7	3.5	2.5	2.1	1.7	1.4	1.4	1.3	1.2
Health professions (nursing, pre-med, etc.)	9.8	9.9	10.3	10.7	13.7	16.1	18.7	16.5	13.3	13.2	12.4	14.6	13.7
History or political science	55.7	5.6	5.5	5.0	4.2	3.1	2.7	[*]	2.7	2.6	2.4	2.4	2.4
Humanities (other)	7.4	7.0	5.9	5.4	4.8	4.2	4.9	3.5	3.1	2.5	2.5	2.1	2.7
Fine arts (applied and performing)	10.3	10.6	10.5	10.4	10.3	9.7	9.8	8.3	7.1	6.3	6.2	5.9	4.9
Mathematics or statistics	4.5	4.3	4.2	3.8	3.5	2.9	2.2	1.6	1.3	1.1	0.8	0.7	0.8
Physical sciences	1.2	1.1	0.9	1.0	0.9	0.8	0.8	1.1	1.2	1.3	1.4	1.3	1.3
Pre-professional	2.3	2.3	2.1	2.3	2.8	3.9	5.1	--	--	--	--	--	--
Social sciences	[*]	[*]	[*]	[*]	12.5	12.2	11.1	[*]	9.3	8.9	8.2	8.0	7.6
Other technical	0.9	1.2	1.1	1.6	1.8	2.6	2.7	2.0	6.5	6.7	6.5	6.5	7.0
Other non-technical	5.2	4.8	4.5	4.1	3.6	5.0	4.5	3.5	9.1	8.8	10.3	9.1	8.6
Undecided	1.8	1.6	1.9	2.1	2.2	2.3	4.8	4.9	4.7	5.5	5.1	5.3	5.3
CAREER PLANS (AGGREGATED) [1,3]													
Artist (including performer)	8.9	8.1	7.8	7.6	7.6	7.2	8.0	4.5	7.1	6.5	8.2	8.1	7.7
Business	3.3	3.3	3.3	3.6	4.2	4.4	4.8	[*]	8.5	10.0	11.6	13.8	15.8
Clergy or other religious worker	0.8	0.3	0.2	0.3	0.2	0.2	0.2	0.4	0.4	0.4	0.2	0.2	0.2
College teacher	1.5	0.9	0.9	0.8	0.9	0.6	0.6	1.0	0.8	0.6	0.3	0.3	0.3
Doctor (M.D. or D.D.S.)	1.7	1.5	1.3	1.3	1.5	2.0	2.8	3.4	3.5	3.3	3.3	3.0	3.4
Education (elementary)	15.7	17.6	19.4	19.3	16.6	13.8	11.1	8.2	6.7	5.8	8.1	7.5	6.8
Education (secondary)	18.4	18.8	18.1	17.2	14.4	11.0	8.4	5.9	5.2	4.5	4.4	3.9	3.3
Engineer	0.2	0.2	0.2	0.3	0.4	0.2	0.3	0.7	0.8	1.1	1.5	1.5	2.2
Farmer, rancher, or forester	0.2	0.1	0.1	0.2	0.4	0.7	0.7	1.0	1.3	1.5	1.4	1.5	1.3
Health professional (non-M.D.)	6.6	6.3	5.7	6.0	6.4	8.8	10.4	11.6	12.5	12.8	10.8	10.5	9.7
Lawyer (or judge)	0.7	0.6	0.6	0.8	1.0	1.4	2.0	2.5	2.3	2.5	3.0	3.4	3.4
Nurse	5.3	5.4	6.1	6.0	8.7	8.6	9.8	9.2	10.2	9.9	9.1	8.8	7.7
Research scientist	1.9	1.6	1.7	1.4	1.6	1.5	1.5	2.4	1.4	1.5	1.7	1.6	1.7
Other	31.0	25.2	23.7	24.3	24.5	26.1	24.9	[*]	26.9	25.9	25.4	25.2	24.8
Undecided	[*]	9.9	10.8	11.0	11.8	13.5	14.4	11.6	12.6	13.8	10.9	10.7	11.6

[*] Results were not comparable to those of other years due to changes in question text or order.

[1] Figures for the years 1966-1976 are from annual Norms Reports. Figures from 1977-1990 computed from disaggregated majors/careers (see Appendix E)

[2] List of disaggregated majors was expanded in 1970, 1973, 1978 and 1982.

[3] List of careers for 1973-1976 not directly comparable to other years.

1979	1980	1981	1982	1983	1984	1985	1986	1987	1988	1989	1990	***DEGREE, MAJOR AND CAREER PLANS***
												HIGHEST ACADEMIC DEGREE PLANNED AT ANY COLLEGE
1.8	2.3	2.3	1.7	1.9	1.5	2.1	2.0	2.0	1.8	0.9	1.3	None
--	--	--	--	1.4	0.9	1.0	0.9	1.4	0.7	0.6	0.7	Vocational certificate
8.9	9.5	9.5	9.8	8.2	8.1	7.1	6.9	6.2	4.5	5.0	6.3	Associate or equivalent
37.5	38.1	38.2	38.8	36.6	37.4	38.1	36.4	34.7	32.3	31.6	27.6	Bachelor's degree (B.A., B.S., etc.)
32.1	30.1	31.2	30.2	30.7	31.2	31.7	33.8	34.5	36.8	37.6	38.1	Master's degree (M.A., M.S., etc.)
8.0	7.3	7.2	7.6	8.0	8.7	8.6	9.2	10.0	11.4	11.5	12.5	Ph.D. or Ed.D.
5.5	5.9	5.6	5.7	6.0	6.1	6.0	5.6	5.4	5.9	6.0	6.6	M.D., D.D.S., D.V.M., or D.O.
3.5	3.7	3.5	3.8	3.9	3.7	3.4	3.6	4.2	4.8	4.9	4.9	LL.B. or J.D. (law)
0.4	0.4	0.3	0.3	0.6	0.5	0.3	0.2	0.2	0.3	0.2	0.2	B.D. or M.Div. (divinity)
2.3	2.6	2.3	2.1	2.7	2.0	1.7	1.5	1.4	1.6	1.7	1.8	Other
												HIGHEST ACADEMIC DEGREE AT FRESHMAN COLLEGE
4.2	4.6	4.5	3.8	3.6	3.4	3.5	3.2	3.4	3.7	3.7	3.6	None
--	--	--	--	2.1	1.2	1.4	1.3	2.3	0.9	1.0	1.5	Vocational certificate
29.8	28.4	29.8	30.4	24.6	25.2	24.4	23.5	21.8	17.9	19.3	25.3	Associate or equivalent
50.6	51.2	50.5	50.4	52.8	54.3	54.2	55.5	55.7	57.3	57.5	51.5	Bachelor's degree (B.A., B.S., etc.)
10.2	9.8	10.1	10.1	9.9	10.6	11.3	11.9	12.0	14.2	13.0	12.6	Master's degree (M.A., M.S., etc.)
1.2	1.3	1.2	1.3	1.6	1.5	1.5	1.5	1.5	2.0	1.8	1.7	Ph.D. or Ed.D.
1.2	1.4	1.1	1.3	1.4	1.2	1.2	1.2	1.1	1.2	1.1	1.1	M.D., D.D.S., D.V.M., or D.O.
0.7	0.8	0.7	0.9	1.0	0.8	0.7	0.6	0.7	1.0	0.9	0.8	LL.B. or J.D. (law)
0.2	0.3	0.2	0.3	0.6	0.3	0.2	0.2	0.2	0.2	0.2	0.2	B.D. or M.Div. (divinity)
1.9	2.2	1.8	1.6	2.5	1.5	1.6	1.2	1.3	1.7	1.5	1.8	Other
												MAJOR PLANS (AGGREGATED) [1]
1.7	1.8	2.2	1.4	0.9	1.0	1.0	0.9	0.8	1.0	0.5	0.7	Agriculture (including forestry)
3.9	3.8	3.7	3.8	3.4	4.2	3.4	3.8	3.7	3.5	3.6	3.7	Biological sciences
23.1	24.5	25.0	25.7	26.0	27.5	27.5	27.0	26.0	24.0	23.3	20.0	Business
12.5	11.6	10.8	9.0	8.9	9.6	10.4	12.1	13.3	13.9	13.3	14.1	Education
2.5	3.2	3.1	3.6	3.5	3.0	3.0	2.9	2.7	2.6	2.9	2.7	Engineering
1.2	1.1	1.1	1.0	1.2	1.2	1.3	1.5	1.5	1.6	1.7	1.6	English
12.9	13.3	13.4	13.9	15.4	14.8	13.0	11.3	10.1	11.4	12.4	14.7	Health professions (nursing, pre-med, etc.)
2.2	2.2	2.1	2.0	2.1	2.4	2.7	2.9	3.1	3.8	3.7	3.5	History or political science
2.6	2.4	2.6	2.6	2.2	2.4	2.6	2.7	3.1	2.9	2.6	2.5	Humanities (other)
5.2	5.0	4.8	4.3	3.9	3.5	3.4	3.9	4.2	4.0	3.9	4.1	Fine arts (applied and performing)
0.6	0.6	0.6	0.7	0.8	0.9	0.8	0.7	0.6	0.6	0.6	0.7	Mathematics or statistics
1.2	1.0	1.0	1.0	1.0	1.1	0.9	1.0	0.9	1.0	1.2	0.9	Physical sciences
--	--	--	--	--	--	--	--	--	--	--	--	Pre-professional
7.8	6.8	6.2	5.5	5.8	6.4	7.3	7.7	7.9	8.8	9.4	9.7	Social sciences
6.9	8.6	9.4	10.7	10.2	7.2	5.8	4.7	3.9	3.7	3.6	4.4	Technical (other)
9.5	8.7	8.9	8.8	8.5	8.9	9.8	9.4	10.3	9.5	9.6	9.4	Nontechnical (other)
5.6	5.5	5.4	5.5	5.7	6.2	6.9	7.5	7.6	7.6	7.9	7.1	Undecided
												CAREER PLANS (AGGREGATED) [1]
8.1	7.8	7.8	7.6	7.0	6.4	7.3	7.6	8.1	7.5	7.2	6.6	Artist (including performer)
16.7	17.9	18.2	19.3	19.5	21.2	22.7	22.6	22.0	21.1	19.6	16.6	Business
0.1	0.1	0.1	0.1	0.1	0.1	0.1	0.1	0.1	0.1	0.1	0.2	Clergy or other religious worker
0.2	0.2	0.2	0.2	0.2	0.2	0.2	0.3	0.3	0.3	0.4	0.3	College teacher
3.5	3.6	3.4	3.6	4.0	4.0	3.8	3.9	3.8	4.0	4.1	4.3	Doctor (M.D. or D.D.S.)
7.0	6.9	6.4	5.5	5.7	6.1	6.7	7.9	8.8	9.7	8.7	9.2	Education (elementary)
3.4	2.7	2.7	2.1	2.4	2.8	3.1	3.5	3.9	4.0	4.0	4.6	Education (secondary)
2.3	2.9	2.9	3.6	3.3	2.9	2.9	2.8	2.6	2.5	2.6	2.4	Engineer
1.2	1.1	1.3	0.9	0.5	0.5	0.7	0.4	0.4	0.4	0.4	0.4	Farmer, rancher, or forester
9.1	8.6	8.5	8.1	8.5	8.4	7.4	6.8	7.2	7.0	7.2	7.2	Health professional (non-M.D.)
3.4	3.5	3.4	3.9	3.6	3.7	3.7	4.0	4.5	5.3	5.4	5.5	Lawyer (or judge)
7.0	7.2	7.3	7.7	8.4	7.5	6.2	5.1	4.0	4.4	4.8	6.5	Nurse
1.3	1.3	1.2	1.2	1.2	1.2	1.2	1.1	1.2	1.3	1.4	1.2	Research scientist
25.4	24.8	25.1	25.3	24.5	22.5	21.9	20.7	20.7	19.2	21.2	23.3	Other
11.4	11.3	11.3	10.8	11.3	12.3	12.1	13.2	12.6	12.9	13.0	11.8	Undecided

[1] Figures for the years 1966-1976 are from annual Norms Reports. Figures from 1977-1990 computed from disaggregated majors/careers (see Appendix E)

[2] List of disaggregated majors was expanded in 1970, 1973, 1978 and 1982.

[3] List of careers for 1973-1976 not directly comparable to other years.

DEGREE, MAJOR AND CAREER PLANS

	1966	1967	1968	1969	1970	1971	1972	1973	1974	1975	1976	1977	1978
MAJOR PLANS (DISAGGREGATED) [1]													
Arts and Humanities													
Art, fine and applied	--	--	--	--	--	--	--	--	--	--	--	3.0	2.8
English, language and literature	--	--	--	--	--	--	--	--	--	--	--	1.3	1.2
History	--	--	--	--	--	--	--	--	--	--	--	0.5	0.5
Journalism	--	--	--	--	--	--	--	--	--	--	--	1.7	1.7
Language (except English)	--	--	--	--	--	--	--	--	--	--	--	0.9	0.9
Music	--	--	--	--	--	--	--	--	--	--	--	1.6	1.5
Philosophy	--	--	--	--	--	--	--	--	--	--	--	0.1	0.1
Theater or drama	--	--	--	--	--	--	--	--	--	--	--	--	1.0
Speech or drama	--	--	--	--	--	--	--	--	--	--	--	0.9	--
Speech	--	--	--	--	--	--	--	--	--	--	--	--	0.2
Theology or religion	--	--	--	--	--	--	--	--	--	--	--	0.2	0.1
Other arts and humanities	--	--	--	--	--	--	--	--	--	--	--	0.9	0.6
Biological Sciences													
Biology (general)	--	--	--	--	--	--	--	--	--	--	--	1.8	1.8
Biochemistry or biophysics	--	--	--	--	--	--	--	--	--	--	--	0.4	0.4
Botany	--	--	--	--	--	--	--	--	--	--	--	0.2	0.2
Marine (life) sciences	--	--	--	--	--	--	--	--	--	--	--	0.5	0.4
Microbiology or bacteriology	--	--	--	--	--	--	--	--	--	--	--	0.4	0.4
Zoology	--	--	--	--	--	--	--	--	--	--	--	0.5	0.5
Other biological sciences	--	--	--	--	--	--	--	--	--	--	--	0.7	0.7
Business													
Accounting	--	--	--	--	--	--	--	--	--	--	--	5.8	6.3
Business administration (general)	--	--	--	--	--	--	--	--	--	--	--	4.2	4.9
Finance	--	--	--	--	--	--	--	--	--	--	--	0.3	0.4
Marketing	--	--	--	--	--	--	--	--	--	--	--	1.3	1.7
Management	--	--	--	--	--	--	--	--	--	--	--	2.3	2.8
Secretarial studies	--	--	--	--	--	--	--	--	--	--	--	6.2	5.9
Other business	--	--	--	--	--	--	--	--	--	--	--	1.0	1.1
Education													
Business education	--	--	--	--	--	--	--	--	--	--	--	0.5	0.3
Elementary education	--	--	--	--	--	--	--	--	--	--	--	4.9	4.4
Music or art education	--	--	--	--	--	--	--	--	--	--	--	0.7	0.6
Physical education or recreation	--	--	--	--	--	--	--	--	--	--	--	2.4	2.1
Secondary education	--	--	--	--	--	--	--	--	--	--	--	0.9	0.8
Special education	--	--	--	--	--	--	--	--	--	--	--	3.4	3.1
Other education	--	--	--	--	--	--	--	--	--	--	--	0.8	0.8
Engineering													
Aeronautical or astronautical	--	--	--	--	--	--	--	--	--	--	--	0.2	0.2
Civil	--	--	--	--	--	--	--	--	--	--	--	0.2	0.3
Chemical	--	--	--	--	--	--	--	--	--	--	--	0.3	0.4
Electrical or electronic	--	--	--	--	--	--	--	--	--	--	--	0.3	0.4
Industrial	--	--	--	--	--	--	--	--	--	--	--	0.1	0.1
Mechanical	--	--	--	--	--	--	--	--	--	--	--	0.2	0.3
Other engineering	--	--	--	--	--	--	--	--	--	--	--	0.5	0.6
Physical Sciences													
Astronomy	--	--	--	--	--	--	--	--	--	--	--	0.0	0.0
Atmospheric sciences	--	--	--	--	--	--	--	--	--	--	--	0.0	0.0
Chemistry	--	--	--	--	--	--	--	--	--	--	--	0.6	0.7
Earth science	--	--	--	--	--	--	--	--	--	--	--	0.2	0.1
Marine sciences	--	--	--	--	--	--	--	--	--	--	--	0.2	0.2
Mathematics	--	--	--	--	--	--	--	--	--	--	--	0.7	0.8
Physics	--	--	--	--	--	--	--	--	--	--	--	0.1	0.2
Statistics	--	--	--	--	--	--	--	--	--	--	--	0.0	0.0
Other physical sciences	--	--	--	--	--	--	--	--	--	--	--	0.2	0.1
Professional													
Architecture or urban planning	--	--	--	--	--	--	--	--	--	--	--	0.4	0.4
Home economics	--	--	--	--	--	--	--	--	--	--	--	1.8	1.3
Health technology	--	--	--	--	--	--	--	--	--	--	--	3.7	3.8
Library or archival sciences	--	--	--	--	--	--	--	--	--	--	--	0.1	0.1
Nursing	--	--	--	--	--	--	--	--	--	--	--	8.4	7.6
Pharmacy	--	--	--	--	--	--	--	--	--	--	--	0.6	0.6
Predentistry, premedicine, prevet	--	--	--	--	--	--	--	--	--	--	--	2.8	2.9
Therapy (physical, occupational, etc.)	--	--	--	--	--	--	--	--	--	--	--	2.8	2.6
Other professional	--	--	--	--	--	--	--	--	--	--	--	1.6	1.6

[1] Data collected in disaggregated form but not reported in 1966-1976.

1979	1980	1981	1982	1983	1984	1985	1986	1987	1988	1989	1990	***DEGREE, MAJOR AND CAREER PLANS***
												MAJOR PLANS (DISAGGREGATED) [1]
												Arts and Humanities
3.0	3.1	2.9	2.7	2.4	2.0	2.1	2.4	2.7	2.3	2.3	2.2	Art, fine and applied
1.2	1.1	1.1	1.0	1.2	1.2	1.3	1.5	1.5	1.6	1.7	1.6	English, language and literature
0.4	0.4	0.4	0.3	0.3	0.4	0.4	0.4	0.5	0.5	0.6	0.6	History
1.9	1.7	2.0	1.9	1.7	1.7	2.0	2.0	1.9	1.9	1.8	1.7	Journalism
0.7	0.6	0.7	0.7	0.6	0.8	0.8	0.9	0.8	0.9	0.8	0.7	Language (except English)
1.4	1.2	1.3	1.0	1.0	0.9	0.9	0.9	0.9	0.9	0.7	0.9	Music
0.1	0.1	0.1	0.1	0.1	0.1	0.1	0.1	0.1	0.1	0.1	0.1	Philosophy
1.0	0.9	0.9	0.9	0.7	0.7	0.8	0.7	0.8	0.8	0.7	0.8	Theater or drama
--	--	--	--	--	--	--	--	--	--	--	--	Speech or drama
0.2	0.2	0.2	0.2	0.2	0.2	0.1	0.1	0.1	0.2	0.2	0.1	Speech
0.1	0.1	0.1	0.1	0.1	0.0	0.1	0.1	0.1	0.1	0.1	0.1	Theology or religion
0.7	0.7	0.8	0.8	0.7	0.8	0.8	0.9	1.3	1.0	0.9	0.8	Other arts and humanities
												Biological Sciences
1.6	1.6	1.5	1.5	1.6	1.7	1.8	2.0	1.8	1.7	1.7	1.7	Biology (general)
0.4	0.4	0.4	0.4	0.5	0.6	0.4	0.4	0.4	0.4	0.4	0.4	Biochemistry or biophysics
0.1	0.1	0.1	0.1	0.0	0.1	0.0	0.0	0.0	0.0	0.0	0.0	Botany
0.4	0.3	0.3	0.2	0.2	0.3	0.2	0.3	0.4	0.4	0.5	0.7	Marine (life) sciences
0.4	0.3	0.3	0.4	0.3	0.4	0.2	0.3	0.3	0.2	0.2	0.1	Microbiology or bacteriology
0.4	0.5	0.4	0.4	0.3	0.4	0.4	0.3	0.3	0.3	0.3	0.3	Zoology
0.6	0.6	0.7	0.8	0.5	0.7	0.4	0.5	0.5	0.5	0.5	0.5	Other biological sciences
												Business
6.0	6.4	6.4	6.8	7.1	7.1	7.1	6.9	6.6	6.4	6.5	5.8	Accounting
5.5	6.2	6.4	6.4	6.2	6.5	6.8	6.9	6.3	6.5	5.7	4.7	Business administration (general)
0.4	0.4	0.5	0.6	0.7	0.9	1.0	1.2	1.1	1.2	1.1	0.6	Finance
1.9	1.9	2.1	2.1	2.4	2.4	2.8	2.7	3.5	2.8	2.8	2.2	Marketing
2.8	3.3	3.4	3.7	3.5	4.3	4.5	4.6	4.2	4.0	3.8	3.2	Management
5.2	4.9	4.6	4.8	4.4	4.5	3.7	2.8	2.4	1.5	1.7	1.8	Secretarial studies
1.3	1.4	1.6	1.3	1.7	1.8	1.6	1.9	1.9	1.6	1.7	1.7	Other business
												Education
0.3	0.2	0.2	0.2	0.2	0.2	0.3	0.3	0.3	0.3	0.3	0.2	Business education
4.7	4.6	4.6	4.2	4.4	5.0	5.6	7.0	7.4	8.5	7.9	8.7	Elementary education
0.5	0.5	0.4	0.4	0.4	0.3	0.3	0.4	0.4	0.4	0.5	0.5	Music or art education
2.3	1.7	1.5	1.1	1.0	1.0	0.9	0.9	0.9	0.7	0.8	0.8	Physical education or recreation
0.8	0.8	0.9	0.7	0.9	1.2	1.4	1.6	2.0	2.0	2.1	2.2	Secondary education
3.3	3.1	2.6	1.8	1.6	1.4	1.3	1.3	1.1	1.1	1.1	1.2	Special education
0.6	0.7	0.6	0.6	0.4	0.5	0.6	0.6	1.2	0.9	0.6	0.5	Other education
												Engineering
0.2	0.3	0.2	0.3	0.3	0.3	0.4	0.4	0.4	0.5	0.4	0.5	Aeronautical or astronautical
0.3	0.3	0.3	0.2	0.2	0.2	0.2	0.2	0.2	0.2	0.3	0.3	Civil
0.5	0.6	0.7	0.7	0.6	0.4	0.4	0.4	0.4	0.4	0.4	0.4	Chemical
0.4	0.6	0.6	0.8	0.9	0.8	0.8	0.7	0.7	0.6	0.6	0.5	Electrical or electronic
0.2	0.2	0.1	0.2	0.2	0.2	0.2	0.2	0.1	0.1	0.2	0.1	Industrial
0.3	0.4	0.4	0.4	0.4	0.4	0.4	0.3	0.3	0.3	0.3	0.3	Mechanical
0.6	0.8	0.8	1.0	0.9	0.7	0.6	0.7	0.6	0.5	0.7	0.6	Other engineering
												Physical Sciences
0.0	0.0	0.0	0.0	0.0	0.0	0.0	0.0	0.0	0.1	0.1	0.0	Astronomy
0.0	0.0	0.0	0.0	0.0	0.0	0.0	0.0	0.0	0.0	0.0	0.0	Atmospheric sciences
0.6	0.6	0.6	0.6	0.6	0.6	0.5	0.6	0.5	0.5	0.5	0.4	Chemistry
0.2	0.1	0.1	0.1	0.1	0.1	0.1	0.1	0.0	0.1	0.1	0.1	Earth science
0.2	0.1	0.1	0.1	0.1	0.1	0.1	0.1	0.1	0.1	0.2	0.2	Marine sciences
0.6	0.6	0.6	0.7	0.8	0.9	0.8	0.7	0.6	0.6	0.6	0.7	Mathematics
0.1	0.1	0.1	0.1	0.1	0.2	0.1	0.1	0.2	0.1	0.2	0.1	Physics
0.0	0.0	0.0	0.0	0.0	0.0	0.0	0.0	0.0	0.0	0.0	0.0	Statistics
0.1	0.1	0.1	0.1	0.1	0.1	0.1	0.1	0.1	0.1	0.1	0.1	Other physical sciences
												Professional
0.6	0.5	0.4	0.4	0.3	0.4	0.3	0.5	0.5	0.6	0.7	0.9	Architecture or urban planning
1.4	1.2	0.9	0.8	0.8	0.9	0.8	0.6	0.8	0.6	0.4	0.4	Home economics
3.4	3.2	2.6	2.4	2.7	2.1	1.8	1.5	1.8	1.4	1.2	1.6	Health technology
0.1	0.1	0.1	0.0	0.0	0.0	0.0	0.0	0.0	0.0	0.0	0.0	Library or archival sciences
6.8	7.0	7.1	7.6	8.2	7.6	6.1	5.0	3.9	4.4	4.9	7.0	Nursing
0.5	0.4	0.4	0.4	0.6	0.7	0.7	0.7	0.8	1.2	1.1	1.2	Pharmacy
2.9	3.2	2.9	3.0	3.2	3.1	3.2	2.9	2.5	3.0	3.1	3.4	Predentistry, premedicine, prevet
2.7	2.7	3.0	2.9	3.4	3.4	3.0	2.7	2.9	2.8	3.3	3.1	Therapy (physical, occupational, etc.)
1.7	1.6	1.6	1.5	1.5	1.7	1.4	1.3	1.7	1.4	1.5	1.5	Other professional

[1] Data collected in disaggregated form but not reported in 1966-1976.

DEGREE, MAJOR AND CAREER PLANS

DEGREE, MAJOR AND CAREER PLANS	1966	1967	1968	1969	1970	1971	1972	1973	1974	1975	1976	1977	1978
MAJOR PLANS (DISAGGREGATED) [1]													
Social Sciences													
Anthropology	--	--	--	--	--	--	--	--	--	--	--	0.1	0.1
Economics	--	--	--	--	--	--	--	--	--	--	--	0.2	0.2
Geography	--	--	--	--	--	--	--	--	--	--	--	0.0	0.0
Political science	--	--	--	--	--	--	--	--	--	--	--	1.9	1.9
Psychology	--	--	--	--	--	--	--	--	--	--	--	3.3	3.4
Social work	--	--	--	--	--	--	--	--	--	--	--	3.2	2.9
Sociology	--	--	--	--	--	--	--	--	--	--	--	0.8	0.7
Other social sciences	--	--	--	--	--	--	--	--	--	--	--	0.4	0.3
Ethnic studies	--	--	--	--	--	--	--	--	--	--	--	--	--
Women's studies	--	--	--	--	--	--	--	--	--	--	--	--	--
Technical Fields													
Building trades	--	--	--	--	--	--	--	--	--	--	--	0.0	0.0
Data processing/computer programming	--	--	--	--	--	--	--	--	--	--	--	1.3	1.4
Drafting or design	--	--	--	--	--	--	--	--	--	--	--	0.2	0.3
Electronics	--	--	--	--	--	--	--	--	--	--	--	0.1	0.1
Mechanics	--	--	--	--	--	--	--	--	--	--	--	0.0	0.0
Other technical	--	--	--	--	--	--	--	--	--	--	--	0.3	0.2
Other Majors													
Agriculture	--	--	--	--	--	--	--	--	--	--	--	1.4	1.6
Communications (radio, T.V.)	--	--	--	--	--	--	--	--	--	--	--	1.1	1.4
Computer science	--	--	--	--	--	--	--	--	--	--	--	0.9	1.2
Forestry	--	--	--	--	--	--	--	--	--	--	--	0.6	0.4
Law enforcement	--	--	--	--	--	--	--	--	--	--	--	1.4	1.4
Military science	--	--	--	--	--	--	--	--	--	--	--	0.0	0.0
Other fields	--	--	--	--	--	--	--	--	--	--	--	1.4	1.1
Undecided	--	--	--	--	--	--	--	--	--	--	--	5.3	5.3
CAREER PLANS (DISAGGREGATED) [1]													
Accountant or actuary	--	--	--	--	--	--	--	--	--	--	--	5.7	6.2
Actor or entertainer	--	--	--	--	--	--	--	--	--	--	--	1.0	1.0
Architect or urban planner	--	--	--	--	--	--	--	--	--	--	--	0.5	0.5
Artist	--	--	--	--	--	--	--	--	--	--	--	2.4	2.1
Business, clerical	--	--	--	--	--	--	--	--	--	--	--	4.9	4.6
Business executive	--	--	--	--	--	--	--	--	--	--	--	6.1	7.3
Business owner	--	--	--	--	--	--	--	--	--	--	--	0.8	1.0
Business, sales	--	--	--	--	--	--	--	--	--	--	--	1.2	1.3
Clergy or other religious worker	--	--	--	--	--	--	--	--	--	--	--	0.2	0.2
Clinical psychologist	--	--	--	--	--	--	--	--	--	--	--	1.4	1.4
College teacher	--	--	--	--	--	--	--	--	--	--	--	0.3	0.3
Computer programmer	--	--	--	--	--	--	--	--	--	--	--	2.4	3.0
Conservationist or forester	--	--	--	--	--	--	--	--	--	--	--	1.1	0.8
Dentist (including orthodontist)	--	--	--	--	--	--	--	--	--	--	--	0.5	0.6
Dietitian or home economist	--	--	--	--	--	--	--	--	--	--	--	1.1	1.0
Engineer	--	--	--	--	--	--	--	--	--	--	--	1.5	2.2
Farmer, rancher, or forester	--	--	--	--	--	--	--	--	--	--	--	0.4	0.5
Foreign service worker	--	--	--	--	--	--	--	--	--	--	--	0.7	0.7
Homemaker (full-time)	--	--	--	--	--	--	--	--	--	--	--	0.3	0.3
Interior decorator	--	--	--	--	--	--	--	--	--	--	--	1.1	1.0
Interpreter (translator)	--	--	--	--	--	--	--	--	--	--	--	0.4	0.3
Laboratory technician or hygienist	--	--	--	--	--	--	--	--	--	--	--	3.3	3.0
Law enforcement officer	--	--	--	--	--	--	--	--	--	--	--	1.0	0.9
Lawyer (or judge)	--	--	--	--	--	--	--	--	--	--	--	3.4	3.4
Military service (career)	--	--	--	--	--	--	--	--	--	--	--	0.2	0.4
Musician (performer, composer)	--	--	--	--	--	--	--	--	--	--	--	1.2	1.2
Nurse	--	--	--	--	--	--	--	--	--	--	--	8.8	7.7
Optometrist	--	--	--	--	--	--	--	--	--	--	--	0.2	0.1
Pharmacist	--	--	--	--	--	--	--	--	--	--	--	0.7	0.6
Physician	--	--	--	--	--	--	--	--	--	--	--	2.5	2.8
School counselor	--	--	--	--	--	--	--	--	--	--	--	0.4	0.3
School principal, superintendent	--	--	--	--	--	--	--	--	--	--	--	0.0	0.0
Research scientist	--	--	--	--	--	--	--	--	--	--	--	1.6	1.7
Social or welfare worker	--	--	--	--	--	--	--	--	--	--	--	4.5	3.9
Statistician	--	--	--	--	--	--	--	--	--	--	--	0.1	0.1
Therapist (occupational, physical, etc.)	--	--	--	--	--	--	--	--	--	--	--	3.6	3.4
Elementary teacher	--	--	--	--	--	--	--	--	--	--	--	7.5	6.8
Secondary teacher	--	--	--	--	--	--	--	--	--	--	--	3.5	3.0
Veterinarian	--	--	--	--	--	--	--	--	--	--	--	1.6	1.6
Writer or journalist	--	--	--	--	--	--	--	--	--	--	--	2.4	2.4
Skilled worker	--	--	--	--	--	--	--	--	--	--	--	0.4	0.4
Other	--	--	--	--	--	--	--	--	--	--	--	8.4	8.3
Undecided	--	--	--	--	--	--	--	--	--	--	--	10.7	11.6

[1] Data collected in disaggregated form but not reported in 1966-1976.

1979	1980	1981	1982	1983	1984	1985	1986	1987	1988	1989	1990	***DEGREE, MAJOR AND CAREER PLANS***
												MAJOR PLANS (DISAGGREGATED) [1]
												Social Sciences
0.1	0.1	0.1	0.1	0.1	0.1	0.1	0.1	0.1	0.2	0.2	0.2	Anthropology
0.3	0.3	0.3	0.3	0.3	0.3	0.3	0.3	0.3	0.3	0.3	0.3	Economics
0.0	0.0	0.0	0.0	0.0	0.0	0.0	0.0	0.0	0.0	0.0	0.1	Geography
1.8	1.8	1.7	1.7	1.8	2.0	2.3	2.5	2.6	3.3	3.1	2.9	Political science
3.7	3.2	3.1	3.1	3.3	3.9	4.7	5.0	5.2	5.9	6.3	6.1	Psychology
2.8	2.4	1.9	1.5	1.5	1.5	1.6	1.7	1.5	1.5	1.6	2.1	Social work
0.6	0.5	0.5	0.3	0.4	0.4	0.4	0.4	0.5	0.6	0.6	0.6	Sociology
0.3	0.3	0.3	0.2	0.2	0.2	0.2	0.2	0.3	0.3	0.4	0.3	Other social sciences
--	--	--	0.0	0.0	0.0	0.0	0.0	0.0	0.0	0.0	0.0	Ethnic studies
--	--	--	0.0	0.0	0.0	0.0	0.0	0.0	0.0	0.0	0.0	Women's studies
												Technical Fields
0.0	0.0	0.0	0.0	0.0	0.0	0.0	0.0	0.0	0.0	0.0	0.1	Building trades
1.6	2.3	2.9	3.7	3.2	1.9	1.8	1.3	0.8	0.8	0.9	0.9	Data processing/computer programming
0.3	0.4	0.4	0.3	0.3	0.2	0.3	0.3	0.3	0.2	0.2	0.3	Drafting or design
0.1	0.1	0.1	0.1	0.1	0.1	0.1	0.1	0.0	0.0	0.1	0.0	Electronics
0.0	0.0	0.0	0.0	0.0	0.0	0.0	0.0	0.0	0.0	0.0	0.0	Mechanics
0.1	0.2	0.2	0.2	0.2	0.2	0.2	0.2	0.1	0.3	0.2	0.2	Other technical
												Other Majors
1.3	1.4	1.8	1.1	0.7	0.9	0.8	0.7	0.7	0.9	0.4	0.6	Agriculture
1.7	1.9	2.1	2.1	2.1	2.2	2.6	2.8	3.0	3.1	3.0	2.5	Communications (radio, T.V.)
1.4	2.4	3.2	4.0	3.7	2.7	1.6	1.3	0.9	1.0	1.0	1.4	Computer science
0.4	0.4	0.4	0.3	0.2	0.1	0.2	0.2	0.1	0.1	0.1	0.1	Forestry
1.0	0.9	0.7	1.0	1.0	0.8	1.0	1.0	1.0	1.0	1.0	1.0	Law enforcement
0.0	0.0	0.0	0.0	0.0	0.0	0.1	0.0	0.0	0.1	0.0	0.1	Military science
1.7	1.3	1.5	1.5	1.4	1.6	1.9	1.7	1.9	1.4	1.9	2.1	Other fields
5.6	5.5	5.4	5.5	5.7	6.2	6.9	7.5	7.6	7.6	7.9	7.1	Undecided
												CAREER PLANS (DISAGGREGATED) [1]
5.8	6.2	6.1	6.5	6.7	6.8	7.1	6.5	6.4	6.4	6.3	5.5	Accountant or actuary
1.1	1.0	1.0	1.0	0.9	0.9	1.0	1.0	1.1	1.1	0.9	0.9	Actor or entertainer
0.8	0.8	0.5	0.6	0.5	0.5	0.5	0.7	0.7	0.8	0.8	1.1	Architect or urban planner
2.1	2.4	2.2	2.1	1.9	1.6	1.6	1.9	2.2	1.8	1.8	1.6	Artist
4.1	3.9	3.8	3.5	3.6	3.5	3.1	2.4	2.2	1.6	1.7	2.0	Business, clerical
8.2	9.2	9.4	10.1	10.0	11.4	11.8	12.1	11.5	11.0	9.9	8.3	Business executive
1.2	1.3	1.5	1.5	1.5	1.7	2.0	2.3	2.3	2.4	2.0	1.5	Business owner
1.5	1.2	1.2	1.2	1.3	1.3	1.8	1.7	1.8	1.3	1.4	1.3	Business, sales
0.1	0.1	0.1	0.1	0.1	0.1	0.1	0.1	0.1	0.1	0.1	0.2	Clergy or other religious worker
1.6	1.4	1.4	1.4	1.4	1.7	2.0	2.1	2.4	2.6	2.5	2.5	Clinical psychologist
0.2	0.2	0.2	0.2	0.2	0.2	0.2	0.3	0.3	0.3	0.4	0.3	College teacher
3.3	4.9	6.4	8.0	7.0	4.6	3.2	2.5	1.8	1.8	1.9	2.2	Computer programmer
0.7	0.7	0.7	0.5	0.3	0.2	0.4	0.3	0.2	0.2	0.3	0.3	Conservationist or forester
0.6	0.7	0.5	0.5	0.6	0.5	0.4	0.5	0.5	0.5	0.5	0.6	Dentist (including orthodontist)
0.7	0.7	0.8	0.6	0.5	0.5	0.4	0.4	0.4	0.3	0.4	0.3	Dietitian or home economist
2.3	2.9	2.9	3.6	3.3	2.9	2.9	2.8	2.6	2.5	2.6	2.4	Engineer
0.5	0.4	0.6	0.4	0.2	0.3	0.3	0.1	0.2	0.2	0.1	0.1	Farmer, rancher, or forester
0.6	0.6	0.6	0.7	0.7	0.8	1.1	1.2	1.3	1.4	1.2	1.0	Foreign service worker
0.4	0.2	0.3	0.2	0.1	0.1	0.2	0.2	0.2	0.1	0.2	0.4	Homemaker (full-time)
1.1	1.0	1.0	1.0	0.8	0.8	1.1	1.0	1.2	0.9	0.9	0.8	Interior decorator
0.3	0.3	0.3	0.3	0.3	0.4	0.3	0.3	0.3	0.3	0.3	0.2	Interpreter (translator)
2.7	2.3	1.9	2.0	1.9	1.5	1.1	1.1	1.0	0.6	0.6	0.6	Laboratory technician or hygienist
0.7	0.6	0.4	0.5	0.6	0.5	0.6	0.6	0.6	0.5	0.4	0.5	Law enforcement officer
3.4	3.5	3.4	3.9	3.6	3.7	3.7	4.0	4.5	5.3	5.4	5.5	Lawyer (or judge)
0.3	0.2	0.2	0.2	0.3	0.3	0.3	0.3	0.2	0.2	0.2	0.3	Military service (career)
1.1	0.9	1.0	0.9	0.9	0.7	0.8	0.8	0.8	0.8	0.7	0.7	Musician (performer, composer)
7.0	7.2	7.3	7.7	8.4	7.5	6.2	5.1	4.0	4.4	4.8	6.5	Nurse
0.2	0.2	0.2	0.2	0.3	0.3	0.2	0.2	0.2	0.3	0.2	0.2	Optometrist
0.6	0.5	0.5	0.5	0.7	0.8	0.8	0.8	1.0	1.3	1.2	1.2	Pharmacist
2.9	2.9	2.9	3.1	3.4	3.5	3.4	3.4	3.3	3.5	3.6	3.7	Physician
0.4	0.3	0.3	0.2	0.3	0.3	0.3	0.4	0.4	0.4	0.5	0.6	School counselor
0.0	0.0	0.0	0.0	0.0	0.0	0.0	0.0	0.0	0.0	0.0	0.0	School principal, superintendent
1.3	1.3	1.2	1.2	1.2	1.2	1.2	1.1	1.2	1.3	1.4	1.2	Research scientist
3.9	3.2	2.6	2.0	2.1	2.1	2.3	2.3	2.2	2.2	2.1	2.3	Social or welfare worker
0.1	0.1	0.1	0.1	0.1	0.1	0.1	0.1	0.1	0.1	0.1	0.0	Statistician
3.5	3.4	3.6	3.3	3.8	3.8	3.5	3.2	3.5	3.4	3.8	3.6	Therapist (occupational, physical, etc.)
7.0	6.9	6.4	5.5	5.7	6.1	6.7	7.9	8.8	9.7	8.7	9.2	Elementary teacher
3.0	2.4	2.4	1.9	2.1	2.5	2.8	3.1	3.5	3.6	3.5	4.0	Secondary teacher
1.4	1.5	1.5	1.5	1.3	1.5	1.4	1.1	1.1	1.1	1.0	1.3	Veterinarian
2.7	2.5	2.6	2.6	2.5	2.4	2.8	2.9	2.8	2.9	2.9	2.6	Writer or journalist
0.4	0.5	0.4	0.3	0.4	0.2	0.3	0.3	0.4	0.2	0.3	0.4	Skilled worker
8.9	8.1	8.1	7.5	7.4	7.7	7.9	7.7	8.3	7.4	9.5	10.4	Other
11.4	11.3	11.3	10.8	11.3	12.3	12.1	13.2	12.6	12.9	13.0	11.8	Undecided

[1] Data collected in disaggregated form but not reported in 1966-1976.

COLLEGE EXPERIENCES AND EXPECTATIONS	1966	1967	1968	1969	1970	1971	1972	1973	1974	1975	1976	1977	1978
PLANNED RESIDENCE FOR FALL													
With parents or relatives	--	--	--	--	--	--	--	41.1	41.6	37.5	42.5	41.5	34.3
Other private home, apartment or room	--	--	--	--	--	--	--	3.6	5.6	4.9	5.9	5.6	4.4
College dormitory	--	--	--	--	--	--	--	53.5	51.1	55.0	49.2	50.7	59.1
Fraternity or sorority house	--	--	--	--	--	--	--	0.1	0.2	0.2	0.2	0.1	0.2
Other campus student housing	--	--	--	--	--	--	--	0.9	0.7	1.4	1.3	1.3	1.2
Other type of housing	--	--	--	--	--	--	--	0.8	0.8	1.0	0.9	0.7	0.8
PREFERRED RESIDENCE FOR FALL													
With parents or relatives	--	--	--	--	--	--	--	--	21.1	19.4	20.6	20.1	17.5
Other private home, apartment or room	--	--	--	--	--	--	--	--	25.8	23.8	28.1	25.2	23.4
College dormitory	--	--	--	--	--	--	--	--	44.8	46.7	41.5	45.2	49.4
Fraternity or sorority house	--	--	--	--	--	--	--	--	3.0	3.0	3.1	3.3	3.9
Other campus student housing	--	--	--	--	--	--	--	--	3.1	4.2	4.0	3.9	3.9
Other type of housing	--	--	--	--	--	--	--	--	2.2	2.9	2.7	2.3	2.0
STUDENTS ESTIMATE CHANCES ARE VERY GOOD THAT THEY WILL [1]													
Be satisfied with this college	--	--	--	--	68.4	--	64.8	59.9	58.8	58.6	56.5	59.2	60.3
Make at least a B average	--	--	--	--	--	--	33.8	36.0	38.6	39.1	41.1	40.5	41.8
Graduate with honors	--	3.0	3.1	3.4	3.8	--	6.6	8.0	8.7	8.7	10.0	10.1	10.2
Be elected to an academic honor society	--	3.0	2.8	2.4	2.5	--	4.6	5.0	5.2	5.2	6.6	6.7	7.5
Get a bachelor's degree (B.A., B.S., etc)	--	--	--	--	--	--	60.7	62.8	58.6	63.3	61.8	62.2	64.5
Be elected to a student office	--	2.0	1.7	1.4	1.3	--	1.5	1.6	1.6	1.7	2.0	2.1	2.2
Join social fraternity, sorority or club	--	33.2	28.9	24.6	21.8	--	19.2	16.6	14.3	16.0	17.4	19.2	20.2
Change major field	--	17.3	15.6	17.3	16.7	--	16.7	15.1	12.4	12.7	12.2	12.7	12.9
Change career choice	--	18.0	16.1	17.9	17.0	--	17.7	14.9	12.7	13.1	12.3	12.8	13.1
Need extra time to complete degree	--	--	--	--	--	--	4.5	4.7	4.5	4.9	4.7	5.0	4.7
Fail one or more courses		2.1	1.3	1.7	2.3	--	1.9	1.9	1.5	1.8	1.5	1.7	1.4
Get tutoring help in specific courses	--	--	--	--	--	--	--	--	--	7.3	8.5	9.5	10.1
Live in a coeducational dorm	--	--	--	--	--	--	--	19.2	17.7	19.1	19.5	20.9	24.9
Seek vocational counseling	--	--	--	--	--	--	13.9	11.9	10.7	9.9	8.2	7.9	7.8
Seek personal counseling	--	--	--	--	--	--	6.0	5.3	5.1	5.1	4.1	4.2	4.3
Get a job to help pay for college expenses	--	--	--	--	--	--	--	--	--	--	40.8	43.0	42.0
Have to work at an outside job	--	--	--	--	--	--	34.4	34.2	33.4	31.3	26.7	27.4	24.2
Work full-time while attending college	--	--	--	--	--	--	--	--	--	--	--	--	--
Participate in student protests or demonstrations		4.2	3.9	--	--	--	--	--	--	--	--	--	2.8
Transfer to another college	--	13.1	12.1	12.7	13.0	--	14.0	14.2	14.2	13.3	13.4	12.1	11.0
Drop out of this college temporarily (excluding transferring)	--	1.1	1.0	1.3	1.5	-- --	1.9	2.0	1.8	1.8	1.6	1.6	1.2
Drop out permanently	--	0.7	0.6	0.7	0.9	--	1.1	1.2	1.0	0.9	0.9	0.9	0.8
Get married while in college	--	8.6	7.5	9.6	8.9	--	9.0	8.0	7.4	7.3	6.8	6.4	5.9
Get married within a year after college	--	27.4	22.6	24.2	21.7	--	18.8	20.2	19.3	18.7	18.2	17.2	17.2
Enlist in the Armed Services before graduating	--	--	--	0.3	0.3	--	1.1	1.1	1.0	--	--	--	--
Be more successful after graduating than most students attending this college	--	--	--	7.0	7.0	--	13.2	15.2	14.7	--	--	--	--
Play varsity athletics	--	--	--	--	--	--	--	--	--	--	--	--	--
Find a job after college graduation in the field for which you were trained	--	--	--	--	--	--	52.5	57.2	56.5	60.8	61.6	68.4	69.1
CONCERN ABOUT ABILITY TO FINANCE COLLEGE EDUCATION													
None (I am confident that I will have sufficient funds)	35.3	34.4	35.0	33.0	32.4	32.4	33.5	33.6	36.1	32.8	31.3	30.4	31.0
Some concern (but I will probably have enough funds)	55.5	56.2	55.9	55.9	55.4	56.4	50.4	48.4	48.0	49.0	51.2	51.3	52.7
Major concern (not sure I will have enough funds to complete college)	9.2	9.3	9.1	11.1	12.2	11.2	16.1	18.0	15.9	18.2	17.5	18.3	16.3

[1] Text, order or number of response options may vary from year to year.

1979	1980	1981	1982	1983	1984	1985	1986	1987	1988	1989	1990	***COLLEGE EXPERIENCES AND EXPECTATIONS***
												PLANNED RESIDENCE FOR FALL
37.2	35.9	30.5	33.2	36.0	33.8	31.4	30.6	29.0	30.5	30.6	24.3	With parents or relatives
6.3	6.0	5.0	4.7	5.9	4.7	6.0	7.2	8.5	6.5	6.9	7.1	Other private home, apartment or room
54.3	55.4	62.1	60.1	55.5	59.3	59.4	58.7	59.2	60.2	58.5	64.8	College dormitory
0.2	0.2	0.2	0.1	0.2	0.1	0.2	0.2	0.2	0.2	0.2	0.1	Fraternity or sorority house
1.3	1.7	1.5	1.1	1.7	1.4	2.1	2.1	2.3	2.0	3.0	2.7	Other campus student housing
0.7	0.8	0.7	0.9	0.7	0.7	0.8	1.1	0.8	0.6	0.8	1.1	Other type of housing
												PREFERRED RESIDENCE FOR FALL
19.4	19.1	17.8	18.7	19.0	18.3	16.7	15.7	13.8	14.7	14.2	--	With parents or relatives
22.9	22.9	23.2	24.5	26.4	26.4	27.1	28.3	31.8	32.0	32.9	--	Other private home, apartment or room
47.4	48.0	48.7	46.3	43.3	43.3	43.6	41.4	39.4	39.1	38.5	--	College dormitory
3.6	4.1	4.4	4.9	4.6	5.2	5.6	6.3	6.9	6.6	5.8	--	Fraternity or sorority house
4.0	3.9	4.0	3.8	4.7	5.0	5.0	5.9	5.9	5.7	6.2	--	Other campus student housing
2.7	2.0	1.9	1.8	2.0	1.8	2.1	2.3	2.1	1.9	2.4	--	Other type of housing
												STUDENTS ESTIMATE CHANCES ARE VERY GOOD THAT THEY WILL [1]
59.6	59.5	60.8	60.5	60.5	60.4	58.0	57.2	57.5	55.5	53.8	55.5	Be satisfied with this college
41.8	42.6	41.7	42.5	42.4	41.6	40.9	40.5	39.3	41.3	40.7	40.9	Make at least a B average
10.6	11.7	10.3	11.0	11.5	11.1	11.4	10.7	11.1	10.8	11.8	12.3	Graduate with honors
7.4	8.1	7.6	7.0	7.4	7.4	7.6	6.8	7.2	7.0	7.7	8.0	Be elected to an academic honor society
63.8	64.4	65.2	65.8	66.4	68.3	67.6	69.1	69.0	72.1	70.1	67.4	Get a bachelor's degree (B.A., B.S., etc)
2.4	2.8	2.7	2.7	2.8	3.1	3.3	3.2	3.1	3.3	3.3	3.4	Be elected to a student office
19.7	19.6	20.9	19.2	18.9	19.1	20.3	19.8	20.1	20.0	19.9	18.9	Join social fraternity, sorority or club
12.9	12.6	13.2	12.7	12.9	13.7	14.2	14.1	14.8	15.3	14.2	12.7	Change major field
13.1	12.8	13.0	12.4	12.7	13.4	13.9	13.6	14.4	14.6	13.7	12.2	Change career choice
5.2	5.2	5.5	5.3	5.2	5.5	6.5	6.6	6.8	7.5	7.5	8.4	Need extra time to complete degree
1.5	1.4	1.4	1.2	1.1	1.1	1.2	1.2	1.0	1.3	1.2	0.9	Fail one or more courses
9.8	10.3	10.7	10.4	10.2	11.5	12.3	12.5	12.7	14.9	14.3	18.1	Get tutoring help in specific courses
24.0	24.5	28.2	27.6	25.5	27.9	28.0	--	--	--	--	--	Live in a coeducational dorm
7.5	6.7	6.8	6.1	6.7	5.9	6.7	6.2	6.0	5.7	4.8	5.6	Seek vocational counseling
4.5	4.4	4.2	3.8	4.0	3.8	4.2	3.7	4.1	4.3	3.8	3.9	Seek personal counseling
41.9	41.9	42.9	40.7	38.9	40.0	39.9	39.6	40.6	38.3	37.9	38.6	Get a job to help pay for college expenses
25.3	25.1	25.4	23.5	23.6	22.6	23.9	23.1	23.9	22.8	22.9	23.0	Have to work at an outside job
--	--	--	3.0	3.2	3.4	3.4	3.4	3.4	3.6	3.7	4.1	Work full-time while attending college
3.6	4.3	3.4	4.1	3.4	3.6	4.3	4.7	5.9	5.9	7.1	8.1	Participate in student protests or demonstrations
12.0	10.8	11.3	10.4	10.4	10.8	11.1	10.1	10.6	12.7	12.6	12.4	Transfer to another college
1.3	1.0	1.2	1.0	1.0	0.9	1.1	0.9	0.9	0.9	1.0	0.8	Drop out of this college temporarily (excluding transferring)
0.9	0.8	1.0	0.8	0.8	0.7	0.7	0.6	0.6	0.7	0.7	0.7	Drop out permanently
6.2	6.2	6.3	6.1	5.8	5.7	5.8	5.5	5.1	5.6	6.0	6.8	Get married while in college
17.7	18.8	19.5	19.2	18.2	18.4	18.3	17.8	16.8	18.7	--	--	Get married within a year after college
--	--	--	--	--	--	--	--	--	--	--	--	Enlist in the Armed Services before graduating
--	--	--	--	--	--	--	--	--	--	--	--	Be more successful after graduating than most students attending this college
--	--	--	--	10.0	10.4	10.7	9.9	10.7	10.7	10.4	10.8	Play varsity athletics
70.2	71.8	72.4	71.5	72.0	73.9	72.3	72.6	73.0	73.4	72.1	73.8	Find a job after college graduation in the field for which you were trained
												CONCERN ABOUT ABILITY TO FINANCE COLLEGE EDUCATION
30.0	28.2	28.1	27.2	28.8	29.6	30.8	31.5	32.3	32.1	32.2	--	None (I am confident that I will have sufficient funds)
53.9	54.8	53.8	53.4	54.5	54.0	53.8	52.4	51.8	51.6	52.7	--	Some concern (but I will probably have enough funds)
16.1	17.0	18.1	19.4	16.8	16.4	15.5	16.2	15.9	16.3	15.1	--	Major concern (not sure I will have enough funds to complete college)

[1] Text, order or number of response options may vary from year to year.

ATTITUDES AND VALUES	1966	1967	1968	1969	1970	1971	1972	1973	1974	1975	1976	1977	1978
PRESENT POLITICAL VIEWS													
Far left	--	--	--	--	2.4	1.9	1.7	1.6	1.7	1.6	1.8	1.8	1.5
Liberal	--	--	--	--	31.5	33.6	31.9	32.0	27.0	28.1	24.5	24.4	23.0
Middle of the road	--	--	--	--	49.4	50.6	51.5	53.5	58.7	57.5	60.5	60.2	61.7
Conservative	--	--	--	--	16.1	13.6	14.4	12.6	12.0	12.3	12.6	12.9	13.3
Far right	--	--	--	--	0.6	0.4	0.5	0.4	0.6	0.5	0.6	0.6	0.5
OBJECTIVES CONSIDERED TO BE ESSENTIAL OR VERY IMPORTANT													
Become accomplished in one of the performing arts (acting, dancing, etc)	13.4	14.6	11.1	13.7	14.8	14.2	13.8	[*]	13.0	13.3	13.0	15.6	14.5
Become an authority in my field	60.8	63.7	54.5	54.3	60.8	54.3	55.7	57.6	57.7	66.0	66.6	72.1	70.0
Obtain recognition from colleagues for contributions to my special field	36.3	34.9	31.6	35.3	33.4	31.6	31.9	--	34.5	38.9	42.1	44.9	47.3
Influence the political structure	--	--	--	12.0	14.0	10.2	12.2	11.1	9.6	10.9	11.7	12.2	11.4
Influence social values	--	--	--	37.1	36.2	29.8	32.0	33.1	29.3	31.9	31.7	32.7	33.6
Raise a family	--	--	--	77.8	72.4	64.7	67.8	58.2	56.9	57.1	56.8	58.9	61.9
Have administrative responsibility for the work of others	21.4	17.7	16.0	16.4	14.7	13.2	17.6	21.9	21.7	26.5	28.5	30.9	32.7
Be very well-off financially	31.6	30.0	27.1	32.1	28.0	28.2	30.2	[*]	36.4	40.3	44.7	50.7	52.7
Help others who are in difficulty	79.5	73.6	70.8	75.0	74.0	71.6	75.1	73.4	70.4	74.4	71.8	73.0	73.7
Make a theoretical contribution to science	7.5	6.1	5.8	5.5	6.2	5.5	7.2	--	10.2	10.1	10.9	10.7	11.5
Write original works (poems, novels, etc)	17.1	16.7	15.2	16.2	15.9	15.2	16.2	--	13.3	13.8	14.4	15.8	14.6
Create artistic work (painting, sculpture, decorating, etc.)	21.1	22.1	18.7	21.2	21.4	20.3	23.0	--	17.4	18.0	17.6	19.2	17.1
Become involved in programs to clean up the environment	--	--	--	--	--	41.6	43.6	32.6	23.9	27.0	26.1	27.8	26.2
Be successful in my own business	40.1	32.8	31.6	33.1	31.9	28.6	32.5	31.3	27.5	33.4	35.4	38.6	40.6
Develop a meaningful philosophy of life	--	87.6	87.4	85.8	79.1	73.5	75.0	73.7	65.1	68.2	64.1	61.5	59.1
Participate in a community action program	--	--	--	--	32.3	28.5	31.9	--	30.4	33.8	32.1	32.4	29.5
Help promote racial understanding	--	--	--	--	--	--	--	--	--	--	--	39.7	37.7
Keep up to date with political affairs	57.5	49.1	51.8	49.8	50.6	40.4	46.6	40.8	34.3	35.1	34.2	35.2	32.1
Become an expert in finance and commerce	5.9	4.0	3.7	9.0	8.6	7.0	9.6	--	--	--	--	--	--
Participate in an organization like the Peace Corps or Vista	30.0	28.0	26.8	--	26.1	22.0	21.0	--	--	--	--	--	--
Become a community leader	21.2	18.9	16.1	14.1	11.5	10.0	11.6	--	--	--	--	--	--
Never be obligated to people	27.5	23.2	21.8	22.6	20.8	19.6	21.1	--	--	--	--	--	--
PERCENT WHO STRONGLY AGREE OR AGREE SOMEWHAT [1]													
Academic/Campus Issues													
Chief benefit of a college education is that it increases one's earning power	--	46.3	48.6	45.4	61.3	51.0	52.9	49.4	--	--	--	--	--
Faculty promotions should be based in part on student evaluations	--	60.6	62.0	66.3	70.6	75.8	76.0	75.3	74.5	73.5	71.9	72.0	73.0
Colleges would be improved if organized sports were de-emphasized	--	20.6	--	--	--	24.9	24.8	23.4	27.1	25.9	25.0	25.0	25.5
College officials have the right to regulate student behavior off campus	--	--	23.6	19.1	16.8	13.4	12.2	10.1	12.4	12.9	12.8	12.8	13.3
Student publications should be cleared by college officials	--	53.5	57.1	52.0	42.6	32.5	32.5	30.4	32.9	33.3	34.2	37.3	36.7
College officials have the right to ban persons with extreme views from speaking on campus	--	36.1	28.8	28.9	30.5	25.3	22.6	20.3	20.0	21.8	22.9	23.2	23.4
Most college officials have been too lax dealing with student protests on campus	--	43.6	50.2	56.2	55.5	42.8	39.0	32.9	31.8	--	--	--	--
Grading in the high schools is too easy	--	--	--	--	--	--	--	--	--	--	57.9	60.4	64.0
College grades should be abolished	--	--	--	--	46.2	43.8	39.2	34.6	28.2	23.1	18.9	17.2	14.1
Students from disadvantaged social backgrounds should be given preferential treatment in college admissions	--	40.8	39.6	39.0	41.9	38.5	40.1	38.1	37.6	36.2	35.7	36.5	34.8
Open admissions (admitting anyone who applies) should be adopted by all publicly supported colleges	--	--	--	--	--	36.7	37.1	33.9	39.2	34.5	33.6	33.7	30.9
Even if it employs open admissions, a college should use the same performance standards in awarding degrees to all students	--	--	--	--	--	76.2	78.0	76.9	76.1	74.6	75.3	75.9	76.3
All college graduates should be able to demonstrate some minimal competency in written English and mathematics	--	--	--	--	--	--	--	--	--	--	--	--	--

[*] Results were not comparable to those of other years due to changes in question text or order.
[1] Text, order or number of response options may vary from year to year.

1979	1980	1981	1982	1983	1984	1985	1986	1987	1988	1989	1990	*ATTITUDES AND VALUES*
												PRESENT POLITICAL VIEWS
1.9	1.9	1.4	1.5	1.5	1.6	1.5	1.5	1.7	2.1	1.5	1.4	Far left
22.0	18.9	18.1	19.4	19.6	21.1	21.2	22.7	22.9	23.2	23.7	24.7	Liberal
61.5	64.0	64.0	63.7	63.7	60.8	60.9	59.8	60.2	57.6	57.1	57.3	Middle of the road
14.0	14.4	15.9	14.9	14.4	15.7	15.7	15.4	14.6	16.2	16.7	16.0	Conservative
0.7	0.8	0.6	0.6	0.7	0.7	0.8	0.7	0.7	0.9	0.9	0.6	Far right
												OBJECTIVES CONSIDERED TO BE ESSENTIAL OR VERY IMPORTANT
13.6	13.2	12.7	12.8	13.1	12.1	11.7	11.3	14.0	11.3	11.5	11.2	Become accomplished in one of the performing arts (acting, dancing, etc)
70.5	71.7	71.4	71.9	71.8	71.6	69.4	71.3	76.4	70.6	64.1	63.6	Become an authority in my field
49.8	52.5	53.1	53.6	54.3	54.2	53.5	54.3	57.3	53.6	54.0	54.0	Obtain recognition from colleagues for contributions to my special field
12.0	12.6	11.8	11.7	11.1	12.4	12.7	12.3	13.6	14.2	17.7	18.6	Influence the political structure
33.9	34.8	33.9	33.6	33.3	34.6	35.1	35.3	38.8	40.7	46.1	48.4	Influence social values
64.8	63.6	66.7	67.9	67.6	69.3	70.3	67.7	[*]	67.3	69.0	70.6	Raise a family
34.5	37.0	38.0	39.1	39.8	40.7	41.1	43.4	43.4	[*]	42.6	41.8	Have administrative responsibility for the work of others
56.7	57.8	60.2	64.9	65.5	67.3	66.8	69.8	72.1	[*]	71.9	70.3	Be very well-off financially
71.4	72.7	71.0	69.4	69.8	69.8	70.9	65.5	66.5	[*]	68.7	71.4	Help others who are in difficulty
11.2	11.5	11.0	10.4	11.1	10.8	10.2	9.5	9.3	[*]	14.1	14.5	Make a theoretical contribution to science
13.8	13.8	12.5	12.1	11.8	11.4	12.1	11.5	12.7	[*]	12.7	12.5	Write original works (poems, novels, etc)
16.7	16.5	14.8	13.9	13.0	12.2	12.4	11.8	13.9	[*]	12.6	12.2	Create artistic work (painting, sculpture, decorating, etc.)
24.6	25.4	22.7	20.5	18.8	18.1	17.5	13.5	14.9	--	24.3	34.3	Become involved in programs to clean up the environment
42.5	43.6	44.1	44.8	45.4	47.3	47.7	44.9	46.4	[*]	40.8	38.0	Be successful in my own business
54.7	52.1	50.4	47.5	45.6	45.2	43.0	40.6	39.2	[*]	41.6	44.3	Develop a meaningful philosophy of life
28.3	30.3	26.1	24.4	23.8	24.1	24.7	20.4	21.6	[*]	25.9	29.1	Participate in a community action program
35.0	35.8	33.2	32.5	32.0	33.4	33.1	29.0	30.2	[*]	37.6	41.2	Help promote racial understanding
33.4	35.0	33.9	33.1	30.4	33.4	--	--	--		36.0	38.9	Keep up to date with political affairs
--	--	--	--	--	--	21.5	20.8	21.5	--	--	--	Become an expert in finance and commerce
--	--	--	--	--	--	--	--	--	--	--	--	Participate in an organization like the Peace Corps or Vista
--	--	--	--	--	--	--	--	--	--	--	--	Become a community leader
--	--	--	--	--	--	--	--	--	--	--	--	Never be obligated to people
												PERCENT WHO STRONGLY AGREE OR AGREE SOMEWHAT [1]
												Academic/Campus Issues
--	--	--	--	--	--	69.3	67.5	65.6	64.7	66.8	66.2	Chief benefit of a college education is that it increases one's earning power
70.7	71.1	70.3	70.0	69.6	69.8	70.6	70.2	--	--	--	75.0	Faculty promotions should be based in part on student evaluations
--	--	--	--	--	--	--	--	--	--	--	36.5	Colleges would be improved if organized sports were de-emphasized
13.9	13.8	13.7	13.2	13.7	13.7	12.9	11.2	--	--	--	--	College officials have the right to regulate student behavior off campus
41.2	42.4	42.9	41.9	42.4	--	--	--	--	--	--	--	Student publications should be cleared by college officials
23.8	24.4	24.5	22.7	23.5	19.1	23.2	23.4	--	--	--	--	College officials have the right to ban persons with extreme views from speaking on campus
--	--	--	--	--	--	--	--	--	--	--	--	Most college officials have been too lax dealing with student protests on campus
60.2	58.0	56.1	54.0	58.2	54.5	49.6	47.9	--	--	--	--	Grading in the high schools is too easy
14.1	13.6	13.2	12.4	12.1	11.4	--	--	--	--	--	--	College grades should be abolished
37.5	37.2	36.8	34.9	35.7	35.8	--	--	--	--	--	--	Students from disadvantaged social backgrounds should be given preferential treatment in college admissions
34.3	33.7	32.8	--	--	--	--	--	--	--	--	--	Open admissions (admitting anyone who applies) should be adopted by all publicly supported colleges
76.6	--	--	--	--	--	--	--	--	--	--	--	Even if it employs open admissions, a college should use the same performance standards in awarding degrees to all students
--	91.0	91.4	91.1	91.6	91.3	--	--	--	--	--	--	All college graduates should be able to demonstrate some minimal competency in written English and mathematics

[*] Results were not comparable to those of other years due to changes in question text or order.
[1] Text, order or number of response options may vary from year to year.

ATTITUDES AND VALUES

PERCENT WHO STRONGLY AGREE OR AGREE SOMEWHAT [1]	1966	1967	1968	1969	1970	1971	1972	1973	1974	1975	1976	1977	1978
Political/Governance Issues													
Federal government is not doing enough to control environmental pollution	--	--	--	--	--	90.8	89.6	89.7	84.4	83.6	84.6	83.5	84.2
Federal government is not doing enough to protect the consumer from faulty goods and services	--	--	--	--	--	77.2	76.8	80.8	77.6	75.6	76.4	73.8	75.7
Government is not promoting disarmament	--	--	--	--	--	--	--	--	--	--	--	--	--
Increase Federal military spending	--	--	--	--	--	--	--	--	--	--	--	--	--
Federal government is not doing enough to promote school desegregation	--	--	--	--	--	53.0	50.2	51.2	--	--	--	--	--
The Federal government should do more to discourage energy consumption	--	--	--	--	--	--	--	--	--	82.9	82.6	83.9	84.4
Federal government should raise taxes to reduce the deficit	--	--	--	--	--	--	--	--	--	--	--	--	--
The Federal government should do more to control the sale of handguns	--	--	--	--	--	--	--	--	--	--	--	--	--
Wealthy people should pay a larger share of taxes than they do now	--	--	--	--	--	--	69.4	69.3	72.9	73.3	73.7	73.3	71.8
A national health care plan is needed to cover everybody's medical costs	--	--	--	--	--	--	--	--	--	--	--	62.3	62.6
Inflation is our biggest domestic problem	--	--	--	--	--	--	--	--	--	--	--	--	--
Abortion should be legal	--	--	--	--	--	--	--	--	--	--	--	55.6	56.9
Marijuana should be legalized	--	--	16.9	22.4	35.2	35.0	43.0	45.2	43.4	43.3	46.1	49.2	47.1
Capital punishment should be abolished	--	--	--	59.0	59.8	62.8	--	--	--	--	--	--	38.2
Women should receive the same salary and opportunities for advancement as men in comparable positions	--	--	--	--	87.1	94.0	95.4	96.2	94.9	96.2	96.1	96.4	96.6
It is important to have laws prohibiting homosexual relationships	--	--	--	--	--	--	--	--	--	--	38.6	40.3	38.5
Divorce laws should be liberalized	--	--	--	35.2	46.9	--	--	--	--	--	--	--	45.8
Personal/Social Issues													
The activities of married women are best confined to the home and family	--	44.3	--	--	36.7	30.6	25.6	18.8	19.4	18.1	19.5	19.8	19.6
Live together before marriage	--	--	--	--	--	--	--	--	38.9	41.2	42.9	42.1	39.6
Sex is OK if people like each other	--	--	--	--	--	--	--	--	29.8	33.2	32.5	33.8	32.5
People should not obey laws which violate their personal values	--	--	--	--	--	--	--	--	31.7	29.9	29.5	30.1	30.3
Parents should be discouraged from having large families	--	34.0	--	--	--	67.5	65.6	63.5	55.0	52.5	49.8	47.7	42.7
Scientists should publish their findings regardless of the possible consequences	--	38.5	49.7	50.8	58.4	--	--	--	--	--	--	--	--
Realistically, an individual can do little to bring about changes in our society	--	29.8	27.9	31.8	34.9	38.7	39.0	37.3	39.5	43.4	41.0	41.5	--
There is too much concern in the courts for the rights of criminals	--	--	--	46.8	44.5	41.1	43.0	43.7	45.6	47.1	54.3	59.2	60.6
Busing is OK if it helps to achieve racial balance in the schools	--	--	--	--	--	--	--	--	--	--	39.0	42.8	43.7
Nuclear disarmament is attainable	--	--	--	--	--	--	--	--	--	--	--	--	--
Employers should be allowed to require drug testing of employees or job applicants	--	--	--	--	--	--	--	--	--	--	--	--	--
The only way to control AIDS is through widespread, mandatory testing	--	--	--	--	--	--	--	--	--	--	--	--	--
Just because a man thinks that a woman has "led him on"" does not entitle him to have sex with her	--	--	--	--	--	--	--	--	--	--	--	--	--
Young more idealistic than old	--	--	--	--	--	--	--	--	70.1	68.9	--	--	--

[1] Text, order or number of response options may vary from year to year.

ATTITUDES AND VALUES

PERCENT WHO STRONGLY AGREE OR AGREE SOMEWHAT [1]

	1979	1980	1981	1982	1983	1984	1985	1986	1987	1988	1989	1990
Political/Governance Issues												
Federal government is not doing enough to control environmental pollution	84.1	83.5	81.8	82.2	82.3	80.3	80.0	79.6	82.5	85.3	87.6	88.7
Federal government is not doing enough to protect the consumer from faulty goods and services	76.7	78.6	74.8	73.1	69.8	66.7	66.2	66.7	69.5	69.1	71.5	71.6
Government is not promoting disarmament	--	--	--	--	--	72.7	73.0	72.8	77.6	75.2	76.2	--
Increase Federal military spending	--	--	--	29.9	28.3	25.2	19.7	19.7	20.2	20.5	19.6	21.8
Federal government is not doing enough to promote school desegregation	--	--	--	--	--	--	--	--	--	--	--	--
The Federal government should do more to discourage energy consumption	84.7	85.7	83.1	80.8	78.4	75.9	74.5	72.2	--	--	--	--
Federal government should raise taxes to reduce the deficit	--	--	--	--	--	--	19.8	19.4	21.1	24.1	25.5	24.2
The Federal government should do more to control the sale of handguns	--	--	--	--	--	--	--	--	--	--	87.6	87.0
Wealthy people should pay a larger share of taxes than they do now	68.5	69.6	70.8	71.7	70.6	69.6	73.1	71.5	--	--	--	--
A national health care plan is needed to cover everybody's medical costs	62.8	60.8	57.8	60.5	62.3	64.6	63.3	65.2	--	--	79.0	77.0
Inflation is our biggest domestic problem	81.4	82.6	81.3	81.9	73.2	--	--	--	--	--	--	--
Abortion should be legal	53.6	53.8	54.7	55.9	54.8	54.2	55.3	59.0	58.7	57.2	65.5	64.8
Marijuana should be legalized	43.6	36.6	31.9	26.4	23.1	20.3	18.9	18.0	15.9	16.4	13.7	16.0
Capital punishment should be abolished	40.7	40.5	35.2	33.5	33.7	29.6	30.2	29.1	27.0	26.0	23.8	24.1
Women should receive the same salary and opportunities for advancement as men in comparable positions	96.1	96.4	96.6	96.6	96.6	96.6	95.9	96.3	--	--	--	--
It is important to have laws prohibiting homosexual relationships	39.0	40.3	39.9	37.6	39.9	38.4	38.3	42.8	44.6	39.9	35.1	34.5
Divorce laws should be liberalized	46.0	43.4	41.2	42.5	42.7	--	--	--	--	--	--	--
Personal/Social Issues												
The activities of married women are best confined to the home and family	21.0	19.0	19.3	17.6	17.2	15.5	16.0	14.3	20.3	20.1	20.4	20.5
Live together before marriage	38.0	37.9	37.7	37.5	39.7	39.9	43.1	46.8	46.9	46.3	45.0	--
Sex is OK if people like each other	33.7	32.4	32.2	32.8	33.6	31.8	--	--	38.8	37.1	36.4	37.9
People should not obey laws which violate their personal values	31.0	29.9	30.0	--	--	--	--	--	--	--	--	--
Parents should be discouraged from having large families	41.1	39.9	37.2	32.3	31.3	--	--	--	--	--	--	--
Scientists should publish their findings regardless of the possible consequences	--	--	--	--	--	--	--	--	--	--	--	49.7
Realistically, an individual can do little to bring about changes in our society	--	--	--	--	--	--	34.7	--	--	--	--	--
There is too much concern in the courts for the rights of criminals	57.0	61.6	64.2	65.5	65.2	--	--	--	65.5	66.0	65.5	63.2
Busing is OK if it helps to achieve racial balance in the schools	46.5	48.2	46.7	49.8	53.5	56.1	56.9	58.4	57.3	54.9	56.0	57.1
Nuclear disarmament is attainable	--	--	--	--	--	--	56.6	56.4	59.6	53.9	--	60.4
Employers should be allowed to require drug testing of employees or job applicants	--	--	--	--	--	--	--	--	--	72.0	78.9	82.1
The only way to control AIDS is through widespread, mandatory testing	--	--	--	--	--	--	--	--	--	67.7	67.5	66.3
Just because a man thinks that a woman has "led him on"" does not entitle him to have sex with her	--	--	--	--	--	--	--	--	--	91.0	92.8	93.3
Young more idealistic than old	--	--	--	--	--	--	--	--	--	--	--	--

[1] Text, order or number of response options may vary from year to year.

FINANCIAL AID	1966	1967	1968	1969	1970	1971	1972	1973	1974	1975	1976	1977	1978
RECEIVED ANY AID FOR FIRST YEAR EDUCATIONAL EXPENSES [1]													
Personal or Family Resources													
Parents and family	--	--	--	--	--	--	--	--	--	--	--	--	73.3
Spouse's income	--	--	--	--	--	--	--	--	--	--	--	--	1.1
Savings from summer work	--	--	--	--	--	--	--	--	--	--	--	--	45.7
Other savings	--	--	--	--	--	--	--	--	--	--	--	--	20.4
Part-time work while attending college	--	--	--	--	--	--	--	--	--	--	--	--	23.7
Part-time work on campus	--	--	--	--	--	--	--	--	--	--	--	--	--
Other part-time work while in college	--	--	--	--	--	--	--	--	--	--	--	--	--
Full-time work while in college	--	--	--	--	--	--	--	--	--	--	--	--	1.5
Aid Which Need Not Be Repaid													
Pell Grant (BEOG prior to 1982) [2]	--	--	--	--	--	--	--	--	--	--	--	--	22.1
Supp. Educational Oppty. Grant (SEOG) [2]	--	--	--	--	--	--	--	--	--	--	--	--	5.7
State scholarship or grant [2]	--	--	--	--	--	--	--	--	--	--	--	--	15.7
College grant or scholarship	--	--	--	--	--	--	--	--	--	--	--	--	12.8
College Work-Study Grant [2]	--	--	--	--	--	--	--	--	--	--	--	--	12.3
Private grant or scholarship	--	--	--	--	--	--	--	--	--	--	--	--	8.1
Student's GI benefits	--	--	--	--	--	--	--	--	--	--	--	--	0.3
GI benefits awarded to student's parent	--	--	--	--	--	--	--	--	--	--	--	--	1.1
GI/military benefits (student's or parents')	--	--	--	--	--	--	--	--	--	--	--	--	--
Social Security dependent's benefits	--	--	--	--	--	--	--	--	--	--	--	--	6.1
Other gov't aid (ROTC, Soc. Sec.,BIA,etc.)	--	--	--	--	--	--	--	--	--	--	--	--	--
Aid Which Must Be Repaid													
Stafford/Guaranteed Student Loan [2]	--	--	--	--	--	--	--	--	--	--	--	--	9.8
Perkins Loan (NDSL prior to 1990) [2]	--	--	--	--	--	--	--	--	--	--	--	--	8.5
College loan	--	--	--	--	--	--	--	--	--	--	--	--	3.6
Loan(s) from other sources	--	--	--	--	--	--	--	--	--	--	--	--	4.0
From sources other than those cited above	--	--	--	--	--	--	--	--	--	--	--	--	3.6
RECEIVED $1,500+ AID FOR FIRST YEAR EDUCATIONAL EXPENSES [1]													
Personal or Family Resources													
Parents and family	--	--	--	--	--	--	--	--	--	--	--	--	33.1
Spouse's income	--	--	--	--	--	--	--	--	--	--	--	--	0.2
Savings from summer work	--	--	--	--	--	--	--	--	--	--	--	--	1.7
Other savings	--	--	--	--	--	--	--	--	--	--	--	--	1.5
Part-time work while attending college	--	--	--	--	--	--	--	--	--	--	--	--	0.5
Part-time work on campus	--	--	--	--	--	--	--	--	--	--	--	--	--
Other part-time work while in college	--	--	--	--	--	--	--	--	--	--	--	--	--
Full-time work while in college	--	--	--	--	--	--	--	--	--	--	--	--	0.1
Aid Which Need Not Be Repaid													
Pell Grant (BEOG prior to 1982) [2]	--	--	--	--	--	--	--	--	--	--	--	--	3.3
Supp. Educational Oppty. Grant (SEOG) [2]	--	--	--	--	--	--	--	--	--	--	--	--	0.3
State scholarship or grant [2]	--	--	--	--	--	--	--	--	--	--	--	--	1.5
College grant or scholarship	--	--	--	--	--	--	--	--	--	--	--	--	2.2
College Work-Study Grant [2]	--	--	--	--	--	--	--	--	--	--	--	--	0.2
Private grant or scholarship	--	--	--	--	--	--	--	--	--	--	--	--	0.7
Student's GI benefits	--	--	--	--	--	--	--	--	--	--	--	--	0.0
GI benefits awarded to student's parent	--	--	--	--	--	--	--	--	--	--	--	--	0.3
GI/military benefits (student's or parents')	--	--	--	--	--	--	--	--	--	--	--	--	--
Social Security dependent's benefits	--	--	--	--	--	--	--	--	--	--	--	--	1.0
Other gov't aid (ROTC, Soc. Sec.,BIA,etc.)	--	--	--	--	--	--	--	--	--	--	--	--	--
Aid Which Must Be Repaid													
Stafford/Guaranteed Student Loan [2]	--	--	--	--	--	--	--	--	--	--	--	--	4.4
Perkins Loan (NDSL prior to 1990) [2]	--	--	--	--	--	--	--	--	--	--	--	--	1.1
College loan	--	--	--	--	--	--	--	--	--	--	--	--	0.9
Loan(s) from other sources	--	--	--	--	--	--	--	--	--	--	--	--	1.4
From sources other than those cited above	--	--	--	--	--	--	--	--	--	--	--	--	1.0

[1] Response and processing options rendered data from 1973-1977 not comparable to 1978-1990.
[2] In 1987-1990, highest response option of "$3,000 or more" was dropped, since these programs have upper limits less than $3,000.

1979	1980	1981	1982	1983	1984	1985	1986	1987	1988	1989	1990	FINANCIAL AID
												RECEIVED ANY AID FOR FIRST YEAR EDUCATIONAL EXPENSES [1]
												Personal or Family Resources
69.1	69.8	70.4	72.8	72.0	70.8	71.5	74.8	76.1	78.6	79.3	78.0	Parents and family
0.9	1.0	1.0	0.8	0.9	1.0	1.0	1.6	1.1	1.3	1.2	2.1	Spouse's income
41.7	42.4	42.5	39.8	39.1	43.9	47.3	49.0	53.1	52.7	52.7	54.1	Savings from summer work
17.8	18.7	19.1	18.5	18.4	19.9	22.4	26.0	28.3	28.5	28.6	31.7	Other savings
23.5	24.2	23.6	24.0	24.0	29.5	32.9	35.0	--	--	--	--	Part-time work while attending college
--	--	--	--	--	--	--	--	19.5	20.9	21.1	22.0	Part-time work on campus
--	--	--	--	--	--	--	--	24.4	24.1	25.6	22.3	Other part-time work while in college
1.7	1.7	1.7	1.5	1.6	1.5	1.9	2.0	1.7	2.0	1.8	2.2	Full-time work while in college
												Aid Which Need Not Be Repaid
32.8	33.1	27.2	24.3	27.5	20.9	21.2	17.9	18.6	21.7	23.0	25.3	Pell Grant (BEOG prior to 1982) [2]
7.1	8.2	5.7	5.8	7.2	5.6	5.1	5.4	6.0	5.9	6.2	7.2	Supp. Educational Oppty. Grant (SEOG) [2]
15.6	16.4	14.3	14.9	16.1	14.1	15.0	14.1	16.7	14.9	15.6	16.8	State scholarship or grant [2]
11.8	13.3	12.1	12.5	13.9	18.1	20.0	18.9	13.3	21.5	21.7	23.6	College grant or scholarship
12.7	15.9	13.3	12.7	14.6	10.7	11.2	11.6	11.0	11.1	11.3	11.4	College Work-Study Grant [2]
7.5	7.7	7.3	7.9	7.9	6.6	5.9	7.2	9.9	9.3	9.5	10.9	Private grant or scholarship
0.4	0.4	0.3	0.3	0.3	0.2	0.3	0.2	--	--	--	--	Student's GI benefits
1.2	1.0	0.9	0.8	0.7	0.5	0.5	0.5	--	--	--	--	GI benefits awarded to student's parent
--	--	--	--	--	--	--	--	0.6	--	--	--	GI/military benefits (student's or parents')
5.9	6.1	6.4	3.6	1.7	--	--	--	--	--	--	--	Social Security dependent's benefits
--	--	--	--	--	1.6	1.4	1.3	0.9	1.3	1.4	2.0	Other gov't aid (ROTC, Soc. Sec.,BIA,etc.)
												Aid Which Must Be Repaid
12.5	19.9	25.6	20.7	21.8	23.4	23.2	25.5	22.4	22.4	22.8	23.4	Stafford/Guaranteed Student Loan [2]
8.1	9.5	8.0	6.5	7.4	6.6	6.1	6.4	4.4	2.9	2.3	7.5	Perkins Loan (NDSL prior to 1990) [2]
3.2	4.2	3.5	3.4	3.6	3.4	3.6	3.8	5.1	5.4	7.6	5.5	College loan
3.6	4.1	4.4	4.3	4.2	3.9	3.9	4.0	5.1	5.6	6.5	6.2	Loan(s) from other sources
3.4	3.5	3.5	2.8	3.5	2.3	2.9	2.7	3.9	3.1	3.2	3.7	From sources other than those cited above
												RECEIVED $1,500+ AID FOR FIRST YEAR EDUCATIONAL EXPENSES [1]
												Personal or Family Resources
29.2	28.9	32.0	37.4	37.6	40.9	42.7	47.1	49.8	51.7	52.9	51.7	Parents and family
0.1	0.2	0.2	0.2	0.2	0.2	0.2	0.4	0.3	0.3	0.2	0.6	Spouse's income
1.7	1.9	2.3	2.7	2.7	2.9	3.5	3.3	4.1	4.7	4.9	5.5	Savings from summer work
1.4	1.8	1.9	2.4	2.3	3.0	3.0	4.0	4.3	4.4	4.9	5.4	Other savings
0.7	0.7	0.9	0.8	0.9	0.9	1.1	1.4	--	--	--	--	Part-time work while attending college
--	--	--	--	--	--	--	--	0.7	0.8	0.9	1.2	Part-time work on campus
--	--	--	--	--	--	--	--	1.0	1.1	1.0	1.1	Other part-time work while in college
0.3	0.2	0.3	0.3	0.3	0.2	0.3	0.4	0.3	0.3	0.4	0.5	Full-time work while in college
												Aid Which Need Not Be Repaid
4.6	4.7	4.3	4.7	6.4	4.7	5.4	4.1	4.5	5.5	6.0	7.8	Pell Grant (BEOG prior to 1982) [2]
0.4	0.5	0.5	0.6	0.8	0.7	0.7	0.9	1.0	1.0	1.0	1.3	Supp. Educational Oppty. Grant (SEOG) [2]
1.6	1.5	1.4	1.6	2.0	1.6	2.1	2.1	3.4	3.0	3.4	3.7	State scholarship or grant [2]
2.0	2.5	2.8	3.5	4.3	5.7	6.3	6.7	5.1	8.3	9.0	10.2	College grant or scholarship
0.3	0.5	0.5	0.6	0.9	0.6	0.9	0.8	0.8	1.0	1.0	1.5	College Work-Study Grant [2]
0.7	0.8	0.8	1.1	1.2	1.0	1.0	1.3	2.0	2.0	2.2	2.6	Private grant or scholarship
0.1	0.1	0.0	0.0	0.0	0.1	0.0	0.1	--	--	--	--	Student's GI benefits
0.3	0.2	0.2	0.1	0.1	0.2	0.1	0.2	--	--	--	--	GI benefits awarded to student's parent
--	--	--	--	--	--	--	--	0.2	--	--	--	GI/military benefits (student's or parents')
1.0	1.3	1.5	0.8	0.4	--	--	--	--	--	--	--	Social Security dependent's benefits
--	--	--	--	--	0.7	0.5	0.6	0.4	0.7	0.7	1.0	Other gov't aid (ROTC, Soc. Sec.,BIA,etc.)
												Aid Which Must Be Repaid
6.4	11.8	18.6	13.3	14.3	16.9	16.1	15.8	12.7	12.4	13.1	14.1	Stafford/Guaranteed Student Loan [2]
1.3	2.2	2.6	1.8	2.0	2.2	1.9	1.8	1.3	0.8	0.8	2.0	Perkins Loan (NDSL prior to 1990) [2]
1.0	1.5	1.4	1.2	1.4	1.6	1.7	1.5	2.0	2.2	3.4	3.1	College loan
1.3	1.9	2.3	2.0	1.9	2.2	2.0	2.1	2.4	2.6	3.5	3.7	Loan(s) from other sources
0.9	0.9	0.9	0.9	1.0	0.8	0.8	0.9	1.4	1.1	1.2	1.5	From sources other than those cited above

[1] Response and processing options rendered data from 1973-1977 not comparable to 1978-1990.

[2] In 1987-1990, highest response option of "$3,000 or more" was dropped, since these programs have upper limits less than $3,000.

Twenty–Five Year Trends for All Freshmen

STUDENT'S DEMOGRAPHICS	1966	1967	1968	1969	1970	1971	1972	1973	1974	1975	1976	1977	1978
SEX													
Male	--	55.6	56.6	56.6	54.8	54.4	53.9	52.8	52.2	53.2	51.8	50.7	48.9
Female	--	44.4	43.4	43.4	45.2	45.6	46.1	47.2	47.8	46.8	48.2	49.3	51.1
AGE													
16 or younger	--	0.2	0.1	0.1	0.1	0.1	0.1	0.1	0.1	0.1	0.1	0.1	0.1
17	--	4.6	4.5	3.8	3.8	3.4	4.0	4.7	3.9	3.7	3.8	3.2	3.3
18	--	76.9	75.6	74.0	73.2	74.1	74.2	74.7	74.4	73.6	74.1	74.3	75.3
19	--	13.6	13.6	14.3	14.4	16.0	15.7	15.3	16.0	16.7	16.6	17.1	17.2
20	--	1.7	2.1	2.1	2.0	2.1	2.0	1.8	2.1	2.0	2.1	2.1	1.8
21 or older [1]	--	3.2	4.2	5.7	6.4	4.4	4.0	3.4	3.4	3.9	3.4	3.3	2.5
RACIAL/ETHNIC BACKGROUND [2]													
White/Caucasian	90.7	89.9	87.3	90.9	[*]	91.4	87.3	88.5	88.6	86.5	86.2	86.9	88.5
African-American/Black [1]	5.0	4.3	5.8	6.0	[*]	6.3	8.7	7.8	7.4	9.0	8.4	8.8	8.1
American Indian	0.6	0.7	0.7	0.3	[*]	0.9	1.1	0.9	0.9	0.9	0.9	0.8	0.8
Oriental/Asian-American	0.7	0.8	1.1	1.7	[*]	0.5	1.1	1.1	0.9	1.5	2.0	1.1	1.1
Mexican-American/Chicano	--	--	--	--	--	1.1	1.5	1.3	1.5	1.7	1.7	1.4	1.0
Puerto Rican-American	--	--	--	--	--	0.2	0.6	0.4	0.6	0.7	0.5	0.9	0.9
Other	3.0	4.4	5.1	1.1	[*]	1.2	1.8	1.5	1.7	1.9	1.8	1.8	1.7
MARITAL STATUS													
No	--	--	--	--	--	97.2	97.7	98.1	98.1	97.8	98.2	98.4	98.8
Yes [1]	--	--	--	--	--	2.8	2.3	1.9	1.9	2.2	1.8	1.6	1.2
CITIZENSHIP STATUS													
Yes	--	--	--	98.0	98.4	--	97.8	97.8	--	--	--	--	--
No [1]	--	--	--	2.0	1.6	--	2.2	2.2	--	--	--	--	--
TWIN STATUS													
No	--	--	--	--	--	--	--	--	--	--	--	98.2	--
Yes, identical	--	--	--	--	--	--	--	--	--	--	--	0.6	--
Yes, fraternal	--	--	--	--	--	--	--	--	--	--	--	1.2	--
VETERAN STATUS													
No	--	--	--	--	96.6	97.2	98.0	98.3	97.8	97.5	97.9	98.3	98.7
Yes [1]	--	--	--	--	3.4	2.9	2.1	1.7	2.2	2.5	2.1	1.7	1.3
STUDENT'S CURRENT RELIGIOUS PREFERENCE (Aggregated) [3]													
Protestant	53.9	49.3	45.9	49.9	51.1	41.5	38.2	46.7	48.2	47.2	45.9	46.3	47.0
Roman Catholic	28.2	30.5	31.3	29.5	30.6	29.5	30.1	34.3	33.3	34.0	35.5	37.4	37.5
Jewish	4.0	4.8	4.4	3.5	4.4	2.8	3.8	5.1	3.7	3.8	3.6	3.7	4.0
Other	7.0	7.5	8.8	3.9	3.9	11.7	13.6	3.7	4.2	4.5	5.0	4.2	3.9
None	6.9	7.9	9.6	13.2	9.8	14.4	14.3	10.1	10.5	10.3	10.0	8.5	7.6
STUDENT'S CURRENT RELIGIOUS PREFERENCE (Disaggregated)													
Baptist	--	--	--	11.5	14.3	--	--	13.2	13.2	13.8	12.6	13.1	13.0
Buddhist	--	--	--	--	--	--	--	--	--	--	--	--	--
Congregational (United Church of Christ) [1]	--	--	--	3.8	2.3	--	--	1.7	1.9	1.6	1.8	2.0	1.9
Eastern Orthodox	--	--	--	--	0.5	--	--	0.6	0.5	0.6	0.6	0.7	0.7
Episcopal	--	--	--	3.6	3.5	--	--	3.2	3.0	3.0	2.9	3.0	3.2
Jewish	--	--	--	3.5	4.4	--	--	5.1	3.7	3.8	3.6	3.7	4.0
Latter Day Saints (Mormon)	--	--	--	0.7	0.3	--	--	0.3	0.4	0.3	0.3	0.3	0.2
Lutheran	--	--	--	6.7	6.3	--	--	5.7	6.6	5.8	6.3	5.6	5.5
Methodist	--	--	--	11.0	10.8	--	--	10.5	10.5	10.4	9.3	10.0	10.3
Muslim (Islamic) [1]	--	--	--	0.1	0.1	--	--	0.1	0.2	0.2	0.2	0.2	0.2
Presbyterian	--	--	--	6.4	6.4	--	--	5.9	5.8	5.9	5.5	5.4	5.8
Quaker (Society of Friends)	--	--	--	0.3	0.3	--	--	0.2	0.2	0.2	0.2	0.2	0.2
Roman Catholic	--	--	--	29.5	30.6	--	--	34.3	33.3	34.0	35.5	37.4	37.5
Seventh Day Adventist	--	--	--	0.3	0.3	--	--	0.3	0.3	0.5	0.5	0.3	0.4
Unitarian-Universalist	--	--	--	0.7	0.6	--	--	0.4	0.4	0.3	0.3	0.3	0.3
Other Protestant	--	--	--	4.9	5.5	--	--	4.7	5.4	4.8	5.6	5.4	5.5
Other religion	--	--	--	3.8	3.8	--	--	3.6	4.0	4.3	4.8	4.0	3.7
None	--	--	--	13.2	9.8	--	--	10.1	10.5	10.3	10.0	8.5	7.6
DISABILITIES [4]													
Hearing	--	--	--	--	--	--	--	--	--	--	--	--	--
Speech	--	--	--	--	--	--	--	--	--	--	--	--	--
Partially sighted/blind	--	--	--	--	--	--	--	--	--	--	--	--	--
Orthopedic	--	--	--	--	--	--	--	--	--	--	--	--	--
Learning disabled	--	--	--	--	--	--	--	--	--	--	--	--	--
Health related	--	--	--	--	--	--	--	--	--	--	--	--	--
Other	--	--	--	--	--	--	--	--	--	--	--	--	--
DISTANCE FROM HOME TO COLLEGE													
10 miles or less [1]	--	--	--	26.5	27.2	23.2	26.4	28.2	--	26.5	29.6	26.5	22.0
11-50 miles	--	--	--	24.4	24.9	26.8	24.9	24.8	--	25.6	26.0	26.5	26.5
51-100 miles	--	--	--	13.1	12.7	14.6	13.8	12.8	--	13.4	13.0	14.4	15.0
101-500 miles	--	--	--	26.3	26.6	27.7	26.0	25.9	--	26.2	23.9	25.3	28.1
More than 500 miles	--	--	--	9.6	8.6	7.7	8.8	8.3	--	8.2	7.5	7.3	8.3

[*] Results were not comparable to those of other years due to changes in question text or order.
[1] Text, order or number of response options may vary from year to year.
[2] Respondent allowed to mark all responses that apply from 1971-1990. Responses may sum to more than 100%.
[3] See Appendix D for a discussion of variation in question texts and aggregation procedures.
[4] Responses from 1978-1982 excluded because they were not recorded in a comparable manner.

STUDENT'S DEMOGRAPHICS	1979	1980	1981	1982	1983	1984	1985	1986	1987	1988	1989	1990
SEX												
Male	48.8	48.5	48.6	49.5	49.0	48.2	48.2	47.7	47.2	46.3	46.2	46.2
Female	51.2	51.5	51.4	50.5	51.0	51.8	51.8	52.3	52.8	53.7	53.8	53.8
AGE												
16 or younger	0.1	0.1	0.1	0.1	0.1	0.1	0.1	0.1	0.1	0.1	0.1	0.1
17	2.9	2.6	2.5	2.5	2.4	2.6	2.5	2.8	2.5	2.6	2.4	2.0
18	74.2	72.6	74.1	74.2	72.7	73.4	72.2	72.1	71.8	73.3	71.6	68.3
19	17.8	18.9	18.8	18.9	19.8	19.1	20.2	19.0	19.7	18.8	21.1	23.3
20	2.0	2.2	1.9	1.8	2.0	2.0	1.9	1.9	2.1	1.7	2.1	2.4
21 or older [1]	3.1	3.8	2.8	2.4	3.1	3.0	3.2	4.0	3.8	3.3	2.8	3.9
RACIAL/ETHNIC BACKGROUND [2]												
White/Caucasian	86.3	86.0	88.5	88.2	86.9	85.7	86.2	85.8	86.0	83.2	84.3	84.3
African-American/Black [1]	9.2	9.2	8.6	8.5	9.0	9.8	9.1	8.5	8.7	9.5	9.2	9.6
American Indian	1.0	0.8	1.0	1.0	1.1	0.9	1.0	0.9	0.9	0.8	0.9	1.3
Oriental/Asian-American	1.4	1.4	1.1	1.4	1.6	1.6	2.0	2.5	2.3	2.9	2.9	2.9
Mexican-American/Chicano	1.2	2.1	0.9	0.9	0.9	1.0	1.2	1.2	1.0	1.8	1.4	1.5
Puerto Rican-American	1.0	0.9	0.6	0.9	0.7	0.8	0.6	0.9	1.2	1.4	0.8	0.5
Other	2.0	1.7	1.5	1.4	1.6	1.7	1.5	2.0	1.6	2.2	2.1	1.8
MARITAL STATUS												
No	98.6	98.4	98.7	98.8	98.6	98.6	98.5	98.0	--	--	--	--
Yes [1]	1.4	1.6	1.3	1.2	1.4	1.4	1.5	2.0	--	--	--	--
CITIZENSHIP STATUS												
Yes	--	--	--	97.7	97.4	97.0	97.6	96.9	98.2	97.7	97.0	97.6
No [1]	--	--	--	2.3	2.6	3.0	2.4	3.1	1.8	2.3	3.0	2.4
TWIN STATUS												
No	--	--	98.2	98.2	98.2	98.2	98.2	98.3	98.2	98.2	98.4	98.2
Yes, identical	--	--	0.6	0.6	0.7	0.6	0.7	0.6	0.7	0.7	0.7	0.7
Yes, fraternal	--	--	1.2	1.2	1.1	1.2	1.1	1.1	1.1	1.1	0.9	1.1
VETERAN STATUS												
No	98.5	98.4	98.7	98.7	--	--	--	--	--	--	--	--
Yes [1]	1.5	1.6	1.3	1.3	--	--	--	--	--	--	--	--
STUDENT'S CURRENT RELIGIOUS PREFERENCE (Aggregated) [3]												
Protestant	33.6	34.0	35.4	33.7	32.0	43.8	46.2	29.5	45.6	42.7	46.6	47.6
Roman Catholic	38.1	38.7	37.0	38.9	39.3	39.3	37.0	36.0	36.0	36.2	33.6	32.1
Jewish	3.6	3.2	3.0	3.0	3.1	3.1	2.8	3.2	2.7	3.2	2.7	2.2
Other	16.6	16.1	17.3	17.2	17.9	6.0	5.5	21.2	5.5	6.2	5.8	6.3
None	8.0	8.1	7.3	7.3	7.6	8.0	8.4	10.0	10.1	11.6	11.3	11.8
STUDENT'S CURRENT RELIGIOUS PREFERENCE (Disaggregated)												
Baptist	--	--	--	--	--	14.3	14.5	--	13.1	13.4	15.4	18.2
Buddhist	--	--	--	--	--	0.2	0.3	--	0.4	0.4	0.3	0.4
Congregational (United Church of Christ) [1]	--	--	--	--	--	1.8	1.5	--	1.6	1.2	1.1	1.2
Eastern Orthodox	--	--	--	--	--	0.7	0.6	--	0.5	0.6	0.7	0.6
Episcopal	--	--	--	--	--	--	2.6	--	2.7	2.5	2.5	2.3
Jewish	--	--	--	--	--	3.1	2.8	--	2.7	3.2	2.7	2.2
Latter Day Saints (Mormon)	--	--	--	--	--	0.2	0.2	--	0.2	0.3	0.3	0.3
Lutheran	--	--	--	--	--	5.6	5.9	--	8.2	6.2	6.4	5.8
Methodist	--	--	--	--	--	10.3	9.9	--	9.2	8.7	9.8	9.7
Muslim (Islamic) [1]	--	--	--	--	--	0.2	0.2	--	0.2	0.3	0.4	0.3
Presbyterian	--	--	--	--	--	--	5.0	--	4.8	4.5	4.8	4.5
Quaker (Society of Friends)	--	--	--	--	--	0.2	0.2	--	0.2	0.2	0.2	0.2
Roman Catholic	--	--	--	--	--	39.3	37.0	--	36.0	36.2	33.6	32.1
Seventh Day Adventist	--	--	--	--	--	0.3	0.3	--	0.2	0.3	0.4	0.2
Unitarian-Universalist	--	--	--	--	--	0.2	--	--	--	--	--	--
Other Protestant	--	--	--	--	--	10.2	5.5	--	4.9	4.8	5.0	4.6
Other religion	--	--	--	--	--	5.6	5.0	--	4.9	5.5	5.1	5.6
None	--	--	--	--	--	8.0	8.4	--	10.1	11.6	11.3	11.8
DISABILITIES [4]												
Hearing	--	--	--	--	0.7	0.9	0.9	0.6	0.7	0.8	--	--
Speech	--	--	--	--	0.3	0.3	0.3	0.2	0.2	0.3	--	--
Partially sighted/blind	--	--	--	--	2.2	1.9	2.1	1.7	1.9	1.9	--	--
Orthopedic	--	--	--	--	0.9	1.0	0.9	0.7	0.8	1.0	--	--
Learning disabled	--	--	--	--	0.7	0.9	1.1	0.8	1.2	1.2	--	--
Health related	--	--	--	--	0.9	1.0	1.2	0.8	1.0	1.2	--	--
Other	--	--	--	--	1.2	1.3	1.2	0.9	1.0	1.0	--	--
DISTANCE FROM HOME TO COLLEGE												
10 miles or less [1]	25.1	23.8	19.6	20.5	21.2	19.4	18.8	17.5	17.7	18.1	17.2	13.3
11-50 miles	25.1	26.5	25.1	25.6	28.9	28.5	27.1	27.7	28.5	26.8	26.8	27.4
51-100 miles	15.0	15.3	16.6	16.3	15.9	15.9	17.1	16.6	16.6	14.7	15.9	18.1
101-500 miles	27.1	26.5	30.8	29.6	25.7	27.7	28.5	28.0	27.5	29.3	29.7	30.0
More than 500 miles	7.8	7.9	7.9	7.9	8.3	8.4	8.6	10.1	9.7	11.2	10.4	11.2

[1] Text, order or number of response options may vary from year to year.
[2] Respondent allowed to mark all responses that apply from 1971-1990. Responses may sum to more than 100%.
[3] See Appendix D for a discussion of variation in question texts and aggregation procedures.
[4] Responses from 1978-1982 excluded because they were not recorded in a comparable manner.

STUDENT'S DEMOGRAPHICS	1966	1967	1968	1969	1970	1971	1972	1973	1974	1975	1976	1977	1978
RATED SELF ABOVE AVERAGE OR TOP 10% IN													
Academic ability	57.4	--	--	--	--	50.6	--	--	53.0	--	51.2	--	--
Athletic ability	35.7	--	--	--	--	36.0	--	--	38.5	--	39.3	--	--
Artistic ability	18.7	--	--	--	--	17.7	--	--	19.5	--	21.5	--	--
Drive to achieve	56.8	--	--	--	--	52.4	--	--	59.9	--	61.5	--	--
Emotional health	--	--	--	--	--	--	--	--	--	--	--	--	--
Leadership ability	38.1	--	--	--	--	34.9	--	--	41.3	--	43.3	--	--
Mathematical ability	35.5	--	--	--	--	32.0	--	--	33.4	--	33.5	--	--
Mechanical ability	24.7	--	--	--	--	22.6	--	--	23.8	--	24.0	--	--
Originality	37.0	--	--	--	--	34.2	--	--	37.4	--	39.0	--	--
Physical health	--	--	--	--	--	--	--	--	--	--	--	--	--
Political conservatism	15.3	--	--	--	--	8.6	--	--	10.5	--	12.1	--	--
Political liberalism	19.1	--	--	--	--	23.0	--	--	20.1	--	18.7	--	--
Popularity	31.9	--	--	--	--	29.2	--	--	30.2	--	30.8	--	--
Popularity with the opposite sex	28.8	--	--	--	--	27.2	--	--	29.4	--	30.2	--	--
Public speaking ability	22.4	--	--	--	--	19.4	--	--	20.7	--	21.7	--	--
Self-confidence (intellectual)	36.0	--	--	--	--	34.8	--	--	40.7	--	42.4	--	--
Self-confidence (social)	29.8	--	--	--	--	27.4	--	--	33.9	--	36.3	--	--
Sensitivity to criticism	27.0	--	--	--	--	25.4	--	--	25.1	--	24.3	--	--
Stubbornness	36.9	--	--	--	--	36.3	--	--	36.9	--	35.8	--	--
Understanding of others	60.1	--	--	--	--	62.5	--	--	65.9	--	66.3	--	--
Writing ability	27.2	--	--	--	--	27.7	--	--	30.5	--	32.6	--	--

PARENT'S DEMOGRAPHICS	1966	1967	1968	1969	1970	1971	1972	1973	1974	1975	1976	1977	1978
ESTIMATED PARENTAL INCOME													
Less than $6,000	19.5	[*]	16.6	14.5	13.6	12.0	14.1	11.1	10.6	11.0	10.7	10.1	8.0
$6,000-9,999	34.2	[*]	32.4	30.0	24.0	22.4	18.6	15.0	13.7	11.7	10.9	10.1	8.3
$10,000-14,999	25.2	[*]	27.2	28.7	31.0	32.3	30.3	29.6	29.0	25.4	23.3	20.9	17.6
$15,000-19,999	9.4	[*]	11.2	12.5	13.2	14.3	14.8	16.8	16.6	17.4	17.2	17.2	16.2
$20,000-24,999	4.6	[*]	5.3	6.2	7.3	8.1	8.9	10.9	12.0	12.6	13.6	14.9	16.3
$25,000-29,999	2.4	[*]	2.5	2.8	3.6	3.8	4.3	5.3	5.9	7.0	7.5	8.4	9.8
$30,000 or more	4.7	[*]	4.8	5.2	--	--	--	--	--	--	--	--	--
$30,000-34,999	--	--	--	--	2.4	2.4	2.9	3.7	3.9	4.7	5.5	6.2	7.7
$35,000-39,999	--	--	--	--	1.3	1.3	1.8	2.2	2.4	2.9	3.3	3.6	4.6
$40,000 or more	--	--	--	--	3.6	3.4	--	--	--	--	--	--	--
$40,000-49,999	--	--	--	--	--	--	1.7	1.9	2.2	2.7	3.1	3.4	4.3
$50,000 or more	--	--	--	--	--	--	2.7	3.4	3.8	4.6	4.9	5.4	7.0
$50,000-59,999	--	--	--	--	--	--	--	--	--	--	--	--	--
$50,000-99,999	--	--	--	--	--	--	--	--	--	--	--	--	--
$60,000-74,999	--	--	--	--	--	--	--	--	--	--	--	--	--
$75,000-99,999	--	--	--	--	--	--	--	--	--	--	--	--	--
$100,000 or more	--	--	--	--	--	--	--	--	--	--	--	--	--
$100,000-149,999	--	--	--	--	--	--	--	--	--	--	--	--	--
$150,000 or more	--	--	--	--	--	--	--	--	--	--	--	--	--
MEDIAN INCOME (in $1,000's)	**9.6**	**[*]**	**10.2**	**11.0**	**12.0**	**12.4**	**12.9**	**14.0**	**14.4**	**15.5**	**16.5**	**17.6**	**20.0**
NUMBER CURRENTLY DEPENDENT ON PARENTS FOR SUPPORT [1]													
One	--	--	--	--	--	--	--	--	--	--	--	--	5.0
Two	--	--	--	--	--	--	--	--	--	--	--	--	8.5
Three	--	--	--	--	--	--	--	--	--	--	--	--	19.2
Four	--	--	--	--	--	--	--	--	--	--	--	--	25.6
Five	--	--	--	--	--	--	--	--	--	--	--	--	22.5
Six or more	--	--	--	--	--	--	--	--	--	--	--	--	19.1
NUMBER OF DEPENDENTS CURRENTLY ATTENDING COLLEGE [2]													
None	--	--	--	--	--	--	--	--	--	--	--	--	66.5
One	--	--	--	--	--	--	--	--	--	--	--	--	24.9
Two	--	--	--	--	--	--	--	--	--	--	--	--	6.2
Three or more	--	--	--	--	--	--	--	--	--	--	--	--	2.4
PARENTS' MARITAL STATUS													
both alive and living with each other	--	--	--	--	--	--	83.1	--	--	--	--	--	--
both alive, divorced or separated	--	--	--	--	--	--	8.7	--	--	--	--	--	--
one or both deceased	--	--	--	--	--	--	8.2	--	--	--	--	--	--

[*] Results were not comparable to those of other years due to changes in question text or order.
[1] Including respondent and parents if applicable.
[2] Other than respondent.

1979	1980	1981	1982	1983	1984	1985	1986	1987	1988	1989	1990	*STUDENT'S DEMOGRAPHICS*
												RATED SELF ABOVE AVERAGE OR TOP 10% IN
--	51.5	--	--	--	--	54.9	54.8	54.2	56.1	55.8	53.7	Academic ability
--	40.3	--	--	--	--	--	--	--	--	--	--	Athletic ability
--	22.2	--	--	--	--	22.8	23.2	24.9	24.7	24.5	25.0	Artistic ability
--	64.4	--	--	--	--	61.6	60.9	59.3	63.7	64.1	66.3	Drive to achieve
--	--	--	--	--	--	60.3	58.7	59.0	58.4	56.4	57.1	Emotional health
--	46.9	--	--	--	--	50.9	51.6	50.6	51.6	51.0	50.9	Leadership ability
--	35.6	--	--	--	--	38.5	39.9	39.8	40.6	39.9	37.4	Mathematical ability
--	25.5	--	--	--	--	--	--	--	--	--	--	Mechanical ability
--	43.3	--	--	--	--	--	--	--	--	--	--	Originality
--	--	--	--	--	--	61.6	61.2	59.0	58.4	58.6	58.5	Physical health
--	13.3	--	--	--	--	--	--	--	--	--	--	Political conservatism
--	14.6	--	--	--	--	--	--	--	--	--	--	Political liberalism
--	33.8	--	--	--	--	43.1	44.3	43.5	43.5	42.9	43.0	Popularity
--	34.3	--	--	--	--	--	--	41.2	41.9	41.1	41.2	Popularity with the opposite sex
--	23.8	--	--	--	--	--	--	29.3	29.5	29.3	28.4	Public speaking ability
--	46.2	--	--	--	--	54.3	54.7	48.6	49.7	50.0	48.3	Self-confidence (intellectual)
--	40.6	--	--	--	--	47.4	48.2	43.8	43.8	43.6	44.0	Self-confidence (social)
--	24.1	--	--	--	--	--	--	--	--	--	--	Sensitivity to criticism
--	37.1	--	--	--	--	--	--	--	--	--	--	Stubbornness
--	70.4	--	--	--	--	--	--	--	--	--	66.8	Understanding of others
--	33.6	--	--	--	--	37.8	39.4	38.8	39.8	39.9	39.0	Writing ability

1979	1980	1981	1982	1983	1984	1985	1986	1987	1988	1989	1990	*PARENT'S DEMOGRAPHICS*
												ESTIMATED PARENTAL INCOME
7.8	7.4	5.7	5.1	5.6	5.8	4.6	3.9	3.6	3.7	3.0	3.0	Less than $6,000
8.1	7.2	5.9	5.3	5.3	5.0	4.2	3.7	3.2	2.9	2.8	3.0	$6,000-9,999
15.2	13.7	11.8	10.2	10.6	9.9	7.1	6.4	5.6	5.1	4.8	4.9	$10,000-14,999
13.9	12.4	10.5	9.1	8.7	8.0	7.1	6.5	6.0	5.4	5.3	5.3	$15,000-19,999
16.6	16.5	15.2	13.2	12.6	11.3	8.6	7.9	7.6	6.9	7.0	6.8	$20,000-24,999
10.3	10.9	11.5	11.5	10.5	10.2	8.8	8.2	7.5	7.0	7.0	6.4	$25,000-29,999
--	--	--	--	--	--	--	--	--	--	--	--	$30,000 or more
8.2	9.4	10.5	12.0	11.3	10.9	11.2	10.4	9.7	9.1	9.3	8.8	$30,000-34,999
5.5	6.1	7.9	8.5	8.6	9.1	9.8	9.7	9.6	9.1	9.0	8.7	$35,000-39,999
--	--	--	--	--	--	--	--	--	--	--	--	$40,000 or more
6.0	7.1	9.0	10.6	11.2	12.2	11.8	12.4	12.4	12.4	12.8	12.6	$40,000-49,999
--	--	--	--	--	--	--	--	--	--	--	--	$50,000 or more
--	--	--	--	--	--	9.5	10.2	10.9	11.6	11.8	11.6	$50,000-59,999
6.3	7.1	9.2	11.3	12.3	13.7	--	--	--	--	--	--	$50,000-99,999
--	--	--	--	--	--	7.0	8.3	9.6	10.7	10.8	11.4	$60,000-74,999
--	--	--	--	--	--	4.3	5.3	6.2	7.0	7.2	7.7	$75,000-99,999
2.1	2.2	2.7	3.3	3.4	4.0	--	--	--	--	--	--	$100,000 or more
--	--	--	--	--	--	3.0	3.6	4.2	4.8	4.8	5.0	$100,000-149,999
--	--	--	--	--	--	3.0	3.6	4.0	4.3	4.5	4.6	$150,000 or more
21.5	**22.8**	**25.4**	**28.1**	**28.4**	**29.9**	**34.3**	**36.5**	**38.5**	**40.6**	**41.4**	**42.5**	**MEDIAN INCOME (in $1,000's)**
												NUMBER CURRENTLY DEPENDENT ON PARENTS FOR SUPPORT [1]
6.2	5.9	5.4	5.8	6.3	6.3	6.9	7.5	9.2	--	--	--	One
10.0	9.9	10.0	10.7	12.1	12.5	13.2	14.5	17.4	--	--	--	Two
19.8	20.6	20.6	21.2	23.6	23.6	22.1	22.3	22.6	--	--	--	Three
25.2	25.7	26.7	27.4	28.9	29.4	28.3	28.2	26.9	--	--	--	Four
21.3	21.3	21.7	20.4	18.5	18.3	18.1	17.1	15.4	--	--	--	Five
17.6	16.6	15.6	14.5	10.6	10.0	11.5	10.4	8.4	--	--	--	Six or more
												NUMBER OF DEPENDENTS CURRENTLY ATTENDING COLLEGE [2]
66.2	66.3	65.6	65.4	66.5	68.0	68.9	69.2	69.5	--	--	--	None
24.5	24.8	24.9	25.0	24.5	23.5	23.4	23.3	23.2	--	--	--	One
6.5	6.5	6.8	6.8	6.4	6.1	5.6	5.5	5.3	--	--	--	Two
2.8	2.5	2.7	2.9	2.6	2.4	2.1	2.0	1.9	--	--	--	Three or more
												PARENTS' MARITAL STATUS
--	--	--	--	--	--	--	74.7	73.7	72.8	72.3	71.2	both alive and living with each other
--	--	--	--	--	--	--	19.4	20.6	21.8	22.6	23.3	both alive, divorced or separated
--	--	--	--	--	--	--	5.9	5.7	5.4	5.1	5.4	one or both deceased

[1] Including respondent and parents if applicable.
[2] Other than respondent.

PARENT'S DEMOGRAPHICS	1966	1967	1968	1969	1970	1971	1972	1973	1974	1975	1976	1977	1978
MOTHER'S EDUCATION													
Grammar school or less	5.9	6.3	6.6	6.4	7.1	5.3	6.0	4.5	5.0	5.0	4.9	4.6	3.7
Some high school	13.5	13.9	15.1	14.4	14.4	13.4	13.2	12.0	11.5	11.6	11.2	11.3	9.6
High school graduate	42.2	42.4	43.4	43.7	42.6	45.0	43.8	42.4	41.8	42.2	42.2	42.9	41.9
Postsecondary school other than college	--	--	--	--	--	--	--	6.8	7.0	6.5	6.8	6.7	7.1
Some college	20.4	19.6	18.8	18.7	18.3	17.9	17.5	14.5	14.6	14.0	13.8	13.4	14.2
College degree	15.3	14.9	13.6	14.0	14.6	15.2	13.2	13.5	13.9	14.0	14.5	14.2	15.6
Some graduate school	--	--	--	--	--	--	2.2	2.0	1.9	2.0	1.9	1.9	2.1
Graduate degree	2.7	2.9	2.5	2.8	3.0	3.1	4.0	4.3	4.4	4.8	4.8	5.0	5.8
MOTHER'S CURRENT OCCUPATION [1]													
Artist	--	--	--	--	--	--	--	--	--	--	1.2	1.2	1.2
Businesswoman	--	--	--	--	--	--	--	--	--	--	6.7	6.9	7.7
Business (clerical)	--	--	--	--	--	--	--	--	--	--	10.0	10.0	10.4
Clergy or religious worker	--	--	--	--	--	--	--	--	--	--	0.1	0.1	0.1
College teacher	--	--	--	--	--	--	--	--	--	--	0.3	0.3	0.3
Doctor or dentist	--	--	--	--	--	--	--	--	--	--	0.2	0.1	0.2
Educator (secondary school)	--	--	--	--	--	--	--	--	--	--	2.5	2.5	2.7
Elementary school teacher	--	--	--	--	--	--	--	--	--	--	5.3	5.2	5.6
Engineer	--	--	--	--	--	--	--	--	--	--	0.1	0.1	0.1
Farmer or forester	--	--	--	--	--	--	--	--	--	--	0.2	0.2	0.2
Health professional (non-MD)	--	--	--	--	--	--	--	--	--	--	1.5	1.5	1.4
Homemaker (full-time)	--	--	--	--	--	--	--	--	--	--	33.9	31.9	31.4
Lawyer	--	--	--	--	--	--	--	--	--	--	0.1	0.1	0.1
Nurse	--	--	--	--	--	--	--	--	--	--	5.9	6.4	6.5
Research scientist	--	--	--	--	--	--	--	--	--	--	0.1	0.1	0.1
Skilled worker	--	--	--	--	--	--	--	--	--	--	1.8	1.9	1.9
Semiskilled or unskilled worker	--	--	--	--	--	--	--	--	--	--	5.8	6.0	5.3
Social worker	--	--	--	--	--	--	--	--	--	--	--	1.1	1.0
Unemployed	--	--	--	--	--	--	--	--	--	--	9.3	9.5	8.6
Other	--	--	--	--	--	--	--	--	--	--	15.1	15.0	15.2
MOTHER'S CURRENT RELIGIOUS PREFERENCE (Aggregated) [2]													
Protestant	--	--	--	--	57.2	--	--	--	54.0	53.3	50.8	50.8	51.1
Roman Catholic	--	--	--	--	31.8	--	--	--	35.2	35.6	37.2	38.6	38.2
Jewish	--	--	--	--	5.2	--	--	--	4.2	4.2	4.1	4.1	4.4
Other	--	--	--	--	3.0	--	--	--	3.0	3.3	4.1	3.5	3.4
None	--	--	--	--	2.9	--	--	--	3.7	3.7	3.8	3.1	2.9
MOTHER'S CURRENT RELIGIOUS PREFERENCE (Disaggregated)													
Baptist	--	--	--	--	15.5	--	--	--	14.2	14.9	13.2	13.7	13.4
Buddhist	--	--	--	--	--	--	--	--	--	--	--	--	--
Congregational (United Church of Christ) [3]	--	--	--	--	2.7	--	--	--	2.2	1.9	2.0	2.2	2.1
Eastern Orthodox	--	--	--	--	0.6	--	--	--	0.6	0.7	0.7	0.8	0.7
Episcopal	--	--	--	--	4.2	--	--	--	3.7	3.6	3.4	3.6	3.6
Jewish	--	--	--	--	5.2	--	--	--	4.2	4.2	4.1	4.1	4.4
Latter Day Saints (Mormon)	--	--	--	--	0.3	--	--	--	0.4	0.3	0.3	0.2	0.2
Lutheran	--	--	--	--	7.0	--	--	--	7.3	6.5	7.0	6.1	6.0
Methodist	--	--	--	--	12.4	--	--	--	12.0	12.0	10.6	11.3	11.5
Muslim (Islamic) [3]	--	--	--	--	0.1	--	--	--	0.1	0.1	0.2	0.2	0.2
Presbyterian	--	--	--	--	7.6	--	--	--	6.9	7.1	6.5	6.2	6.8
Quaker (Society of Friends)	--	--	--	--	0.2	--	--	--	0.2	0.2	0.2	0.2	0.2
Roman Catholic	--	--	--	--	31.8	--	--	--	35.2	35.6	37.2	38.6	38.2
Seventh Day Adventist	--	--	--	--	0.3	--	--	--	0.3	0.5	0.6	0.3	0.4
Unitarian-Universalist	--	--	--	--	0.5	--	--	--	0.5	0.4	0.4	0.4	0.4
Other Protestant	--	--	--	--	5.9	--	--	--	5.7	5.2	5.9	5.8	5.8
Other religion	--	--	--	--	2.9	--	--	--	2.9	3.2	3.9	3.3	3.2
None	--	--	--	--	2.9	--	--	--	3.7	3.7	3.8	3.1	2.9

[1] Data for this item collected but not reported in 1969-1975
[2] See Appendix D for a discussion of variation in question texts and aggregation procedures.
[3] Text, order or number of response options may vary from year to year.

1979	1980	1981	1982	1983	1984	1985	1986	1987	1988	1989	1990	***PARENT'S DEMOGRAPHICS***
												MOTHER'S EDUCATION
4.3	4.2	3.1	3.0	3.3	3.4	3.1	3.0	2.8	3.1	2.7	2.7	Grammar school or less
10.3	9.7	8.7	8.0	8.2	7.9	7.6	6.8	5.8	6.1	5.7	6.1	Some high school
41.0	41.6	41.7	41.2	40.6	39.4	38.2	36.3	35.7	34.0	34.8	34.4	High school graduate
6.7	6.8	6.7	7.3	7.5	7.7	7.7	7.8	8.6	8.0	8.0	7.6	Postsecondary school other than college
14.4	14.2	14.5	14.6	14.9	15.2	16.0	16.4	16.2	16.7	16.7	16.9	Some college
15.2	15.6	16.7	17.0	16.3	17.0	17.0	18.1	18.8	19.1	19.6	19.4	College degree
2.2	2.1	2.1	2.1	2.2	2.3	2.5	2.9	2.9	3.0	2.9	2.9	Some graduate school
5.8	5.9	6.4	6.8	7.1	7.1	7.8	8.7	9.2	9.7	9.7	9.9	Graduate degree
												MOTHER'S CURRENT OCCUPATION [1]
1.2	1.2	1.3	1.4	1.4	1.3	1.5	1.6	1.5	1.6	1.5	1.4	Artist
8.2	8.8	9.8	10.1	10.8	11.1	12.6	13.4	14.3	14.2	14.3	14.0	Businesswoman
10.6	11.1	11.3	11.5	11.3	11.5	11.1	11.3	11.9	11.1	11.2	10.2	Business (clerical)
0.1	0.1	0.1	0.1	0.1	0.1	0.1	0.1	0.1	0.1	0.2	0.1	Clergy or religious worker
0.3	0.3	0.3	0.3	0.3	0.3	0.3	0.4	0.4	0.4	0.4	0.4	College teacher
0.2	0.2	0.2	0.3	0.3	0.3	0.3	0.3	0.4	0.4	0.4	0.4	Doctor or dentist
2.7	2.8	3.2	3.3	3.0	3.1	3.4	3.6	3.7	4.0	3.9	4.0	Educator (secondary school)
5.5	5.4	5.8	5.9	5.2	5.5	5.6	5.9	6.2	6.7	6.8	6.9	Elementary school teacher
0.1	0.1	0.1	0.1	0.1	0.1	0.2	0.2	0.2	0.2	0.2	0.2	Engineer
0.3	0.3	0.4	0.4	0.3	0.3	0.3	0.3	0.4	0.3	0.4	0.5	Farmer or forester
1.5	1.6	1.7	1.8	1.9	1.8	1.8	1.8	1.9	1.9	2.0	2.1	Health professional (non-MD)
28.6	28.1	23.2	22.8	25.1	23.8	22.3	20.6	18.0	18.0	16.2	15.0	Homemaker (full-time)
0.1	0.1	0.1	0.1	0.1	0.2	0.2	0.2	0.3	0.3	0.3	0.3	Lawyer
6.7	6.7	7.5	7.7	7.4	7.6	7.6	7.5	7.7	7.6	7.8	8.0	Nurse
0.1	0.1	0.1	0.1	0.2	0.1	0.1	0.1	0.1	0.1	0.1	0.1	Research scientist
1.9	2.0	1.9	2.0	2.0	1.9	2.0	2.1	2.5	2.1	2.2	2.3	Skilled worker
5.8	5.9	5.8	5.9	5.8	5.4	5.3	5.1	4.8	4.4	5.1	5.1	Semiskilled or unskilled worker
1.2	1.1	1.2	1.2	1.2	1.3	1.2	1.2	1.3	1.4	1.4	1.3	Social worker
8.9	8.6	8.5	8.0	7.1	7.0	7.0	6.7	6.2	6.1	5.8	5.7	Unemployed
16.0	15.7	17.4	17.2	16.5	17.1	17.2	17.6	17.9	19.1	19.9	21.8	Other
												MOTHER'S CURRENT RELIGIOUS PREFERENCE (Aggregated) [2]
36.7	36.9	38.1	36.5	34.6	46.9	49.6	32.6	49.9	46.9	50.8	51.2	Protestant
39.1	39.6	37.7	39.4	40.0	39.7	37.6	37.0	37.1	37.7	35.4	34.3	Roman Catholic
3.9	3.5	3.3	3.3	3.4	3.4	3.1	3.6	3.1	3.7	3.0	2.5	Jewish
16.6	16.1	17.3	17.2	18.2	5.9	5.3	21.6	5.2	6.1	5.5	6.1	Other
3.6	3.8	3.6	3.5	3.8	4.1	4.4	5.3	4.9	5.7	5.3	5.9	None
												MOTHER'S CURRENT RELIGIOUS PREFERENCE (Disaggregated)
--	--	--	--	--	14.5	14.6	--	13.5	13.8	15.5	17.7	Baptist
--	--	--	--	--	0.3	0.4	--	0.5	0.6	0.5	0.6	Buddhist
--	--	--	--	--	1.9	1.7	--	1.8	1.4	1.2	1.3	Congregational (United Church of Christ) [3]
--	--	--	--	--	0.8	0.7	--	0.6	0.6	0.7	0.6	Eastern Orthodox
--	--	--	--	--	--	2.9	--	3.1	2.9	3.0	2.8	Episcopal
--	--	--	--	--	3.4	3.1	--	3.1	3.7	3.0	2.5	Jewish
--	--	--	--	--	0.2	0.2	--	0.3	0.3	0.3	0.3	Latter Day Saints (Mormon)
--	--	--	--	--	6.2	6.4	--	8.8	6.9	7.2	6.6	Lutheran
--	--	--	--	--	11.2	10.9	--	10.3	9.7	11.0	10.8	Methodist
--	--	--	--	--	0.2	0.2	--	0.2	0.3	0.4	0.3	Muslim (Islamic) [3]
--	--	--	--	--	--	5.7	--	5.5	5.4	5.7	5.3	Presbyterian
--	--	--	--	--	0.2	0.2	--	0.2	0.2	0.3	0.3	Quaker (Society of Friends)
--	--	--	--	--	39.7	37.6	--	37.1	37.7	35.4	34.3	Roman Catholic
--	--	--	--	--	0.3	0.3	--	0.3	0.3	0.4	0.3	Seventh Day Adventist
--	--	--	--	--	0.3	--	--	--	--	--	--	Unitarian-Universalist
--	--	--	--	--	11.3	6.0	--	5.5	5.4	5.5	5.2	Other Protestant
--	--	--	--	--	5.4	4.7	--	4.5	5.2	4.6	5.2	Other religion
--	--	--	--	--	4.1	4.4	--	4.9	5.7	5.3	5.9	None

[1] Data for this item collected but not reported in 1969-1975
[2] See Appendix D for a discussion of variation in question texts and aggregation procedures.
[3] Text, order or number of response options may vary from year to year.

PARENT'S DEMOGRAPHICS	1966	1967	1968	1969	1970	1971	1972	1973	1974	1975	1976	1977	1978
FATHER'S EDUCATION													
Grammar school or less	9.4	10.3	10.4	10.0	10.7	8.8	9.2	7.2	7.8	7.5	7.5	6.9	5.8
Some high school	15.7	16.2	17.2	16.7	16.0	15.8	15.1	14.0	13.2	13.5	13.0	13.1	11.4
High school graduate	29.1	29.0	30.1	30.2	29.1	30.9	30.3	28.4	28.9	28.9	28.5	29.5	28.3
Postsecondary school other than college	--	--	--	--	--	--	--	4.3	4.5	4.1	4.3	4.3	4.4
Some college	19.1	18.0	17.8	17.6	17.0	16.9	16.2	14.4	14.2	13.7	13.3	13.2	13.5
College degree	16.9	16.5	16.0	16.8	17.7	18.4	16.1	17.2	17.3	17.8	18.5	18.5	19.8
Some graduate school	--	--	--	--	--	--	2.4	2.4	2.2	2.2	2.3	2.2	2.5
Graduate degree	9.7	9.9	8.5	8.8	9.5	9.3	10.7	12.1	12.0	12.3	12.6	12.4	14.1
FATHER'S CURRENT OCCUPATION [1]													
Artist	--	0.8	0.8	0.8	0.9	0.8	0.8	--	0.7	0.7	0.9	0.9	0.8
Businessman	--	31.1	30.1	29.5	30.1	29.7	30.0	--	27.6	26.4	29.0	28.5	29.6
Clergy or religious worker	--	1.1	0.9	1.0	1.1	0.9	0.9	--	1.0	1.0	1.1	1.1	1.1
College teacher	--	0.7	0.7	0.7	0.8	0.8	0.9	--	1.2	1.2	0.9	0.8	0.9
Doctor or dentist	--	2.4	2.0	2.0	2.1	1.9	2.0	--	2.0	2.2	2.2	2.0	2.3
Educator (secondary school)	--	2.0	1.9	2.0	2.2	2.2	2.3	--	2.0	2.0	3.0	2.9	3.3
Elementary school teacher	--	0.3	0.3	0.3	0.4	0.3	0.3	--	0.6	0.7	0.6	0.6	0.5
Engineer	--	7.0	7.0	7.1	7.1	7.5	7.7	--	6.7	6.9	8.8	8.5	9.2
Farmer or forester	--	6.9	6.6	5.9	5.7	6.8	5.9	--	5.2	4.4	4.0	3.8	3.5
Health professional (non-MD)	--	1.1	1.1	1.3	1.2	1.2	1.2	--	1.0	1.1	1.3	1.3	1.3
Lawyer	--	1.4	1.2	1.2	1.3	1.2	1.3	--	1.4	1.4	1.3	1.3	1.4
Military career	--	1.6	1.6	1.8	1.7	2.0	1.8	--	1.5	1.6	2.0	1.9	1.8
Research scientist	--	0.5	0.6	0.5	0.6	0.6	0.6	--	0.6	0.6	0.6	0.6	0.7
Skilled worker	--	12.7	13.0	13.5	12.4	12.3	12.4	--	18.2	17.6	11.2	11.4	11.0
Semiskilled or unskilled worker	--	11.7	13.0	12.5	12.6	11.4	11.3	--	9.5	9.5	10.0	10.1	8.4
Unemployed	--	0.9	1.1	1.2	1.4	1.4	2.0	--	2.1	3.1	2.4	2.6	2.4
Other	--	17.8	18.3	18.7	18.4	19.0	18.5	--	18.7	19.7	20.7	21.8	21.6
FATHER'S CURRENT RELIGIOUS PREFERENCE (Aggregated) [2]													
Protestant	--	--	--	--	--	--	--	--	51.5	50.7	48.6	48.6	49.1
Roman Catholic	--	--	--	--	--	--	--	--	33.7	34.2	35.5	37.4	36.9
Jewish	--	--	--	--	--	--	--	--	4.4	4.4	4.2	4.2	4.6
Other	--	--	--	--	--	--	--	--	2.9	3.1	3.8	3.2	3.0
None	--	--	--	--	--	--	--	--	7.6	7.6	7.9	6.6	6.4
FATHER'S CURRENT RELIGIOUS PREFERENCE (Disaggregated)													
Baptist	--	--	--	--	--	--	--	--	13.4	14.0	12.6	13.0	13.0
Buddhist	--	--	--	--	--	--	--	--	--	--	--	--	--
Congregational (United Church of Christ) [3]	--	--	--	--	--	--	--	--	2.1	1.8	1.9	2.0	1.9
Eastern Orthodox	--	--	--	--	--	--	--	--	0.6	0.7	0.7	0.8	0.8
Episcopal	--	--	--	--	--	--	--	--	3.3	3.2	3.1	3.2	3.2
Jewish	--	--	--	--	--	--	--	--	4.4	4.4	4.2	4.2	4.6
Latter Day Saints (Mormon)	--	--	--	--	--	--	--	--	0.3	0.2	0.3	0.2	0.1
Lutheran	--	--	--	--	--	--	--	--	7.2	6.4	6.8	6.0	5.9
Methodist	--	--	--	--	--	--	--	--	11.5	11.5	10.1	10.8	11.0
Muslim (Islamic) [3]	--	--	--	--	--	--	--	--	0.2	0.2	0.2	0.2	0.2
Presbyterian	--	--	--	--	--	--	--	--	6.7	6.9	6.2	6.1	6.5
Quaker (Society of Friends)	--	--	--	--	--	--	--	--	0.2	0.2	0.2	0.2	0.2
Roman Catholic	--	--	--	--	--	--	--	--	33.7	34.2	35.5	37.4	36.9
Seventh Day Adventist	--	--	--	--	--	--	--	--	0.3	0.4	0.5	0.2	0.4
Unitarian-Universalist	--	--	--	--	--	--	--	--	0.4	0.3	0.3	0.3	0.3
Other Protestant	--	--	--	--	--	--	--	--	5.5	5.1	5.9	5.8	5.8
Other religion	--	--	--	--	--	--	--	--	2.7	2.9	3.6	3.0	2.8
None	--	--	--	--	--	--	--	--	7.6	7.6	7.9	6.6	6.4

[1] Data for this item collected but not reported in 1973.
[2] See Appendix D for a discussion of variation in question texts and aggregation procedures.
[3] Text, order or number of response options may vary from year to year.

1979	1980	1981	1982	1983	1984	1985	1986	1987	1988	1989	1990	***PARENT'S DEMOGRAPHICS***
												FATHER'S EDUCATION
6.2	6.2	5.1	4.5	4.9	4.9	4.3	4.1	3.7	4.1	3.4	3.8	Grammar school or less
12.1	11.7	10.5	10.0	10.4	9.7	9.5	8.7	8.0	7.3	7.5	7.4	Some high school
28.0	29.4	29.2	29.6	29.3	29.2	28.5	27.4	27.2	26.9	27.7	28.0	High school graduate
4.3	4.3	4.5	4.6	4.8	5.1	5.0	5.0	5.3	4.8	5.1	4.9	Postsecondary school other than college
13.4	13.0	13.4	13.4	13.7	13.8	14.0	14.1	14.1	14.5	14.6	15.3	Some college
19.4	19.1	20.1	20.1	19.5	19.9	19.6	20.3	20.7	21.1	21.7	21.1	College degree
2.4	2.3	2.4	2.3	2.3	2.3	2.7	2.7	2.7	2.8	2.5	2.4	Some graduate school
14.2	14.1	14.9	15.4	15.1	15.0	16.4	17.8	18.3	18.6	17.6	17.1	Graduate degree
												FATHER'S CURRENT OCCUPATION [1]
0.8	0.8	0.8	0.9	0.9	0.8	0.9	0.8	0.9	0.9	0.8	0.7	Artist
29.3	28.8	29.0	29.6	29.2	29.2	29.2	30.2	30.7	29.8	29.7	27.5	Businessman
1.0	1.0	1.1	1.0	0.9	0.9	1.0	1.0	0.9	0.9	1.0	1.1	Clergy or religious worker
0.9	0.9	0.9	1.0	0.9	0.9	0.9	1.0	0.9	0.9	0.9	0.8	College teacher
2.2	2.2	2.2	2.2	2.2	2.1	2.1	2.3	2.4	2.4	2.2	2.1	Doctor or dentist
3.3	3.2	3.6	3.5	3.4	3.4	3.5	3.6	3.6	3.9	3.6	3.6	Educator (secondary school)
0.6	0.6	0.6	0.6	0.6	0.6	0.7	0.7	0.8	0.9	0.9	0.9	Elementary school teacher
8.6	8.7	8.8	9.0	8.6	8.5	8.5	8.4	8.3	8.2	7.7	7.8	Engineer
3.7	3.9	4.4	3.9	3.9	3.7	3.9	3.1	3.4	2.9	2.9	3.2	Farmer or forester
1.3	1.2	1.3	1.4	1.3	1.3	1.3	1.4	1.3	1.3	1.3	1.3	Health professional (non-MD)
1.5	1.5	1.5	1.6	1.4	1.5	1.5	1.7	1.7	1.8	1.6	1.6	Lawyer
1.7	1.7	1.9	1.8	1.8	1.6	1.6	1.7	1.8	1.7	1.8	2.2	Military career
0.6	0.6	0.6	0.6	0.6	0.5	0.6	0.6	0.6	0.6	0.5	0.4	Research scientist
10.9	11.3	11.0	11.1	10.8	10.9	10.4	10.4	10.1	10.1	10.3	10.3	Skilled worker
8.9	9.3	8.1	8.3	8.7	8.4	8.7	7.6	7.3	7.0	7.9	7.9	Semiskilled or unskilled worker
2.5	2.7	2.1	2.1	3.2	2.8	2.8	2.6	2.4	2.3	2.3	2.4	Unemployed
22.1	21.6	21.9	21.4	21.7	22.7	22.4	23.0	22.9	24.2	24.5	26.0	Other
												FATHER'S CURRENT RELIGIOUS PREFERENCE (Aggregated) [2]
35.8	36.1	37.4	35.8	33.9	45.0	47.3	31.5	47.7	44.7	48.7	48.9	Protestant
37.7	38.1	36.1	37.8	38.0	38.4	36.4	35.4	35.6	35.9	34.4	33.0	Roman Catholic
4.1	3.6	3.4	3.5	3.6	3.6	3.3	3.7	3.3	3.8	3.2	2.7	Jewish
15.8	15.2	16.6	16.5	17.5	5.4	4.8	20.8	4.9	5.7	5.1	5.6	Other
6.6	6.9	6.6	6.5	7.0	7.6	8.2	8.6	8.6	9.9	8.8	9.8	None
												FATHER'S CURRENT RELIGIOUS PREFERENCE (Disaggregated)
--	--	--	--	--	13.9	13.9	--	13.0	13.2	14.9	17.4	Baptist
--	--	--	--	--	0.3	0.4	--	0.5	0.5	0.5	0.5	Buddhist
--	--	--	--	--	1.8	1.6	--	1.6	1.2	1.1	1.1	Congregational (United Church of Christ) [3]
--	--	--	--	--	0.9	0.7	--	0.6	0.7	0.8	0.7	Eastern Orthodox
--	--	--	--	--	--	2.6	--	2.8	2.6	2.6	2.5	Episcopal
--	--	--	--	--	3.6	3.3	--	3.3	3.8	3.2	2.7	Jewish
--	--	--	--	--	0.2	0.2	--	0.2	0.3	0.3	0.3	Latter Day Saints (Mormon)
--	--	--	--	--	6.0	6.2	--	8.8	6.7	7.1	6.6	Lutheran
--	--	--	--	--	10.7	10.3	--	9.8	9.2	10.4	9.9	Methodist
--	--	--	--	--	0.2	0.2	--	0.3	0.4	0.5	0.4	Muslim (Islamic) [3]
--	--	--	--	--	--	5.5	--	5.3	5.1	5.5	5.0	Presbyterian
--	--	--	--	--	0.2	0.2	--	0.1	0.2	0.2	0.2	Quaker (Society of Friends)
--	--	--	--	--	38.4	36.4	--	35.6	35.9	34.4	33.0	Roman Catholic
--	--	--	--	--	0.2	0.2	--	0.2	0.3	0.4	0.2	Seventh Day Adventist
--	--	--	--	--	0.2	--	--	--	--	--	--	Unitarian-Universalist
--	--	--	--	--	10.9	5.9	--	5.3	5.2	5.4	5.0	Other Protestant
--	--	--	--	--	4.9	4.2	--	4.1	4.8	4.1	4.7	Other religion
--	--	--	--	--	7.6	8.2	--	8.6	9.9	8.8	9.8	None

[1] Data for this item collected but not reported in 1973.
[2] See Appendix D for a discussion of variation in question texts and aggregation procedures.
[3] Text, order or number of response options may vary from year to year.

HIGH SCHOOL EXPERIENCES AND ACHIEVEMENTS

HIGH SCHOOL EXPERIENCES AND ACHIEVEMENTS	1966	1967	1968	1969	1970	1971	1972	1973	1974	1975	1976	1977	1978
YEAR GRADUATED FROM HIGH SCHOOL													
Current year (year of the survey)	--	--	--	--	--	90.4	91.6	93.1	92.3	92.3	92.6	92.6	94.1
Last year	--	--	--	--	--	--	--	2.9	3.4	3.1	3.1	3.3	2.9
Two years ago	--	--	--	--	--	--	--	0.7	1.0	0.9	1.0	0.9	0.8
Three years ago	--	--	--	--	--	--	--	2.0	2.0	2.2	2.0	1.9	1.4
High school equivalency certificate	--	--	--	--	--	--	--	0.7	0.7	0.8	0.8	0.8	0.5
Never completed high school	--	--	--	--	--	--	--	0.6	0.7	0.6	0.5	0.4	0.3
TYPE OF SECONDARY SCHOOL													
Public	83.8	--	--	83.6	83.2	--	84.5	--	--	--	--	--	--
Private: nondenominational [1]	3.9	--	--	3.9	2.5	--	4.1	--	--	--	--	--	--
Private: denominational [1]	12.3	--	--	12.5	14.3	--	11.3	--	--	--	--	--	--
AVERAGE GRADE IN HIGH SCHOOL													
A or A+	5.7	5.2	4.6	4.3	5.3	5.7	6.7	7.5	7.5	8.0	8.4	8.6	10.5
A-	9.7	9.2	8.7	8.2	9.2	9.3	10.6	9.8	11.3	10.3	11.3	11.1	12.8
B+	17.0	16.6	15.9	15.6	17.4	17.4	18.8	20.6	19.1	19.2	20.6	20.3	20.1
B	22.3	23.1	23.1	23.7	24.3	25.0	25.8	25.6	26.7	26.1	26.6	27.6	26.4
B-	14.8	15.3	15.5	15.6	16.2	16.4	14.4	15.5	13.6	15.0	13.2	13.6	12.7
C+	16.1	16.1	16.5	16.9	15.9	15.4	14.3	10.9	12.7	11.7	11.6	11.4	10.5
C	13.6	13.6	14.9	14.7	11.0	10.1	9.0	9.7	8.7	9.1	7.8	7.0	6.8
D	0.8	0.8	0.9	0.9	0.7	0.6	0.5	0.4	0.5	0.5	0.4	0.4	0.3
ACADEMIC RANK IN HIGH SCHOOL													
Top quarter [1]	--	--	51.2	50.7	42.2	41.8	43.5	--	--	--	--	--	45.7
Second quarter	--	--	27.6	26.6	31.3	31.3	33.5	--	--	--	--	--	34.1
Third quarter	--	--	17.2	18.2	22.3	23.0	20.3	--	--	--	--	--	18.1
Fourth quarter	--	--	4.0	4.7	4.2	4.0	2.7	--	--	--	--	--	2.1
Top 20 percent	--	--	--	--	--	--	--	--	--	--	--	--	--
Second 20 percent	--	--	--	--	--	--	--	--	--	--	--	--	--
Middle 20 percent	--	--	--	--	--	--	--	--	--	--	--	--	--
Fourth 20 percent	--	--	--	--	--	--	--	--	--	--	--	--	--
Bottom 20 percent	--	--	--	--	--	--	--	--	--	--	--	--	--
HAVE MET/EXCEEDED RECOMMENDED YEARS OF HIGH SCHOOL STUDY [2]													
English (4 years)	--	--	--	--	--	--	--	--	--	--	--	--	--
Mathematics (3 years)	--	--	--	--	--	--	--	--	--	--	--	--	--
Foreign language (2 years)	--	--	--	--	--	--	--	--	--	--	--	--	--
Physical science (2 years)	--	--	--	--	--	--	--	--	--	--	--	--	--
Biological science (2 years)	--	--	--	--	--	--	--	--	--	--	--	--	--
History or American government (1 year)	--	--	--	--	--	--	--	--	--	--	--	--	--
Computer science (1/2 year)	--	--	--	--	--	--	--	--	--	--	--	--	--
Art and/or music (1 year)	--	--	--	--	--	--	--	--	--	--	--	--	--
HAVE HAD SPECIAL TUTORING OR REMEDIAL WORK IN													
English	--	--	--	--	--	--	--	--	--	--	--	--	--
Reading	--	--	--	--	--	--	--	--	--	--	--	--	--
Mathematics	--	--	--	--	--	--	--	--	--	--	--	--	--
Social studies	--	--	--	--	--	--	--	--	--	--	--	--	--
Science	--	--	--	--	--	--	--	--	--	--	--	--	--
Foreign language	--	--	--	--	--	--	--	--	--	--	--	--	--
WILL NEED SPECIAL TUTORING OR REMEDIAL WORK IN [1]													
English	--	--	--	--	--	--	--	--	--	--	--	12.9	14.0
Reading	--	--	--	--	--	--	--	--	--	--	--	7.3	8.1
Mathematics	--	--	--	--	--	--	--	--	--	--	--	25.6	24.9
Social studies	--	--	--	--	--	--	--	--	--	--	--	2.5	4.0
Science	--	--	--	--	--	--	--	--	--	--	--	10.1	12.9
Foreign language	--	--	--	--	--	--	--	--	--	--	--	11.6	14.2

[1] Text, order or number of response options may vary from year to year.
[2] Based on recommendations of the National Commission on Excellence in Education

HIGH SCHOOL EXPERIENCES AND ACHIEVEMENTS

1979	1980	1981	1982	1983	1984	1985	1986	1987	1988	1989	1990	*HIGH SCHOOL EXPERIENCES AND ACHIEVEMENTS*
												YEAR GRADUATED FROM HIGH SCHOOL
92.8	92.1	93.8	94.0	93.3	93.5	93.4	92.2	92.5	93.6	93.4	92.4	Current year (year of the survey)
3.3	3.4	2.7	2.8	2.8	2.9	2.6	2.8	2.9	2.3	2.8	2.9	Last year
0.9	1.0	0.7	0.8	0.8	0.7	0.7	0.9	0.8	0.7	0.7	0.9	Two years ago
1.8	2.1	1.7	1.5	1.9	1.7	1.9	2.4	2.2	1.9	1.8	2.4	Three years ago
0.8	0.9	0.7	0.7	1.0	1.0	1.1	1.4	1.4	1.3	1.1	1.2	High school equivalency certificate
0.4	0.5	0.3	0.2	0.2	0.2	0.2	0.3	0.2	0.2	0.2	0.2	Never completed high school
												TYPE OF SECONDARY SCHOOL
85.7	86.2	--	--	84.5	83.6	--	--	--	--	--	--	Public
3.2	3.2	--	--	4.3	4.4	--	--	--	--	--	--	Private: nondenominational [1]
11.1	10.7	--	--	11.2	12.0	--	--	--	--	--	--	Private: denominational [1]
												AVERAGE GRADE IN HIGH SCHOOL
9.2	9.1	9.2	9.6	9.4	9.3	9.1	10.7	10.3	11.0	10.4	10.2	A or A+
11.5	11.7	11.4	11.4	11.0	10.7	11.6	11.8	10.9	12.6	12.8	12.4	A-
19.3	19.2	19.3	19.3	18.6	18.6	19.0	18.3	19.4	18.5	18.8	18.3	B+
27.0	27.0	26.7	26.5	25.8	25.2	25.5	24.8	22.4	24.8	25.8	25.3	B
13.7	13.3	14.2	13.9	14.2	14.4	13.9	14.1	17.0	14.2	14.4	14.5	B-
11.8	11.8	11.8	12.0	12.7	13.0	12.3	12.5	10.0	11.5	11.1	12.2	C+
7.1	7.5	7.1	7.1	7.8	8.3	8.1	7.3	9.5	7.0	6.3	6.7	C
0.4	0.4	0.3	0.4	0.5	0.5	0.5	0.4	0.4	0.4	0.3	0.3	D
												ACADEMIC RANK IN HIGH SCHOOL
--	--	--	--	--	--	--	--	--	--	--	--	Top quarter [1]
--	--	--	--	--	--	--	--	--	--	--	--	Second quarter
--	--	--	--	--	--	--	--	--	--	--	--	Third quarter
--	--	--	--	--	--	--	--	--	--	--	--	Fourth quarter
38.2	39.0	39.2	39.6	39.4	39.7	41.0	41.7	--	--	--	--	Top 20 percent
23.1	23.0	23.6	23.2	22.8	22.4	22.6	22.3	--	--	--	--	Second 20 percent
32.3	31.4	30.4	30.6	30.6	30.1	28.9	28.8	--	--	--	--	Middle 20 percent
5.6	5.7	6.0	5.8	6.2	6.7	6.4	6.1	--	--	--	--	Fourth 20 percent
0.9	1.0	0.8	0.9	1.0	1.1	1.1	1.1	--	--	--	--	Bottom 20 percent
												HAVE MET/EXCEEDED RECOMMENDED YEARS OF HIGH SCHOOL STUDY [2]
--	--	--	--	89.2	92.6	92.4	93.6	93.5	94.9	--	95.8	English (4 years)
--	--	--	--	83.3	85.4	85.3	88.1	88.4	91.5	--	91.4	Mathematics (3 years)
--	--	--	--	64.2	65.8	65.5	71.1	73.4	78.6	--	76.1	Foreign language (2 years)
--	--	--	--	55.6	51.8	54.4	53.6	49.4	49.5	--	48.1	Physical science (2 years)
--	--	--	--	35.9	33.8	35.0	35.5	34.0	34.7	--	33.1	Biological science (2 years)
--	--	--	--	--	98.5	99.0	98.9	99.2	99.1	--	98.8	History or American government (1 year)
--	--	--	--	--	52.2	57.5	59.1	57.8	58.1	--	53.7	Computer science (1/2 year)
--	--	--	--	--	61.3	61.3	63.0	64.1	66.8	--	72.3	Art and/or music (1 year)
												HAVE HAD SPECIAL TUTORING OR REMEDIAL WORK IN
6.3	6.6	5.2	5.3	--	5.6	--	--	--	--	5.6	--	English
6.4	6.8	5.1	5.1	--	5.4	--	--	--	--	5.3	--	Reading
7.8	8.3	7.0	7.6	--	9.0	--	--	--	--	10.4	--	Mathematics
5.2	6.0	3.9	3.9	--	4.0	--	--	--	--	4.1	--	Social studies
4.9	5.7	3.8	3.9	--	4.3	--	--	--	--	4.7	--	Science
4.1	4.0	3.1	3.3	--	3.7	--	--	--	--	4.5	--	Foreign language
												WILL NEED SPECIAL TUTORING OR REMEDIAL WORK IN [1]
11.8	11.9	11.6	11.3	--	12.1	--	--	--	--	11.3	--	English
5.2	5.2	4.7	4.4	--	4.8	--	--	--	--	4.9	--	Reading
21.9	21.1	21.4	22.1	--	24.6	--	--	--	--	26.5	--	Mathematics
2.7	2.9	2.6	2.6	--	2.9	--	--	--	--	3.2	--	Social studies
9.3	9.5	9.0	9.3	--	10.3	--	--	--	--	10.0	--	Science
8.7	8.7	7.6	7.5	--	8.7	--	--	--	--	9.9	--	Foreign language

[1] Text, order or number of response options may vary from year to year.
[2] Based on recommendations of the National Commission on Excellence in Education

HIGH SCHOOL EXPERIENCES AND ACHIEVEMENTS

ACTIVITIES REPORTED IN THE LAST YEAR	1966	1967	1968	1969	1970	1971	1972	1973	1974	1975	1976	1977	1978
Frequently or Occasionally [1]													
Played a musical instrument	51.4	44.6	39.7	39.9	38.5	37.7	--	--	--	--	--	--	43.9
Stayed up all night	60.2	63.3	57.3	63.8	61.2	59.9	--	--	--	--	--	--	67.0
Participated in organized demonstrations	15.5	16.3	--	--	--	--	--	--	--	--	--	--	16.8
Worked in a local, state, or national political campaign [4]	--	--	12.7	16.4	14.1	13.0	--	--	--	--	--	--	8.9
Came late to class	49.2	56.9	53.6	58.3	58.6	52.9	--	--	--	--	--	--	--
Attended a religious service	--	--	91.0	89.2	87.6	86.0	--	--	--	--	--	--	85.5
Attended a public recital or concert [4]	64.2	--	--	--	--	--	--	--	--	--	--	--	81.6
Overslept and missed a class or appointment	20.4	21.2	18.8	23.9	23.0	21.0	--	--	--	--	--	--	--
Argued with a teacher in class	--	51.8	50.9	53.9	51.5	49.5	--	--	--	--	--	--	--
Was a guest in a teacher's home	--	37.3	--	--	--	--	--	--	--	--	--	--	--
Studied with other students	--	90.7	--	--	--	--	--	--	--	--	--	--	--
Drank beer	53.5	54.7	52.4	56.4	56.6	60.6	--	--	--	--	--	--	73.2
Took sleeping pills	--	5.9	5.8	6.5	5.3	4.3	--	--	--	--	--	--	2.9
Took a tranquilizing pill	--	9.9	8.6	9.5	7.8	6.2	--	--	--	--	--	--	5.1
Took vitamins	--	61.0	59.1	61.3	58.5	58.8	--	--	--	--	--	--	58.8
Tutored another student	--	46.6	46.5	43.5	45.2	42.9	--	--	--	--	--	--	--
Visited an art gallery or museum	--	71.4	70.9	71.4	68.8	66.2	--	--	--	--	--	--	--
Played chess	--	41.5	40.8	40.8	38.4	38.4	--	--	--	--	--	--	--
Performed volunteer work	--	--	--	--	--	--	--	--	--	--	--	--	--
Had vocational counseling	--	58.8	60.3	57.7	52.9	46.7	--	--	--	--	--	--	--
Read poetry not connected with a course	--	--	56.1	57.9	57.2	59.3	--	--	--	--	--	--	--
Wore glasses or contact lenses	--	--	--	--	51.7	--	--	--	--	--	--	--	46.3
Did not complete homework on time [4]	--	74.0	61.3	72.7	71.5	66.7	--	--	--	--	--	--	--
Won a varsity letter in a sport [3]	31.7	32.5	31.5	31.2	30.6	32.8	--	--	--	--	--	--	--
Frequently Only [1]													
Did extra, unassigned reading for a course	--	14.4	11.1	13.5	15.6	14.2	--	--	--	--	--	--	--
Voted in a student election	70.7	72.9	76.9	67.3	68.0	64.4	--	--	--	--	--	--	--
Studied in the library	27.4	[*]	33.2	36.1	32.7	31.2	--	--	--	--	--	--	--
Checked out a book or journal from the school library	51.6	54.4	50.3	47.5	44.3	42.5	--	--	--	--	--	--	--
Missed school due to illness	--	3.2	2.9	3.6	3.4	3.3	--	--	--	--	--	--	--
Typed a homework assignment	25.0	26.5	20.5	23.6	21.6	22.4	--	--	--	--	--	--	--
Smoked cigarettes	16.6	16.5	15.6	15.5	14.8	14.9	--	--	--	--	--	--	13.9
Discussed religion	--	33.4	29.3	28.1	26.9	25.8	--	--	--	--	--	--	--
Discussed politics	--	24.2	29.9	25.9	26.8	21.1	--	--	--	--	--	--	--
Discussed sports	--	44.6	43.5	42.9	42.1	41.7	--	--	--	--	--	--	--
Asked a teacher for advice after class	--	26.2	21.5	24.2	22.6	21.8	--	--	--	--	--	--	--
Felt depressed	--	--	--	--	--	--	--	--	--	--	--	--	--
Felt overwhelmed	--	--	--	--	--	--	--	--	--	--	--	--	--
Used a personal computer	--	--	--	--	--	--	--	--	--	--	--	--	--
Noted [2]													
Was elected president of one or more student organizations	23.3	22.3	20.3	19.7	19.0	18.4	--	--	--	--	--	--	--
Received a high rating in a state or regional music contest	11.1	10.3	9.9	9.9	9.5	10.1	--	--	--	--	--	--	--
Competed in state or regional speech or debate contest	6.8	6.0	5.6	5.5	5.0	4.5	--	--	--	--	--	--	--
Had a major part in a play	19.5	17.7	16.8	16.0	15.1	14.9	--	--	--	--	--	--	--
Won an award in an art competition [4]	5.4	5.3	5.3	5.4	5.5	5.5	--	--	--	--	--	--	--
Edited a school publication [4]	12.6	11.9	11.2	11.0	11.1	11.5	--	--	--	--	--	--	--
Had original writing or poetry published [4]	16.7	16.4	15.7	15.8	15.5	15.1	--	--	--	--	--	--	--
Won an award in a state or regional science contest [4]	2.9	2.5	2.4	2.4	2.3	1.9	--	--	--	--	--	--	--
Was a member of a scholastic honor society	28.3	27.1	25.2	24.3	25.6	24.5	--	--	--	--	--	--	--

[*] Results were not comparable to those of other years due to changes in question text or order.
[1] Response options for these items were "frequently", "occasionally" and "not at all".
[2] Response option for these items was a single bubble to be marked if the student engaged in the indicated activity.
[3] In 1966-1971, response option was a single bubble as noted in [2]. In 1984-1990, response options were as in [1].
[4] Text, order or number of response options may vary from year to year.

HIGH SCHOOL EXPERIENCES AND ACHIEVEMENTS

1979	1980	1981	1982	1983	1984	1985	1986	1987	1988	1989	1990	ACTIVITIES REPORTED IN THE LAST YEAR
												Frequently or Occasionally [1]
42.0	--	41.8	45.5	43.1	42.5	42.3	42.2	--	--	--	38.4	Played a musical instrument
67.9	--	71.1	73.4	71.4	73.5	74.3	76.5	75.2	81.0	78.7	79.1	Stayed up all night
18.1	--	20.1	21.4	20.5	--	--	--	--	35.1	36.7	39.4	Participated in organized demonstrations
8.6	--	8.8	8.2	7.5	8.9	--	--	--	8.7	--	--	Worked in a local, state, or national political campaign [4]
--	--	--	--	--	--	--	--	--	--	--	57.1	Came late to class
84.7	--	85.9	85.9	85.3	84.4	84.9	83.2	83.4	81.7	82.2	83.0	Attended a religious service
79.0	--	78.3	77.4	74.9	73.2	76.6	76.0	--	--	--	--	Attended a public recital or concert [4]
--	--	--	--	24.4	27.2	28.6	30.7	30.3	--	--	--	Overslept and missed a class or appointment
--	--	--	--	--	--	--	--	--	--	41.8	--	Argued with a teacher in class
--	--	--	--	--	--	32.6	32.9	--	30.3	28.9	30.0	Was a guest in a teacher's home
--	--	--	--	--	--	88.2	87.2	88.1	87.3	85.4	84.7	Studied with other students
72.5	--	75.2	75.1	72.3	67.8	66.5	66.5	65.8	65.3	60.3	58.2	Drank beer
2.9	--	2.9	2.9	2.7	--	--	--	--	--	3.0	--	Took sleeping pills
5.3	--	5.1	4.9	4.4	4.2	--	--	--	--	1.7	--	Took a tranquilizing pill
60.1	--	64.7	66.2	65.7	66.7	--	--	--	--	--	56.8	Took vitamins
--	--	--	--	--	--	42.4	41.6	43.4	44.9	44.6	45.5	Tutored another student
--	--	--	--	--	--	--	--	--	--	54.9	52.5	Visited an art gallery or museum
--	--	--	--	--	--	--	--	--	--	--	--	Played chess
--	--	--	--	--	69.8	70.4	69.4	--	--	62.0	63.1	Performed volunteer work
--	--	--	--	--	--	--	--	--	--	--	--	Had vocational counseling
--	--	--	--	--	--	--	--	--	--	--	--	Read poetry not connected with a course
44.3	--	43.9	43.7	43.6	--	--	--	--	--	--	49.0	Wore glasses or contact lenses
--	--	--	--	60.7	67.7	68.6	68.8	68.8	68.8	68.7	67.9	Did not complete homework on time [4]
--	--	--	--	--	45.5	45.8	46.1	47.5	46.6	48.3	50.4	Won a varsity letter in a sport [3]
												Frequently Only [1]
--	--	--	--	--	12.4	11.4	11.8	10.4	10.9	10.1	10.3	Did extra, unassigned reading for a course
--	--	--	--	--	--	--	--	--	--	--	--	Voted in a student election
--	--	--	--	--	--	--	--	--	--	13.3	10.1	Studied in the library
--	--	--	--	--	--	--	--	--	--	--	26.7	Checked out a book or journal from the school library
--	--	--	--	--	3.9	4.2	4.4	4.2	--	--	--	Missed school due to illness
--	--	--	--	--	--	--	--	--	--	--	--	Typed a homework assignment
13.3	--	11.9	11.7	10.9	9.5	9.1	9.8	8.9	10.1	10.2	10.6	Smoked cigarettes
--	--	--	--	--	--	--	--	--	20.9	--	--	Discussed religion
--	--	--	--	--	--	--	--	--	18.5	--	--	Discussed politics
--	--	--	--	--	--	--	--	--	42.7	--	--	Discussed sports
--	--	--	--	--	--	24.1	--	--	--	--	28.5	Asked a teacher for advice after class
--	--	--	--	--	--	8.2	8.4	8.3	10.5	9.0	8.5	Felt depressed
--	--	--	--	--	--	16.0	17.5	16.4	21.5	19.2	20.3	Felt overwhelmed
--	--	--	--	--	--	24.9	24.2	24.6	27.4	29.4	--	Used a personal computer
												Noted [2]
--	--	--	--	--	--	--	--	--	--	--	20.4	Was elected president of one or more student organizations
--	--	--	--	--	--	--	--	--	--	--	11.7	Received a high rating in a state or regional music contest
--	--	--	--	--	--	--	--	--	--	--	6.1	Competed in state or regional speech or debate contest
--	--	--	--	--	--	--	--	--	--	--	12.9	Had a major part in a play
--	--	--	--	--	--	--	--	--	--	--	9.2	Won an award in an art competition [4]
--	--	--	--	--	--	--	--	--	--	--	12.4	Edited a school publication [4]
--	--	--	--	--	--	--	--	--	--	--	13.9	Had original writing or poetry published [4]
--	--	--	--	--	--	--	--	--	--	--	4.6	Won an award in a state or regional science contest [4]
--	--	--	--	--	--	--	--	--	--	--	29.1	Was a member of a scholastic honor society

[1] Response options for these items were "frequently", "occasionally" and "not at all".
[2] Response option for these items was a single bubble to be marked if the student engaged in the indicated activity.
[3] In 1966-1971, response option was a single bubble as noted in [2]. In 1984-1990, response options were as in [1].
[4] Text, order or number of response options may vary from year to year.

COLLEGE CHOICE, APPLICATION AND MATRICULATION

COLLEGE CHOICE, APPLICATION AND MATRICULATION	1966	1967	1968	1969	1970	1971	1972	1973	1974	1975	1976	1977	1978
VERY IMPORTANT REASONS NOTED IN DECIDING TO GO TO COLLEGE [1]													
My parents wanted me to go	--	--	--	--	--	22.9	--	--	--	--	29.3	28.8	28.6
To be able to get a better job	--	--	--	--	--	73.8	--	--	--	--	71.0	77.0	75.4
Could not get a job	--	--	--	--	--	--	--	--	--	--	5.7	6.1	4.4
To get away from home	--	--	--	--	--	--	--	--	--	--	9.1	9.1	7.8
To gain a general education and appreciation of ideas	--	--	--	--	--	59.5	--	--	--	--	64.0	70.9	68.3
To improve my reading and study skills	--	--	--	--	--	22.2	--	--	--	--	35.1	42.6	37.7
There was nothing better to do	--	--	--	--	--	2.2	--	--	--	--	2.6	2.4	1.8
To make me a more cultured person	--	--	--	--	--	28.9	--	--	--	--	32.8	38.9	34.0
To be able to make more money	--	--	--	--	--	49.9	--	--	--	--	53.8	62.1	60.4
To learn more about things that interest me	--	--	--	--	--	68.8	--	--	--	--	72.9	79.3	74.0
To meet new and interesting people	--	--	--	--	--	45.1	--	--	--	--	53.3	59.4	56.6
To prepare myself for grad/prof school	--	--	--	--	--	34.5	--	--	--	--	43.9	45.9	44.2
VERY IMPORTANT REASONS NOTED FOR SELECTING FRESHMAN COLLEGE													
Relatives wanted me to come here [1]	--	--	--	--	--	7.8	[*]	[*]	7.6	8.0	6.8	6.4	5.8
Teacher advised me	--	--	--	--	--	--	--	5.2	5.2	4.8	4.2	4.3	3.9
College has a good academic reputation [1]	--	--	--	--	--	36.1	48.4	49.0	50.4	47.5	43.1	48.0	50.7
College has a good social reputation	--	--	--	--	--	--	--	--	--	--	--	--	--
Offered financial assistance	--	--	--	--	--	--	17.5	16.8	18.6	16.7	13.6	15.4	14.5
College offers special education programs	--	--	--	--	--	32.6	27.0	29.2	30.4	28.2	25.3	29.1	25.8
College has low tuition	--	--	--	--	--	18.8	19.6	26.9	27.5	24.7	18.0	19.4	16.8
Advice of guidance counselor	--	--	--	--	--	7.2	6.9	9.5	9.4	8.4	7.5	8.2	7.6
Wanted to live at home	--	--	--	--	--	12.2	12.6	13.9	13.2	14.1	11.6	12.0	10.0
Wanted to live near home	--	--	--	--	--	--	--	--	--	--	--	--	--
Friend suggested attending	--	--	--	--	--	--	--	--	--	7.1	7.2	8.1	6.6
College representative recruited me	--	--	--	--	--	--	--	--	--	4.2	3.9	4.5	4.2
Athletic department recruited me	--	--	--	--	--	--	--	--	--	--	--	--	--
Graduates go to top grad schools	--	--	--	--	--	--	--	--	--	--	--	--	--
Graduates get good jobs	--	--	--	--	--	--	--	--	--	50.9	--	--	--
Not accepted anywhere else	--	--	--	--	--	3.1	3.4	--	--	--	2.9	3.2	2.7
Advice of someone who attended	--	--	--	--	--	15.7	17.1	18.8	17.8	16.6	14.4	16.2	13.9
Not offered aid by first choice	--	--	--	--	--	--	--	--	--	--	--	--	--
Wanted to live away from home	--	--	--	--	--	--	17.9	15.4	13.7	14.0	--	--	--
THIS COLLEGE IS STUDENT'S													
First choice	--	--	--	--	--	--	--	--	75.6	78.2	76.9	75.2	75.9
Second choice	--	--	--	--	--	--	--	--	19.0	16.9	17.2	18.7	18.5
Less than second choice [1]	--	--	--	--	--	--	--	--	5.5	4.8	5.9	6.1	5.6
NUMBER OF APPLICATIONS SENT TO OTHER COLLEGES													
None (applied to only one college)	--	50.1	50.6	51.3	--	--	47.2	47.7	--	46.3	44.2	40.0	37.0
One	--	19.7	20.2	20.0	--	--	18.7	19.1	--	20.3	19.2	18.4	18.1
Two	--	14.2	13.9	13.8	--	--	14.8	14.5	--	14.2	14.9	16.7	17.8
Three	--	8.5	8.3	7.9	--	--	9.0	8.9	--	9.2	10.9	12.3	13.4
Four	--	4.1	3.8	3.8	--	--	4.7	4.8	--	4.8	5.3	6.0	6.5
Five	--	2.0	1.9	1.8	--	--	2.9	2.7	--	2.7	2.8	3.4	3.7
Six or more	--	1.4	1.4	1.4	--	--	2.6	2.3	--	2.5	2.8	3.1	3.4
NUMBER OF ACCEPTANCES FROM OTHER COLLEGES [2]													
None	--	--	--	--	--	--	--	--	--	30.6	29.1	26.3	22.3
One	--	--	--	--	--	--	--	--	--	30.4	28.5	28.8	29.4
Two	--	--	--	--	--	--	--	--	--	20.0	20.3	22.5	22.9
Three	--	--	--	--	--	--	--	--	--	10.9	12.8	13.1	14.7
Four	--	--	--	--	--	--	--	--	--	4.6	5.2	5.2	6.0
Five	--	--	--	--	--	--	--	--	--	1.7	2.0	2.2	2.5
Six or more	--	--	--	--	--	--	--	--	--	1.8	2.1	1.8	2.3

[*] Results were not comparable to those of other years due to changes in question text or order.
[1] Text, order or number of response options may vary from year to year.
[2] Students who applied to no other colleges not included.

COLLEGE CHOICE, APPLICATION AND MATRICULATION

1979	1980	1981	1982	1983	1984	1985	1986	1987	1988	1989	1990	
												VERY IMPORTANT REASONS NOTED IN DECIDING TO GO TO COLLEGE [1]
29.7	31.5	32.5	33.1	32.0	31.7	[*]	[*]	[*]	[*]	34.4	35.2	My parents wanted me to go
77.7	77.1	76.3	77.9	76.2	75.7	[*]	[*]	[*]	[*]	75.9	78.3	To be able to get a better job
5.1	5.8	5.8	7.4	6.2	5.3	[*]	[*]	[*]	[*]	7.0	7.1	Could not get a job
7.7	8.9	9.5	10.1	10.3	11.1	[*]	[*]	[*]	[*]	15.0	16.0	To get away from home
68.5	66.7	67.4	66.2	63.9	65.1	61.3	61.6	60.7	60.1	62.5	63.1	To gain a general education and appreciation of ideas
39.1	39.3	39.7	39.5	41.8	41.6	40.5	40.3	39.8	39.4	40.5	43.0	To improve my reading and study skills
2.0	2.1	2.3	2.3	2.4	2.0	2.4	2.5	2.5	2.9	2.4	2.3	There was nothing better to do
33.9	34.4	33.5	33.8	31.8	33.8	32.6	32.2	33.5	35.4	35.6	39.8	To make me a more cultured person
63.9	63.4	67.0	69.8	66.7	67.8	69.7	70.6	71.3	72.6	72.2	73.2	To be able to make more money
73.7	74.6	73.3	72.5	71.7	72.3	73.5	74.1	72.4	73.8	72.4	73.1	To learn more about things that interest me
56.3	56.2	55.4	54.6	54.6	56.1	--	--	--	--	--	--	To meet new and interesting people
45.4	46.0	45.4	45.4	47.0	47.9	46.0	47.1	47.2	49.9	51.5	53.1	To prepare myself for grad/prof school
												VERY IMPORTANT REASONS NOTED FOR SELECTING FRESHMAN COLLEGE
5.9	6.4	6.6	6.6	6.3	6.9	6.1	7.7	7.0	7.1	8.5	8.8	Relatives wanted me to come here [1]
4.0	4.4	4.1	4.0	4.0	4.3	4.2	4.4	3.8	4.1	3.8	4.1	Teacher advised me
49.1	50.8	53.0	53.5	52.6	55.7	55.1	59.2	56.1	56.0	52.8	51.3	College has a good academic reputation [1]
--	--	--	--	20.6	22.2	22.5	27.2	26.7	22.6	22.4	21.2	College has a good social reputation
15.9	16.2	15.4	16.7	20.8	20.0	20.2	21.5	20.2	21.4	22.8	25.2	Offered financial assistance
26.4	27.3	26.6	25.5	21.9	22.2	22.2	23.5	22.0	22.0	20.3	21.7	College offers special education programs
16.6	17.0	17.7	20.6	21.3	20.8	21.3	22.4	20.9	21.3	21.9	23.4	College has low tuition
7.5	8.1	7.6	7.7	8.1	8.1	7.7	8.4	7.5	7.5	7.1	7.6	Advice of guidance counselor
11.0	11.1	10.5	11.1	--	--	--	--	--	--	--	--	Wanted to live at home
--	--	--	--	19.7	18.6	17.5	18.8	17.9	19.2	19.0	19.8	Wanted to live near home
7.0	7.3	7.2	7.2	6.7	7.0	7.4	8.4	8.1	8.2	8.3	9.0	Friend suggested attending
4.6	4.9	4.6	4.3	3.0	3.1	3.7	3.7	3.5	3.7	3.7	4.0	College representative recruited me
--	--	--	--	4.2	4.1	4.5	4.6	4.4	4.4	4.7	5.0	Athletic department recruited me
--	--	--	--	25.8	26.2	25.7	25.8	27.5	--	23.9	24.1	Graduates go to top grad schools
--	--	--	--	46.4	46.3	45.7	46.8	47.5	[*]	43.7	42.4	Graduates get good jobs
2.9	2.5	2.7	2.7	--	--	--	--	--	--	--	--	Not accepted anywhere else
14.4	15.1	14.8	14.9	--	--	--	--	--	--	--	--	Advice of someone who attended
--	--	--	--	--	4.0	4.2	4.7	4.2	4.6	5.2	--	Not offered aid by first choice
--	--	--	--	--	--	--	--	--	--	--	--	Wanted to live away from home
												THIS COLLEGE IS STUDENT'S
75.6	75.8	74.5	73.6	73.7	73.3	72.3	71.4	70.3	67.9	68.9	70.7	First choice
18.5	18.4	19.4	19.9	20.2	20.4	20.8	21.3	22.1	23.0	22.9	22.2	Second choice
5.9	5.8	6.1	6.5	6.1	6.3	6.9	7.3	7.7	9.1	8.3	7.1	Less than second choice [1]
												NUMBER OF APPLICATIONS SENT TO OTHER COLLEGES
39.5	39.7	38.0	38.6	37.8	34.9	33.7	35.3	35.2	31.2	31.3	31.9	None (applied to only one college)
17.7	17.1	18.0	16.7	17.6	17.8	21.0	17.2	16.0	15.0	15.3	15.7	One
16.7	16.8	17.2	16.7	16.9	17.4	16.8	16.0	15.7	16.6	16.7	16.7	Two
13.0	13.2	13.3	13.6	13.4	14.0	13.6	14.0	14.2	15.2	15.2	14.9	Three
6.0	6.4	6.6	6.8	6.6	7.4	6.9	7.7	8.3	9.2	9.0	8.9	Four
3.6	3.5	3.4	3.7	3.8	4.0	4.0	4.7	5.0	5.7	5.7	5.5	Five
3.4	3.4	3.6	3.9	3.9	4.4	4.1	5.1	5.7	7.0	6.9	6.6	Six or more
												NUMBER OF ACCEPTANCES FROM OTHER COLLEGES [2]
24.1	22.1	21.6	20.7	19.8	18.9	18.8	19.4	17.9	15.7	16.3	--	None
28.6	28.7	29.1	28.9	28.7	28.3	28.2	27.4	27.1	26.5	25.9	--	One
22.3	23.1	23.5	23.7	23.8	23.5	23.6	22.9	23.4	24.4	23.8	--	Two
14.4	15.1	14.8	15.3	15.7	16.2	16.4	15.9	16.8	17.3	17.1	--	Three
5.9	6.2	6.2	6.5	6.7	7.0	7.1	7.7	8.1	8.7	8.9	--	Four
2.4	2.5	2.4	2.6	2.7	3.0	2.9	3.3	3.4	3.7	4.0	--	Five
2.2	2.3	2.4	2.5	2.6	3.0	2.9	3.4	3.3	3.7	4.1	--	Six or more

[*] Results were not comparable to those of other years due to changes in question text or order.
[1] Text, order or number of response options may vary from year to year.
[2] Students who applied to no other colleges not included.

DEGREE, MAJOR AND CAREER PLANS

DEGREE, MAJOR AND CAREER PLANS	1966	1967	1968	1969	1970	1971	1972	1973	1974	1975	1976	1977	1978
HIGHEST ACADEMIC DEGREE PLANNED AT ANY COLLEGE													
None	5.5	4.2	4.1	2.0	2.1	[*]	3.4	[*]	3.9	3.7	3.2	2.3	2.2
Vocational certificate	--	--	--	--	--	--	--	--	--	--	--	--	--
Associate or equivalent	5.6	7.3	6.7	8.7	7.6	[*]	8.1	[*]	8.5	7.8	8.1	8.3	7.7
Bachelor's degree (B.A., B.S., etc.)	38.7	37.4	38.2	38.2	38.3	[*]	37.3	[*]	36.8	34.7	35.6	35.6	37.2
Master's degree (M.A., M.S., etc.)	31.7	32.5	32.5	32.9	31.2	[*]	27.4	[*]	27.1	28.3	28.6	30.1	30.1
Ph.D. or Ed.D.	9.8	10.4	10.6	10.3	9.7	[*]	8.9	[*]	8.5	9.1	8.7	9.2	8.9
M.D., D.D.S., D.V.M., or D.O.	4.9	4.7	4.2	4.1	4.6	[*]	7.2	[*]	7.5	7.3	7.1	6.2	6.6
LL.B. or J.D. (law)	[*]	[*]	[*]	[*]	3.5	[*]	4.5	[*]	4.4	4.8	4.8	4.8	4.5
B.D. or M.Div. (divinity)	0.3	0.3	0.3	0.4	0.4	[*]	0.4	[*]	0.4	0.6	0.6	0.5	0.4
Other	2.0	1.8	2.1	2.0	2.6	[*]	2.8	[*]	2.9	3.8	3.3	3.0	2.4
HIGHEST ACADEMIC DEGREE AT FRESHMAN COLLEGE													
None	--	--	--	--	--	--	8.2	7.1	8.1	7.2	6.8	5.2	4.7
Vocational certificate	--	--	--	--	--	--	--	--	--	--	--	--	--
Associate or equivalent	--	--	--	--	--	--	26.4	27.8	30.5	29.0	28.3	28.4	25.9
Bachelor's degree (B.A., B.S., etc.)	--	--	--	--	--	--	50.2	49.7	46.4	46.9	48.4	49.7	52.6
Master's degree (M.A., M.S., etc.)	--	--	--	--	--	--	8.2	8.9	8.5	9.0	8.9	9.8	10.3
Ph.D. or Ed.D.	--	--	--	--	--	--	1.4	1.5	1.3	1.5	1.4	1.5	1.5
M.D., D.D.S., D.V.M., or D.O.	--	--	--	--	--	--	1.3	1.6	1.5	1.5	1.4	1.4	1.5
LL.B. or J.D. (law)	--	--	--	--	--	--	0.9	1.0	0.8	1.0	0.9	1.0	1.0
B.D. or M.Div. (divinity)	--	--	--	--	--	--	0.1	0.1	0.1	0.4	0.6	0.4	0.3
Other	--	--	--	--	--	--	3.1	2.3	2.7	3.4	3.3	2.6	2.2
MAJOR PLANS (AGGREGATED) [1,2]													
Agriculture (including forestry)	1.9	2.4	2.2	2.1	2.0	3.2	3.2	2.8	3.8	3.9	3.6	3.6	3.2
Biological sciences	3.7	3.7	3.7	3.3	3.5	3.6	3.9	7.0	6.7	6.3	6.2	4.7	4.6
Business	14.3	16.2	16.4	16.2	16.2	16.4	15.5	17.7	17.9	18.9	20.9	22.2	23.9
Education	10.6	10.5	11.5	11.1	11.6	9.9	7.3	12.2	10.5	9.9	9.3	8.8	8.0
Engineering	9.8	9.5	9.8	10.2	8.6	7.2	6.9	6.6	6.6	7.9	8.5	9.3	10.3
English	4.4	4.0	3.7	3.6	3.0	2.2	1.6	1.5	1.3	1.0	1.0	1.0	1.0
Health professions (nursing, pre-med, etc.)	5.3	5.2	5.3	5.5	7.4	8.8	10.6	10.4	7.5	7.3	6.9	10.0	9.6
History or political science	6.8	6.7	6.8	6.2	5.4	4.2	3.9	[*]	3.7	3.5	3.1	3.0	2.8
Humanities (other)	4.7	4.6	3.8	3.7	3.5	3.1	3.6	2.8	2.5	2.1	2.2	1.9	2.2
Fine arts (applied and performing)	8.4	8.6	8.6	8.7	9.2	9.0	8.8	6.7	6.8	6.2	6.1	5.7	4.8
Mathematics or statistics	4.5	4.2	4.0	3.5	3.3	2.7	2.2	1.7	1.4	1.1	1.0	0.8	0.9
Physical sciences	3.3	3.0	2.7	2.5	2.3	2.0	1.9	2.7	2.6	2.7	2.7	2.3	2.4
Pre-professional	7.2	6.7	6.3	6.3	7.0	8.5	9.4	--	--	--	--	--	--
Social sciences	[*]	[*]	[*]	[*]	8.9	8.6	7.8	[*]	6.8	6.2	5.6	5.4	5.3
Other technical	2.2	2.6	2.8	3.6	3.7	5.1	6.1	5.3	7.7	8.6	7.5	7.2	7.7
Other non-technical	2.7	2.5	2.3	2.3	2.4	3.1	2.7	5.4	9.7	9.5	10.7	9.1	8.7
Undecided	1.9	1.8	2.0	2.3	2.2	2.3	4.6	4.7	4.5	5.0	4.7	4.7	4.6
CAREER PLANS (AGGREGATED) [1,3]													
Artist (including performer)	6.6	5.8	5.8	5.7	6.2	6.0	6.5	3.6	5.7	5.2	6.8	6.8	6.3
Business	11.6	11.2	11.3	11.1	11.4	10.7	10.5	[*]	13.2	13.8	16.4	18.1	19.3
Clergy or other religious worker	1.0	1.2	0.7	0.9	0.8	0.6	0.6	0.8	0.9	0.7	0.6	0.5	0.5
College teacher	1.8	1.2	1.1	1.1	1.0	0.7	0.6	1.0	0.7	0.6	0.4	0.3	0.3
Doctor (M.D. or D.D.S.)	4.8	4.2	3.7	3.4	3.9	4.4	5.5	5.9	5.3	5.1	4.8	4.1	4.5
Education (elementary)	7.6	8.3	9.1	9.0	8.0	6.8	5.6	4.2	3.5	3.0	4.3	4.0	3.7
Education (secondary)	14.1	14.1	14.4	13.1	11.3	8.6	6.5	4.6	4.2	3.5	3.7	3.2	2.7
Engineer	8.9	8.4	8.3	8.3	7.5	5.3	5.3	5.3	4.7	5.9	7.8	8.3	9.1
Farmer, rancher, or forester	1.8	1.9	1.7	1.8	1.8	2.9	2.9	3.1	3.8	3.7	3.0	3.2	2.5
Health professional (non-M.D.)	4.7	4.3	4.1	4.2	4.5	6.1	7.3	8.4	8.9	8.8	7.3	7.2	6.5
Lawyer (or judge)	3.9	3.5	3.4	3.5	3.8	4.3	4.7	4.7	3.9	4.0	4.3	4.4	4.3
Nurse	2.5	2.5	2.7	2.7	4.0	4.1	4.7	4.5	5.1	4.8	4.6	4.5	4.1
Research scientist	3.5	2.9	2.9	2.5	2.6	2.5	2.3	3.1	2.1	2.0	2.4	2.2	2.2
Other	22.8	20.5	19.8	21.5	21.5	23.8	23.0	23.5	25.7	25.2	23.3	23.4	23.0
Undecided	[*]	10.1	11.1	11.3	11.6	13.2	13.9	11.2	12.4	13.7	10.3	9.7	10.6

[*] Results were not comparable to those of other years due to changes in question text or order.
[1] Figures for the years 1966-1976 are from annual Norms Reports. Figures from 1977-1990 computed from disaggregated majors/careers (see Appendix E)
[2] List of disaggregated majors was expanded in 1970, 1973, 1978 and 1982.
[3] List of careers for 1973-1976 not directly comparable to other years.

1979	1980	1981	1982	1983	1984	1985	1986	1987	1988	1989	1990	DEGREE, MAJOR AND CAREER PLANS
												HIGHEST ACADEMIC DEGREE PLANNED AT ANY COLLEGE
1.8	2.4	2.1	1.9	2.1	1.6	2.1	2.0	2.0	1.8	1.1	1.5	None
--	--	--	--	1.5	1.0	1.2	1.2	1.5	0.6	0.9	1.3	Vocational certificate
7.3	8.2	8.4	8.3	7.0	6.7	6.2	6.3	5.3	3.9	4.5	5.5	Associate or equivalent
36.5	37.6	37.8	38.3	36.5	37.6	38.2	36.8	35.3	33.1	32.3	29.0	Bachelor's degree (B.A., B.S., etc.)
32.3	29.7	31.0	30.5	30.4	31.2	31.6	33.0	34.3	36.3	37.0	37.2	Master's degree (M.A., M.S., etc.)
8.7	7.9	7.9	8.2	8.5	9.2	9.2	9.7	10.4	11.7	11.7	12.4	Ph.D. or Ed.D.
6.2	6.4	5.9	6.0	6.3	6.2	6.0	5.6	5.3	5.7	5.7	6.3	M.D., D.D.S., D.V.M., or D.O.
4.4	4.3	4.0	4.3	4.1	4.0	3.6	3.7	4.2	5.0	4.9	4.8	LL.B. or J.D. (law)
0.6	0.5	0.5	0.5	0.7	0.6	0.4	0.3	0.3	0.4	0.3	0.4	B.D. or M.Div. (divinity)
2.4	2.9	2.3	2.1	2.8	2.0	1.7	1.6	1.5	1.5	1.6	1.7	Other
												HIGHEST ACADEMIC DEGREE AT FRESHMAN COLLEGE
4.5	4.7	4.6	4.0	3.8	3.6	3.5	3.3	3.5	3.7	3.7	4.1	None
--	--	--	--	2.2	1.4	1.7	1.6	2.4	0.8	1.3	2.0	Vocational certificate
27.1	26.1	27.7	28.5	23.0	23.3	22.4	21.6	19.6	16.1	18.1	24.4	Associate or equivalent
51.4	51.9	51.2	50.7	52.9	54.5	55.1	56.5	56.5	58.4	58.2	51.2	Bachelor's degree (B.A., B.S., etc.)
10.8	10.4	10.6	10.7	10.4	11.1	11.8	12.0	12.8	14.8	13.2	12.6	Master's degree (M.A., M.S., etc.)
1.5	1.4	1.4	1.5	1.7	1.7	1.7	1.6	1.7	2.0	1.9	1.8	Ph.D. or Ed.D.
1.4	1.6	1.3	1.5	1.6	1.4	1.3	1.2	1.2	1.3	1.1	1.1	M.D., D.D.S., D.V.M., or D.O.
0.9	1.0	0.9	1.0	1.1	0.9	0.8	0.6	0.8	1.1	0.9	0.8	LL.B. or J.D. (law)
0.3	0.4	0.3	0.3	0.7	0.4	0.2	0.2	0.2	0.2	0.2	0.2	B.D. or M.Div. (divinity)
2.0	2.4	1.9	1.7	2.5	1.6	1.6	1.2	1.3	1.6	1.4	1.8	Other
												MAJOR PLANS (AGGREGATED) [1]
3.0	2.9	3.5	2.6	1.9	2.0	2.0	1.8	1.7	1.7	1.2	1.3	Agriculture (including forestry)
4.0	3.7	3.7	3.7	3.8	4.2	3.4	3.9	3.8	3.7	3.7	3.7	Biological sciences
24.3	23.9	23.7	24.2	24.4	26.4	26.8	26.9	27.3	25.6	24.5	21.1	Business
8.4	7.7	7.1	6.0	6.0	6.5	7.1	8.1	8.9	9.3	9.2	9.9	Education
10.6	11.8	12.0	12.6	11.7	11.0	10.7	10.9	9.4	9.5	10.2	9.6	Engineering
0.9	0.9	0.9	0.8	0.9	1.0	1.0	1.2	1.2	1.3	1.3	1.3	English
8.9	9.2	9.0	9.2	10.1	10.0	8.9	8.0	7.2	8.3	9.0	10.7	Health professions (nursing, pre-med, etc.)
2.6	2.6	2.5	2.4	2.4	2.7	3.1	3.2	3.4	4.0	3.9	3.9	History or political science
2.2	2.1	2.2	2.1	1.9	1.9	2.1	2.2	2.8	2.4	2.1	2.3	Humanities (other)
5.1	5.0	4.4	4.2	3.9	3.6	3.8	4.3	4.7	4.4	4.4	5.0	Fine arts (applied and performing)
0.6	0.6	0.6	0.6	0.8	0.8	0.8	0.7	0.6	0.6	0.6	0.7	Mathematics or statistics
2.3	2.0	2.1	1.9	1.8	1.8	1.6	1.7	1.6	1.5	1.6	1.7	Physical sciences
--	--	--	--	--	--	--	--	--	--			Pre-professional
5.5	4.7	4.3	3.9	4.2	4.6	5.2	5.5	5.5	6.3	6.5	6.6	Social sciences
7.9	9.8	10.8	12.5	12.8	9.5	7.9	6.7	5.6	5.0	5.4	5.9	Technical (other)
9.2	8.6	8.4	8.4	8.5	8.6	9.8	8.9	10.0	9.5	9.3	9.8	Nontechnical (other)
4.8	4.7	4.7	4.6	4.9	5.2	5.9	6.5	6.6	6.8	6.9	6.6	Undecided
												CAREER PLANS (AGGREGATED) [1,3]
6.8	6.5	6.6	6.3	6.0	5.7	6.4	6.6	7.4	6.8	6.4	6.0	Artist (including performer)
19.7	19.7	19.6	20.2	20.4	22.2	23.9	24.1	24.6	23.6	21.8	18.4	Business
0.4	0.4	0.5	0.3	0.3	0.3	0.3	0.3	0.3	0.2	0.3	0.3	Clergy or other religious worker
0.3	0.2	0.2	0.2	0.2	0.3	0.3	0.3	0.3	0.4	0.4	0.4	College teacher
4.3	4.4	4.1	4.3	4.6	4.6	4.4	4.3	4.0	4.2	4.3	4.4	Doctor (M.D. or D.D.S.)
3.8	3.8	3.5	3.0	3.1	3.4	3.8	4.4	5.0	5.6	5.0	5.4	Education (elementary)
2.9	2.4	2.2	1.9	2.2	2.3	2.6	3.2	3.4	3.5	3.6	4.0	Education (secondary)
9.3	10.7	10.9	12.0	10.8	10.4	10.0	9.7	8.5	8.6	9.0	8.1	Engineer
2.4	2.2	2.8	2.1	1.5	1.5	1.5	1.4	1.0	1.2	1.0	1.0	Farmer, rancher, or forester
6.2	5.8	5.5	5.4	5.8	5.8	5.2	4.8	5.0	5.3	5.3	5.6	Health professional (non-M.D.)
4.2	4.1	3.9	4.3	3.9	4.1	3.9	4.0	4.5	5.4	5.4	5.2	Lawyer (or judge)
3.7	3.8	3.9	4.0	4.4	4.0	3.3	2.7	2.2	2.5	2.7	3.8	Nurse
1.8	1.7	1.6	1.5	1.5	1.5	1.4	1.4	1.5	1.6	1.6	1.4	Research scientist
23.8	23.8	24.5	25.3	25.1	23.1	22.4	21.2	20.7	19.8	21.6	25.0	Other
10.4	10.1	10.1	9.5	10.1	10.9	10.7	11.6	11.4	11.5	11.6	11.1	Undecided

[1] Figures for the years 1966-1976 are from annual Norms Reports. Figures from 1977-1990 computed from disaggregated majors/careers (see Appendix E)

[2] List of disaggregated majors was expanded in 1970, 1973, 1978 and 1982.

[3] List of careers for 1973-1976 not directly comparable to other years.

DEGREE, MAJOR AND CAREER PLANS

	1966	1967	1968	1969	1970	1971	1972	1973	1974	1975	1976	1977	1978
MAJOR PLANS (DISAGGREGATED) [1]													
Arts and Humanities													
Art, fine and applied	--	--	--	--	--	--	--	--	--	--	--	2.3	2.0
English, language and literature	--	--	--	--	--	--	--	--	--	--	--	1.0	1.0
History	--	--	--	--	--	--	--	--	--	--	--	0.7	0.7
Journalism	--	--	--	--	--	--	--	--	--	--	--	1.3	1.4
Language (except English)	--	--	--	--	--	--	--	--	--	--	--	0.6	0.5
Music	--	--	--	--	--	--	--	--	--	--	--	1.6	1.5
Philosophy	--	--	--	--	--	--	--	--	--	--	--	0.2	0.1
Theater or drama	--	--	--	--	--	--	--	--	--	--	--	--	0.8
Speech or drama	--	--	--	--	--	--	--	--	--	--	--	0.7	--
Speech	--	--	--	--	--	--	--	--	--	--	--	--	0.2
Theology or religion	--	--	--	--	--	--	--	--	--	--	--	0.4	0.3
Other arts and humanities	--	--	--	--	--	--	--	--	--	--	--	0.7	0.5
Biological Sciences													
Biology (general)	--	--	--	--	--	--	--	--	--	--	--	1.9	1.9
Biochemistry or biophysics	--	--	--	--	--	--	--	--	--	--	--	0.5	0.5
Botany	--	--	--	--	--	--	--	--	--	--	--	0.2	0.2
Marine (life) sciences	--	--	--	--	--	--	--	--	--	--	--	0.7	0.6
Microbiology or bacteriology	--	--	--	--	--	--	--	--	--	--	--	0.3	0.3
Zoology	--	--	--	--	--	--	--	--	--	--	--	0.4	0.4
Other biological sciences	--	--	--	--	--	--	--	--	--	--	--	0.7	0.7
Business													
Accounting	--	--	--	--	--	--	--	--	--	--	--	6.4	6.7
Business administration (general)	--	--	--	--	--	--	--	--	--	--	--	6.5	6.9
Finance	--	--	--	--	--	--	--	--	--	--	--	0.5	0.6
Marketing	--	--	--	--	--	--	--	--	--	--	--	1.3	1.6
Management	--	--	--	--	--	--	--	--	--	--	--	3.5	4.0
Secretarial studies	--	--	--	--	--	--	--	--	--	--	--	3.1	3.1
Other business	--	--	--	--	--	--	--	--	--	--	--	0.9	1.0
Education													
Business education	--	--	--	--	--	--	--	--	--	--	--	0.3	0.2
Elementary education	--	--	--	--	--	--	--	--	--	--	--	2.6	2.4
Music or art education	--	--	--	--	--	--	--	--	--	--	--	0.5	0.5
Physical education or recreation	--	--	--	--	--	--	--	--	--	--	--	2.3	2.0
Secondary education	--	--	--	--	--	--	--	--	--	--	--	0.8	0.7
Special education	--	--	--	--	--	--	--	--	--	--	--	1.8	1.7
Other education	--	--	--	--	--	--	--	--	--	--	--	0.5	0.5
Engineering													
Aeronautical or astronautical	--	--	--	--	--	--	--	--	--	--	--	0.8	0.9
Civil	--	--	--	--	--	--	--	--	--	--	--	1.1	1.2
Chemical	--	--	--	--	--	--	--	--	--	--	--	0.7	0.9
Electrical or electronic	--	--	--	--	--	--	--	--	--	--	--	3.1	3.1
Industrial	--	--	--	--	--	--	--	--	--	--	--	0.4	0.5
Mechanical	--	--	--	--	--	--	--	--	--	--	--	1.8	2.0
Other engineering	--	--	--	--	--	--	--	--	--	--	--	1.4	1.7
Physical Sciences													
Astronomy	--	--	--	--	--	--	--	--	--	--	--	0.1	0.1
Atmospheric sciences	--	--	--	--	--	--	--	--	--	--	--	0.1	0.1
Chemistry	--	--	--	--	--	--	--	--	--	--	--	0.9	0.9
Earth science	--	--	--	--	--	--	--	--	--	--	--	0.3	0.3
Marine sciences	--	--	--	--	--	--	--	--	--	--	--	0.3	0.3
Mathematics	--	--	--	--	--	--	--	--	--	--	--	0.8	0.9
Physics	--	--	--	--	--	--	--	--	--	--	--	0.4	0.5
Statistics	--	--	--	--	--	--	--	--	--	--	--	0.0	0.0
Other physical sciences	--	--	--	--	--	--	--	--	--	--	--	0.2	0.2
Professional													
Architecture or urban planning	--	--	--	--	--	--	--	--	--	--	--	1.1	1.1
Home economics	--	--	--	--	--	--	--	--	--	--	--	1.0	0.7
Health technology	--	--	--	--	--	--	--	--	--	--	--	2.4	2.4
Library or archival sciences	--	--	--	--	--	--	--	--	--	--	--	0.0	0.1
Nursing	--	--	--	--	--	--	--	--	--	--	--	4.4	4.1
Pharmacy	--	--	--	--	--	--	--	--	--	--	--	0.7	0.6
Predentistry, premedicine, prevet	--	--	--	--	--	--	--	--	--	--	--	3.3	3.4
Therapy (physical, occupational, etc.)	--	--	--	--	--	--	--	--	--	--	--	1.6	1.5
Other professional	--	--	--	--	--	--	--	--	--	--	--	1.6	1.5

[1] Data collected in disaggregated form but not reported in 1966-1976.

1979	1980	1981	1982	1983	1984	1985	1986	1987	1988	1989	1990	*DEGREE, MAJOR AND CAREER PLANS*
												MAJOR PLANS (DISAGGREGATED) [1]
												Arts and Humanities
2.3	2.4	2.2	2.1	2.1	1.7	1.8	2.1	2.5	2.1	2.1	2.0	Art, fine and applied
0.9	0.9	0.9	0.8	0.9	1.0	1.0	1.2	1.2	1.3	1.3	1.3	English, language and literature
0.6	0.6	0.6	0.5	0.5	0.6	0.7	0.7	0.8	0.8	0.8	0.9	History
1.6	1.5	1.6	1.5	1.4	1.4	1.6	1.6	1.5	1.6	1.4	1.3	Journalism
0.5	0.4	0.5	0.5	0.4	0.5	0.5	0.6	0.6	0.6	0.5	0.5	Language (except English)
1.4	1.3	1.3	1.1	1.0	1.0	1.0	1.1	1.0	1.0	0.9	1.0	Music
0.1	0.1	0.1	0.1	0.1	0.1	0.1	0.1	0.2	0.2	0.2	0.2	Philosophy
0.8	0.8	0.7	0.7	0.6	0.6	0.6	0.6	0.7	0.7	0.6	0.7	Theater or drama
--	--	--	--	--	--	--	--	--	--	--	--	Speech or drama
0.2	0.1	0.1	0.1	0.1	0.1	0.1	0.1	0.2	0.1	0.1	0.1	Speech
0.3	0.2	0.3	0.2	0.2	0.1	0.2	0.2	0.2	0.1	0.1	0.2	Theology or religion
0.5	0.6	0.6	0.6	0.6	0.6	0.7	0.7	1.1	0.8	0.7	0.7	Other arts and humanities
												Biological Sciences
1.7	1.6	1.6	1.5	1.7	1.8	1.7	1.9	1.8	1.8	1.8	1.8	Biology (general)
0.4	0.4	0.4	0.5	0.5	0.6	0.5	0.5	0.5	0.5	0.4	0.4	Biochemistry or biophysics
0.1	0.1	0.1	0.1	0.1	0.1	0.0	0.1	0.0	0.0	0.0	0.0	Botany
0.5	0.4	0.4	0.3	0.3	0.4	0.3	0.4	0.4	0.4	0.5	0.6	Marine (life) sciences
0.3	0.2	0.2	0.3	0.3	0.3	0.2	0.2	0.3	0.2	0.2	0.1	Microbiology or bacteriology
0.4	0.4	0.4	0.4	0.3	0.4	0.3	0.3	0.2	0.3	0.3	0.3	Zoology
0.6	0.6	0.6	0.6	0.6	0.6	0.4	0.5	0.6	0.5	0.5	0.5	Other biological sciences
												Business
6.2	6.2	5.8	6.2	6.3	6.4	6.5	6.2	6.2	6.1	6.1	5.3	Accounting
7.4	7.2	7.4	7.1	7.0	7.4	7.4	7.6	7.5	7.3	6.5	5.5	Business administration (general)
0.7	0.6	0.7	0.9	1.0	1.3	1.6	1.8	2.1	2.0	1.9	1.3	Finance
1.9	1.8	1.9	1.9	2.2	2.3	2.6	2.7	3.4	2.9	3.0	2.5	Marketing
4.2	4.3	4.2	4.4	4.2	5.1	5.3	5.4	5.1	4.9	4.5	4.0	Management
2.7	2.6	2.4	2.5	2.3	2.4	2.0	1.5	1.3	0.8	0.9	1.0	Secretarial studies
1.2	1.2	1.3	1.2	1.4	1.5	1.4	1.7	1.7	1.6	1.6	1.5	Other business
												Education
0.2	0.2	0.2	0.2	0.2	0.2	0.3	0.3	0.3	0.3	0.3	0.2	Business education
2.6	2.6	2.6	2.3	2.4	2.8	3.1	3.9	4.2	4.9	4.6	5.1	Elementary education
0.4	0.4	0.3	0.3	0.3	0.3	0.3	0.3	0.3	0.3	0.4	0.5	Music or art education
2.3	1.7	1.5	1.2	1.2	1.2	1.2	1.3	1.2	1.0	1.1	1.1	Physical education or recreation
0.7	0.7	0.7	0.6	0.8	0.9	1.1	1.3	1.6	1.7	1.8	1.9	Secondary education
1.8	1.7	1.4	1.0	0.9	0.8	0.7	0.7	0.6	0.6	0.6	0.7	Special education
0.4	0.4	0.4	0.4	0.2	0.3	0.4	0.3	0.7	0.5	0.4	0.4	Other education
												Engineering
1.0	1.1	1.2	1.2	1.2	1.3	1.3	1.6	1.5	1.7	1.5	1.4	Aeronautical or astronautical
1.2	1.2	1.1	0.9	0.8	0.9	0.9	0.9	0.9	0.9	1.1	1.2	Civil
1.0	1.1	1.2	1.2	0.9	0.7	0.7	0.7	0.6	0.6	0.7	0.7	Chemical
3.2	3.8	3.6	4.0	4.3	4.1	3.9	3.8	3.1	2.9	3.0	2.5	Electrical or electronic
0.5	0.5	0.5	0.5	0.5	0.4	0.4	0.4	0.3	0.3	0.3	0.3	Industrial
2.0	2.3	2.4	2.5	2.2	2.1	2.1	2.0	1.7	1.8	2.0	2.0	Mechanical
1.7	1.8	2.0	2.3	1.8	1.5	1.4	1.5	1.3	1.3	1.6	1.5	Other engineering
												Physical Sciences
0.1	0.1	0.1	0.1	0.1	0.1	0.1	0.1	0.1	0.1	0.1	0.1	Astronomy
0.1	0.1	0.1	0.1	0.1	0.1	0.1	0.1	0.1	0.1	0.1	0.1	Atmospheric sciences
0.9	0.8	0.8	0.8	0.8	0.8	0.7	0.7	0.6	0.6	0.6	0.6	Chemistry
0.3	0.3	0.3	0.3	0.2	0.2	0.1	0.2	0.1	0.1	0.1	0.2	Earth science
0.3	0.2	0.2	0.1	0.1	0.1	0.1	0.1	0.1	0.1	0.2	0.2	Marine sciences
0.6	0.6	0.6	0.6	0.8	0.8	0.8	0.7	0.6	0.6	0.6	0.7	Mathematics
0.4	0.4	0.4	0.3	0.4	0.4	0.4	0.4	0.4	0.4	0.4	0.4	Physics
0.0	0.0	0.0	0.0	0.0	0.0	0.0	0.0	0.0	0.0	0.0	0.0	Statistics
0.2	0.1	0.2	0.2	0.1	0.1	0.1	0.1	0.2	0.1	0.1	0.1	Other physical sciences
												Professional
1.2	1.2	0.8	0.9	0.7	0.8	0.9	1.0	1.0	1.2	1.3	1.9	Architecture or urban planning
0.8	0.6	0.5	0.4	0.5	0.5	0.5	0.4	0.5	0.4	0.2	0.2	Home economics
2.2	2.1	1.6	1.5	1.8	1.4	1.3	1.1	1.2	1.0	0.9	1.1	Health technology
0.0	0.0	0.0	0.0	0.0	0.0	0.0	0.0	0.0	0.0	0.0	0.0	Library or archival sciences
3.6	3.8	3.8	4.0	4.4	4.1	3.3	2.7	2.2	2.5	2.8	4.2	Nursing
0.5	0.4	0.4	0.4	0.5	0.6	0.6	0.6	0.6	1.0	0.9	1.0	Pharmacy
3.2	3.4	3.0	3.1	3.2	3.2	3.1	2.9	2.5	2.8	3.0	3.2	Predentistry, premedicine, prevet
1.6	1.6	1.8	1.7	2.0	2.1	1.9	1.8	1.9	2.0	2.3	2.3	Therapy (physical, occupational, etc.)
1.6	1.5	1.4	1.3	1.3	1.4	1.3	1.2	1.6	1.3	1.3	1.3	Other professional

[1] Data collected in disaggregated form but not reported in 1966-1976.

DEGREE, MAJOR AND CAREER PLANS

	1966	1967	1968	1969	1970	1971	1972	1973	1974	1975	1976	1977	1978
MAJOR PLANS (DISAGGREGATED) [1]													
Social Sciences													
Anthropology	--	--	--	--	--	--	--	--	--	--	--	0.1	0.1
Economics	--	--	--	--	--	--	--	--	--	--	--	0.3	0.4
Geography	--	--	--	--	--	--	--	--	--	--	--	0.0	0.0
Political science	--	--	--	--	--	--	--	--	--	--	--	2.3	2.1
Psychology	--	--	--	--	--	--	--	--	--	--	--	2.3	2.3
Social work	--	--	--	--	--	--	--	--	--	--	--	1.8	1.7
Sociology	--	--	--	--	--	--	--	--	--	--	--	0.6	0.5
Other social sciences	--	--	--	--	--	--	--	--	--	--	--	0.3	0.3
Ethnic studies	--	--	--	--	--	--	--	--	--	--	--	--	--
Women's studies	--	--	--	--	--	--	--	--	--	--	--	--	--
Technical Fields													
Building trades											--	0.5	0.6
Data processing/computer programming	--	--	--	--	--	--	--	--	--	--	--	1.5	1.6
Drafting or design	--	--	--	--	--	--	--	--	--	--	--	0.5	0.6
Electronics	--	--	--	--	--	--	--	--	--	--	--	0.9	0.8
Mechanics	--	--	--	--	--	--	--	--	--	--	--	0.4	0.4
Other technical	--	--	--	--	--	--	--	--	--	--	--	0.5	0.5
Other Majors													
Agriculture	--	--	--	--	--	--	--	--	--	--	--	2.3	2.3
Communications (radio, T.V.)	--	--	--	--	--	--	--	--	--	--	--	1.4	1.5
Computer science	--	--	--	--	--	--	--	--	--	--	--	1.0	1.4
Forestry	--	--	--	--	--	--	--	--	--	--	--	1.3	0.9
Law enforcement	--	--	--	--	--	--	--	--	--	--	--	2.0	1.8
Military science	--	--	--	--	--	--	--	--	--	--	--	0.1	0.1
Other fields	--	--	--	--	--	--	--	--	--	--	--	1.2	1.0
Undecided	--	--	--	--	--	--	--	--	--	--	--	4.7	4.6
CAREER PLANS (DISAGGREGATED) [1]													
Accountant or actuary	--	--	--	--	--	--	--	--	--	--	--	6.2	6.3
Actor or entertainer	--	--	--	--	--	--	--	--	--	--	--	0.9	0.9
Architect or urban planner	--	--	--	--	--	--	--	--	--	--	--	1.5	1.5
Artist	--	--	--	--	--	--	--	--	--	--	--	1.9	1.6
Business, clerical	--	--	--	--	--	--	--	--	--	--	--	2.6	2.5
Business executive	--	--	--	--	--	--	--	--	--	--	--	8.4	9.3
Business owner	--	--	--	--	--	--	--	--	--	--	--	2.4	2.5
Business, sales	--	--	--	--	--	--	--	--	--	--	--	1.1	1.2
Clergy or other religious worker	--	--	--	--	--	--	--	--	--	--	--	0.5	0.5
Clinical psychologist	--	--	--	--	--	--	--	--	--	--	--	1.0	1.0
College teacher	--	--	--	--	--	--	--	--	--	--	--	0.3	0.3
Computer programmer	--	--	--	--	--	--	--	--	--	--	--	2.8	3.5
Conservationist or forester	--	--	--	--	--	--	--	--	--	--	--	2.0	1.4
Dentist (including orthodontist)	--	--	--	--	--	--	--	--	--	--	--	0.9	1.0
Dietitian or home economist	--	--	--	--	--	--	--	--	--	--	--	0.6	0.5
Engineer	--	--	--	--	--	--	--	--	--	--	--	8.3	9.1
Farmer, rancher, or forester	--	--	--	--	--	--	--	--	--	--	--	1.2	1.1
Foreign service worker	--	--	--	--	--	--	--	--	--	--	--	0.5	0.5
Homemaker (full-time)	--	--	--	--	--	--	--	--	--	--	--	0.2	0.1
Interior decorator	--	--	--	--	--	--	--	--	--	--	--	0.6	0.5
Interpreter (translator)	--	--	--	--	--	--	--	--	--	--	--	0.2	0.2
Laboratory technician or hygienist	--	--	--	--	--	--	--	--	--	--	--	2.1	1.9
Law enforcement officer	--	--	--	--	--	--	--	--	--	--	--	1.7	1.5
Lawyer (or judge)	--	--	--	--	--	--	--	--	--	--	--	4.4	4.3
Military service (career)	--	--	--	--	--	--	--	--	--	--	--	1.0	1.1
Musician (performer, composer)	--	--	--	--	--	--	--	--	--	--	--	1.5	1.4
Nurse	--	--	--	--	--	--	--	--	--	--	--	4.5	4.1
Optometrist	--	--	--	--	--	--	--	--	--	--	--	0.2	0.2
Pharmacist	--	--	--	--	--	--	--	--	--	--	--	0.8	0.6
Physician	--	--	--	--	--	--	--	--	--	--	--	3.2	3.5
School counselor	--	--	--	--	--	--	--	--	--	--	--	0.3	0.2
School principal, superintendent	--	--	--	--	--	--	--	--	--	--	--	0.0	0.0
Research scientist	--	--	--	--	--	--	--	--	--	--	--	2.2	2.2
Social or welfare worker	--	--	--	--	--	--	--	--	--	--	--	2.7	2.3
Statistician	--	--	--	--	--	--	--	--	--	--	--	0.1	0.1
Therapist (occupational, physical, etc.)	--	--	--	--	--	--	--	--	--	--	--	2.1	2.0
Elementary teacher	--	--	--	--	--	--	--	--	--	--	--	4.0	3.7
Secondary teacher	--	--	--	--	--	--	--	--	--	--	--	2.9	2.5
Veterinarian	--	--	--	--	--	--	--	--	--	--	--	1.4	1.3
Writer or journalist	--	--	--	--	--	--	--	--	--	--	--	1.9	1.9
Skilled worker	--	--	--	--	--	--	--	--	--	--	--	1.9	1.7
Other	--	--	--	--	--	--	--	--	--	--	--	7.2	7.0
Undecided	--	--	--	--	--	--	--	--	--	--	--	9.7	10.6

[1] Data collected in disaggregated form but not reported in 1966-1976.

1979	1980	1981	1982	1983	1984	1985	1986	1987	1988	1989	1990	*DEGREE, MAJOR AND CAREER PLANS*
												MAJOR PLANS (DISAGGREGATED) [1]
												Social Sciences
0.1	0.1	0.1	0.1	0.1	0.1	0.1	0.1	0.1	0.2	0.2	0.2	Anthropology
0.4	0.4	0.4	0.4	0.4	0.4	0.4	0.5	0.5	0.5	0.4	0.4	Economics
0.0	0.0	0.0	0.0	0.0	0.0	0.0	0.0	0.0	0.0	0.0	0.0	Geography
2.0	2.0	1.9	1.9	1.9	2.1	2.4	2.5	2.6	3.2	3.1	3.0	Political science
2.6	2.2	2.2	2.1	2.3	2.7	3.2	3.4	3.5	4.1	4.2	4.2	Psychology
1.6	1.4	1.1	0.9	0.9	0.9	1.0	1.0	0.9	0.9	1.0	1.2	Social work
0.5	0.4	0.3	0.2	0.3	0.3	0.3	0.3	0.3	0.4	0.4	0.4	Sociology
0.3	0.2	0.2	0.2	0.2	0.2	0.2	0.2	0.2	0.2	0.3	0.2	Other social sciences
--	--	--	0.0	0.0	0.0	0.0	0.0	0.0	0.0	0.0	0.0	Ethnic studies
--	--	--	0.0	0.0	0.0	0.0	0.0	0.0	0.0	0.0	0.0	Women's studies
												Technical Fields
0.4	0.5	0.3	0.3	0.3	0.3	0.4	0.3	0.2	0.2	0.4	0.9	Building trades
1.8	2.4	3.0	4.0	3.8	2.4	2.1	1.6	1.1	1.1	1.0	0.9	Data processing/computer programming
0.6	0.7	0.7	0.6	0.7	0.6	0.6	0.6	0.4	0.4	0.5	0.6	Drafting or design
0.7	1.0	0.8	0.9	0.7	0.6	0.5	0.5	0.3	0.2	0.4	0.3	Electronics
0.4	0.6	0.6	0.5	0.6	0.4	0.5	0.5	0.6	0.2	0.5	0.6	Mechanics
0.4	0.5	0.6	0.6	0.7	0.7	0.6	0.5	0.4	0.4	0.5	0.7	Other technical
												Other Majors
2.1	2.2	2.6	1.9	1.3	1.6	1.4	1.2	1.4	1.2	0.8	0.9	Agriculture
1.8	1.9	2.1	2.1	2.1	2.0	2.5	2.5	2.9	2.9	2.7	2.3	Communications (radio, T.V.)
1.8	2.5	3.5	4.4	4.5	3.4	2.3	1.9	1.6	1.7	1.6	1.7	Computer science
0.9	0.7	0.9	0.7	0.6	0.4	0.6	0.6	0.3	0.5	0.4	0.4	Forestry
1.5	1.4	1.1	1.5	1.6	1.5	1.7	1.4	1.6	1.6	1.5	1.7	Law enforcement
0.1	0.1	0.1	0.1	0.1	0.1	0.2	0.1	0.1	0.1	0.1	0.2	Military science
1.4	1.1	1.3	1.2	1.2	1.4	1.6	1.4	1.6	1.4	1.7	1.9	Other fields
4.8	4.7	4.7	4.6	4.9	5.2	5.9	6.5	6.6	6.8	6.9	6.6	Undecided
												CAREER PLANS (DISAGGREGATED) [1]
5.7	5.8	5.5	5.8	5.9	6.0	6.3	5.9	5.9	5.9	5.8	4.8	Accountant or actuary
1.0	0.9	0.9	0.9	0.8	0.8	1.0	1.0	1.1	1.0	0.9	0.9	Actor or entertainer
1.7	1.7	1.3	1.4	1.2	1.3	1.4	1.5	1.5	1.7	1.8	2.4	Architect or urban planner
1.7	1.9	1.8	1.7	1.7	1.5	1.5	1.6	2.1	1.7	1.7	1.5	Artist
2.3	2.2	2.1	1.9	2.0	2.0	1.8	1.4	1.4	1.0	1.1	1.2	Business, clerical
9.8	10.1	10.2	10.5	10.6	11.9	12.7	12.9	13.1	12.4	11.2	9.3	Business executive
2.8	2.6	2.8	2.7	2.7	3.0	3.3	3.7	3.9	3.9	3.4	2.9	Business owner
1.4	1.2	1.1	1.2	1.2	1.3	1.6	1.6	1.7	1.4	1.4	1.4	Business, sales
0.4	0.4	0.5	0.3	0.3	0.3	0.3	0.3	0.3	0.2	0.3	0.3	Clergy or other religious worker
1.1	0.9	0.9	0.9	0.9	1.2	1.3	1.4	1.5	1.7	1.6	1.6	Clinical psychologist
0.3	0.2	0.2	0.2	0.2	0.3	0.3	0.3	0.3	0.4	0.4	0.4	College teacher
4.0	5.3	6.9	8.8	8.5	6.1	4.4	3.5	2.7	2.7	2.6	2.6	Computer programmer
1.2	1.0	1.3	0.9	0.7	0.6	0.8	0.8	0.5	0.7	0.6	0.6	Conservationist or forester
0.9	0.9	0.7	0.7	0.7	0.6	0.6	0.6	0.5	0.5	0.5	0.6	Dentist (including orthodontist)
0.4	0.4	0.4	0.3	0.3	0.3	0.2	0.2	0.2	0.2	0.2	0.2	Dietitian or home economist
9.3	10.7	10.9	12.0	10.8	10.4	10.0	9.7	8.5	8.6	9.0	8.1	Engineer
1.2	1.2	1.5	1.2	0.8	0.9	0.7	0.6	0.5	0.5	0.4	0.4	Farmer, rancher, or forester
0.5	0.5	0.5	0.5	0.6	0.7	0.9	1.0	1.0	1.1	0.9	0.8	Foreign service worker
0.2	0.1	0.2	0.1	0.1	0.1	0.1	0.1	0.1	0.1	0.1	0.2	Homemaker (full-time)
0.6	0.5	0.5	0.5	0.4	0.5	0.6	0.6	0.7	0.5	0.5	0.5	Interior decorator
0.2	0.2	0.2	0.2	0.2	0.2	0.2	0.2	0.2	0.2	0.2	0.2	Interpreter (translator)
1.7	1.5	1.2	1.3	1.3	1.0	0.8	0.7	0.7	0.5	0.5	0.4	Laboratory technician or hygienist
1.2	1.2	0.9	1.2	1.2	1.1	1.3	1.1	1.3	1.2	1.1	1.4	Law enforcement officer
4.2	4.1	3.9	4.3	3.9	4.1	3.9	4.0	4.5	5.4	5.4	5.2	Lawyer (or judge)
1.1	0.9	1.0	0.9	1.1	1.2	1.1	1.3	1.0	1.1	0.9	1.3	Military service (career)
1.3	1.2	1.2	1.1	1.1	0.9	1.1	1.1	1.1	1.1	1.0	1.0	Musician (performer, composer)
3.7	3.8	3.9	4.0	4.4	4.0	3.3	2.7	2.2	2.5	2.7	3.8	Nurse
0.2	0.2	0.2	0.2	0.3	0.3	0.2	0.2	0.2	0.3	0.2	0.2	Optometrist
0.6	0.5	0.4	0.4	0.6	0.7	0.7	0.7	0.8	1.1	1.0	1.1	Pharmacist
3.4	3.5	3.4	3.6	3.9	4.0	3.8	3.7	3.5	3.7	3.8	3.8	Physician
0.3	0.2	0.2	0.2	0.2	0.2	0.2	0.3	0.3	0.3	0.4	0.4	School counselor
0.0	0.0	0.0	0.0	0.0	0.0	0.0	0.0	0.0	0.0	0.0	0.0	School principal, superintendent
1.8	1.7	1.6	1.5	1.5	1.5	1.4	1.4	1.5	1.6	1.6	1.4	Research scientist
2.3	1.9	1.5	1.1	1.3	1.3	1.3	1.4	1.4	1.4	1.3	1.4	Social or welfare worker
0.1	0.1	0.1	0.1	0.1	0.1	0.1	0.1	0.1	0.1	0.1	0.1	Statistician
2.1	2.0	2.1	2.0	2.3	2.4	2.2	2.1	2.3	2.3	2.6	2.7	Therapist (occupational, physical, etc.)
3.8	3.8	3.5	3.0	3.1	3.4	3.8	4.4	5.0	5.6	5.0	5.4	Elementary teacher
2.6	2.2	2.0	1.7	2.0	2.1	2.4	2.9	3.1	3.2	3.2	3.6	Secondary teacher
1.2	1.2	1.2	1.2	1.0	1.1	1.1	0.9	0.8	0.9	0.8	1.0	Veterinarian
2.2	2.0	2.2	2.1	2.0	2.0	2.2	2.3	2.4	2.5	2.3	2.1	Writer or journalist
1.5	1.8	1.7	1.6	1.5	1.3	1.6	1.4	1.3	0.7	1.3	2.1	Skilled worker
7.6	7.0	7.2	6.6	6.4	6.5	6.9	6.8	7.2	6.8	8.6	9.7	Other
10.4	10.1	10.1	9.5	10.1	10.9	10.7	11.6	11.4	11.5	11.6	11.1	Undecided

[1] Data collected in disaggregated form but not reported in 1966-1976.

COLLEGE EXPERIENCES AND EXPECTATIONS	1966	1967	1968	1969	1970	1971	1972	1973	1974	1975	1976	1977	1978
PLANNED RESIDENCE FOR FALL													
With parents or relatives	--	--	--	--	--	--	--	42.2	42.2	39.2	43.7	41.8	35.7
Other private home, apartment or room	--	--	--	--	--	--	--	5.2	6.0	6.8	6.8	6.7	5.5
College dormitory	--	--	--	--	--	--	--	49.9	49.4	50.9	46.7	48.7	56.0
Fraternity or sorority house	--	--	--	--	--	--	--	0.5	0.7	0.5	0.5	0.5	0.5
Other campus student housing	--	--	--	--	--	--	--	1.2	0.9	1.6	1.4	1.5	1.5
Other type of housing	--	--	--	--	--	--	--	1.0	0.8	1.0	0.9	0.8	0.8
PREFERRED RESIDENCE FOR FALL													
With parents or relatives	--	--	--	--	--	--	--	--	22.5	21.8	22.3	21.7	18.9
Other private home, apartment or room	--	--	--	--	--	--	--	--	28.1	26.5	29.3	26.3	24.6
College dormitory	--	--	--	--	--	--	--	--	39.9	41.3	37.7	41.8	45.9
Fraternity or sorority house	--	--	--	--	--	--	--	--	3.8	3.3	3.6	3.8	4.4
Other campus student housing	--	--	--	--	--	--	--	--	3.2	4.0	3.9	3.9	3.9
Other type of housing	--	--	--	--	--	--	--	--	2.6	3.2	3.1	2.5	2.3
STUDENTS ESTIMATE CHANCES ARE VERY GOOD THAT THEY WILL [1]													
Be satisfied with this college	--	--	--	--	64.7	--	59.4	54.1	52.7	53.2	50.8	54.0	55.5
Make at least a B average	--	--	--	--	--	--	32.7	34.8	37.2	38.6	40.6	40.4	41.4
Graduate with honors	--	3.7	3.7	4.1	4.8	--	7.8	9.4	9.7	10.3	11.0	11.4	11.4
Be elected to an academic honor society	--	2.9	2.6	2.3	2.5	--	4.5	4.9	5.2	5.4	6.5	6.9	7.4
Get a bachelor's degree (B.A., B.S., etc)	--	--	--	--	--	--	60.3	61.7	58.7	62.3	61.7	62.6	64.7
Be elected to a student office	--	2.3	2.1	1.9	1.8	--	1.9	2.0	1.9	2.0	2.2	2.5	2.5
Join social fraternity, sorority or club	--	30.8	26.7	22.6	20.4	--	17.3	14.8	13.0	14.5	15.3	17.3	17.9
Change major field	--	16.6	14.5	16.3	15.9	--	16.5	14.6	12.2	12.3	11.4	12.2	12.2
Change career choice	--	17.6	15.4	17.1	16.2	--	17.0	14.0	11.8	12.2	11.2	11.8	11.9
Need extra time to complete degree	--	--	--	--	--	--	4.8	5.0	4.6	4.9	4.7	4.9	4.6
Fail one or more courses	--	2.9	1.9	2.4	3.2	--	2.6	2.4	2.0	2.1	1.8	1.9	1.6
Get tutoring help in specific courses	--	--	--	--	--	--	--	--	--	6.8	7.8	8.8	9.2
Live in a coeducational dorm	--	--	--	--	--	--	--	18.5	17.6	18.9	20.0	22.5	25.6
Seek vocational counseling	--	--	--	--	--	--	13.0	10.7	9.5	8.7	7.2	7.1	6.9
Seek personal counseling	--	--	--	--	--	--	6.2	5.7	5.1	5.3	4.0	4.3	4.3
Get a job to help pay for college expenses	--	--	--	--	--	--	--	--	--	--	40.4	42.7	41.1
Have to work at an outside job	--	--	--	--	--	--	34.7	33.6	32.7	31.0	25.8	26.4	23.4
Work full-time while attending college	--	--	--	--	--	--	--	--	--	--	--	--	--
Participate in student protests or demonstrations		4.7	4.1	--	--	--	--	--	--	--	--	--	3.1
Transfer to another college	--	13.0	12.2	12.7	12.4	--	13.0	13.3	13.9	13.2	13.3	11.9	10.9
Drop out of this college temporarily (excluding transferring)	--	1.1	0.9	1.1	1.3	--	1.8	1.9	1.7	1.7	1.5	1.5	1.2
Drop out permanently	--	0.6	0.5	0.5	0.7	--	1.1	1.1	1.0	1.0	1.0	0.9	0.8
Get married while in college	--	7.6	6.6	8.2	7.7	--	7.6	6.7	6.2	6.1	5.5	5.1	4.8
Get married within a year after college	--	22.9	19.2	20.8	19.2	--	16.9	17.8	17.2	16.6	16.0	15.2	15.2
Enlist in the Armed Services before graduating	--	--	--	1.1	1.6	--	2.5	1.7	1.6	--	--	--	--
Be more successful after graduating than most students attending this college	--	--	--	10.9	11.0	--	17.4	19.2	18.3	--	--	--	--
Play varsity athletics	--	--	--	--	--	--	--	--	--	--	--	--	--
Find a job after college graduation in the field for which you were trained	--	--	--	--	--	--	52.4	57.1	55.3	59.3	59.8	66.1	67.4
CONCERN ABOUT ABILITY TO FINANCE COLLEGE EDUCATION													
None (I am confident that I will have sufficient funds)	35.1	34.4	35.2	34.2	33.8	33.9	35.6	35.8	39.0	36.7	35.1	33.9	34.6
Some concern (but I will probably have enough funds)	56.3	57.0	56.3	55.6	55.1	55.6	49.4	47.5	46.3	47.0	48.8	49.4	50.6
Major concern (not sure I will have enough funds to complete college)	8.6	8.6	8.4	10.2	11.1	10.4	15.0	16.6	14.7	16.4	16.1	16.7	14.8

[1] Text, order or number of response options may vary from year to year.

1979	1980	1981	1982	1983	1984	1985	1986	1987	1988	1989	1990	*COLLEGE EXPERIENCES AND EXPECTATIONS*
												PLANNED RESIDENCE FOR FALL
37.4	35.9	30.3	33.1	35.9	33.1	30.7	29.8	29.5	30.4	29.5	22.6	With parents or relatives
7.3	7.3	5.9	5.8	6.6	5.2	6.2	8.0	8.4	6.8	7.4	6.5	Other private home, apartment or room
52.4	53.3	60.6	58.2	54.5	59.1	59.8	58.4	58.5	59.3	58.9	66.8	College dormitory
0.6	0.6	0.7	0.5	0.5	0.4	0.5	0.6	0.7	0.6	0.5	0.3	Fraternity or sorority house
1.5	1.9	1.7	1.4	1.7	1.5	2.1	2.2	2.2	2.3	3.0	2.9	Other campus student housing
0.8	0.9	0.8	0.9	0.7	0.7	0.8	1.0	0.7	0.6	0.7	0.9	Other type of housing
												PREFERRED RESIDENCE FOR FALL
20.6	20.4	18.5	19.4	19.6	18.7	17.1	16.4	14.4	14.9	14.2	--	With parents or relatives
24.4	23.7	24.7	25.8	27.3	26.8	27.6	29.2	31.9	32.3	33.6	--	Other private home, apartment or room
44.0	45.1	45.8	43.8	41.1	42.0	42.0	39.7	38.4	37.6	36.8	--	College dormitory
4.3	4.6	4.9	5.0	5.0	5.8	6.2	6.8	7.5	7.3	6.7	--	Fraternity or sorority house
3.8	3.9	4.0	3.8	4.6	4.9	4.8	5.4	5.5	5.7	6.1	--	Other campus student housing
2.9	2.3	2.3	2.2	2.3	1.9	2.3	2.5	2.2	2.1	2.5	--	Other type of housing
												STUDENTS ESTIMATE CHANCES ARE VERY GOOD THAT THEY WILL [1]
54.3	54.0	55.8	55.4	54.7	55.2	53.6	52.5	52.6	51.3	49.7	50.9	Be satisfied with this college
40.8	41.3	40.6	41.3	40.7	40.6	40.0	39.8	39.0	41.7	41.0	41.3	Make at least a B average
11.5	12.1	11.2	11.8	12.0	11.8	12.1	11.3	11.9	11.9	12.6	13.5	Graduate with honors
7.3	7.7	7.4	6.7	6.9	7.1	7.3	6.6	7.1	7.2	7.5	8.1	Be elected to an academic honor society
64.1	63.5	64.8	65.0	64.9	67.3	66.9	67.6	68.2	71.3	68.5	66.1	Get a bachelor's degree (B.A., B.S., etc)
2.7	2.9	2.8	2.8	2.8	3.1	3.4	3.2	3.3	3.4	3.4	3.5	Be elected to a student office
17.2	16.9	18.1	16.1	16.2	16.6	17.9	17.2	18.1	18.2	17.9	17.2	Join social fraternity, sorority or club
12.3	11.8	12.1	11.9	12.0	12.7	13.1	13.1	13.9	14.4	13.3	12.4	Change major field
11.8	11.5	11.5	11.0	11.2	11.8	12.3	12.1	12.9	13.1	12.2	11.4	Change career choice
5.1	5.2	5.6	5.2	5.2	5.4	6.3	6.5	6.7	7.1	7.4	8.2	Need extra time to complete degree
1.8	1.7	1.7	1.4	1.3	1.3	1.4	1.4	1.4	1.4	1.4	1.3	Fail one or more courses
9.1	9.4	9.8	9.4	9.3	10.5	11.2	11.0	11.0	12.7	12.6	15.9	Get tutoring help in specific courses
25.3	25.6	28.8	28.2	26.1	28.6	28.4	--	--	--	--	--	Live in a coeducational dorm
6.7	6.0	6.1	5.6	5.9	5.4	6.0	5.4	5.3	5.0	4.4	5.1	Seek vocational counseling
4.5	4.2	4.1	3.6	3.8	3.5	4.0	3.5	3.8	3.8	3.4	3.7	Seek personal counseling
40.5	40.0	40.7	39.1	36.6	37.5	37.5	36.7	38.2	35.4	34.7	36.0	Get a job to help pay for college expenses
23.6	23.5	23.4	21.3	20.9	20.2	21.1	20.3	21.3	20.0	20.1	20.2	Have to work at an outside job
--	--	--	3.2	3.3	3.5	3.5	3.6	3.5	3.5	3.6	4.0	Work full-time while attending college
3.8	4.5	3.7	4.1	3.5	3.9	4.6	4.7	5.7	5.4	6.3	7.1	Participate in student protests or demonstrations
12.0	10.7	11.1	10.5	10.4	10.6	10.7	10.0	10.5	12.0	11.8	12.8	Transfer to another college
1.3	1.2	1.3	1.1	1.1	1.1	1.2	1.2	1.0	1.1	1.1	1.1	Drop out of this college temporarily (excluding transferring)
1.1	0.9	1.0	0.8	0.9	0.8	0.8	0.8	0.7	0.9	0.8	1.0	Drop out permanently
5.1	5.1	5.1	4.8	4.5	4.5	4.6	4.4	4.1	4.4	4.8	5.4	Get married while in college
15.6	16.6	17.2	16.6	15.6	15.7	15.8	15.3	14.2	15.8	--	--	Get married within a year after college
--	--	--	--	--	--	--	--	--	--	--	--	Enlist in the Armed Services before graduating
--	--	--	--	--	--	--	--	--	--	--	--	Be more successful after graduating than most students attending this college
--	--	--	--	14.6	15.2	15.3	14.2	15.0	14.8	14.6	15.4	Play varsity athletics
68.3	69.6	70.8	69.6	68.8	71.0	69.6	69.6	69.9	70.7	69.5	70.6	Find a job after college graduation in the field for which you were trained
												CONCERN ABOUT ABILITY TO FINANCE COLLEGE EDUCATION
33.8	32.3	32.4	31.6	33.5	33.8	35.5	36.3	37.2	36.7	35.7	--	None (I am confident that I will have sufficient funds)
51.7	52.2	51.6	51.2	51.7	51.7	50.8	49.6	49.0	49.0	51.2	--	Some concern (but I will probably have enough funds)
14.5	15.4	16.0	17.2	14.9	14.5	13.7	14.1	13.8	14.3	13.1	--	Major concern (not sure I will have enough funds to complete college)

[1] Text, order or number of response options may vary from year to year.

ATTITUDES AND VALUES	1966	1967	1968	1969	1970	1971	1972	1973	1974	1975	1976	1977	1978
PRESENT POLITICAL VIEWS													
Far left	--	--	--	--	3.1	2.8	2.4	2.2	2.2	2.1	2.2	1.9	1.8
Liberal	--	--	--	--	33.5	35.3	32.8	32.6	28.0	28.8	25.6	25.1	23.6
Middle of the road	--	--	--	--	45.4	46.8	48.3	50.7	55.1	53.8	56.0	56.6	57.8
Conservative	--	--	--	--	17.1	14.5	15.8	13.9	13.9	14.5	15.2	15.6	16.1
Far right	--	--	--	--	1.0	0.7	0.8	0.6	0.8	0.7	1.0	0.8	0.8
OBJECTIVES CONSIDERED TO BE ESSENTIAL OR VERY IMPORTANT													
Become accomplished in one of the performing arts (acting, dancing, etc)	10.8	11.3	8.8	11.3	12.8	11.9	11.8	[*]	11.4	11.7	11.6	13.4	12.8
Become an authority in my field	66.0	67.8	58.3	59.1	66.8	60.0	60.6	62.5	62.2	69.7	70.1	74.8	72.6
Obtain recognition from colleagues for contributions to my special field	42.6	41.2	36.9	41.0	39.9	37.3	36.9	--	39.0	43.2	45.9	48.4	50.3
Influence the political structure	--	--	--	16.3	18.3	14.1	15.7	14.6	12.5	14.4	15.2	15.7	14.6
Influence social values	--	--	--	33.9	34.0	28.0	30.4	31.1	27.2	30.0	29.7	30.8	31.1
Raise a family	--	--	--	71.4	67.5	60.2	64.8	56.4	55.0	56.6	57.2	58.8	61.8
Have administrative responsibility for the work of others	28.6	24.9	22.5	24.0	21.7	19.7	24.1	27.2	25.6	30.6	31.9	34.4	35.6
Be very well-off financially	43.8	43.5	40.8	44.5	39.1	40.1	41.2	[*]	45.8	49.5	53.1	58.2	59.7
Help others who are in difficulty	68.5	61.8	58.9	65.5	64.9	62.7	66.7	64.3	61.3	66.0	63.1	65.1	65.5
Make a theoretical contribution to science	13.3	11.5	10.5	10.3	10.2	9.0	10.6	--	13.0	13.5	14.0	14.1	14.5
Write original works (poems, novels, etc)	14.2	13.8	12.8	13.7	14.0	13.2	13.9	--	11.9	12.1	12.6	13.8	12.7
Create artistic work (painting, sculpture, decorating, etc.)	15.1	15.5	13.5	15.6	16.2	15.4	17.5	--	13.9	14.2	14.3	15.7	14.1
Become involved in programs to clean up the environment	--	--	--	--	--	42.9	44.6	34.3	25.9	28.8	27.7	29.4	27.5
Be successful in my own business	53.0	46.4	45.0	45.8	43.9	41.9	44.7	41.9	37.9	43.6	45.0	47.1	47.9
Develop a meaningful philosophy of life	--	82.9	82.5	81.7	75.6	68.1	70.8	69.0	61.1	64.2	60.8	59.0	56.5
Participate in a community action program	--	--	--	--	29.4	25.9	29.1	--	27.5	30.4	28.8	29.4	26.7
Help promote racial understanding	--	--	--	--	--	--	--	--	--	--	--	35.8	33.8
Keep up to date with political affairs	57.8	50.6	51.7	51.4	52.8	42.8	48.7	42.4	36.6	38.6	37.4	39.9	36.6
Become an expert in finance and commerce	13.5	11.5	10.2	16.6	15.8	13.5	16.2	--	--	--	--	--	--
Participate in an organization like the Peace Corps or Vista	21.0	18.9	18.4	--	19.6	16.2	15.8	--	--	--	--	--	--
Become a community leader	26.1	23.8	21.0	17.6	15.2	13.3	14.9	--	--	--	--	--	--
Never be obligated to people	28.3	24.8	23.5	24.5	22.7	21.3	23.1	--	--	--	--	--	--
PERCENT WHO STRONGLY AGREE OR AGREE SOMEWHAT [1]													
Academic/Campus Issues													
Chief benefit of a college education is that it increases one's earning power	--	56.0	57.8	53.6	66.7	59.2	59.7	55.8	--	--	--	--	--
Faculty promotions should be based in part on student evaluations	--	62.2	63.2	67.5	71.3	76.0	76.3	74.8	73.7	72.6	71.4	72.1	72.3
Colleges would be improved if organized sports were de-emphasized	--	20.8	--	--	--	26.0	25.8	24.8	28.5	27.3	26.8	26.3	26.6
College officials have the right to regulate student behavior off campus	--	--	23.3	19.9	17.0	13.8	12.8	11.4	13.7	14.2	14.0	14.0	14.5
Student publications should be cleared by college officials	--	52.2	56.4	52.0	42.8	32.5	32.5	30.8	32.7	33.5	34.0	36.3	35.9
College officials have the right to ban persons with extreme views from speaking on campus	--	39.5	31.7	32.2	33.2	27.8	25.5	23.1	22.6	24.3	25.2	25.2	25.1
Most college officials have been too lax dealing with student protests on campus	--	47.8	54.5	60.3	58.5	46.5	42.6	36.8	35.0	--	--	--	--
Grading in the high schools is too easy	--	--	--	--	--	--	--	--	--	--	57.7	61.0	63.7
College grades should be abolished	--	--	--	--	44.4	42.6	38.5	34.8	29.3	24.8	21.0	19.2	15.9
Students from disadvantaged social backgrounds should be given preferential treatment in college admissions	--	43.3	41.6	41.4	44.0	40.1	40.9	38.8	38.4	37.4	37.0	37.4	35.5
Open admissions (admitting anyone who applies) should be adopted by all publicly supported colleges	--	--	--	--	--	37.2	37.6	35.3	40.0	36.0	34.7	34.6	32.2
Even if it employs open admissions, a college should use the same performance standards in awarding degrees to all students	--	--	--	--	--	--	79.4	78.0	77.3	75.9	76.7	77.2	77.8
All college graduates should be able to demonstrate some minimal competency in written English and mathematics	--	--	--	--	--	--	--	--	--	--	--	--	--

[*] Results were not comparable to those of other years due to changes in question text or order.

[1] Text, order or number of response options may vary from year to year.

1979	1980	1981	1982	1983	1984	1985	1986	1987	1988	1989	1990	*ATTITUDES AND VALUES*
												PRESENT POLITICAL VIEWS
2.0	2.1	1.6	1.8	1.9	2.0	1.8	2.0	2.3	2.3	1.9	1.8	Far left
22.5	19.6	18.1	18.9	19.2	20.1	20.6	22.0	22.2	22.0	21.7	22.6	Liberal
57.9	60.0	59.6	59.8	60.3	57.4	56.7	56.0	56.0	53.9	53.6	54.7	Middle of the road
16.6	17.1	19.6	18.4	17.5	19.3	19.5	18.7	18.3	20.2	21.3	19.7	Conservative
0.9	1.2	1.1	1.0	1.2	1.2	1.4	1.3	1.3	1.6	1.5	1.2	Far right
												OBJECTIVES CONSIDERED TO BE ESSENTIAL OR VERY IMPORTANT
12.3	12.0	11.5	11.7	11.8	11.0	10.8	10.5	12.6	11.3	11.1	10.8	Become accomplished in one of the performing arts (acting, dancing, etc)
72.8	73.1	72.9	73.5	72.5	73.0	71.2	71.8	77.2	70.6	65.8	65.4	Become an authority in my field
52.2	54.4	54.6	55.3	55.2	55.3	55.2	54.7	58.3	53.6	55.0	54.9	Obtain recognition from colleagues for contributions to my special field
15.4	16.2	15.0	14.8	13.9	15.0	15.6	14.5	16.4	14.2	19.9	20.6	Influence the political structure
31.9	32.2	31.6	31.1	30.7	32.1	32.9	32.5	36.0	40.7	41.1	42.9	Influence social values
64.9	63.1	66.5	67.1	66.1	68.5	69.8	67.0	[*]	67.3	68.8	69.5	Raise a family
36.9	38.7	39.7	40.5	40.6	42.0	42.8	44.2	45.1	[*]	43.6	42.9	Have administrative responsibility for the work of others
62.7	63.3	65.2	68.9	69.3	71.2	70.9	73.2	75.6	[*]	75.4	73.7	Be very well-off financially
63.7	64.7	62.9	61.6	61.7	61.9	63.4	57.2	58.7	[*]	59.7	62.0	Help others who are in difficulty
14.3	14.9	14.4	14.2	14.5	13.6	13.4	12.6	12.4	[*]	17.1	17.1	Make a theoretical contribution to science
12.4	12.5	11.8	11.6	11.2	11.0	11.7	11.3	12.8	[*]	12.5	12.2	Write original works (poems, novels, etc)
14.1	14.4	13.0	12.4	12.0	11.3	11.5	10.9	13.3	[*]	12.5	12.2	Create artistic work (painting, sculpture, decorating, etc.)
26.0	26.7	24.8	22.9	21.2	20.5	20.3	15.9	17.7	--	26.1	33.9	Become involved in programs to clean up the environment
49.0	49.3	49.4	49.7	49.6	51.6	51.8	49.0	50.7	[*]	45.1	43.3	Be successful in my own business
52.9	50.4	49.0	46.7	44.1	44.6	43.3	40.6	39.4	[*]	40.8	43.2	Develop a meaningful philosophy of life
26.0	27.4	24.1	22.8	22.1	22.2	22.8	18.5	19.8	[*]	23.3	25.9	Participate in a community action program
32.1	33.1	31.0	30.7	30.3	31.6	32.0	27.2	29.0	[*]	35.3	38.0	Help promote racial understanding
38.1	40.0	39.2	38.2	35.1	38.0	--	--	--	--	39.4	42.4	Keep up to date with political affairs
--	--	--	--	--	--	25.9	25.2	27.6	--	--	--	Become an expert in finance and commerce
--	--	--	--	--	--	--	--	--	--	--	--	Participate in an organization like the Peace Corps or Vista
--	--	--	--	--	--	--	--	--	--	--	--	Become a community leader
--	--	--	--	--	--	--	--	--	--	--	--	Never be obligated to people
												PERCENT WHO STRONGLY AGREE OR AGREE SOMEWHAT [1]
												Academic/Campus Issues
--	--	--	--	--	--	71.8	70.7	69.4	69.0	70.9	70.7	Chief benefit of a college education is that it increases one's earning power
70.6	71.1	70.2	70.0	69.6	70.0	70.7	70.3	--	--	--	74.9	Faculty promotions should be based in part on student evaluations
--	--	--	--	--	--	--	--	--	--	--	35.8	Colleges would be improved if organized sports were de-emphasized
15.3	15.2	14.9	14.5	15.3	15.0	14.3	12.4	--	--	--	--	College officials have the right to regulate student behavior off campus
40.3	41.2	41.5	40.6	41.0	--	--	--	--	--	--	--	Student publications should be cleared by college officials
25.7	26.1	26.4	24.5	25.5	21.6	25.3	25.6	--	--	--	--	College officials have the right to ban persons with extreme views from speaking on campus
--	--	--	--	--	--	--	--	--	--	--	--	Most college officials have been too lax dealing with student protests on campus
60.0	59.7	57.6	54.5	58.2	54.1	50.1	48.7	--	--	--	--	Grading in the high schools is too easy
16.2	15.6	15.3	14.7	14.7	13.9	--	--	--	--	--	--	College grades should be abolished
38.2	37.9	37.2	35.5	36.6	37.3	--	--	--	--	--	--	Students from disadvantaged social back-grounds should be given preferential treatment in college admissions
35.2	34.7	33.6	--	--	--	--	--	--	--	--	--	Open admissions (admitting anyone who applies) should be adopted by all publicly supported colleges
77.6	--	--	--	--	--	--	--	--	--	--	--	Even if it employs open admissions, a college should use the same performance standards in awarding degrees to all students
--	90.3	90.6	90.5	90.7	90.4	--	--	--	--	--	--	All college graduates should be able to demonstrate some minimal competency in written English and mathematics

[*] Results were not comparable to those of other years due to changes in question text or order.
[1] Text, order or number of response options may vary from year to year.

ATTITUDES AND VALUES

PERCENT WHO STRONGLY AGREE OR AGREE SOMEWHAT [1]	1966	1967	1968	1969	1970	1971	1972	1973	1974	1975	1976	1977	1978
Political/Governance Issues													
Federal government is not doing enough to control environmental pollution	--	--	--	--	--	90.5	89.6	88.1	82.6	81.1	82.4	81.2	81.5
Federal government is not doing enough to protect the consumer from faulty goods and services	--	--	--	--	--	76.2	75.4	75.6	72.9	71.3	71.2	68.7	70.3
Government is not promoting disarmament	--	--	--	--	--	--	--	--	--	--	--	--	--
Increase Federal military spending	--	--	--	--	--	--	--	--	--	--	--	--	--
Federal government is not doing enough to promote school desegregation	--	--	--	--	--	51.7	48.4	48.6	--	--	--	--	--
The Federal government should do more to discourage energy consumption	--	--	--	--	--	--	--	--	--	80.7	79.7	81.8	81.9
Federal government should raise taxes to reduce the deficit	--	--	--	--	--	--	--	--	--	--	--	--	--
The Federal government should do more to control the sale of handguns	--	--	--	--	--	--	--	--	--	--	--	--	--
Wealthy people should pay a larger share of taxes than they do now	--	--	--	--	--	--	72.9	72.7	75.5	76.0	76.2	75.2	73.4
A national health care plan is needed to cover everybody's medical costs	--	--	--	--	--	--	--	--	--	--	--	61.3	60.7
Inflation is our biggest domestic problem	--	--	--	--	--	--	--	--	--	--	--	--	--
Abortion should be legal	--	--	--	--	--	--	--	--	--	--	--	55.7	56.7
Marijuana should be legalized	--	--	19.4	25.6	38.4	38.7	46.6	48.2	46.7	47.2	48.9	52.9	49.5
Capital punishment should be abolished	--	--	--	53.9	56.3	57.6	--	--	--	--	--	--	32.6
Women should receive the same salary and opportunities for advancement as men in comparable positions	--	--	--	--	81.3	87.8	91.3	91.9	91.5	92.2	92.0	92.3	92.7
It is important to have laws prohibiting homosexual relationships	--	--	--	--	--	--	--	--	--	--	47.0	48.6	46.3
Divorce laws should be liberalized	--	--	--	41.6	51.5	--	--	--	--	--	--	--	48.6
Personal/Social Issues													
The activities of married women are best confined to the home and family	--	56.6	--	--	47.8	42.2	37.0	30.4	29.8	28.3	28.4	27.7	27.3
Live together before marriage	--	--	--	--	--	--	--	--	45.3	47.8	48.8	48.3	45.8
Sex is OK if people like each other	--	--	--	--	--	--	--	--	46.0	50.1	49.4	50.4	48.6
People should not obey laws which violate their personal values	--	--	--	--	--	--	--	--	33.6	31.8	31.9	32.0	32.2
Parents should be discouraged from having large families	--	42.2	--	--	--	68.5	67.4	65.4	59.8	57.4	55.1	52.5	47.8
Scientists should publish their findings regardless of the possible consequences	--	43.7	54.2	55.2	61.2	--	--	--	--	--	--	--	--
Realistically, an individual can do little to bring about changes in our society	--	32.9	32.1	36.1	39.0	42.9	43.1	41.1	43.7	47.9	44.3	44.4	--
There is too much concern in the courts for the rights of criminals	--	--	--	54.3	51.6	48.1	50.3	50.1	51.5	53.5	59.7	64.3	65.4
Busing is OK if it helps to achieve racial balance in the schools	--	--	--	--	--	--	--	--	--	--	37.0	40.6	41.5
Nuclear disarmament is attainable	--	--	--	--	--	--	--	--	--	--	--	--	--
Employers should be allowed to require drug testing of employees or job applicants	--	--	--	--	--	--	--	--	--	--	--	--	--
The only way to control AIDS is through widespread, mandatory testing	--	--	--	--	--	--	--	--	--	--	--	--	--
Just because a man thinks that a woman has "led him on" does not entitle him to have sex with her	--	--	--	--	--	--	--	--	--	--	--	--	--
Young more idealistic than old	--	--	--	--	--	--	--	--	72.4	71.5	--	--	--

[1] Text, order or number of response options may vary from year to year.

ATTITUDES AND VALUES

PERCENT WHO STRONGLY AGREE OR AGREE SOMEWHAT [1]

	1979	1980	1981	1982	1983	1984	1985	1986	1987	1988	1989	1990
Political/Governance Issues												
Federal government is not doing enough to control environmental pollution	80.8	79.8	77.6	78.6	80.0	77.7	78.0	78.0	80.9	83.9	86.3	87.9
Federal government is not doing enough to protect the consumer from faulty goods and services	70.8	71.6	65.7	64.4	61.9	57.7	58.2	58.5	62.0	61.0	64.7	68.4
Government is not promoting disarmament	--	--	--	--	--	65.6	66.0	66.0	70.9	66.7	68.1	--
Increase Federal military spending	--	--	--	38.8	36.9	32.5	26.8	26.9	26.2	26.3	24.5	25.1
Federal government is not doing enough to promote school desegregation	--	--	--	--	--	--	--	--	--	--	--	--
The Federal government should do more to discourage energy consumption	82.7	83.0	79.9	77.6	75.0	72.1	71.7	69.7	--	--	--	--
Federal government should raise taxes to reduce the deficit	--	--	--	--	--	--	22.8	--	24.8	27.8	28.8	28.6
The Federal government should do more to control the sale of handguns	--	--	--	--	--	--	--	--	--	--	78.2	77.1
Wealthy people should pay a larger share of taxes than they do now	70.2	70.3	71.0	72.1	70.7	69.7	73.3	72.1	--	--	--	--
A national health care plan is needed to cover everybody's medical costs	61.0	58.1	54.8	57.5	59.4	61.4	60.5	62.1	--	--	75.8	73.7
Inflation is our biggest domestic problem	80.0	80.7	78.7	78.9	68.6	--	--	--	--	--	--	--
Abortion should be legal	53.3	53.6	53.9	54.8	54.8	53.8	54.9	58.6	58.7	57.0	64.7	64.9
Marijuana should be legalized	46.0	39.3	34.0	29.4	25.7	22.9	21.8	21.3	19.3	19.3	16.7	18.6
Capital punishment should be abolished	34.5	34.5	30.1	28.4	28.9	26.0	26.6	25.4	23.8	23.0	21.3	21.5
Women should receive the same salary and opportunities for advancement as men in comparable positions	92.4	93.3	92.7	92.5	92.5	92.4	91.4	92.0	--	--	--	--
It is important to have laws prohibiting homosexual relationships	47.3	48.9	48.6	47.2	49.0	47.8	47.9	52.2	53.2	49.0	45.4	44.4
Divorce laws should be liberalized	48.7	46.3	44.2	44.6	44.7	--	--	--	--	--	--	--
Personal/Social Issues												
The activities of married women are best confined to the home and family	28.2	26.6	26.9	25.5	24.5	22.4	22.4	20.3	26.0	25.6	25.9	25.2
Live together before marriage	44.0	43.4	42.7	42.8	44.8	45.1	47.4	51.1	52.1	51.3	50.7	--
Sex is OK if people like each other	49.3	47.9	47.0	48.2	48.8	46.8	--	--	51.9	50.0	49.7	51.0
People should not obey laws which violate their personal values	33.3	32.3	32.5	--	--	--	--	--	--	--	--	--
Parents should be discouraged from having large families	46.0	44.8	42.0	37.3	36.0	--	--	--	--	--	--	--
Scientists should publish their findings regardless of the possible consequences	--	--	--	--	--	--	--	--	--	--	--	53.1
Realistically, an individual can do little to bring about changes in our society	--	--	--	--	--	--	37.2	--	--	--	--	--
There is too much concern in the courts for the rights of criminals	62.4	65.9	69.1	69.8	68.8	--	--	--	68.3	69.1	68.5	66.3
Busing is OK if it helps to achieve racial balance in the schools	44.1	45.8	43.8	46.8	50.7	53.6	54.4	56.1	55.5	53.7	56.0	56.7
Nuclear disarmament is attainable	--	--	--	--	--	--	54.2	54.6	58.0	60.4	--	60.9
Employers should be allowed to require drug testing of employees or job applicants	--	--	--	--	--	--	--	--	--	71.0	77.8	80.4
The only way to control AIDS is through widespread, mandatory testing	--	--	--	--	--	--	--	--	--	67.7	67.2	66.4
Just because a man thinks that a woman has "led him on" does not entitle him to have sex with her	--	--	--	--	--	--	--	--	--	83.8	86.4	86.9
Young more idealistic than old	--	--	--	--	--	--	--	--	--	--	--	--

[1] Text, order or number of response options may vary from year to year.

FINANCIAL AID	1966	1967	1968	1969	1970	1971	1972	1973	1974	1975	1976	1977	1978
RECEIVED ANY AID FOR FIRST YEAR EDUCATIONAL EXPENSES [1]													
Personal or Family Resources													
Parents and family	--	--	--	--	--	--	--	--	--	--	--	--	71.8
Spouse's income	--	--	--	--	--	--	--	--	--	--	--	--	0.9
Savings from summer work	--	--	--	--	--	--	--	--	--	--	--	--	47.1
Other savings	--	--	--	--	--	--	--	--	--	--	--	--	20.5
Part-time work while attending college	--	--	--	--	--	--	--	--	--	--	--	--	24.9
Part-time work on campus	--	--	--	--	--	--	--	--	--	--	--	--	--
Other part-time work while in college	--	--	--	--	--	--	--	--	--	--	--	--	--
Full-time work while in college	--	--	--	--	--	--	--	--	--	--	--	--	2.1
Aid Which Need Not Be Repaid													
Pell Grant (BEOG prior to 1982) [2]	--	--	--	--	--	--	--	--	--	--	--	--	21.7
Supp. Educational Oppty. Grant (SEOG) [2]	--	--	--	--	--	--	--	--	--	--	--	--	5.7
State scholarship or grant [2]	--	--	--	--	--	--	--	--	--	--	--	--	15.2
College grant or scholarship	--	--	--	--	--	--	--	--	--	--	--	--	12.5
College Work-Study Grant [2]	--	--	--	--	--	--	--	--	--	--	--	--	11.2
Private grant or scholarship	--	--	--	--	--	--	--	--	--	--	--	--	7.4
Student's GI benefits	--	--	--	--	--	--	--	--	--	--	--	--	0.7
GI benefits awarded to student's parent	--	--	--	--	--	--	--	--	--	--	--	--	1.1
GI/military benefits (student's or parents')	--	--	--	--	--	--	--	--	--	--	--	--	--
Social Security dependent's benefits	--	--	--	--	--	--	--	--	--	--	--	--	5.5
Other gov't aid (ROTC, Soc. Sec.,BIA,etc.)	--	--	--	--	--	--	--	--	--	--	--	--	--
Aid Which Must Be Repaid													
Stafford/Guaranteed Student Loan [2]	--	--	--	--	--	--	--	--	--	--	--	--	10.4
Perkins Loan (NDSL prior to 1990) [2]	--	--	--	--	--	--	--	--	--	--	--	--	8.0
College loan	--	--	--	--	--	--	--	--	--	--	--	--	3.6
Loan(s) from other sources	--	--	--	--	--	--	--	--	--	--	--	--	3.7
From sources other than those cited above	--	--	--	--	--	--	--	--	--	--	--	--	3.9
RECEIVED $1,500+ AID FOR FIRST YEAR EDUCATIONAL EXPENSES [1]													
Personal or Family Resources													
Parents and family	--	--	--	--	--	--	--	--	--	--	--	--	31.1
Spouse's income	--	--	--	--	--	--	--	--	--	--	--	--	0.1
Savings from summer work	--	--	--	--	--	--	--	--	--	--	--	--	2.9
Other savings	--	--	--	--	--	--	--	--	--	--	--	--	1.8
Part-time work while attending college	--	--	--	--	--	--	--	--	--	--	--	--	0.8
Part-time work on campus	--	--	--	--	--	--	--	--	--	--	--	--	--
Other part-time work while in college	--	--	--	--	--	--	--	--	--	--	--	--	--
Full-time work while in college	--	--	--	--	--	--	--	--	--	--	--	--	0.3
Aid Which Need Not Be Repaid													
Pell Grant (BEOG prior to 1982) [2]	--	--	--	--	--	--	--	--	--	--	--	--	3.2
Supp. Educational Oppty. Grant (SEOG) [2]	--	--	--	--	--	--	--	--	--	--	--	--	0.3
State scholarship or grant [2]	--	--	--	--	--	--	--	--	--	--	--	--	1.5
College grant or scholarship	--	--	--	--	--	--	--	--	--	--	--	--	2.5
College Work-Study Grant [2]	--	--	--	--	--	--	--	--	--	--	--	--	0.3
Private grant or scholarship	--	--	--	--	--	--	--	--	--	--	--	--	0.8
Student's GI benefits	--	--	--	--	--	--	--	--	--	--	--	--	0.3
GI benefits awarded to student's parent	--	--	--	--	--	--	--	--	--	--	--	--	0.3
GI/military benefits (student's or parents')	--	--	--	--	--	--	--	--	--	--	--	--	--
Social Security dependent's benefits	--	--	--	--	--	--	--	--	--	--	--	--	1.1
Other gov't aid (ROTC, Soc. Sec.,BIA,etc.)	--	--	--	--	--	--	--	--	--	--	--	--	--
Aid Which Must Be Repaid													
Stafford/Guaranteed Student Loan [2]	--	--	--	--	--	--	--	--	--	--	--	--	4.5
Perkins Loan (NDSL prior to 1990) [2]	--	--	--	--	--	--	--	--	--	--	--	--	1.0
College loan	--	--	--	--	--	--	--	--	--	--	--	--	1.0
Loan(s) from other sources	--	--	--	--	--	--	--	--	--	--	--	--	1.2
From sources other than those cited above	--	--	--	--	--	--	--	--	--	--	--	--	1.5

[1] Response and processing options rendered data from 1973-1977 not comparable to 1978-1990.
[2] In 1987-1990, highest response option of "$3,000 or more" was dropped, since these programs have upper limits less than $3,000.

1979	1980	1981	1982	1983	1984	1985	1986	1987	1988	1989	1990	***FINANCIAL AID***
												RECEIVED ANY AID FOR FIRST YEAR EDUCATIONAL EXPENSES [1]
												Personal or Family Resources
67.9	68.8	69.2	71.8	70.8	69.8	70.3	73.4	76.5	78.2	79.8	78.7	Parents and family
0.8	0.9	0.9	0.8	0.9	0.9	0.9	1.5	1.1	1.2	1.1	1.6	Spouse's income
43.0	43.1	43.5	41.3	40.5	45.5	48.4	50.1	54.9	54.4	54.3	55.5	Savings from summer work
17.9	18.6	19.0	18.5	18.4	19.9	22.1	26.0	28.4	28.6	28.6	31.7	Other savings
24.3	24.8	23.6	23.7	23.7	28.0	30.8	33.1	--	--	--	--	Part-time work while attending college
--	--	--	--	--	--	--	--	18.5	19.4	17.6	20.8	Part-time work on campus
--	--	--	--	--	--	--	--	24.1	23.3	24.3	21.8	Other part-time work while in college
2.2	2.3	2.0	1.9	1.8	1.7	2.2	2.3	1.9	2.1	2.0	2.3	Full-time work while in college
												Aid Which Need Not Be Repaid
31.5	31.5	26.0	23.2	26.5	19.8	19.9	16.9	17.5	19.8	21.6	23.2	Pell Grant (BEOG prior to 1982) [2]
7.2	8.0	5.7	5.7	6.8	5.4	4.8	5.3	5.8	5.2	6.0	6.8	Supp. Educational Oppty. Grant (SEOG) [2]
15.1	16.0	13.8	14.4	15.7	13.6	14.1	13.5	16.1	13.5	15.0	16.0	State scholarship or grant [2]
11.3	12.8	11.4	11.9	13.3	16.7	18.5	17.8	12.9	20.0	20.3	22.2	College grant or scholarship
11.7	14.5	12.0	11.8	13.4	9.4	10.0	10.4	9.8	8.4	10.1	10.4	College Work-Study Grant [2]
6.8	7.2	6.8	7.3	7.4	6.3	5.6	7.0	9.5	9.1	9.2	10.6	Private grant or scholarship
0.8	0.9	0.7	0.6	0.5	0.5	0.6	0.7	--	--	--	--	Student's GI benefits
1.1	1.1	1.0	0.8	0.8	0.6	0.5	0.5	--	--	--	--	GI benefits awarded to student's parent
--	--	--	--	--	--	--	--	0.6	--	--	--	GI/military benefits (student's or parents')
5.3	5.7	5.8	3.2	2.1	--	--	--	--	--	--	--	Social Security dependent's benefits
--	--	--	--	--	2.1	1.8	1.9	1.7	2.4	2.5	3.2	Other gov't aid (ROTC, Soc. Sec.,BIA,etc.)
												Aid Which Must Be Repaid
13.2	20.9	26.3	20.8	21.8	23.4	23.0	25.2	22.2	21.2	22.7	22.7	Stafford/Guaranteed Student Loan [2]
7.8	9.1	7.6	6.2	6.8	6.2	5.7	6.1	4.5	3.0	2.4	7.6	Perkins Loan (NDSL prior to 1990) [2]
3.4	4.3	3.7	3.5	3.7	3.5	3.7	4.1	5.3	5.8	7.7	6.0	College loan
3.5	4.0	4.2	4.1	4.0	3.8	3.8	4.2	5.0	5.4	6.3	6.2	Loan(s) from other sources
3.7	3.8	3.7	3.0	3.6	2.3	2.5	2.5	3.4	2.8	3.1	3.2	From sources other than those cited above
												RECEIVED $1,500+ AID FOR FIRST YEAR EDUCATIONAL EXPENSES [1]
												Personal or Family Resources
28.1	28.1	31.5	36.8	37.0	40.8	42.4	46.4	50.5	52.4	53.6	53.2	Parents and family
0.1	0.2	0.3	0.2	0.3	0.2	0.3	0.4	0.3	0.3	0.3	0.5	Spouse's income
3.0	3.1	3.6	4.2	4.0	4.5	5.0	4.7	5.8	6.7	6.8	7.4	Savings from summer work
1.8	2.1	2.2	2.6	2.7	3.2	3.4	4.3	4.8	5.0	5.4	5.9	Other savings
1.1	1.0	1.1	1.1	1.1	1.0	1.3	1.3	1.2	--	--	--	Part-time work while attending college
--	--	--	--	--	--	--	--	0.7	0.8	0.9	1.2	Part-time work on campus
--	--	--	--	--	--	--	--	--	1.3	1.2	1.2	Other part-time work while in college
0.4	0.4	0.4	0.3	0.3	0.3	0.4	0.5	0.5	0.5	0.5	0.6	Full-time work while in college
												Aid Which Need Not Be Repaid
4.5	4.7	4.4	4.8	6.4	4.6	5.0	4.0	4.3	5.2	5.8	7.1	Pell Grant (BEOG prior to 1982) [2]
0.4	0.6	0.5	0.6	0.8	0.8	0.7	0.8	1.0	1.0	1.0	1.3	Supp. Educational Oppty. Grant (SEOG) [2]
1.5	1.6	1.5	1.5	2.1	1.7	2.2	2.1	3.4	3.1	3.4	3.8	State scholarship or grant [2]
2.2	2.7	3.0	3.5	4.3	5.8	6.5	6.7	5.2	8.2	8.9	9.9	College grant or scholarship
0.3	0.6	0.5	0.7	1.0	0.6	0.9	0.8	0.8	1.0	1.0	1.4	College Work-Study Grant [2]
0.8	1.0	1.0	1.2	1.2	1.1	1.0	1.3	2.0	2.1	2.2	2.7	Private grant or scholarship
0.4	0.4	0.3	0.3	0.1	0.3	0.2	0.4	--	--	--	--	Student's GI benefits
0.3	0.3	0.3	0.3	0.2	0.3	0.1	0.2	--	--	--	--	GI benefits awarded to student's parent
--	--	--	--	--	--	--	--	0.5	--	--	--	GI/military benefits (student's or parents')
1.0	1.3	1.4	0.7	0.8	--	--	--	--	--	--	--	Social Security dependent's benefits
--	--	--	--	--	1.2	0.9	1.2	1.1	1.4	1.5	1.9	Other gov't aid (ROTC, Soc. Sec.,BIA,etc.)
												Aid Which Must Be Repaid
6.8	12.3	19.1	13.4	14.2	16.8	16.0	15.6	12.5	12.3	13.1	13.6	Stafford/Guaranteed Student Loan [2]
1.2	2.1	2.4	1.7	1.9	2.1	1.8	1.7	1.4	0.9	0.9	2.1	Perkins Loan (NDSL prior to 1990) [2]
1.1	1.7	1.5	1.5	1.4	1.7	1.7	1.7	2.2	2.4	3.5	3.3	College loan
1.3	1.7	2.2	1.9	1.8	2.2	1.9	2.1	2.5	2.6	3.4	3.6	Loan(s) from other sources
1.5	1.4	1.3	1.2	1.3	1.0	0.8	0.9	1.4	1.1	1.4	1.4	From sources other than those cited above

[1] Response and processing options rendered data from 1973-1977 not comparable to 1978-1990.
[2] In 1987-1990, highest response option of "$3,000 or more" was dropped, since these programs have upper limits less than $3,000.

Appendix A

Research Methodology

Appendix A
Research Methodology

Developing the National Norms

The trends data reported here have been weighted to provide a normative picture of the American college freshman population for persons engaged in policy analysis, human resource planning, campus administration, educational research, guidance and counseling, as well as for the general community of students and parents. This Appendix describes the procedures used to weight the annual freshman survey results to produce the national normative estimates.

The National Population

For the purposes of the CIRP, the population of institutions has been defined as all institutions of higher education listed in the Opening Fall Enrollment (OFE) files of the U.S. Department of Education's Higher Education General Information Survey (HEGIS, since 1986 known as IPEDS—Integrated Postseconday Education Data System). An institution is considered eligible if it was operating at the time of the HEGIS/IPEDS survey and had a first-time full-time (FTFT) freshman class of at least 25 students. In addition, a small number of institutions or their branches are included even though their separate enrollments were not available from the OFE files, because they were part of prior HEGIS/IPEDS populations and are known to be functioning with FTFT students. Generally, the OFE files available for any given year lag one or two years behind. The 1990 population figures, for example, were obtained from the OFE file for Fall, 1988. In 1990, the national population included 2,727 institutions.

It should be noted that the population reflects institutions of "higher education," rather than "postsecondary education." Most proprietary, special vocational or semiprofessional institutions are not included in the population. Two-year colleges offering AA degrees or those described at "terminal vocational" are included.

Institutional Stratification Design

The institutions identified as part of the national population are divided into 37 stratification groups based on institutional race (predominantly white vs. predominantly black), type (two-year college, four-year college, university[1]), control (public, private nonsectarian, Roman Catholic and Protestant) and, for four-year colleges and universities, the "selectivity level" of the institution (for two–year colleges, enrollment is used in place of selectivity). Selectivity, defined as the average composite SAT score of the entering class, was made an integral part of the stratification design in 1968, and was revised and updated in 1975. Figure A1 shows the distribution of institutions across the 37 stratification cells.

It should be noted that the dividing lines between low, medium and high selectivity levels are different for different types of institutions, as shown below:

	Universities				Four–year institutions							
	Public		Private		Public		Nonsectarian		Catholic		Protestant	
Between	SAT V+M	ACT	SAT V+M	ACT	SAT V+M	ACT	SAT V+M	ACT	SAT V+M	ACT	SAT V+M	ACT
Low–medium	1000	22.5	1050	24.0	935	21.0	950	21.5	950	21.5	975	22.0
Medium–high	1100	25.0	1175	27.0	1025	23.0	1025	23.0	1025	23.0	1050	24.0
High–Very high	—	—	—	—	—	—	1175	27.0	—	—	—	—

Changes in stratification assignment do occur; institutional requests for review are honored each year. Appendix C lists the 1990 stratification cell assignments of all institutions that have participated in the CIRP freshman survey.

Having defined the population in terms of the stratification cell scheme, the OFE file is used to compute the male and female FTFT population in each cell. These population counts form the target counts of the weighting procedure.

IDENTIFYING THE NORMS SAMPLE

Generally speaking, an institution is included in the National Norms sample if it provided a representative sample of its FTFT population. The percentage required of a sample is based on the type of institution from which it was collected:

Four–year colleges	85%
Universities	75%
Two–year colleges	50%

Institutions whose sample proportions were less than but close to these cutoffs are included if the method used to administer the survey showed no systematic biases in freshman class coverage.

[1]For stratification purposes, a university is defined as an institution that offers doctoral degrees. Institutions that offer postbaccalaureate programs but do not offer doctoral degrees are considered four–year colleges.

Figure A1: 1990 Data Bank Population

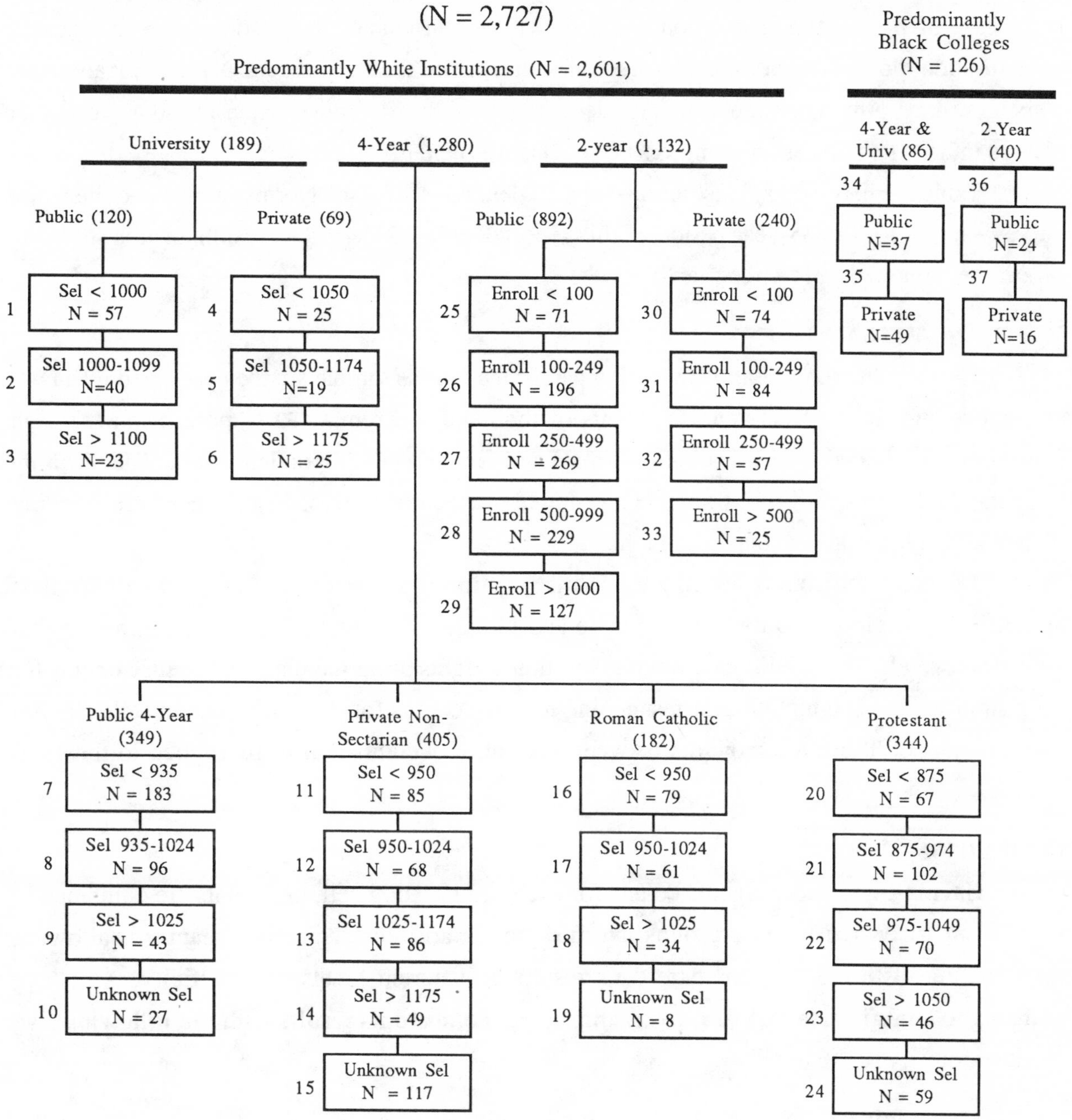

Selectivity (SEL), used to define strata for four-year colleges and universities, is an estimate of the mean score of entering freshmen on the Verbal plus Mathematical portions of the Scholastic Aptitude Test (or the converted SAT math and verbal equivalents from the American College Test composite). The method of estimation is described in detail in Astin and Henson (1977).

Enrollment (ENROLL), used to define strata for two-year colleges, is based on the total number of first-time, full-time entrants.

The stratification design presented here is used to group schools to develop population weights and should not be used as measure of institutional or program quality.

Information about the FTFT population and the method of survey administration are obtained from participating institutions at the time they return their completed surveys. In the event an institution did not return FTFT information, counts from the most recent OFE survey are used. This procedure, although not optimal, is adequate unless the institution experienced a substantial change in its FTFT population changed since the last HEGIS/IPEDS survey.

Table A1 lists the total institutional and student counts for the Norms sample and the entire survey sample for the 25-year period of this report. Table A2 describes results of this selection procedure in more detail for the year 1990.

WEIGHTING THE SAMPLE

Those institutions identified as being part of the Norms sample are then weighted by a two-step procedure. In the first step, the counts of the male and female FTFT population for each institution are divided by that institution's male and female FTFT respondent count. The resulting weights, when applied, bring the male and female respondent counts up to the corresponding counts for the population at that institution.

The weighted counts for all participating institutions in each stratification cell are then summed, and divided into the national male and female FTFT counts for all institutions in that stratification cell. The resulting between-institution weights bring the male and female counts for each stratification cell up to the corresponding national counts for that stratification cell. The last two columns of Table A2 show the between-institution weights that were applied to the 1990 sample.

COMPARISON GROUPS

Having computed weighted counts for each stratification cell, the counts are combined to form comparison (or Norms) groups. Norms groups are hierarchically organized, allowing participating institutions to compare their results at different levels of specificity. A college assigned to stratification cell #14, for example, can compare its results with the following five Norms groups:

Private nonsectarian, very high selectivity
Private nonsectarian
All private 4-year colleges
All 4-year colleges
All institutions

Table A3 shows the 1990 distribution of schools and respondents across the 35 Norms groups normally printed in the annual *American Freshman* report. The results reported here represent the "all institutions" group—the overall summary of all weighted stratificataion cell counts.

Table A1

Number of Institutional and Student Participants in the CIRP Freshman Surveys, 1966–1990

	Counts for Trends Data				Survey Counts	
	Number of		Percent		Number of	
Year	Institutions	Freshmen	Male	Female	Institutions	Freshmen
1966	251	206,865	54.3	45.7	307	254,480
1967	252	185,848	55.6	44.4	359	280,650
1968	358	243,156	56.6	43.4	435	301,448
1969	270	169,190	56.6	43.4	390	260,016
1970	275	180,684	54.8	45.2	425	272,268
1971	326	171,509	54.4	45.6	487	288,526
1972	373	188,900	53.9	46.1	527	307,656
1973	360	189,733	52.8	47.2	579	318,178
1974	364	189,724	52.2	47.8	576	311,950
1975	366	186,406	53.2	46.8	562	314,069
1976	393	215,890	51.8	48.2	592	328,381
1977	374	198,641	50.7	49.3	548	299,467
1978	383	187,603	48.9	51.1	566	289,641
1979	362	190,151	48.8	51.2	560	289,814
1980	355	187,124	48.5	51.5	540	291,491
1981	368	192,248	48.6	51.4	537	284,938
1982	350	188,692	49.5	50.5	492	267,185
1983	358	190,368	49.0	51.0	489	254,317
1984	345	182,370	48.2	51.8	526	271,685
1985	365	192,453	48.2	51.8	546	279,985
1986	372	204,491	47.7	52.3	552	290,429
1987	390	209,627	47.2	52.8	562	289,875
1988	402	222,296	46.3	53.7	585	308,007
1989	403	216,362	46.2	53.8	587	295,966
1990	382	194,181	46.2	53.8	574	276,798
		4,884,512	50.8	49.2		7,227,220

Table A2

Institutional Sample and Population Weights Used to Compare the 1990 Freshman Norms

Stratification Cell for Sampling[2]	Number of Institutions: Population	Participants: Total	Participants: Used in Norms	Cell Weights[1] Applied to Data Collected from: Men	Women
Public universities					
1. Less than 1,000	57	15	9	4.38	4.54
2. 1,000 - 1,099	40	12	7	6.54	6.68
3. 1,100 or more	23	12	9	2.96	2.77
Private universities					
4. Less than 1,050	25	14	8	3.55	3.18
5. 1,050 - 1,174	19	12	12	1.89	1.99
6. 1,175 or more	25	14	10	2.63	2.28
Public four–year colleges					
7,10. Less than 935 or unknown	210	41	19	16.34	15.09
8. 935 - 1,024	96	26	15	7.92	7.14
9. 1,025 or more	43	14	10	3.87	6.79
Private nonsectarian four–year colleges					
11,15. Less than 950 or unknown	202	35	16	7.43	7.98
12. 950 - 1,024	68	29	21	2.09	2.31
13. 1,025 - 1,174	86	49	33	2.97	2.29
14. 1,175 or more	49	40	34	1.32	1.50
Catholic four–year colleges					
16,19. Less than 950 or unknown	87	25	13	4.30	5.47
17. 950 - 1,024	61	33	20	4.22	3.04
18. 1,025 or more	34	18	13	1.82	2.03
Protestant four–year colleges					
20,24. Less than 875 or unknown	126	20	9	12.46	12.15
21. 875 - 974	102	36	26	4.15	4.43
22. 975 - 1,049	70	33	25	2.56	2.69
23. 1,050 or more	46	31	23	2.18	2.03
Public two–year colleges					
25,26. Less than 249	267	6	6	56.55	44.09
27,28. 250-999	498	12	7	91.65	129.58
29. 1,000 or more	127	5	3	36.81	67.14
Private two–year colleges					
30. Less than 100	74	4	4	23.57	6.84
31. 100 - 249	84	11	11	8.23	7.37
32,33. 250 or more	82	5	5	15.32	26.81
Predominantly black colleges					
34,36. public 4-year and 2-year	61	8	4	14.83	15.95
35,37. private 4-year and 2-year	65	14	10	7.76	4.70

[1]Ratio between the number of 1990 first-time, full-time students enrolled in all colleges and the number of first-time, full-time students enrolled at colleges in the 1990 CIRP sample.

[2]Categories within 4-year college and university types are based on selectivity, while categories within 2-year college types are based on freshman enrollment.

Table A3

Number of Institutions and Students Used in Computing the Weighted National Norms in Fall 1990

Norm Group	Number of Institutions in the 1990 Norms	Number of Entering First-time, Full-time Freshmen: Unweighted Participants	Weighted: Number	Weighted: % Men	Weighted: % Women
All institutions	382	194,181	1,582,514	46.23	53.77
All universities	55	84,171	377,023	49.20	50.80
All four-year colleges	291	102,513	634,178	45.63	54.37
All two-year colleges	36	7,497	571,312	44.94	55.06
All black colleges[1]	14	4,866	66,909	41.72	58.28
Public universities	25	55,129	289,789	48.88	51.12
low selectivity	9	21,999	117,636	47.75	52.25
medium selectivity	7	13,699	104,789	49.69	50.31
high selectivity	9	19,431	67,364	49.60	50.40
Private universities	30	29,042	87,234	50.26	49.74
low selectivity	8	7,700	29,841	46.30	53.70
medium selectivity	12	10,682	25,820	46.75	53.25
high selectivity	10	10,660	31,573	56.88	43.12
Public four-year colleges	48	32,969	384,381	46.04	53.96
low selectivity [2]	23	11,809	223,439	45.55	54.45
medium selectivity	15	13,087	115,528	44.94	55.06
high selectivity	10	8,073	45,415	51.26	48.74
Private four-year colleges	243	69,544	249,797	44.98	55.02
Nonsectarian four-year colleges	109	35,731	114,941	46.96	53.04
low selectivity [2]	21	5,712	46,645	47.25	52.75
medium selectivity	21	7,190	20,243	43.66	56.34
high selectivity	33	9,034	26,790	50.41	49.59
very high selectivity	34	13,795	21,263	45.09	54.91
Protestant four-year colleges	88	21,384	91,334	45.30	54.70
low selectivity [2]	40	7,583	55,281	44.59	55.41
medium selectivity	25	6,620	19,410	46.58	53.42
high selectivity	23	7,181	16,643	46.18	53.82
Catholic four-year colleges	46	12,429	43,521	39.11	60.89
low selectivity [2]	13	2,336	14,010	32.12	67.88
medium selectivity	20	4,171	16,176	39.76	60.24
high selectivity	13	5,922	13,335	45.66	54.34
Public two-year colleges	16	4,728	517,415	45.32	54.68
Private two-year colleges	20	2,769	53,898	41.34	58.66
Public black colleges	4	2,133	47,318	41.71	58.29
Private black colleges	11	2,782	20,399	42.57	57.43
Eastern region	140	67,904	635,149	47.16	52.84
Midwestern region	99	57,404	385,015	45.96	54.04
Southern region	96	40,102	345,386	43.33	56.67
Western region	46	28,722	216,155	48.55	51.45

[1]Black colleges are also included in the appropriate four-year college or university norm group according to their type.

[2]Includes those institutions with unknown selectivity.

NOTE: The weighted counts may not always sum to identical totals due to rounding error.

Appendix B

The 1990 Student Information Form

PLEASE PRINT (one letter or number per box)

NAME: FIRST | M I | LAST

ADDRESS:

CITY: | STATE: | ZIP: | PHONE: — —

When were you born? Month (01–12) Day (01–31) Year

1990 STUDENT INFORMATION FORM

DIRECTIONS

Your responses will be read by an optical mark reader. Your careful observance of these few simple rules will be most appreciated.

- Use only black lead pencil (No. 2 is ideal).
- Make heavy black marks that fill the oval.
- Erase cleanly any answer you wish to change.
- Make no stray markings of any kind.

EXAMPLE:
Will marks made with ballpoint or felt-tip marker be properly read? Yes . . . ◯ No . . . ⬬

Dear Student:

The information in this form is being collected as part of a continuing study of higher education conducted jointly by the American Council on Education and the University of California at Los Angeles. Your voluntary participation in this research is being solicited in order to achieve a better understanding of how students are affected by their college experiences. Detailed information on the goals and design of this research program are furnished in research reports available from the Higher Education Research Institute at UCLA. Identifying information has been requested in order to make subsequent mail follow-up studies possible. Your response will be held in the strictest professional confidence.

Sincerely,
Alexander W. Astin, Director
Higher Education Research Institute

PLEASE USE #2 PENCIL

FORM NO.: 112105

PLEASE PROVIDE YOUR SOCIAL SECURITY NO. | Mark here if directed: GRP. CODE A | GRP. CODE B

(0 1 2 3 4 5 6 7 8 9 in each column)

1. Your sex: Male . . . ◯ Female . . . ◯

2. How old will you be on December 31 of this year? (Mark one)
16 or younger . . ◯ 17 ◯ 18 ◯ 19 ◯ 20 ◯ 21–24 ◯ 25–29 ◯ 30–39 ◯ 40–54 ◯ 55 or older ◯

3. Are you a twin? (Mark one)
No . . . ◯ Yes, identical . . ◯ Yes, fraternal . . ◯

4. In what year did you graduate from high school? (Mark one)
1990 ◯ 1989 ◯ 1988 ◯ 1987 or earlier ◯ Did not graduate but passed G.E.D. test ◯ Never completed high school ◯

5. Are you enrolled (or enrolling) as a: (Mark one)
Full-time student? ◯ Part-time student? ◯

6. How many miles is this college from your permanent home? (Mark one)
5 or less ◯ 6–10 ◯ 11–50 ◯ 51–100 ◯ 101–500 ◯ Over 500 ◯

7. What was your average grade in high school? (Mark one)
A or A+ ◯ A– ◯ B+ ◯ B ◯ B– ◯ C+ ◯ C ◯ D ◯

8. What were your scores on the SAT and/or ACT?
SAT VERBAL . . . .
SAT MATH . . . .
ACT Composite . . . .

9. During high school (grades 9-12) how many years did you study each of the following subjects? (Mark one for each item)

	None	½	1	2	3	4	5 or more
English	◯	◯	◯	◯	◯	◯	◯
Mathematics	◯	◯	◯	◯	◯	◯	◯
Foreign Language	◯	◯	◯	◯	◯	◯	◯
Physical Science	◯	◯	◯	◯	◯	◯	◯
Biological Science	◯	◯	◯	◯	◯	◯	◯
History/Am. Govt.	◯	◯	◯	◯	◯	◯	◯
Computer Science	◯	◯	◯	◯	◯	◯	◯
Arts and/or Music	◯	◯	◯	◯	◯	◯	◯

10. Prior to this term, have you ever taken courses for credit at this institution?
◯ Yes ◯ No

11. Since leaving high school, have you ever taken courses at any other institution? (Mark all that apply in each column)

	For Credit	Not for Credit
No	◯	◯
Yes, at a junior or comty. college	◯	◯
Yes, at a 4-yr. college or university	◯	◯
Yes, at some other postsecondary school (For ex., technical, vocational, business)	◯	◯

12. Where do you plan to live during the fall term? (Mark one)
With parents or relatives ◯
Other private home, apt. or rm. ◯
College dormitory ◯
Fraternity or sorority house ◯
Other campus student housing ◯
Other ◯

13. Is this college your: (Mark one)
First choice? ◯ Second choice? ◯ Third choice? ◯ Less than third choice? ◯

14. To how many colleges other than this one did you apply for admission this year?
No other ◯ 1 ◯ 2 ◯ 3 ◯ 4 ◯ 5 ◯ 6 or more ◯

15. What is the highest academic degree that you intend to obtain? (Mark one in each column)

	Highest Planned	Highest Planned at this college
None	◯	◯
Vocational certificate	◯	◯
Associate (A.A. or equivalent)	◯	◯
Bachelor's degree (BA, BS, etc.)	◯	◯
Master's degree (MA, MS, etc.)	◯	◯
Ph.D. or Ed.D.	◯	◯
M.D., D.O., D.D.S., or D.V.M.	◯	◯
LL.B., or J.D. (Law)	◯	◯
B.D. or M.DIV. (Divinity)	◯	◯
Other	◯	◯

16. Is English your native language?
◯ Yes ◯ No

17. Are you a:
◯ U.S. citizen
◯ Permanent resident (green card)
◯ Neither

18. Are your parents: (Mark one)
Both alive and living with each other? ◯
Both alive, divorced or separated? ◯
One or both deceased? ◯

19. How would you describe the racial composition of the high school you last attended and the neighborhood where you grew up? (Mark one in each row)

	Completely non-White	Mostly non-White	Roughly half non-White	Mostly White	Completely White
High school I last attended	◯	◯	◯	◯	◯
Neighborhood where I grew up	◯	◯	◯	◯	◯

20. How much of your first year's educational expenses (room, board, tuition, and fees) do you expect to cover from each of the sources listed below? (Mark one answer for each possible source)

	None	$1–$499	$500–$999	$1,000–$1,499	$1,500–$1,999	$2,000–$3,000	Over $3,000
a. My Own or Family Resources							
Parents, other relatives or friends	○	○	○	○	○	○	○
Spouse	○	○	○	○	○	○	○
Savings from summer work	○	○	○	○	○	○	○
Other savings	○	○	○	○	○	○	○
Part-time on campus job	○	○	○	○	○	○	○
Part-time job off campus	○	○	○	○	○	○	○
Full-time job while in college	○	○	○	○	○	○	○
b. Aid Which Need Not Be Repaid							
Pell Grant	○	○	○	○	○	○	
Supplemental Educational Opportunity Grant	○	○	○	○	○	○	
State Scholarship or Grant	○	○	○	○	○	○	
College Work-Study Grant	○	○	○	○	○	○	
College Grant/Scholarship (other than above)	○	○	○	○	○	○	○
Other private grant	○	○	○	○	○	○	○
Other Government Aid (ROTC, BIA, GI/military benefits, etc.)	○	○	○	○	○	○	○
c. Aid Which Must Be Repaid							
Stafford/Guaranteed Student Loan	○	○	○	○	○	○	
Perkins Loan	○	○	○	○	○	○	
Other College Loan	○	○	○	○	○	○	○
Other Loan	○	○	○	○	○	○	○
d. Other Than Above	○	○	○	○	○	○	○

21. Are you: (Mark all that apply)

- White/Caucasian ○
- Black/African-American ○
- American Indian ○
- Asian-American/Oriental ○
- Mexican-American/Chicano ○
- Puerto Rican-American ○
- Other ○

22. Current religious preference: (Mark one in each column)

	Your's	Father's	Mother's
Baptist	Ⓨ	Ⓕ	Ⓜ
Buddhist	Ⓨ	Ⓕ	Ⓜ
Congregational	Ⓨ	Ⓕ	Ⓜ
Eastern Orthodox	Ⓨ	Ⓕ	Ⓜ
Episcopal	Ⓨ	Ⓕ	Ⓜ
Islamic	Ⓨ	Ⓕ	Ⓜ
Jewish	Ⓨ	Ⓕ	Ⓜ
LDS (Mormon)	Ⓨ	Ⓕ	Ⓜ
Lutheran	Ⓨ	Ⓕ	Ⓜ
Methodist	Ⓨ	Ⓕ	Ⓜ
Presbyterian	Ⓨ	Ⓕ	Ⓜ
Quaker	Ⓨ	Ⓕ	Ⓜ
Roman Catholic	Ⓨ	Ⓕ	Ⓜ
Seventh Day Adventist	Ⓨ	Ⓕ	Ⓜ
Other Protestant	Ⓨ	Ⓕ	Ⓜ
Other Religion	Ⓨ	Ⓕ	Ⓜ
None	Ⓨ	Ⓕ	Ⓜ

23. Do you consider yourself a born-again Christian? ○ Yes ○ No

24. For the activities below, indicate which ones you did during the past year. If you engaged in an activity frequently, mark Ⓕ. If you engaged in an activity one or more times, but not frequently, mark Ⓞ (occasionally). Mark Ⓝ (Not at all) if you have not performed the activity during the past year.

(Mark one for each item)

	Frequently	Occasionally	Not at all
Attended a religious service	Ⓕ	Ⓞ	Ⓝ
Was bored in class	Ⓕ	Ⓞ	Ⓝ
Participated in organized demonstrations	Ⓕ	Ⓞ	Ⓝ
Won a varsity letter for sports	Ⓕ	Ⓞ	Ⓝ
Failed to complete a homework assignment on time	Ⓕ	Ⓞ	Ⓝ
Tutored another student	Ⓕ	Ⓞ	Ⓝ
Did extra (unassigned) work/reading for a class	Ⓕ	Ⓞ	Ⓝ
Studied with other students	Ⓕ	Ⓞ	Ⓝ
Was a guest in a teacher's home	Ⓕ	Ⓞ	Ⓝ
Smoked cigarettes	Ⓕ	Ⓞ	Ⓝ
Drank beer	Ⓕ	Ⓞ	Ⓝ
Drank wine or liquor	Ⓕ	Ⓞ	Ⓝ
Stayed up all night	Ⓕ	Ⓞ	Ⓝ
Spoke a language other than English at home	Ⓕ	Ⓞ	Ⓝ
Felt overwhelmed by all I had to do	Ⓕ	Ⓞ	Ⓝ
Felt depressed	Ⓕ	Ⓞ	Ⓝ
Studied in the library	Ⓕ	Ⓞ	Ⓝ
Performed volunteer work	Ⓕ	Ⓞ	Ⓝ
Visited an art gallery or museum	Ⓕ	Ⓞ	Ⓝ
Took vitamins	Ⓕ	Ⓞ	Ⓝ
Came late to class	Ⓕ	Ⓞ	Ⓝ
Wore glasses or contact lenses	Ⓕ	Ⓞ	Ⓝ
Played a musical instrument	Ⓕ	Ⓞ	Ⓝ
Checked out a book or journal from the school library	Ⓕ	Ⓞ	Ⓝ
Asked a teacher for advice after class	Ⓕ	Ⓞ	Ⓝ

25. Rate yourself on each of the following traits as compared with the average person your age. We want the most accurate estimate of how you see yourself.

(Mark one in each row)

	Highest 10%	Above Average	Average	Below Average	Lowest 10%
Academic ability	○	○	○	○	○
Artistic ability	○	○	○	○	○
Competitiveness	○	○	○	○	○
Cooperativeness	○	○	○	○	○
Drive to achieve	○	○	○	○	○
Emotional health	○	○	○	○	○
Leadership ability	○	○	○	○	○
Mathematical ability	○	○	○	○	○
Physical health	○	○	○	○	○
Popularity	○	○	○	○	○
Popularity with the opposite sex	○	○	○	○	○
Public speaking ability	○	○	○	○	○
Self-confidence (intellectual)	○	○	○	○	○
Self-confidence (social)	○	○	○	○	○
Understanding of others	○	○	○	○	○
Writing ability	○	○	○	○	○

26. What is your best estimate of your parents' total income last year? Consider income from all sources before taxes. (Mark one)

- ○ Less than $6,000
- ○ $6,000–9,999
- ○ $10,000–14,999
- ○ $15,000–19,999
- ○ $20,000–24,999
- ○ $25,000–29,999
- ○ $30,000–34,999
- ○ $35,000–39,999
- ○ $40,000–49,999
- ○ $50,000–59,999
- ○ $60,000–74,999
- ○ $75,000–99,999
- ○ $100,000–149,99
- ○ $150,000 or mor

27. What is the highest level of formal education obtained by your parents?

(Mark one in each column)

	Father	Mother
Grammar school or less	○	○
Some high school	○	○
High school graduate	○	○
Postsecondary school other than college	○	○
Some college	○	○
College degree	○	○
Some graduate school	○	○
Graduate degree	○	○

28. During high school, I: (Mark any that apply)

- Was elected president of one or more student organizations ○
- Received a high rating in a state or regional music contest ○
- Competed in a state or regional speech or debate contest ○
- Had a major part in a play ○
- Won an award in an art competition ○
- Edited a school publication ○
- Had original writing or poetry published ○
- Won an award in a state or regional science contest ○
- Was a member of a scholastic honor society ○

29. In deciding to go to college, how important to you was each of the following reasons?

(Mark one answer for each possible reason)

	Very Important	Somewhat Important	Not Important
My parents wanted me to go	Ⓥ	Ⓢ	Ⓝ
I could not find a job	Ⓥ	Ⓢ	Ⓝ
Wanted to get away from home	Ⓥ	Ⓢ	Ⓝ
To be able to get a better job	Ⓥ	Ⓢ	Ⓝ
To gain a general education and appreciation of ideas	Ⓥ	Ⓢ	Ⓝ
To improve my reading and study skills	Ⓥ	Ⓢ	Ⓝ
There was nothing better to do	Ⓥ	Ⓢ	Ⓝ
To make me a more cultured person	Ⓥ	Ⓢ	Ⓝ
To be able to make more money	Ⓥ	Ⓢ	Ⓝ
To learn more about things that interest me	Ⓥ	Ⓢ	Ⓝ
To prepare myself for graduate or professional school	Ⓥ	Ⓢ	Ⓝ

30. Mark only three responses, one in each column.

Ⓜ Your mother's occupation
Ⓕ Your father's occupation
Ⓨ Your probable career occupation

NOTE: If your father or mother is deceased, please indicate his or her last occupation.

	Y	F	M
Accountant or actuary	Ⓨ	Ⓕ	Ⓜ
Actor or entertainer	Ⓨ	Ⓕ	Ⓜ
Architect or urban planner	Ⓨ	Ⓕ	Ⓜ
Artist	Ⓨ	Ⓕ	Ⓜ
Business (clerical)	Ⓨ	Ⓕ	Ⓜ
Business executive (management, administrator)	Ⓨ	Ⓕ	Ⓜ
Business owner or proprietor	Ⓨ	Ⓕ	Ⓜ
Business salesperson or buyer	Ⓨ	Ⓕ	Ⓜ
Clergy (minister, priest)	Ⓨ	Ⓕ	Ⓜ
Clergy (other religious)	Ⓨ	Ⓕ	Ⓜ
Clinical psychologist	Ⓨ	Ⓕ	Ⓜ
College teacher	Ⓨ	Ⓕ	Ⓜ
Computer programmer or analyst	Ⓨ	Ⓕ	Ⓜ
Conservationist or forester	Ⓨ	Ⓕ	Ⓜ
Dentist (including orthodontist)	Ⓨ	Ⓕ	Ⓜ
Dietitian or home economist	Ⓨ	Ⓕ	Ⓜ
Engineer	Ⓨ	Ⓕ	Ⓜ
Farmer or rancher	Ⓨ	Ⓕ	Ⓜ
Foreign service worker (including diplomat)	Ⓨ	Ⓕ	Ⓜ
Homemaker (full-time)	Ⓨ	Ⓕ	Ⓜ
Interior decorator (including designer)	Ⓨ	Ⓕ	Ⓜ
Interpreter (translator)	Ⓨ	Ⓕ	Ⓜ
Lab technician or hygienist	Ⓨ	Ⓕ	Ⓜ
Law enforcement officer	Ⓨ	Ⓕ	Ⓜ
Lawyer (attorney) or judge	Ⓨ	Ⓕ	Ⓜ
Military service (career)	Ⓨ	Ⓕ	Ⓜ
Musician (performer, composer)	Ⓨ	Ⓕ	Ⓜ
Nurse	Ⓨ	Ⓕ	Ⓜ
Optometrist	Ⓨ	Ⓕ	Ⓜ
Pharmacist	Ⓨ	Ⓕ	Ⓜ
Physician	Ⓨ	Ⓕ	Ⓜ
School counselor	Ⓨ	Ⓕ	Ⓜ
School principal or superintendent	Ⓨ	Ⓕ	Ⓜ
Scientific researcher	Ⓨ	Ⓕ	Ⓜ
Social, welfare or recreation worker	Ⓨ	Ⓕ	Ⓜ
Statistician	Ⓨ	Ⓕ	Ⓜ
Therapist (physical, occupational, speech)	Ⓨ	Ⓕ	Ⓜ
Teacher or administrator (elementary)	Ⓨ	Ⓕ	Ⓜ
Teacher or administrator (secondary)	Ⓨ	Ⓕ	Ⓜ
Veterinarian	Ⓨ	Ⓕ	Ⓜ
Writer or journalist	Ⓨ	Ⓕ	Ⓜ
Skilled trades	Ⓨ	Ⓕ	Ⓜ
Other	Ⓨ		
Undecided	Ⓨ		
Laborer (unskilled)		Ⓕ	Ⓜ
Semi-skilled worker		Ⓕ	Ⓜ
Other occupation		Ⓕ	Ⓜ
Unemployed		Ⓕ	Ⓜ

31. Mark one in each row:

① Disagree Strongly
② Disagree Somewhat
③ Agree Somewhat
④ Agree Strongly

	4	3	2	1
The Federal government is not doing enough to protect the consumer from faulty goods and services	④	③	②	①
The Federal government is not doing enough to control environmental pollution	④	③	②	①
The Federal government should raise taxes to reduce the deficit	④	③	②	①
There is too much concern in the courts for the rights of criminals	④	③	②	①
Federal military spending should be increased	④	③	②	①
Abortion should be legal	④	③	②	①
The death penalty should be abolished	④	③	②	①
If two people really like each other, it's all right for them to have sex even if they've known each other for only a very short time	④	③	②	①
The activities of married women are best confined to home and family	④	③	②	①
Marijuana should be legalized	④	③	②	①
Busing is O.K. if it helps to achieve racial balance in the schools	④	③	②	①
It is important to have laws prohibiting homosexual relationships	④	③	②	①
The chief benefit of a college education is that it increases one's earning power	④	③	②	①
Employers should be allowed to require drug testing of employees or job applicants	④	③	②	①
The best way to control AIDS is through widespread, mandatory testing	④	③	②	①
Just because a man thinks that a woman has "led him on" does not entitle him to have sex with her	④	③	②	①
The federal government should do more to control the sale of handguns	④	③	②	①
A national health care plan is needed to cover everybody's medical costs	④	③	②	①
Colleges would be improved if organized sports were de-emphasized	④	③	②	①
Nuclear disarmament is attainable	④	③	②	①
Scientists should publish their findings regardless of the possible consequences	④	③	②	①
Faculty promotions should be based in part on student evaluations	④	③	②	①
Racial discrimination is no longer a major problem in America	④	③	②	①

32. During your last year in high school, how much time did you spend during a typical week doing the following activities?

Hours per week:	None	Less than 1 hour	1-2	3-5	6-10	11-15	16-20	Over 20
Studying/homework	◯	◯	◯	◯	◯	◯	◯	◯
Socializing with friends	◯	◯	◯	◯	◯	◯	◯	◯
Talking with teachers outside of class	◯	◯	◯	◯	◯	◯	◯	◯
Exercising/sports	◯	◯	◯	◯	◯	◯	◯	◯
Partying	◯	◯	◯	◯	◯	◯	◯	◯
Working (for pay)	◯	◯	◯	◯	◯	◯	◯	◯
Volunteer work	◯	◯	◯	◯	◯	◯	◯	◯
Student clubs/groups	◯	◯	◯	◯	◯	◯	◯	◯
Watching TV	◯	◯	◯	◯	◯	◯	◯	◯

33. Which of the following are important to you in your long-term choice of career occupation?
(Mark one in each row)

	Essential	Very Important	Somewhat Important	Not Important
Job openings generally available	Ⓔ	Ⓥ	Ⓢ	Ⓝ
Rapid career advancement possible	Ⓔ	Ⓥ	Ⓢ	Ⓝ
High anticipated earnings	Ⓔ	Ⓥ	Ⓢ	Ⓝ
Well-respected or prestigious occupation	Ⓔ	Ⓥ	Ⓢ	Ⓝ
Great deal of independence	Ⓔ	Ⓥ	Ⓢ	Ⓝ
Chance for steady progress	Ⓔ	Ⓥ	Ⓢ	Ⓝ
Can make an important contribution to society	Ⓔ	Ⓥ	Ⓢ	Ⓝ
Can avoid pressure	Ⓔ	Ⓥ	Ⓢ	Ⓝ
Can work with ideas	Ⓔ	Ⓥ	Ⓢ	Ⓝ
Can be helpful to others	Ⓔ	Ⓥ	Ⓢ	Ⓝ
Able to work with people	Ⓔ	Ⓥ	Ⓢ	Ⓝ
Intrinsic interest in the field	Ⓔ	Ⓥ	Ⓢ	Ⓝ
The work would be challenging	Ⓔ	Ⓥ	Ⓢ	Ⓝ

34. Below are some reasons that might have influenced your decision to attend this particular college. How important was each reason in your decision to come here? (Mark one answer for each possible reason)

	Very Important	Somewhat Important	Not Important
My relatives wanted me to come here	Ⓥ	Ⓢ	Ⓝ
My teacher advised me	Ⓥ	Ⓢ	Ⓝ
This college has a very good academic reputation	Ⓥ	Ⓢ	Ⓝ
This college has a good reputation for its social activities	Ⓥ	Ⓢ	Ⓝ
I was offered financial assistance	Ⓥ	Ⓢ	Ⓝ
This college offers special educational programs	Ⓥ	Ⓢ	Ⓝ
This college has low tuition	Ⓥ	Ⓢ	Ⓝ
My guidance counselor advised me	Ⓥ	Ⓢ	Ⓝ
I wanted to live near home	Ⓥ	Ⓢ	Ⓝ
A friend suggested attending	Ⓥ	Ⓢ	Ⓝ
A college rep. recruited me	Ⓥ	Ⓢ	Ⓝ
The athletic department recruited me	Ⓥ	Ⓢ	Ⓝ
This college's graduates gain admission to top graduate/professional schools	Ⓥ	Ⓢ	Ⓝ
This college's graduates get good jobs	Ⓥ	Ⓢ	Ⓝ
I was attracted by the religious affiliation/orientation of the college	Ⓥ	Ⓢ	Ⓝ
I wanted to go to a school about the size of this college	Ⓥ	Ⓢ	Ⓝ

35. How would you characterize your political views? (Mark one)

- Far left ◯
- Liberal ◯
- Middle-of-the-road ◯
- Conservative ◯
- Far right ◯

36. Below is a list of different undergraduate major fields grouped into general categories. Mark only one oval to indicate your probable field of study.

ARTS AND HUMANITIES
- Art, fine and applied ○
- English (language and literature) ○
- History ○
- Journalism ○
- Language and Literature (except English) ○
- Music ○
- Philosophy ○
- Speech ○
- Theater or Drama ○
- Theology or Religion ○
- Other Arts and Humanities ○

BIOLOGICAL SCIENCE
- Biology (general) ○
- Biochemistry or Biophysics ○
- Botany ○
- Marine (Life) Science ○
- Microbiology or Bacteriology ○
- Zoology ○
- Other Biological Science ○

BUSINESS
- Accounting ○
- Business Admin. (general) ○
- Finance ○
- Marketing ○
- Management ○
- Secretarial Studies ○
- Other Business ○

EDUCATION
- Business Education ○
- Elementary Education ○
- Music or Art Education ○
- Physical Education or Recreation ○
- Secondary Education ○
- Special Education ○
- Other Education ○

ENGINEERING
- Aeronautical or Astronautical Eng. ○
- Civil Engineering ○
- Chemical Engineering ○
- Electrical or Electronic Engineering ○
- Industrial Engineering ○
- Mechanical Engineering ○
- Other Engineering ○

PHYSICAL SCIENCE
- Astronomy ○
- Atmospheric Science (incl. Meteorology) ○
- Chemistry ○
- Earth Science ○
- Marine Science (incl. Oceanography) ○
- Mathematics ○
- Physics ○
- Statistics ○
- Other Physical Science ○

PROFESSIONAL
- Architecture or Urban Planning ○
- Home Economics ○
- Health Technology (medical, dental, laboratory) ○
- Library or Archival Science ○
- Nursing ○
- Pharmacy ○
- Predental, Premedicine, Preveterinary ○
- Therapy (occupational, physical, speech) ○
- Other Professional ○

SOCIAL SCIENCE
- Anthropology ○
- Economics ○
- Ethnic Studies ○
- Geography ○
- Political Science (gov't., international relations) ○
- Psychology ○
- Social Work ○
- Sociology ○
- Women's Studies ○
- Other Social Science ○

TECHNICAL
- Building Trades ○
- Data Processing or Computer Programming ○
- Drafting or Design ○
- Electronics ○
- Mechanics ○
- Other Technical ○

OTHER FIELDS
- Agriculture ○
- Communications (radio, TV, etc.) ○
- Computer Science ○
- Forestry ○
- Law Enforcement ○
- Military Science ○
- Other Field ○
- Undecided ○

37. Please indicate the importance to you personally of each of the following: (Mark one for each item)

Ⓔ Essential — Ⓥ Very Important — Ⓢ Somewhat Important — Ⓝ Not Important

	E	V	S	N
Becoming accomplished in one of the performing arts (acting, dancing, etc.)	Ⓔ	Ⓥ	Ⓢ	Ⓝ
Becoming an authority in my field	Ⓔ	Ⓥ	Ⓢ	Ⓝ
Obtaining recognition from my colleagues for contributions to my special field	Ⓔ	Ⓥ	Ⓢ	Ⓝ
Influencing the political structure	Ⓔ	Ⓥ	Ⓢ	Ⓝ
Influencing social values	Ⓔ	Ⓥ	Ⓢ	Ⓝ
Raising a family	Ⓔ	Ⓥ	Ⓢ	Ⓝ
Having administrative responsibility for the work of others	Ⓔ	Ⓥ	Ⓢ	Ⓝ
Being very well off financially	Ⓔ	Ⓥ	Ⓢ	Ⓝ
Helping others who are in difficulty	Ⓔ	Ⓥ	Ⓢ	Ⓝ
Making a theoretical contribution to science	Ⓔ	Ⓥ	Ⓢ	Ⓝ
Writing original works (poems, novels, short stories, etc.)	Ⓔ	Ⓥ	Ⓢ	Ⓝ
Creating artistic work (painting, sculpture, decorating, etc.)	Ⓔ	Ⓥ	Ⓢ	Ⓝ
Becoming successful in a business of my own	Ⓔ	Ⓥ	Ⓢ	Ⓝ
Becoming involved in programs to clean up the environment	Ⓔ	Ⓥ	Ⓢ	Ⓝ
Developing a meaningful philosophy of life	Ⓔ	Ⓥ	Ⓢ	Ⓝ
Participating in a community action program	Ⓔ	Ⓥ	Ⓢ	Ⓝ
Helping to promote racial understanding	Ⓔ	Ⓥ	Ⓢ	Ⓝ
Keeping up to date with political affairs	Ⓔ	Ⓥ	Ⓢ	Ⓝ

38. What is your best guess as to the chances that you will: (Mark one for each item)

Ⓥ Very Good Chance — Ⓢ Some Chance — Ⓛ Very Little Chance — Ⓝ No Chance

	V	S	L	N
Change major field?	Ⓥ	Ⓢ	Ⓛ	Ⓝ
Change career choice?	Ⓥ	Ⓢ	Ⓛ	Ⓝ
Fail one or more courses?	Ⓥ	Ⓢ	Ⓛ	Ⓝ
Graduate with honors?	Ⓥ	Ⓢ	Ⓛ	Ⓝ
Be elected to a student office?	Ⓥ	Ⓢ	Ⓛ	Ⓝ
Get a job to help pay for college expenses?	Ⓥ	Ⓢ	Ⓛ	Ⓝ
Work full time while attending college?	Ⓥ	Ⓢ	Ⓛ	Ⓝ
Join a social fraternity, sorority, or club?	Ⓥ	Ⓢ	Ⓛ	Ⓝ
Play varsity/intercollegiate athletics?	Ⓥ	Ⓢ	Ⓛ	Ⓝ
Be elected to an academic honor society?	Ⓥ	Ⓢ	Ⓛ	Ⓝ
Make at least a "B" average?	Ⓥ	Ⓢ	Ⓛ	Ⓝ
Need extra time to complete your degree requirements?	Ⓥ	Ⓢ	Ⓛ	Ⓝ
Get tutoring help in specific courses?	Ⓥ	Ⓢ	Ⓛ	Ⓝ
Have to work at an outside job during college?	Ⓥ	Ⓢ	Ⓛ	Ⓝ
Seek vocational counseling?	Ⓥ	Ⓢ	Ⓛ	Ⓝ
Seek individual counseling on personal problems?	Ⓥ	Ⓢ	Ⓛ	Ⓝ
Get a bachelor's degree (B.A., B.S., etc.)?	Ⓥ	Ⓢ	Ⓛ	Ⓝ
Participate in student protests or demonstrations?	Ⓥ	Ⓢ	Ⓛ	Ⓝ
Drop out of this college temporarily (exclude transferring)?	Ⓥ	Ⓢ	Ⓛ	Ⓝ
Drop out permanently (exclude transferring)?	Ⓥ	Ⓢ	Ⓛ	Ⓝ
Transfer to another college before graduating?	Ⓥ	Ⓢ	Ⓛ	Ⓝ
Be satisfied with your college?	Ⓥ	Ⓢ	Ⓛ	Ⓝ
Find a job after college in the field for which you were trained?	Ⓥ	Ⓢ	Ⓛ	Ⓝ
Get married while in college? (skip if married)	Ⓥ	Ⓢ	Ⓛ	Ⓝ
Participate in volunteer or community service work	Ⓥ	Ⓢ	Ⓛ	Ⓝ

39. The Higher Education Research Institute at UCLA actively encourages the colleges that participate in this survey to conduct local studies of their students. If these studies involve collecting follow-up data, it is necessary for the institution to know the students' ID numbers so that follow-up data can be linked with the data from this survey. If your college asks for a tape copy of the data and signs an agreement to use it only for research purposes, do we have your permission to include your ID number in such a tape? Yes ○ No ○

The remaining ovals are provided for items specifically designed by your college rather than the Higher Education Research Institute. If your college has chosen to use the ovals, please observe carefully the supplemental directions given to you.

40. Ⓐ Ⓑ Ⓒ Ⓓ Ⓔ **44.** Ⓐ Ⓑ Ⓒ Ⓓ Ⓔ **48.** Ⓐ Ⓑ Ⓒ Ⓓ Ⓔ
41. Ⓐ Ⓑ Ⓒ Ⓓ Ⓔ **45.** Ⓐ Ⓑ Ⓒ Ⓓ Ⓔ **49.** Ⓐ Ⓑ Ⓒ Ⓓ Ⓔ
42. Ⓐ Ⓑ Ⓒ Ⓓ Ⓔ **46.** Ⓐ Ⓑ Ⓒ Ⓓ Ⓔ
43. Ⓐ Ⓑ Ⓒ Ⓓ Ⓔ **47.** Ⓐ Ⓑ Ⓒ Ⓓ Ⓔ

THANK YOU!

3508-Questar/914-54321

Appendix C

Institutional Participation, 1966–1990

Institutions Participating in the CIRP Freshman Survey Program, 1966-1990[a]

Institution	Strat Cell	# of Years	90	89	88	87	86	85	84	83	82	81	80	79	78	77	76	75	74	73	72	71	70	69	68	67	66
Abilene Christian University	11	16	X	@	@	@	@	@				X	X	@	@	@	@			@			@	@	@		
Academy of the New Church	22	1	@																								
Adelphi University	04	20	X	X	X				X	X		X	X	X	X	X	X	X	X	X	X	@	@	X	@		X
Adrian College	21	25	X	@	@	@	@	@	@	@	@	@	X	@	@	@	@	@	@	@	@	X	@	@	@	@	@
Agnes Scott College	23	10	@	@	@	@	@	@	@						@	@	@										
Alabama A&M University	34	16	@	@									X	X	X	@	@	@		@	@	X	@	X	@	@	@
Alabama State University	34	14							X	X	X	@	@	@	X	X		X	@	@	@	@	@				
Alaska Pacific University	11	3		@								X	X														
Albany Business College	31	2														@	@										
Albertus Magnus College	17	16	X	@	@	@	@	@	@	@	@	@	@	@	@	@	@	@									
Albion College	23	13	X	X	@	@	@	@	X	@	X	X	X	X	X												
Albright College	23	1										X															
Alcorn State University	34	1																		X							
Alderson-Broaddus College	21	3													X	X	@										
Alexander City State Junior College	27	2														@				@							
Alfred University	13	11	X	X											X	@					X	X	@	@	@	@	@
Alice Lloyd College	31	10											@	@	@	@	@	@	@	@	@	@					
Allegheny College	13	25	@	@	@	@	@	@	@	@	@	@	@	@	@	@	@	@	@	@	@	@	@	@	@	@	@
Allentown College of St Francis de Sales	17	17		@	X	@	@	@	@	@	@	@	@	@	X	@	@	@	@	@							
Alliance College	11	2												@	@												
Alma College	23	15	@	@	@	@	@	@	@	@	@	@	@	@	@	@	@										
Alvin Community College	27	1																X									
American College of Applied Arts	11	3	X		X	X																					
American International College	11	3	X	@	X																						
American University	05	25	@	@	@	@	@	@	@	@	@	@	@	@	@	@	X	@	X	X	X	X	X	@	@	@	@
Amherst College	14	24		@	X	@	@	@	X	@	@	@	@	@	@	@	@	@	@	@	@	@	@	@	@	@	@
Anderson College	32	15	@	@	@	@	@	@		@		@		@		@		@		@	@	@	@				
Anderson University	21	1																	@								
Andrew College	31	5	@	@	@	@	X																				
Andrews University	21	13								X	X	@	@	@	@	@	X	X	@	@	X	X					
Antioch College-Washington/Baltimore	13	2																			X	X					
Antioch University	13	9	@	@	X	@	X	@	@	@										X							
Appalachian State University	07	8												@	@	@		@	@	@	@	@					
Aquinas College	17	25	@	@	@	@	@	@	@	@	@	@	@	@	@	@	@	@	@	@	@	@	@	@	@	@	@
Aquinas Junior College	30	7													@	X	X	@	@	@	@						
Arizona State University	01	3																							X	@	@
Arkansas College	21	15	@	X	@	@	@	@	@	@	@	@	@	X	X	@		@									
Assumption College	18	1																	@								
Athens College	20	6																				@	X	@	@	X	X
Atlanta Christian College	15	1		@																							
Atlanta College of Art	11	4			@	X	@	X																			
Atlantic Christian College	20	1									@																

[a] Participation in the ACE•UCLA Cooperative Institutional Research Program (CIRP) for a given year is indicated by an "@" or an "X." Insitutions providing data judged to be representative of their first-time, full-time freshman class and included in the national norms report are indicated by an "@." Campuses that participate in the survey but whose data were not included in the norms report are noted by an "X." Participation for 1989 is shown for those institutions that had submitted their data in time to be included in this publication.

Institution	Strat Cell	# of Years	90	89	88	87	86	85	84	83	82	81	80	79	78	77	76	75	74	73	72	71	70	69	68	67	66
Atlantic Community College	28	2																			@	×					
Atlantic Union College	20	4	×		×		×	×																			
Augsburg College	23	25	×	×	×	@	@	@	@	@	@	@	×	×	@	@	@	×	×	×	×	×	@	@	@	@	@
Augustana College (IL)	23	21	@	@	@	@	@	@	@	@	@	@	@	@	@	@	@	@	@	@	@	×	@				
Augustana College (SD)	22	21		@	@	@	@	@	@	@	@	@	@	@	@	@	@	@	@	@	@	@	@	@			
Aurora University	21	1		×																							
Austin College	23	25	@	@	@	@	@	@	@	@	@	@	@	@	@	@	@	@	@	@	@	@	@	@	@	@	@
Austin Peay State University	07	18				×	×	@	×	@	×	@	@	×	@	@	@	@	@	×	×	@	@				
Averett College	21	18	@	@	@							@	@	×	×	@	@	@	@	×		×	@	×	@	@	@
Azusa Pacific University	11	11	@						×	×	×	×	×	×	@	@	×		×								
Babson College	13	8	@	@	@	@	@	@									×	×									
Bacone College	31	1												@													
Baker University	21	12	×	×	×	×	×		@		@	×	@	@	@				@								
Bakersfield College	28	2				×	×																				
Baldwin-Wallace College	22	3	@	×	@																						
Ball State University	01	2																					×	×			
Baptist Bible College of Pennsylvania	24	8																@	@	@	@	@	@	@	@		
Baptist College-Charleston	21	3													×			×					×				
Barat College	18	6									×		@	×	×	×	@										
Bard College	13	20	@	@	@	@	@	@	@	@	@	×	×		@	@	×	×	@	×	@	@	@				
Barnard College	14	12	×	×			×	×	@	@	@	@	×	×	@	@											
Barrington College	12	3													@		@		@								
Barry University	16	4		×	×	@													@								
Barton County Community College	27	2								@	@																
Bates College	14	25	×	×	×	×	×	@	@	@	@	@	@	@	@	@	@	@	@	×	@	@	@	@	@	@	@
Bay Path Junior College	32	11							@	@									@	@	@	@	@	@	@	@	@
Baylor University	04	25	@	@	@	@	×	@	@	@	@	×	×	×	@	@	@	@	@	@	@	×	@	@	@	@	@
Beaver College	22	10			@	@									@	@	@	@	@	@	×	@					
Bee County College	28	6																		@	@	@	×	×	@		
Belhaven College	22	1														×											
Bellarmine College	17	6	×	×				×									×	×	×								
Bellarmine-Ursuline College	16	8																		×	×	×	×	@	@	@	@
Bellevue College	11	1												×													
Belmont Abbey College	16	2		@														@									
Beloit College	13	23	@	@	@	@	@	@	@	@	@	@	@	@	@	@			@	@	@	@	×	@	@	@	@
Benedict College	35	11			×		×	@	@	@	@	×	@	×	@	@											
Benedictine College	16	19	×	×	@	@	@	@	@	@	@	@	@	×	@	×	@	@	@	@	@						
Bennett College (NY)	31	3																	@	@	@						
Bennett College (NC)	35	8	@	@	@	@					×	@	@	×													
Bennington College	14	11							×									@	×	@	@	@	@	@	@	@	@
Bentley College	12	2															@		@								
Berea College	11	23	@	@			@	@	@	@	@	@	@	@	@	@	@	@	@	@	@	@	@	@	@	@	@
Bergen Community College	29	9														×	@	@	@	@	×	×	@	×			
Berkshire Community College	27	4			@		@				@	@															
Berry College	12	14	@	@	@	@	@	@	@	×	@	@	@	×		@					@						
Bethany College (KS)	21	5						@	@							@	@	×									
Bethany College (WV)	13	9	×	@	@		@	@	@	@	@	@															
Bethany Lutheran College	31	25	@	@	@	@	@	@	@	@	@	@	@	@	@	@	@	@	@	@	@	@	@	@	@	@	@
Bethel College	22	1	@																								

Institution	Strat Cell	# of Years	90	89	88	87	86	85	84	83	82	81	80	79	78	77	76	75	74	73	72	71	70	69	68	67	66
Biola University	11	1	@																								
Birmingham-Southern College	22	17	@	@	@	x	x	x	x	x	@	x	x	x	x	@	@	@	x								
Bishop College	35	5					x								x			x	x		@						
Black Hawk College	29	10															@	x	@	x		x	x	@	x	x	@
Black Hills State College	07	5	x	x	x	x	x																				
Blackburn College	13	9							x		x		@	x	@	x	@	@	x								
Bloomfield College	20	16				@	@	x	@	@	x	x	x	x	@	@	x	@	x	x	x						
Bloomsburg University of Pennsylvania	08	13	@	@	@	@	@	@	x	@	@	@	@	@	@												
Bluefield State College	34	1																		x							
Bluffton College	21	3																	@		@	@					
Boise State University	07	1																									x
Boston College	05	6			x		x		x																@	@	@
Boston University	05	13			x		x		x		@		x	@	x	@	@	x	x	@	x						
Bowdoin College	14	25	@	x	x	x	x	x	@	@	@	x	x	@	@	x	@	@	@	@	@	@	@	@	@	@	@
Bowie State University	34	18	@	@	x	x		x				@	x	x	@	@	x	x	@	@	@	@			@		@
Bowling Green State University	01	8	x											@	@	@	@	@	@	@							
Bradford College	11	9	x	@	@	@						@						@	@	@		@					
Bradley University	04	25	@	@	x	x	x	@	x	x	x	x	@	@	@	@	@	@	@	x	@	@	@	@	@	@	@
Brandeis University	06	24	@	@	x	x	x	@	@	@	@	@	@	@	@	@	@	@	@	@	@	@	@		@	@	@
Brenau College	11	10	@	@	@	@			x	@					x	x		x	@								
Brevard College	32	20		@	@	@	@	@	@	@	@	@	@	@	@	@	@	@	@	@	@	@	@				
Brewton-Parker College	32	5												@	@	@	@	x									
Briarcliff College	12	9															x		@		x	x	x	@	@	@	@
Bridgewater College	21	3	x	@	@																						
Brigham Young University	04	4					@	x					x									x					
Bronx Community College	28	8	x	x	@	@	x	x																	@	@	
Brown University	06	5			@				@						@	x	@										
Bryan College	15	2																@			@						
Bryant College	12	5															x	x	x	@			x				
Bryn Mawr College	14	16	@	@	@	@	@	@	@	@	@	@	@		@	@	x	@	x								
Bucknell University	14	6		x	x	x			x			x	x														
Buena Vista College	21	24	@	@	@		@	x	x	@	@	@	@	x	x	@	@	@	@	@	@	@	@	@	@	@	@
Bunker Hill Community College	29	1															@										
Butler University	05	6	@	@								@	@	@	@												
Cabrini College	16	3	x	x				x																			
Cal Institute of the Arts	15	1																x									
Caldwell College	16	6	x	@	@	@	@	x																			
Caldwell Community College	27	3								x					x				x								
Calif Baptist College	21	1	@																								
Calif College of Arts and Crafts	11	8	x	@	x	@	x	x									x		x								
Calif Institute of Technology	06	22	@				@	@	@	@	@	@	@	@	@	@	@	@	@	@	@	@	@	@	@	@	@
Calif State U-Bakersfield	07	5	x		x									x			@	@									
Calif State U-Chico	07	4											x			x	@	@									
Calif State U-Dominguez Hills	07	6				@	x						x	x	x	x											
Calif State U-Fresno	08	5											x											x	x	x	@
Calif State U-Fullerton	08	18								x	x	x	x	x	@	@	@	x	x	@	@	x	@	@	@	@	@
Calif State U-Long Beach	08	3					@	x	x																		
Calif State U-Los Angeles	08	3	x	x	x																						
Calif State U-Northridge	08	1																	x								

Institution	Strat Cell	# of Years	90	89	88	87	86	85	84	83	82	81	80	79	78	77	76	75	74	73	72	71	70	69	68	67	66
Calif State U-Stanislaus	08	14			x		x	x	x	x							x	x	@	x	x		x	@		@	@
California Lutheran University	21	11	x	@	@	@		@		@		x		x		x			x		@						
California University of Pennsylvania	08	3																					@		@	x	
Calvin College	22	23	@	@	@	@	@	@	@	@	@	@	@		@	@	@	@	@	@	@	x	@	@	@	@	
Campbellsville College	21	1	@																								
Canisius College	17	13	@	@	@	@	@	@	x	@	x	@	x	@	@												
Capital University	22	4	x	x						@						x											
Cardinal Stritch College	16	22	x	x	@		x		@	x	x	x		@	@	@	@	@	@	x	@	x	x	@	@	@	@
Carl Albert Junior College	25	2										@		@													
Carleton College	14	23	@	@	@	x	@	@	@	@	@	@	@	@	@	@	@	@	@	@	@	@	@	@	@		
Carlow College	18	13		@	@	@	@	@	@	@	@	@	@	@	@	@											
Carnegie-Mellon University	06	14	x	@	@	@	@	@	x						@	@	x	@					x	x	@		
Carroll College (MT)	18	9				x			x						@	x	x	@	@	x		@					
Carroll College (WI)	23	25	@	@	@	@	@	@	@	@	@	@	@	@	@	@	@	@	@	@	@	@	@	@	@	@	@
Carson-Newman College	21	21	x	x	x	@	@	@	x	@	x	x	x	x	x	@	@	@	@	x	x	@	@				
Carthage College	22	2		@										@													
Cascade College	11	1																							@		
Case Western Reserve University	05	6					@	@	x																@	x	x
Castleton State College	07	5	x	x	x	@	x																				
Catawba College	21	9	@	@	@	@	@	@	x	@	@																
Catholic University of America	05	14	@	x	@	@	@	@	x		@	@	@	@	@						@	x					
Cazenovia College	32	12									@	@	@	@	@	@	@	@	@			@	@		@		
Cedar Crest College	22	18	@	@	@	@	@	@	@	@	@	x	x	@	@	@	@	@	@	@							
Centenary College (LA)	23	4		@	x	@	x																				
Centenary College (NJ)	21	4	x				x														@	@					
Central Connecticut State College	08	4	x	x	x	x																					
Central Methodist College	21	5	x														@	@	@			@					
Central State University	34	3													x						x	x					
Central Technical Community College	27	12												x	x	x	x	@	x	@	@	@	@	@	@		
Central Virginia Community College	27	1															x										
Central Washington University	08	1	@																								
Centre College of Kentucky	13	20	@	x	@	@	@	@	@	@	@	@	@	@	@	@	@	@	@	@	@	@					
Cerritos College	28	10		x													x	x	x		@	x	x	x	@	@	
Chaminade University of Honolulu	16	5												x			x	x	x	@							
Champlain College	32	8				@									@	@	@	@	@	@				@			
Chapman College	11	24	x	x	x	x	x	x	x	@	x	x		@	@	x	x	x	@	x	@	x	x	x	@	@	@
Chatham College	13	25	x	@	@	@	@	@	@	@	x	@	@	@	@	@	@	@	@	@	@	@	@	@	@	@	@
Chestnut Hill College	18	1																				@					
Cheyney University of Pennsylvania	34	4	@	@	@	x																					
Chicago State University	34	17			x	x		x	x	x				x	x	x	x	@	x	@	@	x	x	@	@		
Chowan College	32	22	@	@	@	@	@	@	@	@	@	@	@	@	@	@	@	@	@	@	@	@	@	@			
Citrus College	29	6																			x	x		x	x	x	@
City College of San Francisco	29	9														x	@			x	x	x	x	@	@	x	
Claflin College	35	1		@																							
Claremont McKenna College	14	23	@	@	@	@	x	@	x	@	x	@	x	@	@	@	x	@	@	@	@	@	@	@	@		
Clarendon College	26	3																					x	x	@		
Clarion University of Pennsylvania	09	7													@		@						x	@	x	x	x
Clark College	35	17		@	@	@	@		@	@	@	@	@	@	x	@	@	@	@	@	@						
Clark Technical College	27	13											@	x	@	@	@	@	@	@	@	@	x	x	@		
Clark University	14	10	@	@	@	@	@	@														x	x	x	@		

Institution	Strat Cell	# of Years	90	89	88	87	86	85	84	83	82	81	80	79	78	77	76	75	74	73	72	71	70	69	68	67	66
Clarke College	17	9	x	x	x	x	x											@	@	x	@						
Clarkson University	13	2																	x	@							
Clemson University	01	1																	@								
Cleveland Institute of Art	12	14			@		@	x		x	x	@	x		x	x	x	x	x	x	@						
Cleveland State University	08	2																		x	x						
Cochise College	27	5															x	x						x		@	@
Coe College	13	5										@	x		@	@	x										
Cogswell College	11	2														@	@										
Coker College	11	2																@	@								
Colby College	14	23	@	@	@	@	@	@	x	@	@	x	@			x	x	x	x	x	@	@	x	x	@	@	@
Colby-Sawyer College	11	1																			@						
Colgate University	14	10		x		@		@		@		@		@		x		@		@		@					
College of the Atlantic	11	5	@	x	x		@	x																			
College of the Canyons	27	1			x																						
College of the Desert	27	3	x	x	x																						
College of the Holy Cross	18	3	@	x	x																						
College of the Mainland	27	4																	x	x	x				x		
College of the Sequoias	29	15	x	x	x	x	x	@											@	@	@	@	@	@	@	@	@
College of Aeronautics	32	10															x	@	x	x	x	x	x	@		@	@
College of Art and Design	11	6		@	@	x	x	x	x																		
College of Boca Raton	12	4	@	@	@					x																	
College of Charleston	09	14	x	@	@	@	@	x	x											x	x	@		@	@	@	@
College of Ganado	31	1																x									
College of Idaho	22	2	@	x																							
College of Mount Saint Vincent	18	25	@	@	@	@	@	@	@	@	x	@	@	@	@	@	@	@	@	@	@	@	@	@	@	@	@
College of Mt St Joseph on the Ohio	16	7							x	@	@	@	x					@	x								
College of New Rochelle	18	22	@	x	x	@	x	@	@	@	@	x	x	x	x	x	x	@				x	x	@	@	@	@
College of Notre Dame	17	14	@	@	x	x	@	x	x												x	x	x	x	@	@	@
College of Notre Dame of Maryland	18	1											@														
College of Our Lady of the Elms	16	2																			@	@					
College of Saint Benedict	17	22	@	@	@	@	x	x	@		@	@	@	@	@	@	@	@	@	@	@	@	@	@	@		
College of Saint Catherine	17	20	@	@	@	@	@	@	x	x	@	x	@	@	@	@	@	@	@	@	@	@					
College of Saint Elizabeth	12	1	x																								
College of Saint Francis	17	11	@	@	@	@	x					x	@	x				@	@	@							
College of Saint Mary	16	4	@	@	@	x																					
College of Saint Rose	17	3																		@	@	@					
College of Saint Scholastica	17	7							@	@	@			x	@					x	@						
College of Saint Teresa	17	11				@	@	@	@	@	x	@	@	@	@	@											
College of Saint Thomas	18	13	@	@	@	@	@	@	@	@	x	@	@	@		@											
College of Santa Fe	16	5	x															x			x		x	x			
College of Staten Island	29	15			@			@		x	x	x	@	@		@	x	@	x	@	@	x	x				
College of William and Mary	09	9	x	x	@	@			x	x	x	x	x														
College of Wooster	23	9										@	x	@	@	@	@	@	@	@							
College Misericordia	16	11		@	@	@	x	x	x	x	x	@						@	@								
Colorado College	14	11	@	@	@	@	@	x	@	@	x	@									@						
Colorado Mountain College-East Campus	25	4															x	x	x	x							
Colorado State University	02	4	x	x																				x			@
Colorado Women's College	11	4													x		@	@	@								
Columbia College	21	3		@										@								@					
Columbia University	06	11	x	@	@	x	@	x	@	x															@	@	@

Institution	Strat Cell	# of Years	90	89	88	87	86	85	84	83	82	81	80	79	78	77	76	75	74	73	72	71	70	69	68	67	66
Community College of Rhode Island	29	4												@	×	@	×										
Compton Community College	36	11												@		×	×	×			×	×	×	×	×	×	@
Concord College	07	3	×		×	×																					
Concordia College (MN)	23	4															×	×								@	@
Concordia College (NY)	11	9	@	@	@	@	@	@	@	@	@																
Concordia College (OR)	20	16	×	×	×	×			@	@	@	@	@	@	@	@	@	@	@	@							
Concordia College (WI)	31	4												@	@	×	×										
Concordia College	30	2													@					@							
Concordia Lutheran College	20	5		@	@	@	@	×																			
Concordia Teachers College	23	1				×																					
Connecticut College	14	24	×	@	@	@	@	@	@	@	@	@	@	@	@	@	@	@	@	@	@	@		@	@	@	@
Converse College	12	15	@	@	@	@	@	@	@	@	@	@	@	@	@	@	×										
Cooper Union	14	1																			×						
Coppin State College	34	19	×	×	×	×	×		×	×	×	×	×	×	×	×	×	×	×	×	×		×				
Cornell College	23	18	×	@	×	×	@	@	@	@	@	@	@	@	@	@	×	@	@	@							
Cornell Univ-School of Human Ecology	06	2																						×	@		
Cornell University	06	5										×	@					@	×	×							
Corning Community College	28	13			×	@	@	@	@	@	@	@	×	@	@	@										@	
Cottey College	31	5										@							@	@	@	×					
Covenant College	22	8	×		@		@		×			×		@	@	@											
Cowley County Community College	26	9																	×	×	@	×	×	@	@	×	@
Crafton Hills College	27	2		@	×																						
Creighton University	04	4	×	@	@	×																					
Cullman College	30	8													@	@	×	@		@	@	×	@				
Curry College	12	4																		×	×	×	×				
CUNY-Bernard M Baruch College	10	7																	×	×		×	@	×	@	@	
CUNY-Borough of Manhattan Cmty College	29	3																		×	×		×				
CUNY-Brooklyn College	09	2	×																				×				
CUNY-City College	09	16										×	@	@	×	@	×	×	@	×	@	×	@	@	@	@	@
CUNY-Eugenia Maria de Hostos Cmty Coll	28	3															×	×	×								
CUNY-Herbert H Lehman College	10	1																					×				
CUNY-Hunter College	08	3																						×	@		×
CUNY-John Jay College of Criminal Justic	07	12									@		@	@	@	@	@	@	×	@	@	@	×				
CUNY-NY City Technical College	29	3																					×		@	×	
CUNY-Queens College	09	1																					×				
CUNY-Queensborough CC	29	19		@	×	×	@	@	@	@	×	×	×	@	@	@	×	@	@	@	@		@				
CUNY-York College	07	10									×		×	×	×	@	@	×	@	@			@				
D'Youville College	16	11	×	@				×	@							×	@	@	×	@		×	×				
Dakota State College	07	2	×				×																				
Dakota Wesleyan University	20	5							×	@													×	×	@		
Dallas Baptist University	21	3																					×		×	@	
Daniel Payne College	35	3															×	×							×		
Daniel Webster College	11	2	@	@																							
Danville Community College	27	1															@										
Dartmouth College	14	25	@	@	@	@	@	@	@	@	@	@	@	@	@	@	@	@	@	@	@	@	@	@	@	@	@
David Lipscomb College	21	3																					×	×	@		
Davidson College	23	9	@	@	@												@	@	@	@	@	@					
Davis and Elkins College	21	22				×	×	×	@	@	@	@	@	@	@	@	×	@	@	@	@	@	@	@	@	@	@
Defiance College	11	22	×	@	@	@	@	×	×	×	@	@	@	×	×	×	@	×	@		@	@	@	×	@		

Institution	Strat Cell	# of Years	90	89	88	87	86	85	84	83	82	81	80	79	78	77	76	75	74	73	72	71	70	69	68	67	66
Delaware County Community College	28	4																				@	x	x	@		
Delaware State College	34	12					@		@		@					x	x	x				@	@	@	@	@	@
Delaware Valley College of Sci & Agri	11	17									x	@	x	@	@	x	@	@	x	@	@	@	@	@	@	@	@
Delta College	29	2		@											x												
Denison University	13	4	@	@																	x	@					
DePaul University	04	4		x		@		@	x																		
DePauw University	23	20		@	@	@	@		@	@	@	@	@	@	@		@	@	@	@	@	@	@	@	@		
DeVry Institute of Technology (IL)	11	1					x																				
DeVry Institute of Technology (OH)	11	20			x	x		x	x	x	@	@	@	@	@	@	x	@	x	@	@	x	@	@	@		
Dickinson College	14	25	x	@	@	@	@	@	@	@	@	@	@	x	@	@	@	@	@	@	@	@	@	@	@	@	@
Dillard University	35	22	@	@	@	@	x	x	@	@	@	@	@	@	@	@	@	@	@	@	x		@	@	@		
Doane College	21	3																		@	@	@					
Dominican College of Blauvelt	16	25	@	x	x	x	@	@	@	@	@	@	@	@	@	@	@	@	@	@	x	@	@	x	x	@	@
Dominican College of San Rafael	17	25	@	@	x	@	@	@	@	@	@	@	@	x	@	@	@	x	x	@	@	@	@	@	@	@	@
Dominican College-Racine	17	1																		x							
Donnelly College	31	10																x	x	x	x	x	@	@	@	@	@
Douglas College	07	1					x																				
Dowling College	12	1																					x				
Drake University	05	23	@	@	@	@	@	@	@	@	@	@	@	@	x	@	@	x	@	@	@	@	@	x	@		
Drew University	23	12	@	x	x	x	x	x	@	@	x	x	x	x													
Drexel University	13	5					x	x	x					x			x										
Drury College	12	2		@				x																			
Duke University	06	11	@									x	@	@	@	@	@	@	@	x		x					
Dutchess Community College	29	16								@	@	@	@	x	@	@	@	x	@	@		@	x	x	x	@	
Dyersburg State Community College	27	1					x																				
Dyke College	15	2																@	x								
Earlham College	23	23	@	@	@	@	@	@	@	@	@	@	@	@	@	@	@	@	@	@	@	@	@	@	@		
East Carolina University	07	5				@				@	@	@	@														
East Central College	27	3																x	@	x							
East Central University	07	3																			x	x	@				
East Georgia College	25	9	@	@	@	@	@					@	@	@	@												
East Los Angeles College	29	3											@	x					x								
East Stroudsburg University	08	3												@	x	@											
East Texas State University	07	1																		x							
Eastern College	21	5					@												@	@	x	x					
Eastern Mennonite College Inc	21	24		@	@	@	x	@	@	x	x	x	x	x	@	x	@	@	@	@	@	@	@	@	@	@	@
Eastern Montana College	07	6	x							x	x	@	x	@													
Eastern New Mexico University--Roswell	10	1	x																								
Eastern New Mexico University-Portales	07	4	@	@	@	x																					
Eastern Washington University	08	1	x																								
Eastern Wyoming College	25	7							@					@	@	@	@	@	@								
Eckerd College	23	19	@	@	@	x	x	x	x	x		x	x		@	x	@	@	@	@	@	@	@				
Edgewood College	16	2										@	@														
Edmonds Community College	27	1																							x		
Eisenhower College	13	10										x			@	@	@	@	@	x	@	@	@				
Elizabeth City State University	34	17				x	x	x	x	@	@	x	x	@	x	@	x	x	@	@	@	@					
Elizabeth Seton College	32	4															x	x	@	x							
Elizabethtown College	13	22	@	@	@	@	x	@	@	@	@	@	x	@	x	x	@	@	@	@	x	@	@	@			
Elmira College	13	6										@	@	x	x	x						x					

Institution	Strat Cell	# of Years	90	89	88	87	86	85	84	83	82	81	80	79	78	77	76	75	74	73	72	71	70	69	68	67	66
Elon College	21	11	@	@	@	@	@	@	@					@	@						@	×					
Embry-Riddle Aeronautical University	11	4	@	@	@	×																					
Emerson College	12	11	@	@	@	@	@	@	@	@	@	×			×												
Emory and Henry College	22	25	@	@	×	×	@	@	@	@	@	@	×	@	@	@	@	@	×	@	@	@	@	@	@	@	@
Emory University	05	21	@	@	@	@	@	@	@	@	@	@	@	×	@	@	@	@	@	@	@	@					@
Emporia State University (KS)	21	1																		×							
Emporia State University (KS)	07	1																		×							
Erskine College	21	10	@	@	@	@	@	@									×			@	@	@					
Essex County College	29	1																	@								
Eureka College	21	8	@	@		@	×			×			×	@						@							
Evergreen State College	07	16	×	×	×	×	×	@		×	×	×	×	×		×	×	×	×	×							
Fairfield University	18	10	×	@	@				×					@	@	@	@	@	@								
Fairhaven College	30	5																×	×	×	×		×				
Fairleigh Dickinson U-Rutherford Campus	13	1					×																				
Fairleigh Dickinson U-Teaneck Campus	13	15	@	@	×	@							×	×	×	×	@	@	×	@	×	×	×				
Fairmont State College	07	20	×	×	×	×	×		@		@	×	@	@		@	×	×	@	×	×	×			@	@	@
Feather River College	26	1															×										
Felician College	16	3											×	×	×												
Ferris State University	07	1			@																						
Ferrum College	21	5	@	@	@				@	×																	
Findlay College	20	8	×		×		×	@	@											@	@	@					
Fisk University	35	23	@	@	@	@	@	@	@			@	@	@	@	@	@	@	@	@	@	@	@	@	@	@	@
Fitchburg State College	08	2		×									@														
Florida A&M University	34	3		×													@	@									
Florida Atlantic University	07	1			@																						
Florida College	31	11	@	@	@	@									×	@	@				@	@		@	@		
Florida Institute of Technology	13	1										@															
Florida Keys Community College	26	5																		×	×		×	×	@		
Florida Memorial College	35	1																		×							
Florida State University	02	16	×	@	@	@	@	@	@	@	@	@	×	×										@	@	×	@
Fordham University	05	5	@	@	@	@	×																				
Fort Hays State University	08	17			×		×	@	×	@	@	@	×	×					@	×	@		×	×	×	×	@
Fort Lewis College	07	1																					×				
Fort Scott Community College	25	20		×	×	@	@	@	@	×	×	@	@	×	×	@	@	@	@	×	@	@		×			
Fort Valley State College	34	1													@												
Framingham State College	09	16	@	@	×	@								×	×	@	@	×	@	@	@	@	×	@	@		
Franklin and Marshall College	14	25	@	@	×	@	×	@	@	@	@	@	@	@	@	@	@	@	@	@	@	@	@	@	@	@	@
Franklin College	12	7	@									@	@	@	@	@	@										
Franklin Pierce College	11	4	×	×	@	×																					
Franklin University	11	2						×	×																		
Freed-Hardeman College	20	23	@	@	@	@		@	@	@	@	@	@	@	@	@	@	@	@	@	@	@	@	@	@	@	
Fresno City College	29	1															@										
Fresno Pacific College	21	3	@		@		×																				
Friends University	20	2							×							@											
Frostburg State University	07	3																	×	@	@						
Furman University	23	18	@	@	@	@	@	@	@	×	×	@	@	@	@	@	@		@	@	@						
Gallaudet University	11	15						×						×	×	×	×	×	×	×	×	×	×	@	@	@	@
Gannon University	17	12	×				×	@	@	@	×	×	×	×	@	@	@										

Institution	Strat Cell	# of Years	90	89	88	87	86	85	84	83	82	81	80	79	78	77	76	75	74	73	72	71	70	69	68	67	66
Garden City Community College	27	14			@	x	x	@	x	@					x		@	@	@	@	@	@			@		
Gardner Webb College	20	3	@	@	@																						
Garland Junior College	31	6																@	@	@	@	@	@				
Geneva College	21	6	@										@	@						@	@	@					
George Mason University	09	7															x	x	@	x	@	x	@				
George Peabody College for Teachers	11	4																						@	x	@	@
George Washington University	05	2		@	@																						
George Williams College	12	15						@	x					x	x	@	@	@	@		@	@	@	@	@	@	@
Georgetown University	06	5	@		@	@													@	x							
Georgia Institute of Technology	09	25	@	@	x	x	x	@	@	@	@	x	@	x	x	x	@	x	@	x	x	x	@	x	@	@	@
Georgia Southwestern College	07	13	@		@		@					x	x	@	@	@	@		@	@	@	@					
Georgian Court College	16	3			x			@				@															
Gettysburg College	14	22	@	@	@	@	@	@	@	@	x				@	@	@	@	@	@	@	@	@	@	@	@	@
Glassboro State College	08	6	x	@	@	@	@																x				
Goddard College	13	3																	x	x	x						
Gonzaga University	17	21	x	x	x	@	@		@	@	@	@	@		x		@		x	@	x	x	x	x	x	@	@
Gordon Colloge	13	5	@	@	x	@	x																				
Goshen College	22	3					@	x												@							
Goucher College	13	9	x	x	@	@				x		@		@	@	@											
Grace Theological Seminary	21	3			x	x	x																				
Graceland College	22	1																	x								
Grambling State University	34	1																x									
Grand Canyon College	21	3																	x			@	@				
Grand Rapids Baptist College	20	5	@			x	x	@													x						
Grand Valley State College	08	1																		x							
Grandview College	11	21			x	x	x	x	x	x	@	x	@	x	x	@	@	x	@	x	@	x	x	x	@		
Grayson County College	27	15	@		x							@	@	@	@	@	@	@	@	@	@	@	@	@			
Green River Community College	29	1																					x				
Greenfield Community College	28	1																					x				
Greensboro College	21	3	@	@			x																				
Grinnell College	14	21	@	@	@	@	@	@	@	@	@	@	@	@	@				x		x	x	x	@	@	@	@
Grove City College	13	1										@															
Guilford College	23	24	@	x	@	@	x	x	x	@	x	x	x	x	@	x	@	x	x	@	@	@		@	@	@	@
Gulf Coast Community College	28	13								@	@	@	x		x	@	@	@	@	@	@	@	x				
Gustavus Adolphus College	23	20	@	@	@	@	@	@	@	@	@	@	@	@	@	@	@	@	@	x	@		@				
Gwynedd-Mercy College	16	1																@									
GMI Engineering & Management Institute	13	25	@	@	@	@	@	@	@	x	@	x	@	@	@	@	@	@	x	@	@	@	@	@	@	@	@
Hamilton College	14	23	@	@	@	x	x	@	@	x	@	@	@	@	@	@	@	@	@	@	x	x	@	@	@		
Hamline University	23	25	@	@	@	@	x	x	@	@	@	@	@	x	@	@	@	@	@	@	@	@	@	@	@	@	@
Hampden-Sydney College	22	21	@	@	@	@	@	@	@	@	@	@	@	@	@	@	@	@	@	@	@	@	@				
Hampshire College	13	6	x												x		x	x	x	x							
Hampton University	35	2														@						@					
Hannibal-Lagrange College	20	15	x	x	@	@	@								@			@	@	@	@	@	@	@	@	@	
Harcum Junior College	32	7					@	@	@	@	@	@	@														
Harding University	21	18						x	x	x	@	@	x	@	@	@	@	@	@	@	@	@	@	@	@		
Harriman College	31	4														@	@	@		@							
Harris-Stowe State College	07	2																					x	x			
Harrisburg Area Community College	29	4																				x	x	x		x	
Harvard University	06	5																					x	x	x	x	x

Institution	Strat Cell	# of Years	90	89	88	87	86	85	84	83	82	81	80	79	78	77	76	75	74	73	72	71	70	69	68	67	66
Harvey Mudd College	14	23	@	@	@	@	@	@	@	@	@	@	@	@	@	@	@	@	@	@	@			@	@	@	@
Haverford College	14	21	@	@	@	@	@	@	@	x	x	x	@			@	@			@	@	@	@	@	x	@	@
Hawthorne College	31	4																	x	x	x	@					
Heidelberg College	21	6									x		@		@		@		x			@					
Hendrix College	22	12		@	@		@	@	@	@	@	@	@	@	@	x											
Henry Ford Community College	29	3																							@	@	@
Herkimer County Community College	28	15		@		@		@		@		@		@		@	x		x	x	@	@	x	x	@		
Hesston College	31	4	@	@	@	x																					
High Point College	22	1	@																								
Highland Community College	27	6																			@	x	x	@	@	@	
Hillsborough Community College	28	1																		@							
Hillsdale College	12	1										@															
Hiram College	12	21	@	@	@	@	@	x	@	@	@	@	@	x	x	x	@	x	@	@	@	@	@				
Hobart and William Smith Colleges	14	13	@	@						x	x		x	x	x	x	@	x	@	@	@						
Hocking Technical College	29	9	x	x	@	x	@	@					x	x						x							
Hofstra University	04	12			@				x		@		@		@	@	@	@	@	@	@	@					
Hollins College	13	21	@	@	@	@	@	@	x	x	@	x		x				@	x	x	x	x	@	@	@	@	@
Holy Cross Junior College	30	1																						x			
Holy Names College	17	9									x	x	x	x	x	x	x	x	x								
Holy Redeemer College	19	3							@	x	@																
Hood College	13	15	@	@	@	@	@	@	@	@	@	@	@	@	@	@	@										
Hope College	13	8			x					x							x	x	@	@	@	x					
Houghton College	23	8	@					x	x	@	@	x	x	x													
Houston Baptist University	21	4					@																x	@	x		
Howard Community College	26	2																	x	x							
Howard University	35	22	x	x			x	x	@	x	@	x	x	x	@	@	@	x	x	x	x	x		@	x	x	x
Humphreys College	30	19		x	x	x		x	@	@			x	x	x	x	@	@	x	x	@	@		x	x	x	
Huntington College	21	19	@	@	@	@	@	@				@	x	x	@		x	@	x	@	@	x	@	@	@		
Huron College	20	10														@	@	@	x	@	x	x	x	@	@		
Huston-Tillotson College	35	4							x							x				x					@		
Idaho State University	07	10	x		x	x											x	x					x	@	@	x	@
Illinois Benedictine College	17	7	x		x	x		@		@				x			x										
Illinois Central College	29	1																							@		
Illinois Institute of Technology	13	12			x	@	x	x	x	x			x										@	@	@	@	@
Immaculata College (PA)	17	1	@																								
Immaculata College (IL)	12	2																								@	@
Immaculate Heart College	17	8															x	x			x	@		x	@	x	@
Indian Hills Cmty College-Centerville	26	5																					x	x	@	@	@
Indian River Community College	28	7												x						@			@	@	@	x	@
Indiana Institute of Technology	12	5										x				x	x	@	x								
Indiana U-Purdue U-Indianapolis	01	8	x										x	x	x	x	x	x	x								
Indiana University	01	16	x	x	x	x	x	x	x	x	x	x	x	x		x	x				x		x				
Indiana University of Pennsylvania	09	1						x																			
Indiana Wesleyan University	21	10		@	@	x	x	@	x		x	@	@	@													
International Junior College of Business	32	1															@										
Inver Hills Community College	28	1															@										
Iona College	17	1																	@								
Iowa State University	02	22	@	@	x	@	@	@	@	@	@	@	@	@	@	@	@	@	@	@	@	@		x	@		
Iowa Wesleyan College	21	25	@	@	@	@	@	@	@	@	@	@	@	x	@	@	@	@	@	@	@	@	@	@	@	@	@

Institution	Strat Cell	# of Years	90	89	88	87	86	85	84	83	82	81	80	79	78	77	76	75	74	73	72	71	70	69	68	67	66
Itasca Community College	27	6								@													@	@	@	@	@
Ithaca College	13	7														x	x	x	x	x	x	@					
Jackson State University	34	11										x	x	x	@	x	x	x	x	x	x	x					
Jacksonville State University	07	1	@																								
James Madison University	08	1																				@					
Jamestown Business College	32	1															@										
Jamestown Community College	28	8		@				x		@			@			@			@			x				x	
Jefferson Community College	27	23	@	@	@	@	@	@	@	@	@	@	@	@	@	@	@	@	@	@	@	@	x	@	@		
Jefferson Technical College	27	1												@													
Jersey City State College	07	1													x												
John A Gupton College	30	2																@		x							
John Brown University	11	7		@		@		@		x		@			@							@					
John Carroll University	18	1	@																								
John Tyler Community College	26	2																						x	@		
Johns Hopkins University	06	25	@	@	@	@	@	@	@	@	@	@	@	@	@	@	@	@	@	@	@	@	@	@	@	@	@
Johnson C Smith University	35	24	@	@	@	@	@	@	@	@	@	@	@	@	@		@	@	@	@	@	@	@	@	@	@	@
Johnston College	23	2																	@	x							
Judson College	11	5					@					x	@	x	@												
Juniata College	13	12	@	@	@	@		x	@	@	@	@	@	x	x												
Kalamazoo College	13	16			x	x	x	x	x	x	x	x	@	@	@	@	@	x	@	x							
Kalamazoo Valley Community College	27	1																x									
Kansas City Art Institute	11	17	@	x	@	@	@	x	x	@	@	x	@	@	@	@	x	@			x						
Kansas Wesleyan University	21	13			x		@										x	x	x	x	x	@	@	x	@	@	@
Kean College of New Jersey	08	7										@	@	@	@	@			x	x							
Keene State College	07	12	x		x	@	@	@	@	@	@	@	@	@	@												
Kenai Peninsula Community College	25	1												@													
Kendall College of Art and Design	11	1	x																								
Kent State Univ-Stark	27	4				@									@	@	x										
Kent State University	01	1	@																								
Kent State University-Ashtabula	27	3													@	@	x										
Kent State University-East Liverpool	26	3													@	x	x										
Kent State University-Geauga	26	1															x										
Kent State University-Salem	25	5											@	@	@	x	@										
Kent State University-Trumbull	28	7													x	@	x	x	@	@	@						
Kent State University-Tuscawaras	26	7												@	@	@	@	@	@	@							
Kentucky State University	07	16								x		x	x	x		x	x	x	@	x	@	x	x	x	@	x	@
Kentucky Wesleyan College	20	22	x	x	x	x	x	x	x	@	@	@	@	@	x	x	@		x	x		x	@	x	@	@	
Kenyon College	14	11	x	@	@	@	@	@	@	@	@	@		@													
Keuka College	12	1							x																		
Keystone Junior College	32	21		@	@	@	@	@	@	@	@	@	@	@				@	@	@	@	@	@	@	@	@	@
King College	23	5	x		@		@		x						@												
King's College (PA)	12	10	@	@	@	@	@	@	x	@	@	@															
King's College (NY)	12	4		@	@	@	x																				
Kirkland College	14	10														@	@	@	@	@	@	x	@	@	@		
Kirtland Community College	25	4			@	@	@	x																			
Kishwaukee College	27	13										x	x	@	@	x	x	@	x	@	@	x	@	@			
Kittrell College	37	2																	@		@						
Knox College	13	13	x			@	@	@	@	x	x	x	x	@	@	@	@										

Institution	Strat Cell	# of Years	90	89	88	87	86	85	84	83	82	81	80	79	78	77	76	75	74	73	72	71	70	69	68	67	66
Knoxville College	35	8					×						×	@	×	@		×		×					@		
Kutztown University of Pennsylvania	09	1																					×				
La Roche College	16	7	@	×							×										@	×	×	@			
La Salle University	18	14		@		@		@	@	@	@	@	×		×		×	×	@	×	×						
Laboure' College	31	1																×									
Lafayette College	14	23	@	@	@	@	@	@	@	@	@	@	@	@	@	@	@	@	@	@	@	@	@	@	@		
Lake City Community College	27	19				×		×	@	×	@	@	×	@	×	@	@	×	@	@	@	@			×	@	@
Lake Erie College	12	6		×											×		@	@	@	@							
Lake Forest College	23	25	@	@	@	@	@	@	@	@	@	@	@	@	@	@	@	@	@	@	×	@	@	@	@	@	@
Lake Superior State College	08	1	×																								
Lake-Sumter Community College	26	1													@												
Lakeland College	21	15											@	×	@	×	@	×	@	×	@	@	@	@	@	@	@
Lakeland Community College	28	4						×	×													@	@				
Lakeshore Tech	26	3																×	@	×							
Lamar University	07	6	@	×	@	@	@	×																			
Lambuth College	21	2							@	×																	
Lander College	07	14	@	@	@	@	@	@	@	@	@	@	@	@				@	×								
Langston University	34	3																		×	×	×					
Laredo Junior College	28	5																				×	×	×	×	×	
Lawrence University	13	13	×	@	@	@	×	@	×	@	@							×	×	×	×						
Lawson State Community College	34	14		@			×	×		×		@	@	×	@	@	@			@	@	@	@				
Le Moyne College	18	25	@	@	@	@	×	×	@	@	@	@	@	×	@	@	@	@	@	@	@	@	@	@	@	×	@
Le Moyne-Owen College	35	1																		×							
Lea College	14	1																					×				
Lebanon Valley College	23	25	@	@	@	@	@	@	@	@	@	@	@	@	@	@	@	@	@	@	@	@	@	@	@	@	@
Lee College (KY)	31	3																		@	@	@					
Lee College (TN)	20	1										×															
Lehigh University	06	9							@	@	@	@	@	@	@	@	@										
Lenoir-Rhyne College	21	16	@	×	@	@	×	×	@	×	×					@	@	@	@	@	@	@					
Lesley College	12	9				@	@	@	@	@	@	@	@	@													
Lewis & Clark Community College	26	1																				×					
Lewis and Clark College	13	19	×			@	@	@	@	@	@	×	×	@	@	@	@	@	@	@	×	@	@				
Lewis University	12	12	@	@	@	@	×	@	@	@	@	×	×							×							
Limestone College	11	1				×																					
Lincoln College	31	3																			×		@	@			
Lincoln Memorial University	11	1	×																								
Lincoln Technical Community College	27	1																			@						
Lincoln University	35	15	@	@	@	@	@	@	@	×	@	@									@	@	@	@	@		
Lindenwood College	21	13												×	@	@	@	@	@	@	@	@	@	@	@	@	
Linfield College	22	19	×		@	×	@	×	@	@	@	@	@	@	@	@	×	×	×	@	×	×					
Livingstone College	35	10									×	×	×	×		×	×	@	×	×	@						
Lock Haven University of Pennsylvania	07	24	×	@	×	×	@	×	×	×	×	@	@	@	@	×	@	×	@	@	@	@	@	×	@	@	
Lone Mountain College	17	2																×				×					
Long Island U-C W Post Center	12	4								×				×	×	×											
Long Island University-Southampton	12	13						×	×	×	×	@	×	@	×	@	@	×	×	×							
Longwood College	07	23	@	@	@	@	×	×	×	×	×	@	×	@	@	@	@	@	@	@	@	@	@	@	@		
Lorain County Community College	28	4																×						×	×	@	
Loretto Heights College	11	22				×	×	@	×	×	@	@	×	×	@	×	×	@	@	@	@	@	@	@	@	@	@
Los Angeles City College	29	10												×	×	×	×	@	×	@	@	×	@				

Institution	Strat Cell	# of Years	90	89	88	87	86	85	84	83	82	81	80	79	78	77	76	75	74	73	72	71	70	69	68	67	66
Los Angeles Harbor College	29	1																	×								
Los Angeles Pierce College	29	1																	×								
Los Angeles Southwest College	27	1																	×								
Los Angeles Trade Technical College	29	1																	×								
Los Angeles Valley College	29	1																	×								
Louisiana College	20	6				@	@	@	@					@	@												
Louisiana State U-Alexandria	27	22	@	@	@	@	@	@	@	@	@	@	@	@	@	×	@	@	@	@	@	@			@	×	
Louisiana State U-Eunice	25	13	@	×	@	@	×	×	@	@	@			@				×							×	×	
Louisiana State U-Shreveport	07	3										@													@	×	
Louisiana State University and A and M C	01	3																							@	×	@
Louisiana Tech University	07	7																			@	×	×	×	@	@	@
Loyola College	18	15	@	×	@	@	@	@	@	@	@	@	@	@	@	×	@										
Loyola Marymount University	04	5	@	@						@	@	@															
Loyola University (CA)	17	8																		×	×	×	×	×	@	@	@
Loyola University (LA)	04	21	×	×	@	@	@	@	@	@	@	@	@	@	@	@	×	×	@	×	×		@	@			
Loyola University of Chicago	04	23	@	×	×	×	×	@	@	@	@	@	@	@	@	@	@	@	@	@	@	@	@	@	@		
Luther College	23	14			×	×				×	@	×	@	@	@			×	@	@	@	@	@				
Lycoming College	22	1	@																								
Lynchburg College	12	14	@	@	@	@	×	@	×				@	@	@	×	×	×			×						
Lyndon State College	07	1			×																						
Mac Murray College	23	22	×	×	×	×	×	×	@	×	@	×	@	@				@	@	@	@	@	@	@	@	@	@
Macalester College	14	17	@	@	@	@	@	@	@	@	@	@	×	×	×	×			×	@		×					
MacCormac Junior College	31	16	@	@	@	@	@	@	@	@	@	@	@	@	@	@	@		@								
Madison Area Technical College	29	6				@				@			×			×		×				@					
Madonna College	16	10															×	×		@	@	@	@	@	@	@	@
Maharishi International University	11	10			@	×	×	×	@			×	×		×	×	@										
Maine Maritime Academy	07	4	@	×	×	×																					
Mallinckrodt College of the North Shore	30	1											@														
Manatee Community College	29	14									×	×	×	×	×	×	@	@	@	@	@	@	@	×			
Manchester College	21	14			@	@	@	@	×	@	@			@		@		@		@	@	@	@				
Manhattan College	18	18	@	@	@	@	×	@	@	@	@	@	@	@	@	@	@	×		×		@					
Manhattanville College	13	19	@	@	@	@	@	×	@	@	@	×	@	@	@	@	@	@			×				@		×
Mankato State University	07	1				×																					
Manor Junior College	30	11	@	@	@	@	@			@	×	@	@	@	@												
Mansfield University of Pennsylvania	08	3																	@	@	@						
Maria Regina College	31	8						@	@	@	@	@	@	@	@												
Marian College of Fond du Lac	18	17									@	@	×	@	@	@	@	@	@	@	@	@	@	@	@	@	@
Marietta College	12	25	@	@	@	@	@	@	@	@	@	@	@	@	@	@	@	@	@	@	@	@	@	@	@	@	@
Marist College	12	16	@	@		×		×		×	@	×	×	×	×	@	×	×	×	@	×						
Marjorie Webster Junior College	32	1																				@					
Marlboro College	13	24		×	×	@	@	×	×	×	×	×	×	×	×	×	×	@	@	@	@	@	@	@	@	@	@
Marquette University	04	17	@	@	@	@	@	@	@	@	@	@	@	@	×	×	@	@	@								
Mars Hill College	20	15	@	@	×	×	@					@	@	@	@	@	@	@		×	@	@					
Marshall University	07	1	×																								
Mary Baldwin College	22	23	@	@	@	@	@	×	@	×	@	@	@	×	@	@	×	×	×	×	×	×			@	@	@
Mary Holmes College	35	4						×	×									@					×				
Mary Manse College	17	1																		×							
Mary Washington College	09	2																	@	@							
Marygrove College	16	2															@	@									

Institution	Strat Cell	# of Years	90	89	88	87	86	85	84	83	82	81	80	79	78	77	76	75	74	73	72	71	70	69	68	67	66
Maryknoll Smeinary	18	3																						@	@	@	
Maryland Institute College of Art	11	17	×	×	@	@	×	×	@	@	@	@	@	@	@	×	×		@	×							
Marymount College (KS)	16	23			@	@	@	@	@	@	@	@	×	×	@	×	×	×	×	×	×	@	@	@	@	@	@
Marymount College (NY)	17	12	@	@	@	@	@	@	@	@	@	@	×	×													
Marymount College	32	1	@																								
Marymount Manhattan College	13	17		×	×	@	@	×	@	×	×	×	×	×	×	×	×	@	×	×							
Marymount University	19	12	@	@	@	×	@	×	@	@		×	×	×	×												
Maryville College	21	6				@	@			×		@		@					@								
Marywood College	17	22	×	×	@	×	×	×	@	@	@	@	@	×	×	×	×	@	@	@	@	@	@	@			
Massachusetts Bay Community College	29	8							×		×	@	@	@	@	@	@										
Massachusetts College of Art	08	3	@	×				×																			
Master's College	20	24	@	@	@	@	×	@	@	×	@	@	@	@	@	@	@	@	@	@	@	×	@		@	@	@
Mattatuck Community College	27	1	×																								
Mayville State University	07	11	@	×	×	@	×	@	@	@	@	@	@														
McKendree College	20	6												@	@	@	@	@	×								
McPherson College	20	25	@	@	@	@	@	×	@	@	@	@	@	@	×	×	@	@	×	@	@	@	@	@	@	@	@
Medaille College	11	16								@	@	×	×	×	@	×		×	@	@	@	@	@	×	@		×
Medgar Evers College	10	2														@	@										
Memphis State University	07	3		@		×	×																				
Menlo College	11	1																	×								
Mercer County Community College	29	6																			×	×	×	×	@	@	
Mercer University	22	2	×	×																							
Mercy College	12	1													@												
Mercy College of Detroit	16	9															×	×	×	×	×	@	@	×	@		
Mercyhurst College	16	23	@	@	@	@	@	@	@	×	×	×	@	×	×	@	@	×	×	@	@			×	@	@	@
Meredith College	22	1																	@								
Merrimack College	17	17	×	×		×	@	×	@	@	@	@	@	@					×	@	@	@		@	@		
Mesa College	07	3																							@	×	@
Messiah College	21	2	×		@																						
Miami University	03	25	@	@	@	@	@	@	@	@	@	@	@	@	@	@	@	@	×	@	@	@	@	@	@	@	@
Michigan State University	02	7			×						×											×		@	@	@	@
Mid-American Nazarene College	20	18	×	×	×	×	@	@	×	×	×	@	@	@	@	@	@	@	@	@							
Middlebury College	14	24	@	@	@	×	×		×	×	×	×	×	×	×	×	×	×	×	@	@	×	@	@	@	@	@
Middlesex Community College	28	6								@	@	@	@	@	@												
Middlesex County College	29	7																@	×	@	@		×	@	@		
Midway College	31	21	@	@	@	@	×	@	×	@	@	@		@		×	@	×	×	@	@	@	@	@	@		
Midwestern State University	08	2		×									×														
Millersville University of Pennsylvania	09	2			@			×																			
Milligan College	11	23	@	@	@	@	@	@	@	@	@	@	@	@	@	@	@	@	×	@	@	@	@	@	@		
Mills College	13	23	×	×	×	×	@	@	@	×	×	×	×	@		@	@	×	×		×	×	@	×	@	@	@
Millsaps College	22	8																×	×	×	@	×	×	@	@		
Milton College	11	6																		×	@	×	×	@	×		
Milwaukee School of Engineering	13	5	×		×	×	×	×																			
Minneapolis College of Art & Design	11	4				@	@	×	×																		
Mira Costa College	27	3																		×					×	×	
Mississippi College	22	17	×	×	×	×	×	×	×	×	×	×	×	×	×	@	×	×	×								
Mississippi State University	02	1																	×								
Mississippi University for Women	08	1																				×					
Missouri Baptist College	15	4																		×	×	×	×				
Missouri Valley College	21	6												@	@	@	×	@	@								

Institution	Strat Cell	# of Years	90	89	88	87	86	85	84	83	82	81	80	79	78	77	76	75	74	73	72	71	70	69	68	67	66
Modesto Junior College	29	5																	@		x		x		@	@	
Mohawk Valley Community College	29	1																@									
Molloy College	17	5								x	x	@	x						x								
Monmouth College (IL)	21	16		x						@	@	@	@	@				@	x	@	@	@	@	@	@	@	@
Monmouth College (NJ)	11	8	@	@	@	@	@	@	@	x																	
Monroe County Community College	27	1														x											
Montana College of Mineral Sci & Tech	07	5							x	@	@	x			x												
Montana State University	01	17	@	@	x		@	@	@								@	@	@	@	@	@	@	@	@	@	@
Montay College	30	2	@	@																							
Montclair State College	08	12						x		x				x	x	x	x	x					x	x	x	@	@
Montgomery County Community College	29	1																				@					
Monticello College	11	4																					x	@	@	@	
Moore College of Art	12	5	x	x	x	@	x																				
Moorhead State University	08	1						x																			
Moorpark College	28	4																				x	x	x	x		
Moravian College	23	4	x	x	x														x								
Morehead State University	07	4	x		@			x												x							
Morehouse College	35	23	x	x	@	@	@	@	@	@	@	@	@	@	x	x	@	x	x	x	x	x			@	@	@
Morgan State University	34	20		x	x	x	x	x	x		@	@	@	@	@	@	@	x	x	@	x	x				@	@
Morningside College	22	22	@	@	@	@	@	@	@	@	@	x	@	@	@	@	@	x	@	x	@	@	@	@			
Morris Brown College	35	11	x	x	x	x														@	@	@		x	@	x	x
Morristown College	37	3														@		@					@				
Mount Holyoke College	14	25	@	x	x	x	x	@	@	x	@	@	@	@	@	@	@	@	@	@	@	@	@	@	@	@	@
Mount Mary College	16	2						x	x																		
Mount Mercy College	16	1																@									
Mount Olive College	20	19	@	x	@	@	@	@	@	@	@				@	@	@	@	@	@	@	@	@	@			
Mount Saint Clare College	19	10		x	@	x	@	x	@	@	@	@	@														
Mount Saint Mary College	11	20	x	@	x	@	@	x	@	x	x	@	@	@	@	x	@	@	@	@	@	@					
Mount Saint Mary's College	17	23	@	@	@	@	@	@	@	@	@	@	@	@	@	@	x	@	@	@	@	@	@	@	@		
Mount Saint Mary's College-Chalon Campus	17	12	x	x	x	x	@	@	@	@	x	@			@			x									
Mount Saint Marys College-Doheny Campus	30	4	@	@	@	x																					
Mount Saint Scholastica College	16	4																				@	@	@	@		
Mount San Antonio College	29	13			x											@	@	@	@	x	x	x	x	x	@	@	@
Mount Union College	22	6	x										@				@	@	@	@							
Mount Vernon College	12	12	x		@		x	@	@	@	@	@	@	@	@	@											
Mount Vernon Nazarene College	20	14	x	@	@	@	@	@	x	@	@	@	@	@	@	x											
Muhlenberg College	23	4	@	@		@					@																
Mundelein College	12	19	@	x	@	@	@	@	x	@	x	x	x	x	@	x	x	@	@	x			x				
Muscatine Community College	26	7																		@	x	@	@	x	@	@	
Muskingum College	22	6		@				@								@	@	@	@								
Napa College	27	3																			x				@	@	
Nassau Community College	29	2												x						@							
Nasson College	12	2														x	@										
National College of Education	11	13											x	@	@		@		x	@	x	@	x	@	@	@	@
Nazareth College of Kalamazoo	11	11		x													x	@		x	@	x	x	@	@	@	@
Nazareth College of Rochester	12	25	x	@	@	x	x	@	@	@	@	@	@	x	@	x	x	x	@	@	@	@	@	@	@	@	@
Nebraska Wesleyan University	12	6	@						@	@	@	@	x														
Neumann College	13	3	@	@	x																						
New England College	11	3	@		@	x																					

Institution	Strat Cell	# of Years	90	89	88	87	86	85	84	83	82	81	80	79	78	77	76	75	74	73	72	71	70	69	68	67	66
New Hampshire College	11	1																		@							
New Jersey Institute of Technology	09	25	@	@	x	@	x	x	@	x	x	x	x	@	@	@	x	@	@	x	@	@	@	@	@	@	@
New Mexico Highlands University	07	2				x						x															
New Mexico Junior College	27	10					@					@	x	@	@	@		@	x	x	@						
New Mexico Military Institute	27	3	@		@			x																			
New Mexico State U-Alamagordo	26	5															x	x	x	x	@						
New Mexico State U-Carlsbad	25	2														@	@										
New Mexico State University	01	7																			x	x	x	@	x	@	@
New River Community College	26	1															@										
New York University	05	7																	x	x	x	x		x	x		x
Newbury College	32	2														x	x										
Newport College-Salve Regina	16	1															@										
Newton College	18	8																		x	@	x	@	@	@	@	@
Niagara County Community College	28	9							x										@	@	@	x	@	@	@	@	
Niagara University	17	2	@	@																							
North Adams State College	08	6				@	@	x	x	@	x																
North Carolina A&T State University	34	21	x	x	x	@	x	x	x	x	@	x	@	@	@	@	@	@	@	@	@	@	x				
North Carolina School of the Arts	08	2																		x	x						
North Carolina Wesleyan College	21	19	@	x				x	x	x	x	x	@	@	@	x	x		@	@	@	@	@	@	@		
North Central College	22	5	@	@	x	x								x													
North Dakota State University	02	8		@				@					@				@		@			@				@	@
North Florida Junior College	25	4									@	@	x	@													
North Greenville College	32	14		x								@	x	@	@	@	@	@	@				@	@	@	@	@
North Park College	22	1	@																								
North Shore Community College	28	11	x	x	x	x	x	@	@	x	@	x	@														
Northampton County Area CC	28	20			x	@	x	x	x	x	@	x	@	@	@	x	x	x	@	@	x		@	@	@		
Northeast Missouri State University	08	9	@	@	@	x	@	@	x								x	@									
Northeastern Christian Junior College	31	4																		@				x	@	@	
Northeastern Illinois University	07	11					x	x	x	x	@	x	x	@	x	@	x										
Northeastern Junior College	27	2																			@	@					
Northeastern State University	07	14	@	x	x	x	x	@	@	@	@	@				x	@	x		@							
Northeastern University	04	25	x	x	@	x	@	x	@	@	x	@	x	@	x	@	@	x	x	@	@	@	@	@	@	@	@
Northeastern-Burlington	28	2																							@	@	
Northern Essex Community College	29	9						x	x	x	x		x	x	x					x					x		
Northern Illinois University	02	16	@	@	@	@	@	@	@	@	@	@	@	@	@	@	@	@									
Northern Michigan University	07	1																				@					
Northern Montana College	07	1		@																							
Northern Nevada Community College	26	1																				x					
Northland College	12	16										x	x	@	@	x	@	x	@	x	@	@	@	@	@	@	@
Northwest College-Assemblies of God	24	1																	@								
Northwest Community College	27	4	x																	@	@		@				
Northwest Missouri State University	07	22	@	@	@	@	@	@	@	@	@	@	@	@	@	@	x	x	@				x	@	@	x	@
Northwestern College	22	16	@	@	@	@		@	@	x	x	@	@	@	@	x	@	@	@								
Northwestern University	06	25	@	@	@	@	@	@	@	@	@	@	@	@	@	@	@	@	@	@	@	x	@	x	@	@	@
Notre Dame College (OH)	16	4											@	@	@	@											
Notre Dame College (NH)	16	10	x	@	@	x		@	@	@	@	x	x														
Nyack College	21	4			@		@		@	x																	
Oakland City College	20	11		x	@	x	x	x				x	x	x							x					@	@
Oakland University	08	24	@	@	@	@	@	@	@	@	@	@	@	x	@	x	@	@	@	x	@		x	@	@	@	@

Institution	Strat Cell	# of Years	90	89	88	87	86	85	84	83	82	81	80	79	78	77	76	75	74	73	72	71	70	69	68	67	66
Oakton Community College	28	1									×																
Oakwood College	35	1																		×							
Oberlin College	14	21	@	×	@	@	@	@	@	@	@	×	@		×	×	×	×	@	@				@	@	@	@
Occidental College	14	24	@	@	×	@	@	@	@		×	@	×	×	@	@	@	@	@	@	@	@	×	×	@	@	@
Ohio Dominican College	16	25	@	@	@	@	@	@	×	@	@	@	@	@	@	@	@	@	@	@	@	@	@	@	@	@	@
Ohio Northern University	22	8		×													×	×	×	×	@	×	@				
Ohio State University	01	23	@	@	@	@	@	@	@	@	@	@	@	@	@	@	@	@	@	×	@			@	@	@	@
Ohio State University-Lima	07	2				×							@														
Ohio State University-Mansfield	27	1											@														
Ohio State University-Marion	07	11	@	@	×	×	×	@	@	@	×	@	@														
Ohio State University-Newark	27	1											@														
Ohio University	02	3																				×		×	@		
Ohio University-Chillicothe	25	19		×	@	@	@	@	@	@	@	@	×	@	×	×	@	@	@	@	@	@					
Ohio University-Zanesville	26	1																				×					
Ohio Wesleyan University	22	18			@	@	@	@	@	@	@	@	@	@	@	@	×	@	@	@	@	@					
Oklahoma Baptist University	21	6			×			@					×	×	×	@											
Oklahoma Christian College	11	9															@	×	×	×	@	@	@	@	×		
Oklahoma City University	23	2						@	×																		
Oklahoma State University	01	9				@	@	×												@	@	@			@	@	@
Old Dominion University	08	7				×	×	×											×	@	@	@					
Olivet College	12	1																			×						
Olivet Nazarene College	21	2																		×	×						
Oral Roberts University	12	9										×	@	@	@	@	@	@	@					×			
Orange Coast College	29	17				×	×					×	×	@	×	×	@	×	@	×	×		×	@	×	@	@
Oregon State University	01	2																								×	×
Otis Art Institute of The	11	1						×																			
Ottawa University	21	11												@	@	@	@		@	@	@	@	@	@	@		
Otterbein College	22	17		@	@	@	@	@	@	@	@	@	@	@	×	@	@	@	@	@							
Our Lady of The Lake University	16	15	@		@			@							×	×	×	×	@		×	@	@	@	×	@	@
Pace University	12	16			@	×	×				×		×		@		×	×	×	×	@	@	×	@		×	×
Pace University-White Plains	17	6	@	@	@	@									×		@										
Pacific Union College	21	2		@														@									
Pacific University	12	17	×			×	×	@	×	@	@	@	×	@	@	@	@	@	@	@	@						
Packer Collegiate Institute	30	5																				@	@	×	@	@	
Paducah Junior College	16	3																					×	@	@		
Paine College	35	3				@	×	×																			
Palmer Junior College	31	1																×									
Park College	20	14	×	×	@	×	×	@								@	@	×	×	×	×				@	@	
Parkland College	29	1		×																							
Parsons College	22	5																			@	×	@	@	@		
Passaic County Community College	27	2																	×	×							
Patrick Henry Community College	25	2					@										@										
Penn State U-Allentown Campus	25	15		@	@	@	@	×	@	@	@	@	@	@	@	@	@								@		
Penn State U-Altoona Campus	28	15		@	@	@	@	@	@	@	@	@	@	@	@	@	@								×		
Penn State U-Beaver Campus	27	14			@	@	@	@	@	@	@	@	@	@	@	@	×								×		
Penn State U-Behrend College	08	15		×	@	@	×	×	@	@	@	×	×	×	@	@	×								×		
Penn State U-Berks Campus	27	15		@	@	@	@	×	×	×	@	@	@	@	@	@	@								×		
Penn State U-Capital Campus	06	2																					×	×			
Penn State U-Delaware County Campus	27	15		@	@	@	@	@	@	@	@	@	@	×	@	×	@								×		

Institution	Strat Cell	# of Years	90	89	88	87	86	85	84	83	82	81	80	79	78	77	76	75	74	73	72	71	70	69	68	67	66
Penn State U-Dubois Campus	25	16		@	@	@	@	@	@	@	@	@	@	@	@	@	@	@							x		
Penn State U-Fayette Campus	25	14		@	@	@	@	@	@	@	@	@	@	@	@	@	@										
Penn State U-Hazleton Campus	28	16		@	@	@	@	@	@	@	@	@	x	@	x	x	@	@							x		
Penn State U-McKeesport Campus	07	12				x	x	@	x	x	@	x	x	@	@	@	@										
Penn State U-Mont Alto Campus	27	15		@	@	@	@	@	@	@	@	@	@	@	@	@	x								x		
Penn State U-New Kensington Campus	25	15		@	@	@	@	@	@	@	@	@	@	@	@	@	@								x		
Penn State U-Ogontz Campus	28	15		@	@	@	@	@	@	@	@	@	@	@	@	@	@								x		
Penn State U-Schuylkill Campus	25	15		@	@	@	@	@	@	@	@	@	@	@	x	x	x								x		
Penn State U-Shenango Valley Campus	25	16		@	@	@	@	@	@	@	@	@	@	@	x	@	@	x							x		
Penn State U-Wilkes-Barre Campus	27	16		@	@	@	@	@	@	@	@	@	@	@	@	@	@					@			@		
Penn State U-Worthington Scranton Campus	27	17		@	@	@	@	@	@	@	@	@	@	@	@	@	@	@				@			x		
Penn State U-York Campus	27	16		@	@	@	@	@	@	@	@	@	@	@	@	@	@					@			x		
Pennsylvania State University	02	20		@	@	@	@	x	x	x	x	x	x	@	@	x	@			x	x		x	x	x		@
Pennsylvania Valley Community College	28	4																				@	@	x	x		
Pepperdine University	12	21	@	@	x	x	x	x	x	x	x	x			x	@	x	@	@	@	x	x	x	@	@		
Peru State College	07	8													@				x		x	x		@	@	@	@
Pfeiffer College	20	2																	@	@							
Philadelphia Col of Pharmacy and Science	13	21	x	x	x	@	@	@	@	@	@	@	@	@	@	@	@	@	@	@	@	@	@				
Philadelphia Col of Textiles and Science	13	20	@	@	x	x	@	@	@	@	@	@	@	@	@	x	x	x	x	x	x	x					
Philadelphia College of Bible	11	10				@	@									@	@	x	x	x		@	@	@			
Philander Smith College	35	9	@	x	x															@	x	@	@	@	@		
Phillips University	22	2																	@	@							
Pikeville College	20	5			@	@	@	@	x																		
Pine Manor College	11	23	x	x	@	x	@	@	x	@	@	@	x	@	x	@	@	@	@	@	@	@	@	x	@		
Pitt Community College	27	9													x	x	x	x	x	x	@		x	x			
Pittsburg State University	07	6	x		x					@	@	@	@														
Pitzer College	13	16		x	@	@	@	@	@	x	x	@	x	x	x	@	x	x							@		
Point Loma Nazarene College	20	3	x	x	x																						
Point Park College	11	5	@	@	@	@													x								
Polytechnic University	14	23	@	@	x	x		x	x	x	x	x	x		@	x	@	@	x	@	@	@	@	@	@	@	@
Pomona College	14	10			@		@		x								@	x	x	x	x			x	@		
Prairie State College	29	13												x	x	x	@	x	@	x	@	x	x	@		x	@
Prairie View A&M College	34	1				x																					
Pratt Institute	04	9															x		x	x	x	x	x		@	@	@
Presbyterian College	22	9	@	@	@	@	@		x	@			@				@										
Prescott College	13	3																	x	@	@						
Princeton University	06	25	x	@	@	@	@	@	@	@	@	@	@	@	@	@	@	@	@	@	@	@	@	@	@	@	@
Providence College	18	3																		@	x	@					
Purdue University	02	5																					x	x	x	x	x
Queens College	21	11	@	@							@	x	@	x	@	@	@	@	@								
Quincy College	17	13	x	x	x	@	@	x	@	@	@	@	@	@	@												
Quinnipiac College	11	6	x		x	x	x	x	x																		
Quinsigamond Community College	28	9		x			x	x	@													@	@	@	@	x	
Radcliffe College	06	3																						x	@		x
Radford University	07	2					x	x																			
Rainy River Community College	25	18	@	@	@	@	@	x	x	@	@	@	@	@	@	@	@	@	@						@		
Ramapo College of New Jersey	08	13	x	@	@	x	x	x						x			x	x	x	x	@	x					
Randolph-Macon College	23	11				@	@	@	@			@	@					@	@	@	@	@					

Institution	Strat Cell	# of Years	90	89	88	87	86	85	84	83	82	81	80	79	78	77	76	75	74	73	72	71	70	69	68	67	66
Randolph-Macon Woman's College	23	22	@	@	@	@	@	@	@	@	@	@	@	@	@	@	@	@	@	@	@	@	@		@		
Ranger Junior College	26	6																			@	@	×	@	@	×	
Rappahannock Community College	26	1															×										
Raritan Valley Community College	28	4												×	@		×	@									
Reed College	14	22	@		@	×	×	×	×	×	×	@	×	×	×	@	×	@	×	@	@	×		@	@		×
Regis College (CO)	16	8	@	×	×		×		@		@		@	×													
Regis College (MA)	13	24	@	@	@	@	@	@	@	@	@	@	@	@	@	@	@	@	@	@	@	@	@	@	@	@	
Reinhardt College	32	13	@	@	@	×	@	×									@	@	@	@	@	×	@				
Rensselaer Polytechnic Institute	06	9	×	@									@				@	@	@	×	@	@					
Rhode Island College	08	25	@	×	@	@	@	@	@	@	@	@	@	@	@	@	@	@	@	@	×	@	@	@	@	@	@
Rhode Island School of Design	13	17	@	@	@	@	@	@	@	@	@	@	@		×	@	@								@	×	@
Rhodes College	23	7	@	@	×	@	@	@											@								
Rice University	06	13		×	×	×				×		×		@	@	×	@		@	@	@	@					
Richard Bland College	26	2																@	@								
Ricks College	33	2																								@	@
Rider College	12	25	@	@	@	@	@	@	@	@	@	@	@	@	@	@	@	@	@	@	@	@	@	@	@	×	@
Ringling School of Art and Design	11	5		@	×	×	×	×																			
Rio Grande College/Community College	11	1																				×					
Ripon College	13	1										×															
Roanoke College	22	9	@	@	@	@	×	@							×	@	@										
Roanoke-Chowan Technical College	25	5									×	×	@	@	×												
Robert Morris College (PA)	11	11		@	@	@	×	@	@	×	×	×	×	×													
Robert Morris College (OH)	15	1	×																								
Roberts Wesleyan College	22	7	×	@	@	@	@	@											@								
Rochester Institute of Technology	12	7	@	@	@	×	×	×													×						
Rockford College	13	25	@	@	@	@	@	×	×	@	×	×	×	×	×	@	@	@	@	@	@	@	@	×	×	@	@
Rockhurst College	16	19	×					×	×	@	×	×	×	@	@	@	@	@	@	@	@	×	@	@	@		
Roger Williams College	11	7																×	×	×		×	×	@	×		
Rollins College	13	19	@	@	@	@	@	@	@	@	@	@	@	×	×	×							@	@	@	@	@
Rosary College	17	19	@	@	@	@	@	@	@	@	@	@	×	×	@	@	×	@	×	@	@						
Rosemont College	17	5	@	@													×	@	@								
Russell Sage College	12	20	@	@	@	×	@	@	@	@	@	@	@	@	@	@	@	@	@	@	@	@					
Rutgers Camden College of Arts & Science	08	13	×	×	×	×	@	@	@	@		@	×	×	@	@											
Rutgers University-New Brunswick	03	2										×	×														
Rutgers University-Newark	03	4													@	@	@	×									
Sacramento City College	29	1																									×
Sacred Heart University	16	7	@	×													×	@	×	×	×						
Saginaw Valley State College	08	2													@	×											
Saint Alphonsus College	19	3										×	×	@													
Saint Andrews Presbyterian College	22	18	@	@	@	@	@	@	×	@	@	@	@	@	×	@	@	@	@	@							
Saint Anselm College	17	2																			@	@					
Saint Augustine's College	35	1																				×					
Saint Benedict College	16	2																						@	@		
Saint Bonaventure University	17	1						×																			
Saint Catharine College	30	19	@	@	@	@	@	@	@	@	@	@	@	@	@	@	@	@	@	@	@						
Saint Edward's University	16	24	×	@	@	×	×	@	@	@	×	×	×	@	@	@	@	×	@	@		@	@	@	@	@	@
Saint Francis College	17	14	×	×	×	×		×	@	×	×	@	×	×	@	@				×							
Saint John College	17	9																	@	@	@	@	@	@	@	×	@
Saint John Fisher College	18	15	×	×	@	×											×	×	×	×	@	@	@	@	@	@	@

Institution	Strat Cell	# of Years	90	89	88	87	86	85	84	83	82	81	80	79	78	77	76	75	74	73	72	71	70	69	68	67	66
Saint John's College (KS)	12	13						@	@	@	@	@	@	@	@	@	@	@	@	@							
Saint John's College (NM)	14	1																				@					
Saint John's University (MN)	18	23	@	@	@	@	@	@	X	X	@	@	@	@	@	@	@	@	@	@	@	@	@	@	@		
Saint John's University (NY)	04	4																X	@	@	@						
Saint Joseph's College	17	23	X	@			X	@	@	@	@	@	@	@	@	@	X	@	X	@	@	@	@	@	@	@	@
Saint Joseph's University	18	8	X	@	@										X				@	@	@	@					
Saint Lawrence Seminary	30	3																						@	@	@	
Saint Lawrence University	13	9	X	@	@	@		@			@				@				X			@					
Saint Leo College	16	8	@	@	@	@	@						X	X	X												
Saint Louis Cmty Coll-Florissan Valley	29	8																	X	X	@	X	X	X	@	@	
Saint Louis Cmty Coll-Forest Park	28	4																X	X	X			@				
Saint Louis College of Pharmacy	13	3	@		@	X																					
Saint Louis Conservatory of Music	15	2																	X	X							
Saint Louis University	04	15	X				X			X				X			X	@	X	X	@	X	@	@	@	@	@
Saint Louis University-Parks College	11	9										@	X	@	X	X	X	@	X	X							
Saint Martin's College	16	3			X	X													@								
Saint Mary of the Plains College	16	18	X	X	X	X	@	@	X	@	@	@	X	@	X	@	@	@	@	X							
Saint Mary College	17	19	@	X	X	@	@	@	@	@	@	X	@	@	X	@	@	@	@	@	@						
Saint Mary's College (CA)	18	24	@	@	@	@	@	@	@	@	X	X	X	X	X	X	@	@	@	@	@	@	@	X	@		X
Saint Mary's College (IN)	18	17	@	@	@	@	@	X	X	X		@	@	@	X	@	@	@	@	@							
Saint Mary's College (MD)	09	22	X	@	@	X	X	X	@	X	@	@	@	@	@	@	@	@	@	X			@		@	@	@
Saint Mary's College (MN)	16	20	@	@	@	X	X	X	X	X	@	@	@	X	X	X	X	@	@				@	@	@		
Saint Mary's College	31	3	@	@	@																						
Saint Mary's College of O'Fallon	30	9									X			X	X	X	X	@	@	X	@						
Saint Mary's Dominican College	17	14												X	@	@	@	@	X	@	@	@	@	@	@	@	@
Saint Mary's Junior College	31	1																		@							
Saint Mary's University	16	7		X			@							@	X	@	X	@									
Saint Meinrad College	16	25	@	@	@	@	@	@	@	@	@	X	@	@	@	@	X	@	@	@	@	@	@	@	@	@	@
Saint Michael's College	18	3		@	@	X																					
Saint Norbert College	17	25	@	X	X	X	X	X	X	X	X	X	X	@	X	@	@	@	@	X	X	@	@	@	@	@	@
Saint Olaf College	23	4				@	@					@		@													
Saint Paul's College	30	14						@	@	@	@	@	@	@	@	@	@	@	@	@	@						
Saint Peter's College	16	2											@	@													
Saint Petersburg Junior College	29	2																		X							@
Saint Pius X Seminary	31	1																									@
Saint Vincent College	17	9	@	@	@	X	@	@	X	X	@																
Saint Xavier College	16	8															@	X	X	X	@	X	@	@			
Salem College (NC)	23	25	@	@	@	@	@	@	@	@	@	@	@	@	@	@	@	X	@	@	@	@	@	@	@	@	@
Salem College (WV)	11	4												@	X	X	@										
Salem Community College	31	1													@												
Salisbury State College	07	5		@															X	X	@	@					
Sam Houston State University	07	4																X	@	@	X						
Samford University	21	1				X																					
San Francisco Art Institute	13	4					X	X									X		X								
San Francisco Conservatory of Music	15	0																									
San Jose City College	29	1																									@
San Luis Rey College	18	3																							@	@	@
Santa Barbara City College	29	3																					X		@		@
Santa Clara University	05	13	@	@	@	@	X	@							X	@	X	X	@	X	@						
Sarah Lawrence College	14	10	@		X	@									X	X	X		@	@	@	@					

Institution	Strat Cell	# of Years	90	89	88	87	86	85	84	83	82	81	80	79	78	77	76	75	74	73	72	71	70	69	68	67	66
Schenectady County Community College	27	6												x	@		@		@	@	x						
School of the Art Institute of Chicago	12	8		x	@	x	x	x	x	x	@																
School of the Museum of Fine Arts	11	3				x	x	x																			
School of Visual Arts	11	2					x	x																			
Schreiner College	31	16					@	@	x	@	x		@	@	@	x	x	@	x	@	@	@	@				
Scripps College	13	23	@	@	@	x	x	x	x	@	x	x	x	x	x	x	x	@	x	x	x	x	x	x	@		
Seattle Pacific University	22	11	x					x	x	x	x	@	@	x	x	x	x										
Seattle University	17	15	x					x	x	x	@	@	@	x	x	x	x							@	x	@	@
Seton Hall University	04	8							x							x	x	x	@	x	x	@					
Seton Hill College	17	9	@	@	@	@	@	x	@								@				x						
Shaw College-Detroit	24	1																		x							
Shaw University	35	5											x	x	x			@		x							
Shepherd College	07	3																			x	x	@				
Shippensburg University	08	8		@		x		@		@	@	@	x					@									
Shorter College	20	3	@	@	x																						
Siena College	18	2														@						@					
Siena Heights College	16	1															x										
Silver Lake College	16	5										x	@	@	@	x											
Simmons College	13	18	@	x	@	@	@	x	x	x	x	x	@	@	@	@	@	@	@	@							
Simon's Rock of Bard College	15	6													@	@	x	@	@	@							
Simpson College (IA)	21	21	@	x	x	@	@	x	@	@	@	@	@	@	@	@	@	x	x	@	@	@	@				
Simpson College (CA)	20	1																	@								
Sinclair Community College	28	5																				@	@	@	@	@	
Sioux Falls College	22	2																@	x								
Skidmore College	13	16	@	@	@	x	@	@	x	@	@	@	@	@	@	@	@	@									
Slippery Rock University	08	3										@	x		x												
Smith College	14	15	@	@	@	@	@	@	@	@	@	@	@	@	@	@	@										
Snow College	27	2							x					@													
South Carolina State College	34	8													@	@	@	x	x	@	x	@					
South Dakota State University	02	5	@	@	@	x	x																				
Southeast Missouri State University	07	7	@					x	x							x	x	x		x							
Southeastern Massachusetts University	08	6						@		@									@	x	@	@					
Southern Arkansas University	07	22	@	@	@	@	x	@	@	@	@	@	@	@	@	@	@	@	@	x	@	@	@	@			
Southern Baptist College	20	15	@	@	@	@		@	@	@	@	@	@	@	@	@	@	x									
Southern California College	20	1	x																								
Southern College of Technology	07	3			x	x	x																				
Southern Illinois U-Carbondale	01	7																x		x		@		@	@	@	x
Southern Illinois University-Edwrdsville	08	19	@	@	@	@	@	@	@	@	x	x	x	x			x	x	x	x	@	@	@				
Southern Methodist University	05	13	@	@	x												x	@	x	x	x	x	x	@	@		x
Southern Nazarene University	20	3														@	@	@									
Southern Oregon State College	07	1																	x								
Southern Seminary Junior College	31	3										@			@	@											
Southern Union State Junior College	28	1		x																							
Southern University-Baton Rouge	34	4	x																x	@	@						
Southern University-New Orleans	34	1											@														
Southern Vermont College	19	1	x																								
Southwest State University	07	9															x	x	x	x	x	@	@	x	@		
Southwest Texas State University	07	1					x																				
Southwestern Adventist College	20	1																x									
Southwestern College	22	15			@		x	@	x	x	x	x	x	@	@	@	@	@	@	x							

Institution	Strat Cell	# of Years	90	89	88	87	86	85	84	83	82	81	80	79	78	77	76	75	74	73	72	71	70	69	68	67	66
Southwestern University	22	16	@	@	@	@	@	@	@	@	@	@	@	@	@	@	@	@									
Spalding University	17	12				x		@	@								x	x	x	x	@	@			@	@	@
Spelman College	35	23	@	@	@	@	@	@	x	@	@	@	@	@	@	x	@	@	@	@	@	@	@	@	@		
Spring Arbor College	21	14	@	@	@	@	x	@	@	@	@	@	@	@	@	@											
Spring Hill College	17	24	@		x	@	@	@	@	@	@	@	@	@	@	@	@	@	@	@	@	@	@	@	@	@	@
Springfield College	12	11	@	@													x	x			@	x	@	@	@	@	@
Springfield College in Illinois	31	23	@	@	@	@	@	@	@	@	@	@	@	@	@	@	@	@	@	x	@	@	@	@	@		
Stanford University	06	18	@	@	@	@	@	@	@	@	@	@	@	@	@	@								x	x	x	@
Stark Technical College	27	1																@									
Stephen F. Austin State University	07	1																			x						
Stephens College	11	25	@	x	@	@	@	@	@	@	@	@	@	x	x	x	@	@	@	@	@	@	@	@	@	@	@
Stetson University	23	13	x	x	x	x	@	x	@	@	x	x	@	x								@					
Stevens Institute of Technology	13	25	@	x	@	@	@	@	@	@	@	@	@	@	@	@	@	@	x	x	@	@	@	@	@	@	@
Stillman College	35	2	@	@																							
Stockton State College	08	7	@	@					x							@	@	@	x								
Sue Bennett College	31	12		@	@	@	@	x	@	@	@	@							@	@	@						
Suffolk University	11	7	x	x	x	x	x	@	x																		
Sullivan County Community College	28	3											@	x										x			
Suomi College	32	12								@		@	@			@	x	@	@	@	@	@	@	@			
Susquehanna University	23	15	@	@	@	@	@	@	@	@	@	@	@						@	@	@	@					
Swain School of Design	11	2										@	@														
Swarthmore College	14	25	@	@	@	@	@	@	@	@	@	@	x	x	x	x	@	@	@	@	@	@	@	@	@	@	@
Sweet Briar College	13	19	@	@					@	@	@	@	@	@	@	@	@	@	@	@	@	@	@	@	@		
SUNY at Albany	03	1													@												
SUNY at Binghamton	03	16	@	@	@	@	@	@	@	@	@	@	@	@	@	x	x	x									
SUNY at Buffalo	03	10	@	@	@	@	@	@	@	@	@		@														
SUNY at Stony Brook	03	23	@	@	@	@	x	x	@	@	@	@	x	x	x	x	x	x	x	x	x	x			@	@	@
SUNY A&T College at Alfred	29	20	@	@			@	@	@	@	@	@	@	@	@	@	@	@			@	@	x	x	@	@	
SUNY A&T College at Canton	29	3										x		x	@												
SUNY A&T College at Cobleskill	29	19			@	@	@	@	@	@	@	@	@	@	@	@	@	@	@	@	x	@				@	
SUNY A&T College at Delhi	29	24	@	x	x	x	x	@	@	@	@	@	@	@	@	@	@	@	@	@	@	@	@	@	@	@	
SUNY A&T College at Morisville	29	1										@															
SUNY College at Brockport	08	22	@	x	x	@	@	@	x	x	@	x	x	@	x	x	@	@		x	@	@	@	@	@		
SUNY College at Geneseo	09	23	@	@	@	@	@	@	@	@	x	@	@	@	x	@	@	@	@	@	@	@	@	@	@		
SUNY College at Oswego	09	12									x						@	x	@	@	x	x	x	@	@	@	@
SUNY College at Potsdam	09	22	@	x	x	x	x	x	@	@	@	@	x	x	@	@	@	@	@	x	@				@	@	@
SUNY College at Purchase	09	6		x	x		x		@	@	@																
SUNY College of Environ Scie & Forestry	07	2	@			x																					
SUNY College-Buffalo	09	3								@	@	@															
SUNY College-Cortland	09	7																		@	@	x		x	@	@	@
SUNY College-Fredonia	08	3											x	x	x												
SUNY College-New Platz	08	6		@			x				x	@	@	@													
SUNY College-Old Westbury	10	2												x				@									
Taft College	25	1						x																			
Talladega College	35	17				@			x	@	@	x	@	@	x	@	x	x		@	@	@	@	@	@		
Tarkio College	21	5																					x	@	@	x	x
Taylor University	12	3	@	x	@																						
Tennessee State University	34	2													x							@					
Texas A&I University	07	1															x										

Institution	Strat Cell	# of Years	90	89	88	87	86	85	84	83	82	81	80	79	78	77	76	75	74	73	72	71	70	69	68	67	66
Texas Christian University	04	24	@	@	@	@	@	@	@	@	@	@	@		@	@	x	@	@	@	@	@	@	@	@	@	@
Texas College	35	1						x																			
Texas Lutheran College	21	4			@	@	@	x																			
Texas Southern University	34	6							x		x	@	x	x				x									
Texas Tech University	01	9				x			@		@	@											x	x	x	@	@
Texas Wesleyan College	20	4						@	@	@									@								
Texas Woman's University	01	1													@												
Thiel College	22	12			@	x	x	x	x	x	@	@	@	x	x	x											
Thomas More College	18	6	x	x	x			@	x		x																
Thomas Nelson Community College	27	1															@										
Tougaloo College	35	5	@		@	@	@	x																			
Touro College	11	5		x				x	x	x		x															
Towson State University	08	9	@	x	@	@	@	@	x	@	@																
Transylvania University	12	8														@	x			x	@	@	@	@	@		
Trenton State College	09	8	@	@	@	@	@	@												x	@						
Trevecca Nazarene College	20	1	x																								
Trinity Christian College	12	1																	@								
Trinity College (CT)	14	13	@	@	@	x	@	x	@	@	@	@		@	@	@											
Trinity College (DC)	17	24	@	@	@	@	@	@	@		@	@	@	@	@	x	x	@	@	@	@	@	@	@	@	@	@
Trinity College	16	2	@	@																							
Trinity University	23	15	x	@	x	@	@	@	x		@	@				x	x	@	x	@	x						
Tufts University	06	6		x			x												x				x		@		x
Tulane University	06	23	@	@	@	@	x	x	x	@	@	@	@	@		x	@	x	x	x	x	x		x	@	@	@
Tunxis Community College	27	2															x	@									
Tusculum College	11	2													@	@											
Tuskegee University	35	13	@	@	@	x	@	@	@	@	@	@	x	@	@												
Tyler Junior College	29	2																							x	@	
U of the Arts	12	16		x	x	@		@	@	@	@	x	x	x	x	x	x			x	@	@					
U of the District of Columbia	34	9			x							x	x	x	@	x		x	@	x							
U of the Pacific	04	21	@	x	@	@	@	@	@	@	@	@	@	@	@	@	x				x	x	x	x	@		x
U of the Sacred Heart	16	2																						x	x		
U of the South	23	8	@	@	x	x	x	@	@												@						
U of the Virgin Islands	34	1									@																
U of Akron	01	8																		x	x	x	x	x	@	@	@
U of Alabama	02	1			x																						
U of Alabama-Birmingham	01	2													x								x				
U of Alabama-Huntsville	02	11	x				@	@								@	@	@	x	@	@	@	@				
U of Alaska-Anchorage	10	1		x																							
U of Alaska-Fairbanks	01	8					x	x													x	x	x	x	@		x
U of Arizona	01	7	@	@	@	@	@	x	x																		
U of Arkansas-Little Rock	07	10		@			@	x	x	x	x	x	x	x	x												
U of Arkansas-Pine Bluff	34	24	x	x	@	@	@	@	x	x		@	x	x	x	x	x	x	@	x	@	x	x	x	@	x	@
U of Bridgeport	12	16	x	x	x	x	x	x	x	x	@	x	x	x	x		x	x	x								
U of California-Berkeley	03	23	x	x	x	x	x	x	x	x	x	x	x	x	x	@	@	@	x	x	x	x			x	x	x
U of California-Davis	03	6			@		x										@								@	x	x
U of California-Irvine	03	19			x	@	@	x	x	x	x	x	x	x	x	x	x	x	x	@					@	@	@
U of California-Los Angeles	03	22	@	@	@	@	@	@	x	@	x	x	x	x	x	x	x	@	@				@	x	x	@	x
U of California-Riverside	03	12			@				x			x	x	x	x	x							@	@	@	@	@
U of California-San Diego	03	5			@		@		x															x	@		

Institution	Strat Cell	# of Years	90	89	88	87	86	85	84	83	82	81	80	79	78	77	76	75	74	73	72	71	70	69	68	67	66
U of California-Santa Barbara	03	24	x	x	x	x	x	x	x	x	x	x	x	x	x		x	x	@	x	@	@	x	x	@	x	@
U of California-Santa Cruz	03	22	@	@	@	@	@	@	@	@	x	x	@		@	x		@	@	@	@	@	@	@	@	@	
U of Central Florida	08	5																		@		x	x	x	x		
U of Charleston	11	12		x	x	x	x												x	x		x	x	@	@	@	@
U of Cincinnati	02	4			x			x						@	x												
U of Colorado-Boulder	03	7			x	x																	x	x	x	x	x
U of Colorado-Denver	01	5																@	x	x	x		@				
U of Connecticut	02	13	@			@		@		@		x		x	@	@	@	x	x			x					@
U of Connecticut-Hartford	02	2						x				x															
U of Connecticut-Southeast	25	2						@				@															
U of Connecticut-Stamford	25	2						@				@															
U of Connecticut-Torrington	25	2						x				@															
U of Connecticut-Waterbury	27	2						x				x															
U of Dallas	18	7			x		x																x	@	x	x	@
U of Dayton	17	1																				@					
U of Delaware	02	22				@	@	@	@	@	x	@	@	@	@	x	@	@	x	@	x	@	x	@	@	@	@
U of Denver	04	19		@				x	x			x	x	x	@	x	@	x	x	x	@	x	x	@	@	@	@
U of Detroit	04	8													x		x			x			x	x	@	@	@
U of Evansville	22	5	@	x				x	x	x																	
U of Georgia	02	17				@	@	@	x	x	@	x	x	x	x	x				@	x			x	@	@	@
U of Hartford	12	11				@	@	x			@	@	@	@	x										@	x	x
U of Hawaii-Manoa	01	2	x	x																							
U of Houston-Univ. Park	01	4			x		x	x				x															
U of Idaho	01	4																		x	@					@	@
U of Illinois-Chicago Circle	08	4												x		x	x			x							
U of Illinois-Urbana-Champaign	03	12														@	@	x	@	@	x	@	@	@	@	x	x
U of Indianapolis	21	12			x	x	x	@	x	x	x	x	x	x	x	x											
U of Iowa	02	5																				x	@	@	@		x
U of Kansas	02	5																				x	x	x	@	x	
U of Kentucky	01	10															x	x	@	x	x	x	@		@	x	@
U of La Verne	21	17	@	x	x	x	x	x	x	x	x	x	x	x	x	x	x	x	x								
U of Louisville	01	20	x	x	@	@	@	@	@	@	@	@	@	@	@	x					@	@	@	@	@		@
U of Maine-Augusta	27	4																		x	@	@	@				
U of Maine-Bangor	26	1																		x							
U of Maine-Farmington	07	3																		x	@	@					
U of Maine-Fort Kent	07	5															@	x		x	@	@					
U of Maine-Machias	07	17	@	@	@	x	@	x	@	@	x	x	x							x	@	@	x	@	@		
U of Maine-Orono	02	11	x	@	x	x			@	@	@	@								x	@	@					
U of Maine-Portland	08	5	x	x																x	x	x					
U of Maine-Presque Isle	07	9	@	x	x	@	x							@						x	@	x					
U of Mary Hardin Baylor	22	1			@																						
U of Maryland Eastern Shore	34	3											x	x			@										
U of Maryland-Baltimore County	08	8						@						@	x	x	@	@	x	@							
U of Maryland-College Park	02	1	@																								
U of Massachusetts-Amherst	03	23	@	@	@	@	@	@	@	@	@	@	@	@		@		x	@	@	@	@	@	@	@	@	@
U of Massachusetts-Boston	02	2							x								x										
U of Miami	04	15				@	@	@	@	@	@	@	@		@	@	@	@	@	@	@						
U of Michigan-Ann Arbor	03	11															x	@	x	x	x	x	@	@	@	@	@
U of Michigan-Dearborn	08	3												@	x					@							
U of Michigan-Flint	08	17	@	@	@		x	x	@		x	@	@	@	@	@	@	@	@	@	@						

Institution	Strat Cell	# of Years	90	89	88	87	86	85	84	83	82	81	80	79	78	77	76	75	74	73	72	71	70	69	68	67	66
U of Minnesota-Duluth	01	1															@										
U of Minnesota-Morris	08	6			x			x			x			x			@			x							
U of Minnesota-Twin Cities	02	2		x	x																						
U of Mississippi	01	4																						@	x	x	@
U of Missouri-Columbia	02	15			@	x	x	@	@	@	@	@	@	@									x	x	x	x	x
U of Missouri-Kansas City	01	21	@	@	@	@	@	@	x	@	x	x			x	@	x	x	@	@	@	x	@	@	@		
U of Missouri-Rolla	09	16	@	@	@	@			x		x	@		x			@	@	@		@		@	@	@	x	
U of Missouri-Saint Louis	01	20					x	x	x	x	x	x	@	x	x	x	x	@	x	@	@	@	@	@	@	x	
U of Nebraska-Lincoln	01	6																			x	x	x	x	x	@	
U of Nevada-Reno	01	6															@	x	x	x	@						@
U of New Hampshire	02	9				x			@							@		@	@					@	@	@	@
U of New Haven	11	3	x												@	x											
U of New Mexico	01	8	x								x		x										x	x	@	x	x
U of New Orleans	07	2																							@	x	
U of No. Carolina-Charlotte	08	1																@									
U of North Alabama	07	1	x																								
U of North Carolina-Chapel Hill	03	25	@	@	@	@	@	@	@	@	@	@	@	@	@	x	@	x	@	@	x	@	@	x	x	@	@
U of North Carolina-Greensboro	08	2			x	x																					
U of North Carolina-Wilmington	07	6	x						@				x	x	x	@											
U of North Dakota	02	24	x	x	@	@	@	@	@	@	@	@	@	x	@	@	@	x	@	@	x	x	x	@	@	@	
U of Northern Colorado	08	2																					@		x		
U of Northern Iowa	09	3									@					x	x										
U of Notre Dame	06	16	@	@	@	@	@	@		@	@	@	@	@			@	@	@	@	@						
U of Oregon	01	1														x											
U of Pennsylvania	06	16		x	@									x	x	x	@	x	x	x	@	x	x	x	@	@	@
U of Pittsburgh	02	13	@	@	@	x	x	x	@	@	x	x	x	x													@
U of Pittsburgh-Bradford	07	15	@	@	@	@	@	x	@	x	x	x	x	x	@	x		@									
U of Pittsburgh-Greensburg	27	11	@	@	@	@	@	@	@	@	@	@	@														
U of Pittsburgh-Johnstown	07	14	@	@	@	@	@	@	@	@			x	x	x	x	@				@						
U of Pittsburgh-Titusville	25	17	@	@	@	@	@	@	@	@	@	@	@		@	@	@	@	@			x					
U of Portland	04	7	x	x	x	x	x	x	x																		
U of Puerto Rico	01	3							x																	x	x
U of Redlands	22	25	@	@	@	@	@	@	@	@	@	@	@	@	@	@	@	@	@	@	@	@	@	x	@	@	@
U of Rhode Island	01	8		@										x	@	@	@							x	x		@
U of Richmond	13	10	@	@						@	@	@	@	@	@	x	@										
U of Rochester	05	25	@	@	@	@	x	x	x	@	@	@	@	@	@	@	@	@	@	@	@	@	@	@	@	@	@
U of San Diego	04	20	@	@	@	x	@	@	@	@	@	@	@	@	x	@	@	@						x	@	@	@
U of San Francisco	18	4	x	x	x																	@					
U of Science & Arts of Oklahoma	07	1					x																				
U of Scranton	18	11	@	@				x					@	@	x	@	@	@	@	@							
U of South Carolina	01	25	@	@	@	@	@	@	@	@	@	@	@	@	@	@	@	@	x	@	@	x	@	@	@	@	@
U of South Carolina-Aiken	07	13	x	@	@					x	x	x	@	@	@			@	@	x	@						
U of South Carolina-Beaufort	25	1				x																					
U of South Carolina-Coastal Carolina Col	07	19	x	@	x	x	@	x	x	x	x	x	@	@	@	x	@		x	@	@	@					
U of South Carolina-Lancaster	25	8				@								@	x	x		@	@	@	@						
U of South Carolina-Salkehatchie	25	6	@	@	@	x							@								@						
U of South Carolina-Spartanburg	07	3	x	@																	@						
U of South Carolina-Sumter	25	1				x																					
U of South Carolina-Union	25	9	@	@	x	@									@	@	@			@	x						
U of South Dakota (SD)	07	4																x	@	@		@					

Institution	Strat Cell	# of Years	90	89	88	87	86	85	84	83	82	81	80	79	78	77	76	75	74	73	72	71	70	69	68	67	66
U of South Dakota (SD)	02	1					x																				
U of South Florida	07	3											@	@	@												
U of South Florida-New College	09	7		x	x	@	@	@											@	@							
U of Southern California	05	14	@	@	@	@	@	x	x	x			x		x	x	x	x	x								
U of Southern Colorado	07	3									x															@	@
U of Tampa	12	20	@	@		x	@	@	@	@	@	x	x	x					x	x	x	x	x	x	x	@	@
U of Tennessee-Chattanooga	08	3	x																		@	@					
U of Tennessee-Knoxville	01	21	@	@	x		x	@	x				@	@	@	@	@	@	x	@	x	x	x	x	@	@	@
U of Texas--Austin	02	1													x												
U of Texas-Arlington	07	1													@												
U of Toledo	01	3	@	x																		x					
U of Tulsa	04	10					x											x		x	x	x	x	x	@	x	@
U of Vermont	02	25	@	@	@	@	@	@	@	@	@	@	x	x	x	@	@	x	x	x	x	x	@	@	@	@	@
U of Virginia	03	23	@	@	@	@	@	@	@	@	@	@	@	@	@	@	@	@	@	@	@		x	@	@		@
U of Washington	03	6	x	x	x	x																				@	@
U of Wisconsin-Green Bay	08	1																			x						
U of Wisconsin-La Crosse	08	7		x														@					x	x	x	x	x
U of Wisconsin-Madison	03	1																									x
U of Wisconsin-Milwaukee	02	17			@	@	@	@	@	@	x			x	x	@	x	@	@	@	@	@					@
U of Wisconsin-Parkside	08	4	x	x													x	@									
U of Wisconsin-River Falls	07	1			x																						
U of Wisconsin-Superior	07	2															@	x									
U of Wisconsin-Whitewater	08	20	@	@	@	@	@	x	x	x	x	x	x	x	x	@	@					@	@	@	@	@	
U of Wyoming	01	6						x				x												@	@	@	@
Union College (KY)	20	1																	@								
Union College (NE)	20	18						x	x	x	@		@	x	@	x	@	@	x	@	@	@	@	@	@	@	
Union College	14	17	@	x	@	x	@	x	@	@	@	@	@	@	@	@	x	@	@								
United States Air Force Academy	09	23	@	@	@	@	@	@	@	@	@	@	@	@	@	@	@	@	@	@	@	@	@	@	@		
United States Coast Guard Academy	09	25	@	@	@	@	@	@	@	@	@	@	@	@	@	@	@	@	@	@	@	@	@	@	@	@	@
United States Military Academy	09	24	@	@	@		@	@	@	@	@	@	@	@	@	@	@	@	@	@	@	@	@	@	@	@	@
United States Naval Academy	09	18				@	@	@	@	@	@	@	@	@	@	@	@	@	@	@	@	@	@				
Unity College	11	5							x		x	x	@	@													
University College of Pace University	11	7				x			@				@		x		x		x				x				
Upsala College	22	10								x							x	x	x	@	@	@	x	@	@		
Urbana University	21	3															x	x	x								
Ursinus College	13	8		x	x	@	@				@	@	@	x													
Utah State University	01	2																								x	x
Utica College of Syracuse University	12	2																x	x								
Utica Junior College	34	11			x							@	@	@		@	@	x		@	@	@	@				
US Merchant Marine Academy	09	5												@	@		@	@		@							
Valley Forge Military Junior College	31	15	@	@				@	@	x	@		@	@	@	@	@	@	@	@	@						
Valparaiso University	23	25	@	@	@	@	@	@	@	@	@	@	@	@	x	@	@	@	@	@	@	@	@	@	@	@	@
Vanderbilt University	06	25	@	@	@	@	@	x	@	@	@	@	x	x	x	@	@	x	x	x	x	@	@	@	@	@	@
Vassar College	14	25	@	x	x	x	@	@	@	x	x	x	x	x	x	x	@	@	@	@	@	x	@	@	@	@	@
Vermont Technical College	27	5	@	@	@	@	@																				
Victoria College	27	18		@			@	@	@	@	@	@	@	@	@	@	@	@	@	@	@	@	@				
Villa Julie College	31	1												@													
Villa Maria College	16	1														@											
Villa Maria College of Buffalo	31	17	@	x	@	@	@								@	@	@	@	@	@	@	@	@	@	@	@	

Institution	Strat Cell	# of Years	90	89	88	87	86	85	84	83	82	81	80	79	78	77	76	75	74	73	72	71	70	69	68	67	66
Villanova University	05	11	@	@	@	@	@	@	@		@			@						@	@						
Vincennes University	29	5						@	@	@	@	@															
Virginia Commonwealth University	01	14								×	×	@	@	@	×	@	@	×	×	×		×	×	×			
Virginia Intermont College	20	2				@													×								
Virginia Military Institute	08	25	@	@	@	@	@	@	@	@	@	@	@	@	@	@	@	@	@	@	@	@	@	@	@	@	@
Virginia Polytechnic Inst and State U	02	21				@	@	@	×	×	×	×	@	×	@	@	×	@	@	@	@	@	@	×	@		×
Virginia State University	34	24	@	@	@	@	@	×	@	@	@	@	@	@	@	@	@	@	@	@	@	@	@	×	@	@	
Virginia Union University	35	16			@						×	×	@	×	×	@	@	@	@	×	×	@	@	@	@		
Virginia Wesleyan College	21	9	@	@	@	@	@	@	@	@	@																
Viterbo College	17	5															×	@	×	@	@						
Voorhees College (SC)	35	1																×									
Voorhees College (NY)	31	3																		@	×		@				
Wabash College	13	13	@							@	@	@	@	@	@	@	@	×	@	@	@						
Wagner College	22	13	@		×	×	×	×	×	@	×	@	×	×	×	@											
Wake Forest University	05	6	@	@			@		@			@	@														
Waldorf College	32	5	@	@	@	@	×																				
Walla Walla College	21	3															@	×	@								
Walsh College	17	21		×	×	×	×	@	×	@	×	×	@	@	@	×	@	@	@	@	@	@	@	@			
Warner Pacific College	20	2												×	@												
Warren Wilson College	21	4	@																×	@	@						
Washburn University of Topeka	07	2																								×	@
Washington and Jefferson College	13	11	@	@	@	@	@	@	×	@	@	@	@														
Washington and Lee University	14	25	@	@	@	@	@	@	@	@	@	@	@	@	@	@	@	@	@	@	@	@	@	@	@	@	@
Washington College	13	13	×	@	@	@	@	@	@								×		×	×					×	@	@
Washington State University	02	10															×	×	×	×	×	×	×		@	@	@
Washington University	05	11												×	×	×	×	×		×	×	×			@	@	@
Wayland Baptist University	20	5																				@	@	×	×	@	
Wayne State University	01	8	@	@	@	×									×	×			×			@					
Waynesburg College	21	7	@	@										×	@					@	@	@					
Webb Institute of Naval Architecture	14	18	@	@					@	@	@	@	@	@	@	@	@	@	@	×	@	@		@	×		
Webber College	30	3																		×	×	×					
Weber State College	07	1								×																	
Webster University	12	20	×	×	×	×	×	×	×	×	×	×	×	×	×	×	×	@	×	@	×	@					
Wellesley College	14	23	×	×	@	@	×	@	@	@	@	@	×	×	@	×	@	@	×	×	×	@			@	@	@
Wells College	13	9	×	@	@	×	@	×	×							@			×								
Wentworth Institute of Technology	11	17	×		@	@	×		×				@	@		×	@	×	×	@	@	@			@	@	@
Wesley College	11	1						×																			
Wesleyan College	21	20	@	@	@	@	@	@	@	@	@	@	@	@	@	@			@	@	@				@	@	@
Wesleyan University	14	23	@	@	@	@	@	@	@	@	@	@	@	@	@	@	@	@	@	@	@	@	@	@	@		
West Chester University	08	9	@		@		@		@		@		@	@	@							@					
West Los Angeles College	28	1																	×								
West Virginia State College	07	17				×	×	×	×	×	×	×	×	@	@	@	@			×	×			@	@	×	
West Virginia University	01	7									@					×	×	@	@	×	×						
West Virginia Wesleyan College	21	1																@									
Westbrook College	12	4	×	×	×	×																					
Western Baptist College	24	1													×												
Western Carolina University	07	8															×	@	@	@	×	×	@	@			
Western Connecticut State University	08	1	×																								
Western Illinois University	08	21					×	×	×	×	×	×	×	×	×	@	×	×	@	@	@	@	@	@	@	@	@

Institution	Strat Cell	# of Years	90	89	88	87	86	85	84	83	82	81	80	79	78	77	76	75	74	73	72	71	70	69	68	67	66
Western New England College	11	25	@	x	x	x	x	x	x	@	@	@	@	x	@	@	x	x	x	x	@	@	x	x	@	x	@
Western New Mexico University	07	4	x			x								@	@												
Western Oregon State College	07	2	x					x																			
Western Washington University	09	5		@				@				@					@					x					
Western Wyoming College	27	9					x			x									x	@	@	x	x	@	x		
Westfield State College	08	5	@											x	@	@	@										
Westmar College	21	12	x	@	@	@	@				@	@	@	@					@	@	@						
Westminster College (MO)	22	18	@	@	@	@	@	@	@	@	@	@	@	@	@	@		@	x				@	@			
Westminster College (PA)	22	16	@	@	@	@	@	@	@	@	@	@	@	@	@					@	@	@					
Westminster College	21	3										x				x	x										
Westmont College	13	3	x	x	@																						
Wharton Community Junior College	28	22		@	@	@	@	@	@	@	@	@	@	@	@	@	@	@	@	@	@	@	@		@	@	
Wheaton College (IL)	13	7		@		@		@		@		@		@	@												
Wheaton College (MA)	13	24	@	@	@	@	@	@	@	@	@	@	@	@	@	@	@	@	@	@		@	@	@	@	@	@
Wheeling Jesuit College	16	12	x	x	x	@	@	@	@						@		@	@	@	@							
Wheelock College	11	8			@					@	@	x	@	@	@	@											
Whitman College	13	25	x	x	@	@	x	@	x	@	x	x	x	x	x	x	@	@	@	@	@	@	@	@	@	@	@
Whittier College	13	17		@	@	@	@	@	@	@	@	x	@	@	@	@	@	@	@	@							
Whitworth College	12	4					@	@	@	x																	
Widener University	13	2																@	x								
Wilberforce University	35	9		@	@	@						x	@	@	@	@					x						
Wiley College	35	1			x																						
Wilkes College	13	9	@	@	@	@	@	@	@	@	x																
Willamette University	13	19	@	@	@	@	@	x	x	x	x	x	@	@	x	@	@	@	@	@	@						
William Carey College	20	14		x	x											x	x	x	x	x	x	x	x	x	@	@	@
William Jewell College	22	11		@	@	@	@	@	@	@	x	x	x	@													
William Paterson College	07	15		x	@	@	@	@	@	@	@	@	@	x	x	@	@	x									
William Woods College	12	1	@																								
Williams College	14	25	@	@	@	@	@	@	@	@	@	@	@	@	@	@	@	@	@	@	@	@	@	@	@	@	@
Williamsport Area Community College	29	9	@	@			@	@												@	@	x	x	@			
Willmar Community College	27	4											@	@	@			@									
Wilmington College	21	8	x	@	@	@	x	x	x	x																	
Wilson College	12	2										@			@												
Windham College	12	2																x							x		
Wingate College	11	24	@	@	@	@	@	@	@	@	@	@	@	@	@	@	@	@	@	@	@	@	@	@	@	@	
Winona State University	07	2	@	x																							
Winston-Salem State University	34	20		x	@	x	@		x			x	@	@	@	@	@	@	@	@	x	@	x	@	@	@	
Winthrop College	07	2																@	@								
Wittenberg University	22	25	@	@	@	@	@	@	@	@	@	@	@	@	@	@	@	@	x	@	@	@	@	@	@	@	@
Wofford College	21	20	@	@						@	@	@	@	@	@	@	@	@	@	@	@	@	@	@	@	@	@
Wood Junior College	31	10	@					x						x	@	@	@	@	@	@	@						
Woodbury University	11	7	x	x	x	x	x	x	x																		
Worcester Junior College	30	9														x	x			x		x	@	@	x	@	@
Worcester Polytechnic Institute	14	18	@	@	@	x	@	@	@	@	x	@	x	@	@	@	@	@	@	x							
Worthington Community College	25	19					@	@	@	@	@	@	@	@	x	@	@	@	@	@	@	@	@	@	@		
Wytheville Community College	26	1															@										
Xavier University (LA)	35	18	x	@	x	x	x	x		@	@	@	x	@	@	@	@	@	@	x	@						
Xavier University (OH)	18	8	@					@										x	x	@	x	@		@			

Institution	Strat Cell	# of Years	90	89	88	87	86	85	84	83	82	81	80	79	78	77	76	75	74	73	72	71	70	69	68	67	66
Yale University	06	3																		x	x	x					
Yankton College	11	8							@	x												@	x	x	@	@	@
Yeshiva University	06	1																x									
Yuba College	28	13										@	@	@	x	x	x	@	x	@	@	x	@	@			

Appendix D

Qualifications in Assessing Trends

Appendix D

Qualifications in Assessing Trends

In any multi–year survey research project such as the CIRP, change to the survey instrument is inevitable. A question's text may be changed to more accurately elicit the information desired, or to elicit slightly different information. Different formats or arrangements of the questions may be tried out. The commonly–accepted meanings of the words in a question may change over time. In a few cases, question texts, formats, or order have even been changed inadvertently.

While such changes have, on the whole, been of benefit to the CIRP, they can raise problems in consistency when viewed over the 25–year span of this report. Accordingly, each of the 400–odd items have been evaluated for each year in which it occurs to determine whether year–to–year changes reflect actual changes in the population or are artifacts of the way in which the question was asked.

In many cases where we judged the results to be severely contaminated by such artifacts, the special symbol "[*]" was placed in the report, indicating that data was collected for that item, but was judged to be incomparable to results from other years.

In other cases, however, the effect may not have been severe, or may have been confined to one or two responses in an item. This appendix identifies these cases. Please note that in discussing these possible anomalies, the possibility still exists that they were actually due in whole or in part to an actual change.

CAREER

The career variable was changed substantially in the period 1973–1975. The 48–response option set was replaced by a 62–response set, some of which were not directly comparable with the original. The original response set was restored in 1976. The effect is most pronounced for aggregated careers in education.

MAJOR

Until 1971, students were asked to mark their first, second, and last choices for major. Starting in 1972, students were directed to mark the major they were most likely to choose. Since students prior to 1972 were not likely to select "undecided" as first, second, or last choice, the "undecided" response option showed a substantial increase between 1971 and 1972.

Nine response categories, including specific business and education categories, were added in 1973. "Pre–med, dental, veterinary" was removed from the response set in 1973 and restored in 1977. Additional response categories were added in 1978, 1980, and 1982.

RELIGION

Changes were made in the response set in a number of years, primarily switching from a "short" list (five responses) to a "long" list (17–18 responses). When the short list was used, "Protestant" and "other" represented two of the five options (the others being Roman Catholic, Jewish and none). When the long list was used, "Protestant" represented the sum of all Christian religions other than Roman Catholic, while "other" represented the sum of Buddhist, Moslem (or Islamic) and Other Religion.

It appears that many non–Catholic Christians don't identify their religion as "Protestant." In the years when a short list was used, the percentage of "Protestants" dropped substantially, matched by an increase in the percentage of "other religion." The short list was used in 1972, 1979–83 and 1985.

In 1984, two long–list "Protestant" religions (Episcopal and Presbyterian) were inadvertently left off the list. They were restored in 1985. A 1984 rise in the "other Protestant" response, followed by a drop in 1985, can most probably be attributed to this change in the list. The "Unitarian–Universalist" religion was dropped as of 1985.

HIGH SCHOOL GRADES

The format of the response options was changed in 1973 and again in 1987. In both instances, the original format was restored the following year. The grades most affected by this format change were B– and C+.

ESTIMATED PARENTAL INCOME

Due to inflation, it became necessary to change the response set for this item several times. Each change resulted in some artifactual effects on the data as compared to the previous year. In addition, from 1966–1972, students were allowed to enter their own family income if they were not dependent on their parents. The elimination of this option undoubtedly resulted (at least partially) in the drop in the low–income families observed in 1973.

In 1985, to accommodate a finer discrimination among income ranges at the high end of the spectrum, it was necessary to compress the low–end ranges. Specifically, the six ranges formerly representing incomes of less than $15,000 were replaced by three. This change had a slight effect on the percentage of low–income families between 1984 and 1985, but virtually no effect on the median parental income for those two years.

FINANCIAL AID

Some version of the financial aid question has been asked since the beginning of the Freshman Survey in 1966. It was not until 1978, however, that the various items presented and the response sets were sufficiently standardized to allow their inclusion in this report. A re–ordering of the aid items in 1984 (in which items were grouped by personal, grant or loan sources) may have had some small effects on the results.

MISCELLANEOUS

On a number of occasions, year–to–year comparability of results based on items dealing with opinions, projected future activities or perceived goals and values, many have been adversely affected by changes in the order of their presentation, changes in the text of the item itself or the addition/deletion of other items. These include:

•**Student opinions** between 1971–75, 1975–76 and 1986–87.

•**Goals and values** between 1972–74, 1986–87. Almost all of the goal and value items were dropped from the 1988 results due to extensive order changes and item deletions, resulting in severe contamination of the results.

•**Reason for choosing freshman college** between 1972–73 and 1982–83.

•**Future activities** between 1975–77.

•**Self–ratings** between 1986–87. all 1983 responses were dropped from the report because the response options were not comparable to any other year.

•**Will need remedial work** between 1977–78.

Appendix E

The Precision of the Normative Data and Their Comparisons

Appendix E

The Precision of the Normative Data and Their Comparisons

One of the most common questions asked about CIRP data is our estimate of the standard error, which is normally reported in "plus or minus x percentage points." Using traditional methods of calculating standard error, the percentages reported would be estimated as being accurate within one–tenth of one percent (see Table E1). Since we report our results to the accuracy of 0.1%, it would appear that every change from year to year, no matter how small, is statistically significant. There are three primary reasons why this appearance is somewhat misleading:

1) Traditional methods of computing standard error are based on the assumption that the sample being used was randomly selected from an infinite population. The CIRP Norms sample is derived from students attending a group of institutions that voluntarily chose to participate in the CIRP. In addition, while every effort has been made to maximize the comparability of the institutional sample from year to year (repeat participation runs about 90 percent), comparability is reduced somewhat by non–repeat participation and year–to–year variation in the quality of data collected by continuing institutional participants. This institutional form of "response bias" undoubtedly introduces an unknown amount of non–random variation in the results from year to year.

2) The wording of some questions in the survey instrument, the text and number of response options and the order of their presentation have changed over the years. We have found that even small changes can have a disproportionate effect on the results. While the trend data found in this report have been carefully examined to remove results which have clearly been contaminated by these considerations, some variations caused by order and context effects can still be observed (see Appendix D).

3) Substantial changes in the stratification cell scheme were made in 1968, 1971 and 1975, including the inclusion of cells for historically black colleges, public and private universities, and the use of selectivity levels. These changes resulted in corresponding changes to the weights applied to individual institutions over the period 1966–1975, giving them greater or lesser influence over the national normative results. (Although there have been changes to the stratification cell assignments of individual institutions since 1975, the scale of these changes in

relation to the national normative results are quite small in comparison to other sources of bias).

Instead of relying on the standard error as a measure of changes in the trends, we recommend that observed trends be judged in large part on their consistency. Any result which undergoes a consistent change over three or more years can reasonably be assumed to reflect a real change in the national population of entering freshmen. A change from one year to the next, no matter how large, which is not maintained in following years, may well represent an artifact of the sort described above.

Table E1

Standard Errors of Categorical Response Percentages for Norms Groups of Various Sizes[a]

Number of Actual Participants in a Norms Groups[b]	Standard error			
	1% or 99%	10% or 90%	25% or 75%	50%
2,500	.199	.600	.866	1.000
5,000	.141	.424	.612	.707
7,500	.115	.347	.500	.577
10,000	.100	.300	.433	.500
25,000	.063	.190	.274	.316
50,000	.044	.134	.194	.224
75,000	.036	.110	.158	.183
100,000	.031	.095	.137	.158
150,000	.026	.077	.112	.129
175,000	.024	.071	.104	.120

[a]Assumes simple random sampling of students from an infinite population.
[b]To determine 1990 populations counts, please Appendix A, Table A3, column 2.

Appendix F

Aggregation of Major and Career Responses

Student's Probable Major

Aggregated Category	Disaggregated Categories
Agriculture	Agriculture; Forestry.
Biological Sciences	Biology (general); Biochemistry/biophysics; Botany; Marine (life) science; Microbiology/bacteriology; Zoology; Other.
Business	Accounting; Business administration (general); Finance; Marketing; Management; Secretarial studies; Other business.
Education	Business; Elementary. Music or Art; Physical Education or Recreation; Secondary; Special; Other.
Engineering	Aero-or astronautical; Civil; Chemical; Electrical or Electronic; Industrial; Mechanical; Other.
English	English (language or literature).
Health Professional	Nursing; Pharmacy; Premed, Predent, Prevet; Therapy (physical, occupational, speech).
History/Political Science	History; Political Science.
Humanities (Other)	Language (except English); Philosophy; Theater or drama; Theology or religion; Other arts or humanities.
Fine Arts	Art, fine & applied; Music; Speech; Architecture/urban planning.
Mathematics/Statistics	Mathematics; Statistics.
Physical Sciences	Astronomy; Atmospheric science; Chemistry; Earth science; Marine science; Physics; Other physical sciences.
Social Sciences	Anthropology; Economics; Ethnic Studies, Geography; Psychology; Social work; Sociology; Women's studies; Other social sciences.
Other Technical	Health technology; Data processing/computer programming; Drafting or design; Electronics; Mechanics, Other technical; Computer science.
Other Non-Technical	Journalism; Home economics; Library/archival science; Other professional; Building trades; Communications; Law enforcement; Military science; Other field.

Student's Probable Career

Aggregated Category	Disaggregated Categories
Artist	Actor or entertainer; Artist; Interior decorator; Musician (performer, composer); Writer or journalist.
Business	Accountant or actuary; Business (management); Business owner or proprietor; Business sales rep or buyer.
Clergy	Clergy (minister, priest); clergy (other religious).
College Teacher	College teacher.
Doctor (MD or DDS)	Dentist (including orthodontist); Physician.
Education (secondary)	School counselor; School principal; Teacher (secondary).
Engineer	Engineer.
Farmer or Forester	Conservationist or forester.
Health Professional	Dietitian or home economist; Lab technician or hygienist; Optometrist; Pharmacist; Therapist (physical, occupational, speech); Veterinarian.
Lawyer	Lawyer.
Nurse	Nurse.
Research scientist	Research scientist.
Other	Architect; Business (clerical); Clinical psychologist; Computer programmer; Foreign service worker; Homemaker; Law enforcement officer; Military service (career); Social worker; Statistician; Skilled trades; Other.
Undecided	Undecided.

Father's Career

Aggregated Category	Disaggregated Categories
Artist	Actor or entertainer; Artist; Interior decorator; Musician (performer, composer); Writer or journalist.
Business	Accountant or actuary; Business (management); Business owner or proprietor; Business sales rep or buyer.
Clergy	Clergy (minister, priest); clergy (other religious).
College Teacher	College teacher.
Doctor (MD or DDS)	Dentist (including orthodontist); Physician.
Education (secondary)	School counselor; School principal; Teacher (secondary).
Engineer	Engineer.
Farmer or Forester	Conservationist or forester.
Health Professional	Dietitian or home economist; Lab technician or hygienist; Optometrist; Pharmacist; Therapist (physical, occupational, speech); Veterinarian.
Lawyer	Lawyer.
Military	Military service (career).
Research scientist	Research scientist.
Skilled worker	Skilled trades.
Semi-skilled worker	Semi-skilled labor.
Unskilled worker	Laborer (unskilled).
Unemployed	Unemployed.
Other	Architect; Business (clerical); Clinical psychologist; Computer programmer; Foreign service worker; Homemaker; Law enforcement officer; Social worker; Statistician; Other.

Mother's Career

Aggregated Category	Disaggregated Categories
Artist	Actor or entertainer; Artist; Interior decorator; Musician (performer, composer); Writer or journalist.
Business	Accountant or actuary; Business (management); Business owner or proprietor; Business sales rep or buyer.
Business (clerical)	Business (clerical).
Clergy	Clergy (minister, priest); clergy (other religious).
College Teacher	College teacher.
Doctor (MD or DDS)	Dentist (including orthodontist); Physician.
Education (secondary)	School counselor; School principal; Teacher (secondary).
Engineer	Engineer.
Farmer or Forester	Conservationist or forester.
Health Professional	Dietitian or home economist; Lab technician or hygienist; Optometrist; Pharmacist; Therapist (physical, occupational, speech); Veterinarian.
Homemaker	Homemaker.
Lawyer	Lawyer.
Nurse	Nurse.
Research scientist	Research scientist.
Social/welfare worker	Social worker.
Skilled worker	Skilled trades.
Semi-skilled worker	Semi-skilled labor.
Unskilled worker	Laborer (unskilled).
Unemployed	Unemployed.
Other	Architect; Clinical psychologist; Computer programmer; Foreign service worker; Law enforcement officer; Statistician; Other.

Higher Education Research Institute/CIRP

Current Publications List

October, 1991

The American College Teacher ($12.00)

National Norms for the 1989-90 HERI Faculty Survey

Provides an informative profile of teaching faculty at American colleges and universities. Teaching, research activities and professional development issues are highlighted along with issues related to job satisfaction and stress. December, 1990/ 104 pages.

The Black Undergraduate ($8.00)

Current Status and Trends in the Characteristics of Freshmen

This study examines changes in the characteristics of black college freshmen during the past two decades. A wide variety of characteristics of black college freshmen are considered in the study: family background, academic experience in high school, reasons for attending college, finanical aid, choices of majors and careers, expectations for college, self-concept, values, attitudes, and beliefs. August, 1990/22 pages.

Predicting College Student Retention ($8.00)

Comparative National Data from the 1982 freshman class.

A practical guide for colleges interested in using registrar's data to predict student retention. Focus is on the entering freshmen class of 1982 using results from the 1986 Follow-up Survey. March, 1989/110 pages.

The American College Student

Provides information on the college student experience two and four years after college entry. Student satisfaction, talent development, student involvement, changing values and career development, and retention issues are highlighted along with normative data from student responses to the HERI Follow-up Surveys.

1988 report: Normative data for 1984 and 1986 freshmen. August, 1990/210 pages $15.00

1987 report: Normative data for 1983 and 1985 freshmen. Sept., 1989/130 pages $15.00

1985 report: Normative data for 1981 and 1983 freshmen. March, 1989/44 pages $14.00

The American Freshman: Twenty–Five Year Trends ($25.00)

Provides trends data for entering freshman classes on selected items of the CIRP survey from 1966-1990. The report highlights academic skills and preparation, demographic trends, high school activities and experiences, education and career plans, and student attitudes and values. September, 1991/192 pages.

The Courage and Vision to Experiment ($10.00)

Hampshire College 1970-1990

Summarizes the results of a study of Hampshire College, an experimenting liberal arts institution located in Amherst, Massachusetts. Through an analysis of alumni outcomes, the report emphasizes how the lessons learned from the innovative approach used at Hampshire can be translated to the higher education community at large. January, 1991/190 pages.

The American Freshman: National Norms

Provides national normative data on freshman responses to the annual freshman survey. Please check the year you wish to receive:

Year	Price	Year	Price
1966	7.50__	1979	7.50__
1967	7.50__	1980	7.50__
1968	7.50__	1981	7.50__
1969	7.50__	1982	7.50__
1970	7.50__	1983	8.25__
1971	7.50__	1984	8.25__
1972	7.50__	1985	8.50__
1973	7.50__	1986	12.95 (out of stock)
1974	7.50__	1987	15.00__
1975	7.50__	1988	17.00__
1976	7.50__	1989	19.00__
1977	7.50__	1990	19.00__
1978	7.50__		

Order Form

Please send me the publication(s) checked on the listing above.

Name ______________________________

Title ______________________________

Institution ______________________________

Address ______________________________

City ____________________ State ______ Zip ____________

Daytime Phone ______________________________

Enclosed is: _______Personal Check _______Institutional Check _______Institutional Purchase Order

Total amount enclosed $___________